The Promise of EU Democracy

The Promise of EU Democracy Reconnecting European Citizens?

Edited by

JAN WOUTERS

Jean Monnet Chair ad personam and Full Professor of International Law and International Organizations, KU Leuven, Belgium

JULIE SMITH

Professor of European Politics, Department of Politics and International Studies, University of Cambridge, UK

KOLJA RAUBE

Associate Professor in European Governance and EU External Action, KU Leuven, Belgium

BEN CRUM

Professor of Political Science, Department of Political Science and Public Administration, Vrije Universiteit Amsterdam, the Netherlands

OXFORD
UNIVERSITY PRESS

OXFORD
UNIVERSITY PRESS

Great Clarendon Street, Oxford, OX2 6DP,
United Kingdom

Oxford University Press is a department of the University of Oxford.
It furthers the University's objective of excellence in research, scholarship,
and education by publishing worldwide. Oxford is a registered trade mark of
Oxford University Press in the UK and in certain other countries.

Published in the United States of America by Oxford University Press
198 Madison Avenue, New York, NY 10016, United States of America.

British Library Cataloguing in Publication Data
Data available

Library of Congress Control Number: 2025947886

ISBN 9780198891192

DOI: 10.1093/9780191996191.001.0001

Printed and bound by
CPI Group (UK) Ltd., Croydon, CR0 4YY

MIX
Paper | Supporting responsible forestry
FSC® C013604
FSC www.fsc.org

The manufacturer's authorised representative in the EU for product safety is
Oxford University Press España S.A. of Parque Empresarial San Fernando de Henares,
Avenida de Castilla, 2–28830 Madrid (www.oup.es/en or product.safety@oup.com).
OUP España S.A. also acts as importer into Spain of products made by the manufacturer.

Acknowledgements

The publication of the present volume is the culmination of longstanding collaboration between the authors and the editors. Sustaining the endeavour and bringing it to a conclusion was only possible thanks to the support of many individuals and institutions. First and foremost, just like its sister volume, *Upholding the Rule of Law in the EU*, this volume results from, and draws upon the work accomplished within, the Horizon 2020 project RECONNECT ('Reconciling Europe with its Citizens through Democracy and the Rule of Law', www.reconnect-europe.eu), a four-year multidisciplinary research project (2018–22) with a consortium of eighteen partners, led by Jan Wouters and coordinated by the Leuven Centre for Global Governance Studies at KU Leuven. RECONNECT was given great praise by its external evaluators as having 'delivered exceptional results with significant immediate or potential impact'. As senior investigators in the RECONNECT project we found it imperative to make the research and insights acquired available, not just through the website, a MOOC and numerous other publications, policy briefs and working papers, but also through these two legacy volumes published by Oxford University Press (OUP). As this publication process took time, the two books have evolved in such a manner that they also provide a great number of updates and new insights. We are grateful to OUP for all the trust and support they have given us throughout the publication process, and in particular to Merel Alstein, Peter Daniell, and Charlotte Kershaw. Last but not least, we would like to thank very warmly Niles Webb for his sterling copy-editing services when the manuscript was nearly complete.

Contents

Figures

Tables

Abbreviations

ACP	African, Caribbean, and Pacific
ACTA	Anti-Counterfeiting Trade Agreement
AFSJ	Area of Freedom, Security, and Justice
ALDE	Alliance of Liberals and Democrats for Europe
AMCE	average marginal component effect
AMLA	Anti-Money Laundering Authority
BU	Banking Union
BUDG	Budget Committee (of the Council or the Parliament)
CCP	Common Commercial Policy
CEAS	Common European Asylum System
CEEC	Central and Eastern European countries
CETA	Comprehensive Economic and Trade Agreement
CJEU	Court of Justice of the European Union
CMU	Capital Markets Union
CoFoE	Conference on the Future of Europe
CONT	Budgetary Control Committee of the EP
DG BUDG	Budget Directorate-General of the Commission
DG HOME	Directorate-General on Migration and Home Affairs
EASO	European Asylum Support Office
EBA	European Banking Authority
ECA	European Court of Auditors
ECB	European Central Bank
ECCs	European Citizen Consultations
ECFIN	Economic and Financial Affairs Directorate-General of the Commission
ECI	European Citizens' Initiative
ECOFIN	Economic and Financial Affairs Council
ECON	Economic and Monetary Affairs (Committee of the EP)
ECPs	European Citizens' Panels
ECSC	European Coal and Steel Community
EEC	European Economic Community
EFB	European Fiscal Board
EFC	Economic and Financial Committee of the Council
EFSF	European Financial Stability Facility
EFSM	European Financial Stabilisation Mechanism
EIB	European Investment Bank

EIBG	European Investment Bank Group
EIF	European Investment Fund
EIOPA	European Insurance and Occupational Pensions Authority
EP	European Parliament
EPC	Economic Policy Committee of the Council
EPP	European People's Party
ESAs	European Supervisory Authorities
ESFS	European System of Financial Supervision
ESM	European Stability Mechanism
ESMA	European Securities and Markets Authority
ESM	European Stability Mechanism
ESRB	European Systemic Risk Board
EUAA	European Union Agency for Asylum
EUCO	European Council
EU	European Union
FISC	Sub-committee on tax matters of the European Parliament
FSC	Financial Services Committee of the Council
FTA	Free Trade Agreement
GFC	Global Financial Crisis
IFI	Independent Fiscal Institution
IfSG	*Infektionsschutzgesetz*
IGC	Intergovernmental Conference
IMF	International Monetary Fund
ISCED	International Standard Classification of Education
MEP	Member of the European Parliament
MFF	Multiannual Financial Framework
NGO	Non-governmental organization
NPE	Normative Power Europe
NSA	National Supervisory Authority
OLS	Ordinary Least Squares
PCA	Principal Component Analysis
PES	Party of European Socialists
PHEIC	public health emergency of international concern
PSM	perceived societal marginalization
RCA	Representative Claims Analysis
RECOVER	Recovery and Resilience Task Force of the Commission
RRF	Recovery and Resilience Facility
SB	Supervisory Board
SGP	Stability and Growth Pact
SRB	Single Resolution Board
SRF	Single Resolution Fund
SSM	Single Supervisory Mechanism

TAIEX	Technical Assistance and Information Exchange Instrument
TAX	Taxation and Customs Union Directorate-General of the Commission
TEU	Treaty on European Union
TFEU	Treaty on the Functioning of the European Union
TSCG	Treaty on Stability, Coordination and Governance in the Economic and Monetary Union
TSD	Trade and Sustainable Development
TTIP	Transatlantic Trade and Investment Partnership
UNHRC	United Nations Human Rights Council
WHO	World Health Organization

Contributors

Alex Andrione-Moylan is Juan de la Cierva Fellow at the Institut Barcelona d'Estudis Internacionals (IBEI), Spain. https://orcid.org/0000-0003-0226-9591

Carlos Closa is Vice-President for Organization and Institutional Relations, Spanish National Research Council (CSIC), Madrid, Spain. https://orcid.org/0000-0002-2935-1926

Ben Crum is Professor of Political Science, Department of Political Science and Public Administration, Vrije Universiteit Amsterdam, Netherlands. https://orcid.org/0000-0003-4330-295X

Pieter de Wilde is Professor of European Politics and Society, Faculty of Arts, University of Groningen, Netherlands. https://orcid.org/0000-0003-1878-7780

Viljam Engström is Senior Lecturer in Public International Law, Department of Business and Economics, and Law, Åbo Akademi University, Turku, Finland. https://orcid.org/0000-0002-4908-0158

Cristina Fasone is Associate Professor of Comparative Public Law, Department of Political Science, Luiss University, Rome, Italy; Visiting Professor, Nicolaus Copernicus University, Toruń, Poland. https://orcid.org/0000-0002-8426-8797

Katri Johanna Gadd is University Lecturer, Department of Geography and Geology, University of Turku, Finland.

Felipe González De León is Advisor, Cabinet of the Spanish Secretary of State for Social Security, Ministry of Inclusion, Social Security and Migration, Spain.

Anna Gora, PhD is Research Advisor, Norwegian University of Science and Technology (NTNU), Trondheim, Norway. https://orcid.org/0000-0003-4102-9259

Naman Karl-Thomas Habtom, PhD is Non-Resident Fellow, Quincy Institute for Responsible Statecraft, Washington, DC, United States.

Gisela Hernández is Post-doctoral Researcher, Department of Social Sciences, Heinrich Heine University Düsseldorf, Germany. https://orcid.org/0000-0003-3525-3561

Camille Kelbel is Scientific Advisor at the Fund for Scientific Research (F.R.S.-FNRS), Belgium.

Sylvia Kritzinger is Professor for Methods in the Social Sciences, Department of Government, University of Vienna, Austria.

Julien Navarro is Associate Professor of Political Science, Université Catholique de Lille, France. https://orcid.org/0000-0003-3718-4600

Alvaro Oleart is Post-doctoral Researcher, Department of Political Science and Institute for European Studies, Université Libre de Bruxelles, Belgium. https://orcid.org/0000-0002-9696-4298

Julia Partheymüller is Senior Scientist, Department of Government, University of Vienna, Austria. https://orcid.org/0000-0001-8302-1912

Carolina Plescia, PhD is Associate Professor, University of Vienna, Austria. https://orcid.org/0000-0002-9719-001X

Kolja Raube is Associate Professor in European Governance and EU External Action, KU Leuven, Leuven, Belgium. https://orcid.org/0000-0002-6545-6995

Lise Rye, PhD is Professor of Contemporary European History, Department of Historical Sciences, NTNU, Trondheim, Norway. https://orcid.org/0000-0003-0455-7351

Constantin Schäfer is Director EU Relations & Projects, ifok GmbH, Brussels, Belgium. https://orcid.org/0000-0002-0693-0888

Bernd Schlipphak is Professor of Empirical Research Methods, Department of Political Science, University of Münster, Germany. https://orcid.org/0000-0001-8022-0027

Julie Smith is Professor of European Politics, Department of Politics and International Studies, Cambridge University, Cambridge, United Kingdom. https://orcid.org/0000-0002-1725-5443

Tom Theuns is Senior Assistant Professor, Institute of Political Science, Leiden University, Netherlands.

Oliver Treib is Professor of Comparative Policy Analysis and Research Methods, Department of Political Science, University of Münster, Germany. https://orcid.org/0000-0002-2273-4043

Valentin Voith, MA, was Student Assistant at the Department of Government, University of Vienna, and now works in public administration.

Jan Wouters is Jean Monnet Chair *ad personam* and Full Professor of International Law and International Organizations, KU Leuven, Leuven, Belgium. https://orcid.org/0000-0001-8328-6005

About the Authors

Editors

Ben Crum is Professor of Political Science at the Vrije Universiteit Amsterdam (VU). He researches the ways in which democratic institutions respond to contemporary challenges like internationalization, socioeconomic inequalities, and digitalization. Recent publications of his include *Populist Parties and Democratic Resilience* (Routledge 2023, co-edited with Alvaro Oleart) and 'Why the European Parliament lost the *Spitzenkandidaten*-process' (JEPP (2023) 30(2)).

Kolja Raube is Associate Professor in European Governance and EU External Action at the Faculty of Social Sciences at KU Leuven, Belgium. He is Director of the Joint Bachelor of European Studies and co-editor of the series 'Palgrave Studies in European Union Politics'. He has published widely on EU external action and European parliamentary affairs. His co-edited special issues, articles and chapters have appeared, among others, in the *Journal of Common Market Studies*, the *Journal of European Integration*, *European Security*, the *British Journal of Politics and International Relations* and the *Cambridge Review of International Affairs*.

Julie Smith is Professor of European Politics at Cambridge University and Fellow in Politics of Robinson College, Cambridge. Her research focuses on the history and politics of the European Union, especially democracy in Europe and the UK's relations with the EU. Recent publications include *The Palgrave Handbook on the 2024 European Parliament Elections* (2025), co-edited with Juliet Lodge and Stergios Fotopoulos, and *The Palgrave Handbook on European Referendums* (2021), as editor and contributor. She has published recently in *JCMS—the Journal of Common Market Studies* (2025) and *German Politics* (2025). Her current research focuses on the UK's relations with Germany.

Jan Wouters is Full Professor of International Law and International Organizations, Jean Monnet Chair *ad personam*, Director, Institute for International Law and Leuven Centre for Global Governance Studies (Jean Monnet Centre of Excellence and University Centre of Excellence), Administrator, America Europe Fund, KU Leuven; Visiting Professor, Paris2 and College of Europe; Adjunct Professor, Columbia University. Member of the Belgian Royal Academy; Of Counsel, Omega Law. He has published widely on international and EU law, international organizations, global governance, and corporate and financial law. He recently coordinated a large Horizon2020 Project, RECONNECT, and frequently advises and trains international organizations and governments.

Authors

Alex Andrione-Moylan is Juan de la Cierva Fellow at the Institut Barcelona d'Estudis Internacionals (IBEI), Spain. His research focuses on the (de-)politicization and geopoliticization of European issues and policies, both at the EU level and in the Member States.

Carlos Closa is Vice-President for Organization and Institutional Relations of the Spanish National Research Council (CSIC) and Research Professor at the Institute for Public Goods and Policies (IPP-CSIC). He is also a Senior Fellow at the School of Transnational Governance at the European University Institute (STG-EUI). He has published four volumes in Cambridge University Press and authored articles in *Common Market Law Review, Comparative European Politics, European Law Review, European Political Science, European Law Journal, Journal of Common Market Studies, Journal of European Integration, Journal of European Public Policy, West European Politics, World Politics, European Journal of International Relations*, etc).

Pieter de Wilde holds the Chair in European Politics and Society at the University of Groningen. He was previously a Professor in Political Science and Associate Professor in European Studies at the Norwegian University of Science and Technology (NTNU) in Trondheim and Senior Researcher at the Wissenschaftszentrum Berlin (WZB). Pieter holds a PhD in Political Science from ARENA, Centre for European Studies, University of Oslo. He studies societal conflict and transnationalization in Europe, focusing on politicization, representation and cleavage formation. He has published in the *Journal of European Public Policy* and *European Journal of Political Research* and with Cambridge University Press among others.

Dr Viljam Engström, Adjunct Professor (*Docent*) is Senior Lecturer in Public International Law at Åbo Akademi University, Finland. Engström has been part of two large-scale EU-funded projects: FRAME (2013–17) and RECONNECT (2020–24). Within both projects he has undertaken research on EU migration policies, securitization, and EU fundamental values. Relevant publications include: 'EU delegations as intermediaries of perceptions of the EU: A view from the MENA region' (with Katri Gadd), *Mediterranean Politics* (2024); 'Democratic Legitimacy in EU Migration Policies' (with Katri Gadd and Barbara Grabowska-Moroz), RECONNECT Working Paper 13/1 (2020); and 'Lisbonizing Back and Forth? Strategic Planning and Fundamental Rights in the AFSJ' (with Mikaela Heikkilä), in *European Yearbook on Human Rights* (2015).

Cristina Fasone is Associate Professor of Comparative Public Law at Luiss University, where she is the Director of the BA in Politics, Philosophy, and Economics. Visiting Professor at Nicolaus Copernicus University of Toruń since 2020, she holds a PhD in Comparative Public Law (University of Siena) and has been Max Weber post-doctoral fellow in Law (2013–15) at the EUI. Holder of a Jean Monnet Module 2016–19 'Parliamentary accountability and technical expertise: Budgetary Powers, Information and Communication Technologies and Elections' (PATEU), until January 2024 she has been the coordinator at Luiss research unit of the Horizon Europe Project RED-SPINEL.

Dr Katri Gadd, a human geographer, is University Lecturer at the Department of Geography and Geology, University of Turku, Finland. Gadd has done research, among other things, concerning irregular migrants in Finland and Iraqi women in Iraq and Finland, and the realization of the rights of elderly immigrants in the project 'Access to Justice for Marginalized Groups in an Ageing Society' (AMIS, Research Council of Finland). In 2019–22, Gadd was a researcher at the Åbo Akademi Institute of Human Rights within the Horizon2020 project 'RECONNECT' (EU Commission, 2020– 24), focusing on immigration policies of the European Union. Currently she leads the research project 'Human Rights Incorporated and Acquired—Participatory research on Iraqi women between multiple normative frameworks in Finland' (HuRiIA—الحرية, Kone Foundation).

Felipe González De León is an Advisor in the Cabinet of the Spanish Secretary of State for Social Security. He previously served as an Advisor to the Minister of Inclusion, Social Security, and Migration. He has also worked as a Senior Officer at the Central Bank of Malta and as a Research Associate at the Institute for Public Goods and Policies of the Spanish National Research Council (IPP-CSIC).

Anna Gora is a research advisor at the Norwegian University of Science and Technology (NTNU) in Trondheim and holds a PhD in Political Science from Carleton University in Ottawa. She was a post-doctoral researcher at NTNU on the Horizon 2020 RECONNECT project. Anna has worked on political contestation and democracy in the European Union, including politicization, and political cleavages in public debates. She has published in the *Journal of European Public Policy* and *Political Studies*, among others.

Naman Karl-Thomas Habtom is a foreign and security policy researcher, writer, and editor. He completed a PhD in history at the University of Cambridge, where he focused primarily on contemporary military and diplomatic history. He has published in *Foreign Policy, Survival, War on the Rocks, Lawfare, Bulletin of the Atomic Scientists, Scandinavian Journal of Military History*, and has also edited an academic volume on post-Cold War neutrality. Habtom has written briefs for think tanks such as Carnegie Europe and the Quincy Institute for Responsible Statecraft. He has been a guest researcher at the Swedish Defence University, Université Libre de Bruxelles, and the University of Luxembourg.

Gisela Hernández is a post-doctoral researcher at Heinrich Heine University Düsseldorf. Previously, she was a pre-doctoral researcher at the Institute for Public Goods and Policies of the Spanish National Research Council (IPP-CSIC) and at the Universidad Autónoma de Madrid (UAM). She has published in *Journal of European Public Policy, West European Politics, Journal of Common Market Studies, Hague Journal on the Rule of Law*, and *Politics and Governance.*

Camille Kelbel is Scientific Advisor at the Fund for Scientific Research (F.R.S.-FNRS), Belgium. She was formerly Associate Professor at ESPOL, Université Catholique de Lille (France). Her areas of expertise include political parties and electoral behaviour. Her research has appeared in several leading scholarly journals, including *European Union Politics, Politics and Governance, Revue Française de Science Politique* and *European Political Science.*

Sylvia Kritzinger is Professor of Methods in the Social Sciences at the Department of Government of the University of Vienna. She is one of the principal investigators of the *Austrian National Election Study* (AUTNES) and Director of the research network

Interdisciplinary Value Research. Her research focuses on Citizens' Political Attitudes and Voting Behaviour, Democratic Representation and Political Participation, Voting at 16 and Survey Research. She has published inter alia in *Comparative Political Studies, Political Communication, Electoral Studies, British Journal of Political Science, West European Politics*, and *European Journal of Political Research.*

Julien Navarro is Associate Professor of Political Science at the Université Catholique de Lille, affiliated with both ETHICS EA 7446 and ESPOL-LAB. His research explores the representative link in Europe at the national and EU levels, with a focus on parliamentary behaviour, ideological congruence between citizens and their representatives, democratic satisfaction, and electoral participation. His recent work has been published in *French Politics*, the *European Journal of Political Research*, *European Union Politics*, and *European Political Science.*

Alvaro Oleart is a post-doctoral researcher at the Department of Political Science and the Institute for European Studies of the Université Libre de Bruxelles. His research focuses on the relationship between political conflict and democracy through a decolonial lens in the context of the European Union, focusing on citizen participation processes, political parties, the media, civil society, and transnational social movements. He is the author of the books *Framing TTIP in the European Public Spheres: Towards an Empowering Dissensus for EU Integration* (Palgrave, 2021) and *Democracy Without Politics in EU Citizen Participation: From European Demoi to Decolonial Multitude* (Palgrave, 2023).

Julia Partheymüller is a Senior Scientist at the Department of Government at the University of Vienna, a member of the Vienna Centre for Electoral Research (VieCER), and part of the Austrian National Election Study (AUTNES). Her research focuses on elections, public opinion, and political communication in comparative perspective. She holds a doctoral degree in Social Sciences from the University of Mannheim, and her work has been published in peer-reviewed journals such *Journal of Common Market Studies*, *Electoral Studies*, *West European Politics*, and the *British Journal of Political Science.*

Carolina Plescia is Associate Professor in the Department of Government at the University of Vienna. Currently, she is the principal investigator of the ERC starting grant project DeVOTE. Her research interests range from public opinion, electoral behaviour, and experimental methods, to the role of data in democratic processes. Her research has been published in *Comparative Political Studies*, *European Journal of Political Research*, *Electoral Studies*, and *Political Psychology*, among others. She is the author of *Split-ticket Voting in Mixed-member Electoral Systems: A Theoretical and Methodological Investigation* (ECPR Press 2016) and *The Meanings of Voting for Citizens: A Scientific Challenge, a Portrait, and Implications* (Oxford University Press 2025).

Lise Rye is Professor of Contemporary European History at the Norwegian University of Science and Technology (NTNU). She researches the history of European integration, with the history of the EU, Norway's relations with the EU and the EEA agreement as special fields. The aim of this research is to understand how the development of the EU can be explained, why different forms of integration emerge, and how integration affects democracy, in the Member States and at the European level. Recent publications include 'Where to wriggle? Norwegian politicians' presentations of autonomy within the EEA association', *West European Politics* (2025) 48(5) (with Kristine Graneng), and 'Teaching European Union politics: the perspective of history', in *Teaching European Union Politics* (Edward Elgar Publishing 2024) (with Carine Germond).

Constantin Schäfer works as Director EU Relations & Projects in the area of Deliberation, Open Government & Democracy for ifok in Brussels. He acts as project lead, process designer, and facilitator for participatory projects at the European level and for the Horizon projects CLIMAS and SCALEDEM, which aim to advance democratic innovations. He earned his PhD from the University of Mannheim, before working as post-doctoral researcher at the University of Münster and becoming affiliated with the KU Leuven. He lectures on innovative citizen participation at the University of Mainz and publishes on European integration, political behaviour, and deliberative democracy.

Bernd Schlipphak is Professor of Empirical Methods in the Social Sciences at the Department of Political Science, University of Münster. After receiving his PhD from the University of Freiburg, he worked as a Postdoc in the field of public attitudes toward international politics and the European Union at Salzburg and Göttingen before joining the University of Münster. His main research interests include citizens' attitudes towards and elite communication about international politics. Hence, he is interested in public legitimacy toward international organizations, globalization backlash, and the linkage between domestic and international politics, including the effects of populism and polarization on international politics.

Tom Theuns is Senior Assistant Professor of Political Theory and European Politics at the Institute of Political Science in Leiden. Previously, he held a research position at Utrecht University and a teaching position at the University of Amsterdam. Theuns read for an MPhil in Political Theory at Balliol College, Oxford and defended his PhD in Political Science at Sciences Po Paris in 2017. He defended his *habilitation á diriger des recherches* at Sciences Po Paris in 2024. His habilitation thesis, 'Protecting Democracy in Europe: Pluralism, Autocracy and the Future of the EU', was published by Hurst and Oxford University Press.

Oliver Treib is Professor of Comparative Policy Analysis and Research Methods at the Department of Political Science, University of Münster. He received his Master's degree and PhD in political science from the University of Cologne. Prior to joining the University of Münster, he worked at the Max Planck Institute for the Study of Societies in Cologne, the Institute for Advanced Studies in Vienna, and at the University of Salzburg. His current research revolves around the transformation of political conflict structures in the European multi-level system, public support for democratic innovations, and the protection of democracy against right-wing extremist challengers.

Valentin Voith contributed to this publication during his time as a Master's student in Political Science and as a student assistant in the Department of Government at the University of Vienna. His Master's thesis investigated the issue engagement of political candidates on social media during election campaigns. Following his graduation, he worked as a researcher and evaluator in the field of financial literacy and education, co-authoring several published reports and articles. He is currently employed in public administration.

1
A Promise of EU Democracy? Introductory Remarks

Jan Wouters, Julie Smith, Kolja Raube, and Ben Crum

Democracy has long been contested in Europe as elsewhere, and the democratic experience of the European Union ('EU' or 'Union') has been mixed. Representative democracy emerged alongside the development of the modern European nation state during the nineteenth and twentieth centuries, with political parties the key vehicles for political contestation for many years. By the late twentieth century, (liberal) democracy seemed to have prevailed across much of the continent as the EU and its Member States all aspired to democratic practices (Berman 2019; Mazower 1998). Yet, going into the twenty-first century, far from reaching the 'end of history' heralded by Francis Fukuyama (1992) with the end of the Cold War, polarized political currents have re-emerged, finding themselves in sometimes visceral confrontation with each other in Europe, as in many other parts of the world. Despite, or rather because of, these struggles throughout contemporary European history, European integration has been built on the promise of democracy: that is, not only should the Member States be founded on democratic principles, but the Union should extend these principles to the supranational level and thereby also democratize relations across the Member States and their peoples.

The original European Communities were predicated on rational bureaucracy or 'technocracy', with little attention paid to their democratic underpinnings (Wallace and Smith 1995). The creation of a parliamentary body was in many ways a democratic figleaf at the outset, despite the official ambition of holding direct elections at some future date. The 'Common Assembly' (in the terminology of the 1951 Treaty of Paris establishing the European Coal and Steel Community (ECSC)), which eventually became the European Parliament, was composed of national MPs nominated by their Member States and had very few powers. Still, even then, the Assembly had the power to adopt a motion of censure that could force the members of the High Authority to resign as a body (Article 24, third paragraph, ECSC Treaty). Over the years, and as the EU gradually acquired more competences, a desire grew that not only should the Member States be democratic by constitutional design and practice, but that the Union itself should also meet these criteria (see Chapter 2 of this volume; Lodge 2025; Rye et al. 2020). As the initial

Jan Wouters, Julie Smith, Kolja Raube, and Ben Crum, *A Promise of EU Democracy? Introductory Remarks* In: *The Promise of EU Democracy*. Edited by: Jan Wouters, Julie Smith, Kolja Raube, and Ben Crum, Oxford University Press.
 DOI: 10.1093/9780191996191.003.0001

'permissive consensus' towards European integration seemed to be vanishing, national leaders, including French President Valéry Giscard d'Estaing and German Chancellor Helmut Schmidt, alongside Roy Jenkins as Commission President, looked for ways to connect more directly with citizens of the Member States, for example by means of the direct elections to the European Parliament that were finally introduced in 1979. Moreover, ever since the 1992 Treaty on European Union (TEU, or 'Treaty of Maastricht'), following calls for a 'political' Union, and in light of the Treaty's introduction of a 'citizenship of the Union', the EU and its institutions were expected by many to become more democratic (even though 'political union' at the time referred mainly to moves to cooperation in the areas of foreign policy and security, not wider political cooperation associated with electoral practices). Indeed, the then twelve Member States stated in the preamble of the Maastricht Treaty that they were 'desiring to enhance further the democratic and efficient functioning of the institutions so as to enable them better to carry out, within a single institutional framework, the tasks entrusted to them'.

One key consequence of the Treaty of Maastricht was that the legislative powers of the European Parliament were extended. With the introduction of the co-decision procedure (since the Treaty of Lisbon, referred to as 'ordinary legislative procedure'), the Treaty laid the foundations for the European Parliament to become a fully developed co-legislative body in most policy domains in the wake of several subsequent Treaty changes. Moreover, with the introduction of the notion of citizenship of the Union, the Treaty of Maastricht foresaw that a national of any of the Member States could be directly linked to the Union and enjoy the rights, and be subject to the duties, laid down in the Treaty. This included the right of Union citizens to vote and to stand as a candidate for European and municipal elections in the Member State in which they reside but of which they are not a national, under the same conditions as nationals of that state. Thus, by expanding on democratic institutional credentials and linking the Union directly with the citizens, the promise of democracy became enshrined in the Treaties. This promise was built on the premise that democracy would be a given in the Member States. Article F(1) of the TEU made this famously clear: 'The Union shall respect the national identities of its Member States, whose systems of government are founded on the principles of democracy'. A predecessor of this provision can be found in the European Council's Declaration on Democracy adopted in Copenhagen on 8 April 1978—simultaneously with the decision to fix the dates for the first direct elections of the European Parliament, an event described as 'of outstanding importance for the future of the European Communities and a vivid demonstration of the ideals of democracy shared by the peoples within them'—in which the heads of state and government solemnly declare that 'respect for and maintenance of representative democracy and human rights in each Member State are essential elements of membership of the European Communities' (European Council 1978; Devroe and Wouters 1996: 92).

In their book *Why Nations Fail*, Nobel Prize-winning economists Daron Acemoğlu and James A. Robinson remind us that, according to democratic modernization theory, economic growth within authoritarian regimes will always exist for a limited time only and must ultimately lead to democracy (Acemoğlu and Robinson 2013: 443). It is an open question whether this logic also applies to regional unions such that the more they contribute to economic growth, the greater the pressure to democratize becomes. Regardless, much of the justification of European integration hinges on its supposed contribution to economic growth in the Member States (Milward 1992). Forming a single market would spur economic exchanges between the Member States, while the Union's own market power (Damro 2012) that was thereby created promised to bring economic growth to the rest of the continent, if not larger parts of the world. In accordance with both democratic modernization theory, and in line with Seymour Martin Lipset's ground-breaking theoretical contribution on the socio-economic prerequisites for democratic transformation and consolidation (Lipset 1959; 1960), economic market integration and growth could be expected to go hand in hand with democracy and work as a hedge against authoritarianism (Acemoğlu and Robinson 2013). As a consequence, the more the EU contributes to the economic growth and prosperity of its Member States, the more—so the logic goes—it should also be taking on competences to act and the more these competences should be accompanied by democratic institutions and decision-making procedures.

Yet, such a line of argument has never been fully accepted by politicians who reject such incursions into national sovereignty, whether they be realists of the past such as Charles de Gaulle and Margaret Thatcher or modern-day Eurosceptics reluctant to cede further powers to the EU. Nor will it be readily accepted by all scholars of European integration, many of whom have argued prominently that the Union would never be able to develop democratic credentials due to the lack of a 'demos' or any common supranational identity (Grimm 1995; Scharpf 1999; Bellamy 2019).

Despite such sceptical views, the Union has often expressed ambitions to develop its democratic credentials along three dimensions: to promote democracy externally; to become more democratic in its own internal decision-making; and to strengthen and protect democracy in its Member States. For many years, criticism of the EU's own democratic deficit focused on the fact that powers previously enjoyed by Member States had shifted to the European level, where decisions were now taken by members of national governments in the Council of Ministers, often by qualified majority, without proper oversight by parliamentary bodies (Bogdanor 1989). As a response to this critique, the quest began to empower the European Parliament (see Rye et al. 2020; Lodge 2025).

But the EU's democratic deficit turned out to be a deeper problem that could not simply be resolved by some institutional engineering. As highlighted by Dimitris Chryssochoou in the late 1990s, and as has become even more evident in the

2020s, the gap between the people and elites pressing for European cooperation has increased over time (Chryssochoou 1998). Whereas in the early years of integration there was an assumed 'permissive consensus' (Lindberg and Scheingold 1970) whereby citizens were content with the decisions taken by political elites in the European context, largely because of the perceived advantages in terms of policy outcomes, resulting in a high degree of citizen satisfaction, or 'output legitimacy', over the years such positive approval began to wane. And once citizens became more vocal about European integration, there was a lack of a common European public space in which they could exchange and deliberate upon their competing views (Habermas 1995). From an era of permissive consensus, Europe moved to an era of 'constraining dissensus' (Hooghe and Marks 2009).

From the late 1990s, Europe's leaders began to recognize the need to become closer to their citizens, yet progress proved slow. Calls for openness, proximity to citizens and transparency were voiced in the run-up to the 1997 Amsterdam Treaty (Fossum 2000), though it was at the Nice Summit of December 2000 that EU leaders formally recognized the persistent 'disconnect' between elites and citizens that was thwarting the EU's promise of democracy and thus set in motion deliberations that would continue on and off for the next quarter of a century, starting with the Laeken Declaration of 2001, which in turn led to the Convention on the Future of Europe (2002–03) and paved the way for a Constitutional Treaty that aspired to make the Union not just a union between states but also of citizens (Van Gerven 2005). However, the negative referendum outcomes in France and the Netherlands in the spring of 2005, which put the idea of further treaty reform on hold, demonstrated once again the gap between elites and citizens.

Overall, the contextual conditions to push for and implement transformative agendas both outside and inside the EU seem to have declined, thereby reducing the prospect that the Union will be able credibly to further support and improve democratic conditions vis-à-vis others or, indeed, within its own 'political system' (Börzel and Lebanidze 2017; Hix and Hoyland 2022). Efforts to promote human rights and democracy externally are increasingly seen as self-interested and incoherent, as well as patronizing and 'postcolonial' attempts by the EU to shape the world according to its own image (see Chapter 3 of this volume), a situation compounded by the Union's inability to meet these high standards itself. Meanwhile, the 'other democratic deficit' (Kelemen 2017) created by (some) Member States pursuing democratic backsliding in an attempt to establish illiberal political regimes confronts the Union with an additional dilemma. Clearly, both developments are interlinked: the more the Union's commitment to democracy, whether at the EU level or within the Member States, is compromised, the more it loses its appeal and leverage externally. Moreover, at a time when the United States—previously the world's foremost promoter of democracy—no longer seems to support the Union's efforts in democracy promotion and rather aligns with illiberal anti-democratic forces, there is both an enhanced need for the EU to pursue its democratic objectives alone and a reduced scope for it to be able to do so effectively. Despite darkening democratic clouds, the Union should nonetheless recall that it may be one of the few remaining 'land[s] of the free' (Charlemagne 2025), and take this as inspiration to invest further in its transformational normative power. In that sense, the promise of democracy for and by the EU seems to be ever more pertinent in these challenging times for democracy, which brings us to the core justification for this book.

* * *

While the Union's democratic credentials have seen ups and downs, the present volume brings together contributions that foreground the democratic promise that it holds and ask to what extent the Union has been able to live up to its promise. It offers a comprehensive overview of the state of EU democracy by addressing fundamental questions of the performance of the Union's main democratic mechanisms as well as the democratic character of specific policy domains. In these different ways we can assess the transformations the Union has undergone in moving closer to and further away from its democratic promise. Drawing on the results of the Horizon 2020 (H2020) project RECONNECT ('Reconciling Europe with its Citizens through Democracy and the Rule of Law', www.reconnect-europe.eu), the volume offers a new conceptual angle that articulates the promise of EU democracy (see also Chapter 2 of this volume). In the face of current developments and contestations of democracy outside and inside the Union, such an outlook is arguably more pertinent than ever.

In this regard, a **first premise** underlying this volume is that democracy is an inherently expansive and ever more inclusive process, and that European integration should be seen to be pushing the next frontier of this process, in that it does nothing less than overcome the confinement of democracy within national polities. Crucially, the Union is not merely a system for transnational decision-making aimed at addressing challenges which transcend national borders. The EU prides itself on the democratic character of its Member States, and it aspires to be a democratic political system in and of itself. As Crum reminds us in Chapter 2: 'the EU has come a long way in establishing a system of joint decision-making that can aspire to be democratic'. Over time, the Union has adopted many institutional reforms that have served to enhance its democratic character. For example, several chapters in this volume discuss the roles of European elections and the European Parliament and the nature of public support for EU policies (see Chapters 4, 6, and 7 of this volume).

The **second premise** that runs through the volume stands in contrast with the first: namely, that the EU's promise remains unfulfilled when it comes to pushing the boundaries of democracy. Various contributions demonstrate that the causes of this are both structural and contingent upon conditions in the Union and its Member States (see Chapters 3, 5, 7, and 8 of this volume). Alongside the constraints facing the Union's ability to push for democracy promotion externally (see Chapter 3 of this volume), from a structural perspective deep divides persist *within* the Union. At times, these are amplified further by new divisions that reflect inequalities within the Member States. Indeed, when it comes to matters that are contingent upon national characteristics, we have seen that the impact of democratic EU reform is often frustrated by the reassertion of domestic controls. The 2007 Treaty of Lisbon confirmed the position of the European Parliament as full co-legislator alongside the Council of the EU in most EU policymaking fields. Yet when the Union was faced with subsequent crises (e.g. migration—see Chapter 12 of this volume; and Covid-19—see Chapter 15 of this volume), it typically resorted to non-legislative, and at times even non-Treaty-based, instruments, effectively sidelining the existing institutional framework, i.e., the Treaties, in favour of new intergovernmental mechanisms (e.g. the European Fiscal Compact and the European Stability Mechanism—see Chapter 14 of this volume; or the 2016 EU–Turkey Declaration—see Chapter 15 of this volume).

* * *

In short, this volume offers a comprehensive assessment of the EU and its potential to forge democracy across borders, while at the same time identifying the areas where this potential remains unfulfilled or perverse effects have occurred. It does so by analysing developments in the foundations of the Union, in its main institutions, and in selected policy domains. In order to cover different disciplinary angles and provide answers to the question whether the EU has kept its democratic promise, the volume is a multidisciplinary endeavour, bringing together legal scholars, political scientists, and historians. Given the different disciplinary and thematic perspectives involved, the authors have naturally used different methodological approaches, but all within a common framework that allows them to critically assess the origins and state of the EU's long-standing promise to push for democracy across borders (Chapter 2). Thus, despite the variety of research approaches across the different chapters, the chapters complement each other in methodological terms, and the volume is organized around one coherent message.

The volume is structured as follows. Part I lays out the foundations of democracy, clarifying both the historical understanding of European integration and the theoretical framework that informs the various chapters. In so doing, the EU's democratic promise is situated within its international and historical context, which helps to outline and better understand the Union's evolution over time. Furthermore, this allows for variations in democratic performance across the EU's Member States to be mapped. To this end, the introductory chapters are predominantly conceptual and historical (see Chapters 2, 3, 4, and 5). They focus on the initial conceptual idea of the 'promise of democracy' in European integration (Chapter 2), the Union's struggle to keep its promise of democracy promotion towards the outside world (Chapter 3), and the variation in conceptions of democracy in the EU over time (Chapter 4), as well as the lack of participation of citizens in the democratic processes across EU Member States (Chapter 5).

In Part II, the volume identifies the general mechanisms upon which EU democracy relies. It looks, in particular, at the organization of European elections, the role and performance of the European Parliament, the ongoing contestation of the EU's basic procedures, and the relations between policymaking, information, and citizens' support. The subsequent chapters covering the EU's democratic mechanisms set out institutional arrangements, outline public opinion, and analyse perceptions. They combine legal and political perspectives and incorporate quantitative analyses relating to public support (Chapters 6, 7 8, 9, 10, and 11). These chapters cover a large body of research, each assessing whether the EU has kept its democratic promise through democratic practices, covering European elections and electoral law and practices (Chapters 6 and 7); the pluralist value of processes of constitutional change in the EU (Chapter 8); the state of (mis-)information and public perceptions of EU legitimacy (Chapters 9 and 10) as well as citizen participation in the Conference on the Future of Europe (Chapter 11).

Part III of the volume focuses on a selection of prominent policy fields, in an effort to offer a more precise appraisal of the achievements and limitations of EU democracy in particular contexts. Specifically, the chapters cover policies on migration, trade, fiscal and macroeconomic affairs, and the Covid-19 pandemic. These case studies focusing on selected policy domains bring together qualitative historical and quantitative data analysis in areas of crisis and policy change (Chapters 12, 13, 14, and 15).

* * *

In sum, through its three parts, this volume systematically reviews the Union's democratic achievements as well as its persistent shortcomings. In doing so, it analyses the underlying dynamics that account for the limits of EU democracy and seeks to identify opportunities to push the promise of democracy further. It, thus, offers a multi-faceted and comprehensive account of the state of EU democracy at times when both the democratic achievements of the Union and democracy more broadly are being (con)tested within the EU and its Member States.

References

Acemoğlu, D. and Robinson, J. A. (2013). *Why Nations Fail: the Origins of Power, Prosperity, and Poverty*. London, Faber and Faber.

Bellamy, R. P. (2019). *A Republican Europe of States: Cosmopolitanism, Intergovernmentalism and Democracy in the EU*. Cambridge, Cambridge University Press.

Berman, S. (2019). *Democracy and Dictatorship in Europe – From the Ancient Regime to the Present Day*. Oxford, Oxford University Press.

Bogdanor, V. B. (1989). The June 1989 European Elections and the Institutions of the Community. *Government and Opposition*, 24(2): 199–214.

Börzel, T. A. and Lebanidze, B. (2017). 'The Transformative Power of Europe' Beyond Enlargement: the EU's Performance in Promoting Democracy in its Neighbourhood. *East European Politics*, 33(1): 17–35.

Charlemagne (11 April 2025). The Thing About Europe: it's the Actual Land of the Free Now. *The Economist.*

Chryssochoou, D. N. (1998). *Democracy in the European Union.* London and New York, Tauris Academic Studies.

Damro, C. (2012). Market Power Europe. *Journal of European Public Policy*, 19(5): 682–699.

Devroe, W. and Wouters, J. (1996). *De Europese Unie. Het Verdrag van Maastricht en zijn uitvoering: analyse en perspectieven.* Leuven, Peeters.

European Council (1978). *Declaration on Democracy, Bulletin of the European Communities* 3-1978: 5.

Fossum, J. E. (2000). Constitution-making in the European Union. In Eriksen, E. O. and Fossum, J. E. (eds). *Democracy in the European Union. Integration through Deliberation?* London/New York, Routledge: 111–140.

Fukuyama, F. (1992). *The End of History and the Last Man.* New York, Free Press.

Grimm, D. (1995). Does Europe Need a Constitution? *European Law Journal*, 1(3): 282–302.

Habermas, J. (1995). Remarks on Dieter Grimm's 'Does Europe Need a Constitution?'. *European Law Journal*, 1(3): 303–307.

Hix, S. and Hoyland, B. (2022). *The Political System of the European Union.* London, Bloomsbury.

Hooghe, L. and Marks, G. (2009). A Postfunctionalist Theory of European Integration: From Permissive Consensus to Constraining Dissensus. *British Journal of Political Science*, 39(1): 1–23.

Kelemen, D. (2017). Europe's Other Democratic Deficit: National Authoritarianism in Europe's Democratic Union. *Government and Opposition*, 52(2): 211–238.

Lindberg, L. N. and Scheingold, S. A. (1970). *Europe's Would-Be Polity: Patterns of Change in the European Community.* Englewood Cliffs, NJ, Prentice-Hall.

Lipset S. M. (1959). Some Social Requisites of Democracy: Economic Development and Political Legitimacy. *American Political Science Review*, 53(1): 69–105.

Lipset, S. M. (1960). *Political Man – The Social Bases of Politics.* New York, Doubleday and Company.

Lodge, J. (2025). The European Parliament Elections in 2024: Coming of Age? In Lodge, J., Smith, J., and Fotopoulos, S. (eds). *The Palgrave Handbook on the 2024 European Parliament Elections.* Cham, Springer Verlag: 15–37.

Mazower, M. (1998). *Dark Continent: Europe's Twentieth Century.* New York, Knopf.

Milward, A. (1992). *The European Rescue of the Nation-State.* Berkeley, CA, University of California Press.

Rye, L., Fox, C., and Smith, J. (2020). The Changing Role of the European Parliament in EU Interinstitutional Relations. In Bartolucci, L., Fasone, C., Fox, C., Kelbel, C., Lupo, N., Navarro, J., Rye, L., and Smith, J. (eds). *Working Paper on Interinstitutional Relations in the EU*, Reconnect Deliverable 6.2, available at: D6.2.pdf: 13–26. Accessed 9 August 2025.

Scharpf, F. (1999). *Governing in Europe: Effective and Democratic?* Oxford, Oxford University Press.

Van Gerven, W. (2005). *The European Union: A Polity of States and Peoples.* Stanford, Stanford University Press.

Wallace, W. and Smith, J. (1995). Democracy or Technocracy? European Integration and the Problem of Popular Consent. *West European Politics*, 18(3): 137–157.

PART I

THE PROMISE AND FOUNDATIONS OF EU DEMOCRACY

2
The Promise of EU Democracy: Integration Versus Democracy in the Post-Lisbon Era

Ben Crum[*]

2.1 Introduction

The ideal of democracy is not necessarily demarcated by the borders of nation-states. Certainly, historically, nation-states have offered the prime sites in which the abstract ideal of democracy could be transformed in an institutional practice. However, if the ideal of democracy is about enabling people to have co-ownership of the social laws and norms under which they live (Kant 1793), national boundaries seem an insufficient justification to exclude anyone from that ideal. From this perspective, the European Union (EU) is a critical project as it offers a political context in which the concerns of people outside of one's national borders can become the object of joint democratic deliberation. In other words, while the ideal of democracy has come with the ever-greater inclusion of citizens within the nation-state (Marshall 1950), European integration promises to extend this inclusionary logic beyond national boundaries. This is what I refer to as 'the promise of EU democracy'.

It would be a mistake to think of the promise of democracy as a teleological project that will be fulfilled automatically. European integration was not necessarily initiated with the aim of realizing a form of transnational democracy. Peace and economic prosperity were the prime drivers. Arguably, however, the promise of EU democracy has always been implied by the European project, if only because

* This chapter was first conceived for presentation at the online conference 'Is a Europe in the spirit of the Ventotene Manifesto still possible?', organized by Fondazione Luigi Einaudi, 20–22 January 2021. I have developed its ideas further in presentations for the D66 political party (25 January 2021, available at: https://youtu.be/6JTlKWtIoXU?si=FxEcVbFSCVtQhzCG), Urios—Study Association for International and European Law (6 April 2021), and the Loge Saint Napoleon Amsterdam (27 January 2024). Particular thanks to Julie Smith and Kolja Raube for helpful comments.

Ben Crum, *The Promise of EU Democracy: Integration Versus Democracy in the Post-Lisbon Era* In: *The Promise of EU Democracy*. Edited by: Jan Wouters, Julie Smith, Kolja Raube, and Ben Crum, Oxford University Press.
 DOI: 10.1093/9780191996191.003.0003

its Member States live up to the ideal of democracy—as they are required to by the EU treaties. Still, the realization of EU democracy is a possibility not a destiny, and its realization (or, rather, approximation) eventually depends on political choices and conditions.

Notably, the prevailing tendency in much scholarship of recent decades has been to position European integration exactly in opposition to democracy (Mair 2013: Ch. 4; Bickerton and Tuck 2018). In such arguments, the presumption is that the ideal of democracy is inherently much better fulfilled within the nation-state and that there are structural conditions that will prevent the EU from becoming democratic in any substantial sense. Hence, whenever powers move from the national to the European level, they move from an arena of higher democratic quality to a democratically inferior one.

There is much to be said for such analyses, especially if one considers how democracy has taken a back seat in the ways that European politicians have responded to the series of international crises that they have encountered since 2009, such as the global financial crisis, the refugee crisis, Brexit, Covid, and the invasion of Ukraine (Crum 2013; Kreuder-Sonnen 2016; White 2019). In all these cases, we saw that the EU could only address these crises by bringing new powers to the supranational level while giving little attention to how these powers were to be controlled democratically. However, arguments that insist that democracy is best served by preserving it at the national level neglect the extent to which the international has become intertwined with domestic politics and society. What is more, they ignore the EU's promise of democracy, i.e. the inherent democratic potential in bringing the scope of the democratic community to a higher level.

This chapter seeks to explicate the nature of the democratic promise that can be projected onto the EU, to identify the structural challenges that this promise faces, and to explore whether and under what conditions the promise of democracy and the process of European integration can be reconciled. Section 2.2 offers a theoretical outline of what the EU's democratic promise potentially involves, and relates it to the origins, the objectives, and the structural characteristics of the process of European integration. Section 2.3 zooms in on the most ambitious attempt to institutionalize the promise of EU democracy: the making of a Constitutional Treaty for the EU in the early 2000s. Section 2.4 continues the historical analysis by examining what happened to the EU's democratic vocation in the crisis-ridden period that followed the failure of the Constitutional Treaty. Reflecting on these two episodes, Section 2.5 asks whether European integration and democracy are in fact irreconcilable or whether and how a middle way can be charted that tries to reconcile the two. To help specify the conditions under which the EU may be able to approximate its democratic promise (again), the chapter concludes with three lessons for future attempts to bring the EU on a proper democratic course.

2.2 The European promise of democracy beyond borders

The promise of transnational democracy did not animate European integration from the start. However, as the process evolved, one can see how it actually allowed for transnational concerns to become the object of joint democratic deliberation. Nevertheless, this ability remains structurally constrained in Europe in the absence of a fully integrated public sphere and political culture.

The foundations of European integration were laid as a response to the horrors that the Nazi regime committed in Europe. In 1941, in the midst of the Second World War, Altiero Spinelli envisaged a 'free and united Europe' in the Ventotene Manifesto. The very first requirement to secure such freedom and unity was 'the definitive abolition of the division of Europe into national, sovereign States' (Spinelli and Rossi 1988: 31); Europe was to be a truly integrated whole. The main concerns of Spinelli and his co-author Ernesto Rossi were to secure such integration to overcome the inter-state quarrels of the past and to lay the groundwork for a socialist society and economy. In this grander scheme of things, they had little patience with democracy and democrats. In fact, in line with common socialist doctrine, they declared that 'Democratic political methods are a dead weight during revolutionary crises' (Spinelli and Rossi 1988: 28).

By the time the Treaty of Paris establishing the European Coal and Steel Community was signed in 1951, the moment that European nation-states could have been erased and democratic procedures could have been bypassed had evaporated, if it had ever been there (Hoffmann 1966). Nonetheless, besides a desire to prevent further war on the continent and the pressure (exercised in particular by the United States) to cooperate in the restoration of societies and economies, the founding states of the Treaties of Paris and Rome (1957) were joined politically by an aversion to authoritarianism and a commitment to democracy. This shared commitment to democracy may have been quite thin and involved little more than a commitment to open and periodic elections and to constrained state power. Indeed, democracy may have been valued more for its instrumental role in securing societal and individual freedom than for the intrinsic value of collective self-government (Conway and Depkat 2010). Still, there also was an element in which the transnational interlocking of power was seen as a way to secure and strengthen each other's democracy. Embedding the individual countries into a greater European whole was to serve as a check on any one of them turning to authoritarianism. Obviously, this concern applied to (West-)Germany in particular.

However, as the process of European integration unfolded, a more substantial notion of democracy beyond borders could be projected upon it. This notion is anchored in the idea of democracy as collective self-government, i.e. the Kantian ideal that all citizens should live under laws that they could reasonably have willed themselves (Kant 1793). Importantly, the Kantian ideal is an aspiration. It is unlikely for any piece of democratic legislation to fully command the reasonable consent of all citizens involved. However, a democratic polity is defined by the fact that its institutional structure and the motivations of its actors are systematically geared towards ensuring that all laws can be reasonably justified to the citizens subjected to them (Habermas 1993).

As such, this democratic ideal stands in direct tension to the presence of national borders, which appear as accidental and non-deliberate boundaries on the scope of inclusion under collective self-government (Abizadeh 2012; Näsström 2003). If we conceive of the history of democracy as a joint trajectory of an ever-more inclusive demos and an ever-wider sphere of collective law-making that replaces traditional hierarchies (Marshall 1950), then national boundaries appear as a remnant of a pre-modern order, lacking in the rational justification that democracy requires.

To be sure, collective self-government does not necessarily entail the involvement of all citizens in all decisions. It certainly allows for the compartmentalization of the polity in which (sub-)groups are free to legislate for themselves if the consequences of that legislation are also effectively limited to themselves. However, the promise of democracy across borders is that, where interdependencies exist or are caused by the establishment of collective rules, all those that are affected by them can be brought into the decision-making process. Here European integration promises to break down boundaries that previously existed. It offers a joint political space for the collective deliberation and resolution of cross-national interdependencies (Merlo 2023). Importantly, we thus have to think of European, transnational democracy as supplementary to national democracy (rather than as substituting for it, as per the Ventotene Manifesto), as a means to break through the national boundaries that have traditionally been imposed on democracy whenever the scope or consequences of the decisions justify doing so.

In formal, institutional terms, the EU has come a long way in establishing a system of joint decision-making that can aspire to be democratic. The exercise of European power is subject to an extensive set of checks and balances (Moravcsik 2002). Most notably, the EU can claim no new competences without the prior authorization by all Member States and its exercise of powers is subject to the principles of subsidiarity and proportionality. More importantly, as a rule, EU legislation needs to be passed in two chambers before it can enter into force: first, the Council of Ministers, where it has to command the consent of a super-majority of the democratically elected member governments, and secondly the European Parliament, where it has to command the support of a majority of the European parliamentarians who have been directly elected by the European citizens.

However, democracy is more than just the creation of an institutional space for joint decision-making. As always, democracy is premised on pluralism, the presence of diverse interests and values in society that may well compete with each other (Rawls 1993). Democracy is exactly that set of practices that allows everyone to recognize the collective rules as their own while reasonably conceding that these will not fully match their own interest given the presence of competing interests in the polity. Such concessions require an awareness of these competing interests, the ability to recognize them as legitimate even if they are not one's own, and a willingness to accept them affecting the collective rules. Where democracy works in nation-states, it is because of the presence of a well-working united constitutional framework and culture which allows political conflict to be reconciled in a peaceful and respectful way. Moreover, this usually requires democratic political institutions to be connected to a societal infrastructure of media and a public sphere in which competing interests confront each other and become subject to a process of collective deliberation.

Once we move beyond national borders into the European sphere, the range of pluralism expands (Wolthuis et al. 2025; Chapter 8 of this volume). On top of the established cleavages of domestic politics—like left–right and conservative–progressive—come international dimensions such as differences in national sentiments and national allegiances. Obviously, it is possible to establish institutions for collective decision-making beyond national borders. However, they do not automatically come with a political culture in which the people in the different Member States involved recognize the full range of competing interests and values in other Member States as legitimate. Critically, the social infrastructure of an effectively integrated public sphere and civil society that would facilitate such mutual recognition remains underdeveloped in the EU. The focus of most of the media and public sphere remains at the national level for now. While the visibility of Europe and of the experiences of other EU Member States has certainly increased in these national institutions (Koopmans and Erbe 2004), little of an EU-level public sphere has emerged (Habermas 1995); whatever EU public sphere exists, it operates as a Brussels-centred elite sphere, rather than one that engages the European citizenry at large.

Crucially, in the national context, citizens have come to regard the procedures and practices by which political conflict is reconciled as their own and, hence, as democratic. This is essentially the myth (or promise) of the democratic French revolution, whereby the structures of power that were originally owned by the king were appropriated by the people (Lefort 1986). By contrast, even if the structure of the EU has been the product of deliberate design, it remains essentially the result of negotiations between national governments. In that sense the EU has been founded as a union of states. It may have come to recognize the citizens of these states as direct subjects of the supranational order, but so far it has not granted them the effective power and opportunity to reappropriate and redesign its decision-making structures in accordance with their own will. Indeed, as the EU machinery remains alien and opaque, citizens can only assume that the EU ensures a fair balance between the interests involved. This is supported by the finding that, regardless of the divides that characterize EU politics at present, the foremost issue on which citizens across the political spectrum agree is the expansion of direct citizen participation in EU decision-making (Chapter 10 of this volume).

To sum up, European integration promises to complement national democracies with a transnational democratic sphere that erases the exclusionary boundaries that have divided states historically and, thus, to expand the range of societal pluralism across which collective self-government is possible. However, this promise of EU democracy faces two structural obstacles. First, there is no effective EU public sphere that allows for the collective deliberation of EU decisions. Instead, most EU citizens perceive EU decision-making through the one-sided lens of their national public sphere. Secondly, the EU treaties that define the rules of decision-making and function as a constitution have been enacted by national governments, but have never been appropriated by the people. As a consequence, it remains logical for EU citizens to regard the Union as an external political force, rather than seeing themselves as effective co-authors of EU decision-making.

2.3 Promise unfulfilled: a constitutional treaty for Europe

One cannot engineer a public sphere and its accompanying political culture like one can engineer institutions. Cultural change requires the willing and spontaneous adjustment of individual citizens. Nonetheless, institutional reform may facilitate cultural change. If citizens are invited to engage with EU politics, then their awareness of, and concern about, each other might increase.

Over time, the EU has endeavoured to make a series of institutional reforms that were intended not only to create new inroads into EU decision-making but, ideally, also to contribute to a genuinely shared European public sphere. A critical step was the introduction of direct elections to the European Parliament (EP) in 1979 because it established a collective political focus point rather than assembling the members of the EP from the national parliaments, as had been the case up till then. However, the current set-up of EP elections continues to suffer from major shortcomings. The main deficiency is that the European elections remain under the shadow of national elections (and indeed of national politics more generally) (Reif and Schmitt 1980). Notably, EP elections are still fought on national party lists and in national party districts. Even if national party factions merge into European party groups once they enter the EP, the national parties remain the main conduit back to the (national) constituencies. For the most part, European election campaigns take place in the national context, even if research finds that European topics are increasingly prominent in these campaigns (Gattermann et al. 2021). Apart from the debates that have been organized between the lead candidates of the European parties (de Wilde 2020), there is little of an encompassing political competition at the European level.

The recognition that EU democracy requires more than piecemeal institutional reform very much animated the Constitution project as it emerged in the early

2000s. It was certainly implied in the opening shot of this process, the speech by German foreign minister Joschka Fischer at the Berlin Humboldt University on 20 May 2000. In his speech, Fischer called for the EU to make 'the transition from a union of states to full parliamentarisation as a European Federation' (Fischer 2000). He envisaged a complete overhaul of the EU, putting the EP at its centre and having it control an 'EU government'. Fischer's proposals stood out because of their explicit aim to move beyond the Monnet method of incremental integration and to inspire a wholesale transformation of the EU from a (mere) union of states towards a democratic federation. Thus, he envisaged a pan-European constitutional project that would mobilize the citizens in all Member States that would be willing to take this next step (the 'centre of gravity', as he referred to it). In other words, Fischer recognized that reforming the EU would only take a hold among EU citizens if it were brought about by a collective democratic act.

While many European leaders disagreed with Fischer's proposals, he provoked many of them to share their own visions on the future of Europe (Crum 2003). In December 2001, Belgian Prime Minister Guy Verhofstadt capitalized on this momentum and used his turn as President of the EU to have the Heads of Government adopt the Laeken Declaration (European Council 2001). The Laeken Declaration involved a long list of fundamental and institutional questions on the EU. This list of questions essentially set the agenda for the European Convention that the Declaration established: a body of sixty-six members who were to be delegated by the fifteen EU governments, their national parliaments, the European Commission and the EP, complemented by thirty-nine observers from the thirteen countries that were negotiating EU accession at the time. Concretely, the Laeken Declaration tasked the European Convention 'to consider the key issues arising for the Union's future development and try to identify the various possible responses'.

In the Laeken Declaration, former president of France Valéry Giscard d'Estaing was appointed as chair of the European Convention. Giscard was accompanied by Giulio Amato and Jean-Luc Dehaene, who had been prime ministers of Italy and Belgium respectively, as vice-presidents. From the very first session of the Convention, Giscard set out to turn the Convention into more than a mere consultative and advisory body. Indeed, following closely on Joschka Fischer's call of two years earlier, he sought to turn the Convention into a constituent assembly that would move the EU beyond a union of states. Thus, in his opening speech Giscard called upon the Convention members to aim to build a consensus which would eventually issue in a single proposal: 'If we were to reach consensus on this point, *we would thus open the way towards a Constitution for Europe*' (Giscard d'Estaing 2002, original emphasis).

One and a half years later the European Convention came out with a single comprehensive Constitutional Treaty that envisaged a complete overhaul of the EU treaties (Crum 2012: Ch. 5). The Convention's Constitutional Treaty reorganized and clarified much of the legal procedures of the EU. It also included major institutional reforms, such as the formalization of the European Council, the introduction of a full-time European Council president, a reduction in the size of the European Commission, the elevation of the EP to a full co-legislator with the Council, and the introduction of an Early Warning Mechanism by which national parliaments could object to EU legislation-in-the-making. Notably, the Constitutional Treaty did not move a great deal of new competences to the European level. Rather it sought to ease the exercise of the competences already granted to the EU by expanding the range of domains in which decisions could be taken by a qualified majority instead of unanimity, by simplifying the use of enhanced cooperation among sub-groups of Member States, and by establishing institutional resources available at the EU level, most notably through the establishment of a European External Action Service.

It is hard to overestimate the achievement of having this ambitious and radical package endorsed by almost the whole of the Convention (only eight Convention members adopted their own dissenting 'minority report'). This consensus could only be forged because of the exceptional political skills and commitment of Giscard and the praesidium and staff that surrounded him (Closa 2004; Schönlau 2007; Crum 2012: Ch. 4). So forceful was the substance of the Constitutional Treaty and the Convention consensus behind it that the member governments had no choice but to accept it as the basis of the Intergovernmental Conference (IGC) that was to formally determine the revision of the EU treaties (Crum 2012: Section 7.1). The IGC integrally adopted the Constitutional Treaty's structure while amending seventy-two of its provisions, albeit mostly in minor ways.

While the European Convention was successful in swaying the Member States' governments, it eventually faltered on the spirits that it had invoked by framing itself as a constituent assembly: the EU peoples. As already presaged by Joschka Fischer, if the EU was to be democratized and to move from being a 'union of states' to become what he called a 'European federation', it would require that very process to be thoroughly democratic. In line with this logic, it was widely held that it did not suffice for the Constitutional Treaty to be agreed by the national governments, with subsequent ratification by the national parliaments. Instead, if the new treaty was genuinely constitutional in character, a more demanding and engaging procedure was required: more demanding so that there would be an extra check on these fundamental reforms and more engaging to ensure that these reforms would be actually embraced by the people.

Ten Member States decided that the Constitutional Treaty would be subject to a popular referendum (Crum 2007). This thus involved many more countries than the three countries that had had referendums on previous EU (reform) treaties: Denmark, Ireland, and France. Besides these three were five established Member States—the Netherlands, Luxembourg, the UK, Spain, and Portugal—as well as new Member States the Czech Republic and Poland. Three of these countries could be seen to have committed to a referendum as a sign of confidence (Crum 2012: 137): Luxembourg, Spain, and Portugal. In the other seven, the referendum was also a way to concede to, and to release, some Eurosceptic sentiments, even though the governments involved were generally quite confident that they would secure a positive outcome.

However, in spring 2005, after a solid 77 per cent of the Spanish voters had endorsed the Constitutional Treaty, majorities of 55 per cent in France and 62 per cent in the Netherlands turned against it. These negative outcomes led six of the remaining seven countries that had also envisaged a referendum to suspend their ratification process.[1] Thus, the ratification process unravelled. No pressure was exerted on France and the Netherlands to consider the possibility of a second referendum, partly because the other countries that had committed to a referendum—not least the UK—anticipated the possibility that they would not be able to secure a positive vote either. Instead, the EU Heads of Government put the issue aside by inaugurating a 'period of reflection'.

Eventually, it was the Germany presidency of the first half of 2007 that decided that a new Treaty revision process would be started, but with the abandonment of all constitutional aspirations. Essentially, this strategy allowed almost all of the substance of the reforms included in the Constitutional Treaty to be adopted, but without making them subject to a democratic constituent process. Thus, by October 2007 a very short Intergovernmental Conference reached agreement on the relevant reforms of what became the Treaty of Lisbon. But since the pretensions of a democratic constituent project had been abandoned, the pressure to directly consult the people on its ratification was relieved. Only in the Republic of Ireland was a referendum necessary for constitutional reasons. When the Treaty of Lisbon was first put to the Irish people in June 2008, they rejected it by 53 per cent. However, since this was an isolated case, a declaration was negotiated that sought to assuage the main concerns that had come to the fore in the Irish referendum campaign (Crum 2012: Section 8.3). With that declaration attached, a second referendum yielded a majority of 67 per cent in favour of the treaty (Laffan 2021). The successful referendum in Ireland allowed the Treaty of Lisbon to enter into force on 1 December 2009. Thus, the last comprehensive EU treaty change process that we have seen was completed. However, what had initially promised to be the most ambitious initiative to put the EU on a comprehensive democratic footing was concluded as a rather technical exercise within a closed circle of elected politicians.

[1] Only Luxembourg decided to push ahead with a referendum. On 10 July 2005 the Constitutional Treaty received the support of 57 per cent of the Luxembourg electorate.

2.4 Beyond the constitutional treaty project: managing crises at the cost of democracy

In April 2010, five months after the entry into force of the Treaty of Lisbon, the global financial crisis hit the euro area as credit rating agencies downgraded Greek bonds to junk status. This was only the beginning of a long chain of crises that the EU would come to face, connecting the global financial crisis to the Syrian refugee crisis, Brexit, Covid-19, the Russian invasion of Ukraine, and the re-election of Donald Trump as US President. Each time, these crises forced the EU to adopt new powers and to establish new institutions, for example the European Stability Mechanism, the EU–Turkey migration deal, the common procurement of vaccines, and the reassignment of the European Peace Facility to support Ukraine.

The abandonment of the promise to put the EU on a democratic footing has loomed large over the way these responses have been organized (Fossum 2008; Seubert 2024). Rather than using these crises to mobilize democratic support, EU leaders have adopted a functional approach in which the reforms adopted were deemed to be legitimated by the urgency of the situation and in which democratic popular engagement was shunned rather than sought. In fact, most crisis responses have been concocted exclusively by the Member States' governments and often they have even done so outside of the checks and balances of the EU treaty framework. Bickerton et al. (2015) have aptly labelled this mode of operation 'new intergovernmentalism'. The supranational institutions of the European Commission and the EP only came to be involved when the Member States allowed it. In the process, the Member States frequently bypassed the EU legislative procedures, relying instead on unconventional measures.

The prioritizing of crisis response over democracy was probably most visible during the euro crisis (Schmidt 2020). Not only were citizens and their direct representatives in the EP mostly sidelined, the Member States that were most exposed to the crisis also found that they could only retain their position within the eurozone if they accepted having decisions being imposed upon them by the others. Most notably in Greece, but also in the other states that had to be bailed-out, national democracy was essentially suspended for the sake of soothing the financial markets (Crum 2013). What is more, key collective decisions—like the adoption of the Fiscal Compact and the establishment of the European Stability Mechanism—were adopted outside of the common EU treaty framework, which meant that they were not subject to the fundamental legal principles of the EU treaty framework nor under any control by the EP (Fabbrini and Puetter 2016). Ultimately, a critical role in keeping the euro crisis at bay was played by the European Central Bank (Schmidt 2020: Ch. 6). Typically, operating at marked distance from political oversight, the Bank resorted to various 'innovative' interventions, like its Outright Monetary Transactions programme and its Public Sector Purchase Programme.

Also in the subsequent crises, the EU often stretched its formal competences while shunning democratic engagement and oversight. The adoption of EU migration deals, with the EU–Turkey deal of 2016 as the main example, raises fundamental questions of human rights and democratic accountability (Carrera, den Hartog, and Stefan 2019). In a different way, the financing of the EU's post-pandemic Recovery and Resilience Facility stands on a rather dubious legal footing (de Witte 2021). What is more, again the EP has been mostly sidelined from overseeing the implementation of the facility and the exact allocation of the funds involved (Crum 2020).

Certainly, there remained a simmering sense that the EU still faced a more fundamental democratic challenge. Already in 2008 the European Council appointed a 'Reflection Group' led by former Spanish prime minister Felipe González 'to reflect broadly and deeply on the future of Europe' (Hoffmann and Mayer 2014). However, its recommendations were mostly lost in the whirlwind of the euro crisis. In 2017, the European Commission published a *White Book on the Future of Europe*, which sought to push the debate forward by laying out five scenarios for the future trajectory of the EU (European Commission 2017). The idea was that the White Book would result in a grand debate that would be concluded at the European Council summit in the Romanian city of Sibiu, in the weeks before the EP elections of May 2019. In the end, however, the Sibiu summit only yielded a rather short and symbolic declaration (European Council 2019).

Most recently, in 2021–22, following up on an initial call by French President Emmanuel Macron which was then echoed by Commission President Ursula von der Leyen, the three political institutions of the EU organized a Conference on the Future of Europe (CoFoE). The Conference was organized around a Convention-like Conference Plenary with no less than 383 members representing the EU-level institutions (EP, Council, and Commission), national parliaments, and citizens' initiatives. It furthermore involved sixty-eight observers from EU advisory institutions and civil society. However, the Plenary was only one pillar of a wider initiative which also included a digital platform, a range of national meetings, and, most notably, four EU-wide Citizens Panels. The CoFoE Citizens Panels covered four broad EU policy domains and were each composed of 200 EU citizens who had been randomly selected from the twenty-seven Member States. In May 2022, the Conference delivered its final report which was composed of forty-nine proposals that covered no less than 326 (proposed) measures, as an advice to the three EU-level political institutions, the Council, the EP and the Commission. While the Conference thus successfully completed its work, its contribution to EU democracy has remained rather limited. Since the Conference received remarkably little media coverage, its work has been left unknown to most of the EU citizens. As Oleart (Chapter 11 of this volume) argues, as EU Citizen Panels are organized under the purview of the European Commission, they are marked by a tendency towards depoliticization and detached from the public sphere. While the CoFoE Citizens Panels may have been an impactful experience for the 800 citizens involved, there is little reason to expect that the rest of the EU polity has regarded them as acting on their behalf or in their interest.

All institutions have issued sympathetic responses to the recommendations of the Conference. Only a few proposals were dismissed outright, while for many it was signalled that they were already being taken up by ongoing policy initiatives. The critical bone of contention turned out to be the question of whether a treaty reform process should be initiated to give effect to some of the more radical proposals of the Conference. In fact, the EP adopted a resolution asking the European Council to initiate such a process (EP 2023). However, the European Council declined to respond, while the Commission paid lip service to treaty revision without strongly pushing for it. While the institutions thus found themselves in a stand-off on this fundamental issue, the proposals and experience of the CoFoE were as good as invisible in the 2024 European elections campaign.

As the new College of Commissioners entered office at the end of 2024—in the shadow of wars in Ukraine and Gaza, and in a challenging global environment in which the rise of China undermines Europe's economic prowess while the re-election of Trump as US President threatens its military security—furthering EU democracy seemed to have receded even more as a key concern. Indeed, rather than developing a vision of how to strengthen democracy within the EU, the value of democracy has mostly been invoked in a defensive way as something that distinguishes the EU from most of the rest of the world. Instead of seeking to deepen EU democracy, these external threats to EU democracy are referenced to justify rather restrictive or even securitizing practices. Thus, Greubel and Carbonell (2024) observe a 'clear devaluation of democracy' as a priority in the strategic agenda of the in-coming Commission, and note that:

> Von der Leyen focuses on threats like disinformation and electoral manipulation posed both by external actors (mainly Russia) to the political system and the EU. This shifts the attention regarding the state and future of democracy away from European countries and the current functioning of politics and institutions.

Essentially, then, since the failure of the Convention project, the evolution of the EU has taken place at a considerable and deliberate distance from EU citizens. The trauma of the Constitutional Treaty led EU leaders to suppress any suggestion of engaging in substantial treaty change. The negation of public consultation on EU reform was further justified by the sense of urgency that accompanied the various crises (Kreuder-Sonnen 2016; White 2019). By 2024, preoccupied by external threats, the EU had turned away from delivering on its democratic promise.

2.5 Discussion: can European integration and democracy be reconciled?

Almost twenty years after the failure of the EU Constitutional Treaty, the two structural obstacles to the EU delivering upon its democratic promise—the absence of a collective public sphere and of a democratically authorized constitutional foundation—remain firmly in place. Arguably, they have even become more difficult to overcome. For one, no effective EU public sphere has emerged and the reliance on (new) intergovernmental approaches in dealing with crises may even have deepened the divisions among the Member States and their public debates. What is more, EU leaders have systematically eschewed a broad and inclusive debate that would allow the EU's fundamental structures to be revamped on a genuinely democratic basis. In the absence of a constitutional structure with genuine democratic credentials, the ways in which the EU has addressed the various crises have only risked reinforcing impressions that EU decision-making systematically favours bigger Member States over smaller ones, western Europeans over southern and eastern ones, and corporate interests over those of employees and consumers.

The two obstacles are closely related. It is hard to see how a democratic EU constitution could be adopted without being subject to a truly pan-European debate. EU leaders have a point if they assess that it is close to impossible to conceive of a comprehensive constitutional redesign that can command popular majorities in all twenty-seven EU Member States if the ratification procedures and debates in each Member State remain essentially disconnected from each other (Hooghe and Marks 2009; Bressanelli, Koop, and Reh 2020). This also explains why ever since the agreement on the Treaty of Lisbon, Member State governments have refused to revisit the EU treaties that essentially embody the constitution of EU decision-making.

Thus, the EU appears to face a hard choice between European integration or democracy. From a principled point of view, it may well be concluded that if a democratic EU is not possible under the present conditions, then it would be better to abandon the integration process. This is the way that some in the UK—from the political right and left—argued in favour of Brexit; leaving the EU was a way to regain full democracy at the national level (Bickerton and Tuck 2018). It also resonates in how Peter Mair (2013: Ch. 4) has portrayed European integration as a way for politicians to escape political choices and responsibility. Thus, this line of thought suggests that abandoning European integration would allow nation-states to secure democracy again.

However, this logic runs into two objections. First, by leaving the political system of the EU one does not escape the structure of international power and the transnational interdependencies that are so prominent in the contemporary world. One only gives up on the established political instruments to address these interdependencies in a structured way, however imperfect they may be. Instead, one retreats into the constant jockeying of international negotiations and the power balances that shape them. Secondly, by rejecting integration, one recommits to the established myth of the nation and its God-given boundaries and abandons the promise of extending democracy beyond borders; the promise that we can make it viable to achieve joint democratic decisions with peoples who have been separated from us by historical coincidence.

Ever since the failure of the Constitutional Treaty, EU political leaders seem to have opted for the opposite option: to save the integration project at the cost of democracy. As indicated above, in addressing the euro crisis but also the key challenges of Covid and of refugees fleeing to the EU, European leaders have turned away from seeking democratic authorization and deal with these challenges in a purely instrumental (technocratic) way that suppresses the diversity of political positions on the issue (Wolthuis et al. 2023). Ultimately, however, this strategy risks being self-defeating. It alienates voices that are not heard and that are shut out of the decision-making process; it undermines confidence in democracy as a system of decision-making under conditions of pluralism; and it risks condoning non-democratic practices elsewhere, including in Member States. These consequences undermine the confidence in EU decision-making and, indeed, in the EU as a democratic polity that operates in the service of the EU states and citizens rather than merely ruling over them.

If there is a way out of this dilemma between (further) European integration and democracy, it has to rely on the possibility that the opposition between these two values is not an absolute one but that they allow for some middle way to be found. Essentially, such a middle way would need to commit to continuing the integration project in the spirit of its democratic promise. As underlined in the first section above, democracy is always an aspiration. It is unlikely for any piece of democratic legislation to fully command the reasonable consent of all citizens involved. As it is, EU democracy is structurally impaired. We cannot force a supranational public sphere on the EU. The experience of the European Convention demonstrates furthermore that we cannot force an EU constitutional moment either. However, the very ambition to create a transnational union continues to hold a democratic promise in that it overcomes the national boundaries that have artificially curtailed democratic processes so far. The challenge is to chart a way forward with that promise in mind as well as with the recognition that, as it is, EU democracy is bound to disappoint.

If we recognize EU democracy to be structurally deficient but remain committed to the promise of transnational democracy that it holds, then it is crucial to be more generous and at the same time more modest about the democratic steps that the EU actually takes. Such a reappreciation can start with the way we look back on the Constitution Project and the way its shadow continues to loom over EU decision-making today. If one really counted on a comprehensive democratization of the EU, then the attempt to forge a constitution for Europe in the early 2000s was unlikely to succeed from its very start. Yet, the European Convention came an incredibly long way. Within its confines, the Convention was an exceptional case of transnational deliberation that eventually resulted in an ambitious proposal that rose far beyond the lowest common denominator. Substantively, the proposals of the Convention were also well thought through (if anything, they may have fallen short on ambition), which the EU Member States confirmed by agreeing to them twice, first in the Intergovernmental Conference immediately following the Convention and secondly in adopting almost all of them again in the Treaty of Lisbon. Where the Convention failed was in engaging the national publics in its deliberations. Clearly, it was handicapped by the absence of an EU public sphere. However, the very pressure that the Convention leadership built to come to a consensus internally induced a kind of cognitive closure to the outside world among its members (Crum 2012: Ch. 6). Rather than engaging openly with their constituents, many Convention members tended to identify with the line of thought set out by the Convention and to engage with the public in a rather defensive way.

However, the main problem with the Constitution Project lay in the response of EU politicians once they found out that a consensus among the EU publics was not naturally forthcoming (Crum 2012: Chs 7 and 8). When confronted with the negative referendum results in France and the Netherlands, they did not engage in a public debate about what could be done to improve the Constitutional Treaty, but looked at the referendum results as wholesale rejections. Here it did not help that other Member States were quite happy to withdraw from their earlier commitments to having a referendum themselves (although looking back at it, for the UK, this might have been the better referendum to have had). This response stands in marked contrast to the response, three years later, to the initial No-vote on the Treaty of Lisbon in the Republic of Ireland. It is easy to look cynically at what happened in Ireland (and, previously, also with the Treaty of Nice in Ireland and the Treaty of Maastricht in Denmark) by saying: just have a referendum until you get the right answer. But you can also look at this as the natural way for democracy to evolve, as an ongoing and never-ending conversation between politicians and the people (Laffan 2021). Even if the public may not be convinced a first time, they may come around a second time, if you take them seriously.

If European leaders want the integration process to continue—if only for dealing with the external challenges that they face—*and* they want to do so in the spirit of democracy, then the only way to do so is to engage in bold initiatives in which EU citizens are actively involved and consulted on the decisions being taken and accepting that democracy may lead to decisions being withdrawn or amended. This is a fundamentally different approach than the one that the EU has adopted in the past fifteen years of crisis governance. Among other things, it would require more frequent citizens consultations or referendums on major decisions, more active engagement of the EP and national parliaments in crisis governance and in the monitoring of its subsequent implementation, and turning democratic experiments like citizens' panels into genuine agenda-setting bodies (Chapter 11 of this volume; Abels et al. 2022). Such practices will have their price in the short-term; they may increase the challenge of reaching decisions and, even when EU leaders have been able to reach agreement, slow down their implementation. However, in the long run, such a reorientation can contribute to EU citizens gaining trust in EU decision-making, to the emergence of a transnational public sphere, and to the EU living up to its democratic promise.

2.6 Conclusion

In the Ventotene Manifesto, Spinelli and Rossi derided democrats and the procedures they adhere to:

> At the very moment when the greatest decisiveness and boldness is needed, democrats lose their way, not having the backing of spontaneous popular approval, but rather a gloomy tumult of passions. They think it their duty to form a consensus and they represent themselves as exhortatory preachers, where instead there is a need for leaders who know just what they want (Spinelli and Rossi 1988: 28).

In the present day, political leaders lack the certainty that Spinelli and Rossi called for. In fact, 'leaders who know just what they want' may well be the greatest danger not only for democracy but also for the integration project. Democracy may well be deficient, but it is probably the best and most socially sustainable option we have. This certainly also applies to the EU, even if it remains far removed from being a mature democratic polity. However, if we do not want to give up on the promise of EU democracy then the only way to deal with it is to try again and to continue the conversation with the citizens.

The Constitutional Treaty project brings important lessons for any attempt to democratize the EU, while recognizing the structural constraints that this process faces. Three of these lessons can be highlighted in particular. The first, which Joschka Fischer (2000) had already underlined at the very start of the Constitutional Treaty process, is that credible EU democratization requires substance to go hand in hand with performance. Democratic reforms are only credible if they are enacted through a democratic process. If the EU is to be democratized, this cannot be done by resorting to intergovernmentalism, but only by systematically involving citizens and their directly elected representatives. At the same time, democratic initiatives will only be credible and elicit active engagement in the media and among the public if they can result in substantive democratic reforms. This point underlines the limitations of, for instance, experimenting with European Citizens Panels if their place in the decision-making process remains unclear and they are not given any genuine power (Chapter 11 of this volume).

The second lesson from the Constitutional Treaty project is that once a serious trajectory to democratize the EU is undertaken, it is likely to take on a life of its own. Typically, if one convenes some kind of convention to reflect upon the future of the EU, it is likely to come to think of itself as having constituent power and hence to transcend the mandate that it has been given. This is of course what Giscard actively pursued with the European Convention, and EU leaders are all too aware that this may happen again with any new initiative (and were keen to contain the recent Conference on the Future of Europe to that effect). However, a confident democratic polity should allow such dynamics to unfold and be confident that they can eventually be channelled again and brought to a common resolution.

The third and final lesson is that any serious initiative to democratize the EU is likely to disappoint and fail to deliver the collective democratic experience that it promises. It is a major challenge to build consensus on fundamental concerns within any broadly representative EU body but, if it succeeds, then whatever consensual proposals emerge can be expected to meet major opposition among the public outside. Such opposition may be lessened if the public at large can be engaged in the course of the political deliberations. However, as we know, this is unlikely in the absence of a well-integrated European public sphere. Still, even the shared experience of the failing of a collective proposal and of political conflict may in the long run constitute a next step in the trajectory towards the fulfilment of the EU as a transnational democracy. The promise of EU democracy can only be sustained if European leaders are willing to face the public and the setbacks that that may occasion.

References

Abels, G. et al. (2022). *Next Level Citizen Participation in the EU: Institutionalising European Citizens' Assemblies*. Gütersloh, Bertelsmann Stiftung.

Abizadeh, A. (2012). On the Demos and Its Kin: Nationalism, Democracy, and the Boundary Problem. *American Political Science Review*, 106(4): 867–882.

Bickerton, C., Hodson, D., and Puetter, U. (2015). The New Intergovernmentalism: European Integration in the Post-Maastricht Era. *Journal of Common Market Studies*, 53(4): 703–722.

Bickerton, C. and Tuck, R. (17 August 2018). A Brexit Proposal. *Briefings for Britain*. https://briefingsforbrexit.com/a-brexit-proposal-by-christopher-bickerton-and-richard-tuck/.

Bressanelli, E., Koop, C., and Reh, C. (2020). EU Actors under pressure: politicisation and depoliticisation as strategic responses. *Journal of European Public Policy*, 27(3): 329–341. https://doi.org/10.1080/13501763.2020.1713193.

Carrera, S., den Hertog, L., and Stefan, M. (2019). The EU–Turkey Deal: Reversing Lisbonisation in EU Migration and Asylum Policies. In Carrera, S., Santos Vara, J., and Strik, T. (eds). *Constitutionalising the External Dimensions of EU Migration Policies in Times of Crisis*. Cheltenham, Edward Elgar: 155–174.

Closa, C. (2004). The Convention Method and the Transformation of EU Constitutional Politics. In Eriksen, E. O., Fossum, J. E., and Menéndez, A. J. (eds). *Developing a Constitution for Europe*. London, Routledge: 183–206.

Conway, M. and Depkat, V. (2010). Towards a European History of the Discourse of Democracy: Discussing Democracy in Western Europe 1945–60. In Conway, M. and Patel, K. K. (eds). *Europeanization in the Twentieth Century: Historical Approaches*. Basingstoke/New York, Palgrave Macmillan: 132–156.

Crum, B. (2003). Legislative–Executive Relations in the EU. *Journal of Common Market Studies*, 41(3): 375–395.

Crum, B. (2007). Party Stances in the Referendums on the EU Constitution: Causes and Consequences of Competition and Collusion. *European Union Politics*, 8(1): 61–82.

Crum, B. (2012). *Learning from the EU Constitutional Treaty*. London, Routledge.

Crum, B. (2013). Saving the Euro at the Cost of Democracy? *Journal of Common Market Studies*, 51(4): 614–630.

Crum, B. (2020). How to Provide Political Guidance to the Recovery and Resilience Facility? European Parliament: Directorate-General for Internal Policies/Economic Governance Support Unit (EGOV). https://data.europa.eu/doi/10.2861/939747.

de Wilde, P. (2020). The Fall of the Spitzenkandidaten: Political Parties and Conflict in the 2019 European Elections. In Kritzinger S. et al. (eds). *Assessing the 2019 European Elections*. London, Routledge: 37–53.

de Witte, B. (2021). The European Union's COVID-19 Recovery Plan: The Legal Engineering of an Economic Policy Shift. *Common Market Law Review*, 58(3): 635–682.

European Commission (2017). *White Book on the Future of Europe*. Brussels.

European Council (15 December 2001). The Future of the EU: Declaration of Laeken, SN 273/01, Laeken.

European Council (9 May 2019). The Sibiu Declaration. https://www.consilium.europa.eu/en/press/press-releases/2019/05/09/the-sibiu-declaration/.

European Parliament (22 November 2023). Resolution on Proposals of the European Parliament for the Amendment of the Treaties (2022/2051(INL)). https://www.europarl.europa.eu/doceo/document/TA-9-2023-0427_EN.html.

Fabbrini, S. and Puetter, U. (2016). Integration without Supranationalisation: Studying the Lead Roles of the European Council and the Council in post-Lisbon EU Politics. *Journal of European Integration*, 38(5): 481–495.

Fischer, J. (12 May 2000). From Confederacy to Federation. Speech at the Humboldt University, Berlin.

Fossum, J. E. (2008). European Constitutional Avoidance. Oslo, ARENA/University of Oslo, unpublished paper.

Gattermann, K., de Vreese, C., and van der Brug, W. (2021). Introduction to the Special Issue: No Longer Second-Order? Explaining the European Parliament Elections of 2019. *Politics*, 41(4): 423–432.

Giscard d'Estaing, V. (26 February 2002). Introductory Speech to the Convention on the Future of Europe. SN 1565/02, Brussels.

Greubel, J. and Carbonell, J. (2024). Democracy Demoted. Commentary. Brussels, European Policy Centre. https://www.epc.eu/en/Publications/Democracy-demoted~5db060.

Habermas, J. (1993). *Faktizität und Geltung*. Frankfurt, Suhrkamp.

Habermas, J. (1995). Remarks on Dieter Grimm's 'Does Europe Need a Constitution?'. *European Law Journal*, 1(3): 303–307.

Hoffmann, L. and Mayer, H. (2014). An Expectation–Outcome-Gap Writ Large: The Felipe González Reflection Group Revisited. In Foret, F. and Rittelmeyer, Y. S. (eds). *The European Council and European Governance. The Commanding Heights of the EU*. London, Routledge: 129–146.

Hoffmann, S. (1966). Obstinate or Obsolete? The Fate of the Nation-State and the Case of Western Europe. *Daedalus*, 95(3): 862–915.

Hooghe, L. and Marks, G. (2009). A Postfunctionalist Theory of European Integration: From Permissive Consensus to Constraining Dissensus. *British Journal of Political Science*, 39(1): 1–23.

Kant, I. (1793). On the Common Saying: That May be Correct in Theory, But it is of no Use in Practice. In Gregor, M. (trans. and ed.) (1996). *Practical Philosophy*. Cambridge, Cambridge University Press: 273–311.

Koopmans, R. and Erbe, J. (2004). Towards a European Public Sphere? *Innovation: The European Journal of Social Sciences*, 17(2): 97–118.

Kreuder-Sonnen, C. (2016). Beyond Integration Theory: The (Anti-)Constitutional Dimension of European Crisis Governance. *Journal of Common Market Studies*, 54(6): 1350–1366.

Laffan, B. (2021). Referendums on EU Treaty Reform: Revisiting the Result in Second Referendums. In Smith, J. (ed.). *The Palgrave Handbook of European Referendums*. Cham, Palgrave Macmillan: 563–581.

Lefort, C. (1986). La question de la démocratie. In *Essais sur le politique*. Paris, Seuil: 17–30.

Mair, P. (2013). *Ruling the Void*. London, Polity Press.

Marshall, T. H. (1950). *Citizenship and Social Class and Other Essays*. Cambridge, Cambridge University Press.

Merlo, S. (2023). A Republican Fiscal Constitution for the EMU. *Critical Review of International Social and Political Philosophy*: 1–23.

Moravcsik, A. (2002). Reassessing Legitimacy in the European Union. *Journal of Common Market Studies*, 40(4): 603–624.

Näsström S. (2003). What Globalization Overshadows, *Political Theory* 31(6): 808–834.

Rawls, J. (1993). *Political Liberalism*. New York, Columbia University Press.

Reif, K. and Schmitt, H. (1980). Nine Second-Order National Elections—A Conceptual Framework for the Analysis of European Election Results. *European Journal of Political Research*, 8(1): 3–44.

Schmidt, V. (2020). *Europe's Crisis of Legitimacy*. Oxford, Oxford University Press.

Schönlau, J. (2007). The 'Convention Method'. In Castiglione, D. et al. (eds). *Constitutional Politics in the European Union*. Basingstoke, Palgrave Macmillan: 90–111.

Seubert, S. (2024). The Conference on the Future of Europe as a Chance for Democratic Catching Up? Towards a Citizen-Centred Perspective on Constitutional Renewal in the European Union. *Global Constitutionalism* 13(2): 429–447. doi:10.1017/S2045381723000199.

Spinelli, A. and Rossi, E. (1988 [1941]). *The 1944 Ventotene Manifesto*. Ventotene, The Altiero Spinelli Institute for Federalist Studies. https://www.ssipseminario.it/wp-content/uploads/2020/03/The-Ventotene-Manifesto-Spinelli-Rossi.pdf.

White, J. (2019). *Politics of Last Resort. Governing by Emergency in the European Union*. Oxford: Oxford University Press.

Wolthuis, A. J., Crum, B., Oleart, A., and Overeem, P. (2023). Democracy and Pluralism after European Integration: Incorporating the Contested Character of the EU. *Critical Review of International Social and Political Philosophy*, 28(6), 1136–1160. https://doi.org/10.1080/13698230.2023.2216043.

3

The Promises and Pitfalls of EU 'Democracy Promotion' in the International Arena: A Decolonial Perspective

*Alvaro Oleart and Tom Theuns**

3.1 Introduction: problematizing EU 'democracy promotion' abroad

The European Union (EU) has the ambition—and the promise—of being a powerful normative actor for the promotion of democracy in international affairs. Article 21(2b) of the Treaty on European Union (TEU) boldly declares that 'consolidat[ing] and support[ing] democracy, the rule of law, human rights and the principles of international law' are key goals of EU external action. Were it to live up to these lofty ideals, it would give form to the idea of 'Normative Power Europe' (NPE), first theorized over twenty years ago (Manners 2002; for a critical view, see Staeger 2016).

The narrative of an EU that acts as a democratic actor in international affairs is common. While the democratic quality of the Union itself can be questioned, democratic government is a key criterion of membership in the Union, especially since membership standards were formalized in the Copenhagen criteria (even if there are certain caveats, see Dudley 2020). In fact, EU integration is often applauded for consolidating democracy in the European continent. EU institutions themselves are supposedly legitimated through a delegated mandate from elected Member State governments and through the directly elected European Parliament. After the brutal shocks of totalitarianism and war, the latter half of the twentieth century was broadly perceived to be a period of the development and democratization of Western, Northern, and Southern Europe, and later of many countries in

* The authors thank the participants of the seminar of the International Organization and European Integration research clusters at the Institute of Political Science, Leiden University, for their comments and suggestions; the EU politics workshop of the Politicologenetmaal 2023 hosted by the KU Leuven, especially Elena Escalante Block, Gilles Pittoors, and Jan Pieter Beetz; and the EWIS 2023 workshop 'Critical Perspectives on the European Union's Role as a Global Actor'. Section 3.3 draws on and develops some points from Sampson and Theuns (2023). We also thank the editors of this volume for their constructive comments.

Alvaro Oleart and Tom Theuns, *The Promises and Pitfalls of EU 'Democracy Promotion' in the International Arena: A Decolonial Perspective* In: *The Promise of EU Democracy*. Edited by: Jan Wouters, Julie Smith, Kolja Raube, and Ben Crum, Oxford University Press. © Alvaro Oleart and Tom Theuns 2026.
DOI: 10.1093/9780191996191.003.0004

Central and Eastern Europe following the collapse of the Soviet Union.[1] With this narrative in mind, the EU's professed commitment to democracy, and the potential of peaceful European integration more generally, could serve as a model for other regions of the world seeking to develop and democratize.

The EU is also a powerful actor in economic terms. This wealth could be used to support pro-democratic civil society abroad in its struggle to achieve and consolidate democratic self-rule, as well as subsidize the costs of democratic transition. However, several aspects limit the EU's ability to promote democracy effectively and coherently. There is a post-colonial paradox of supposedly 'promoting democracy' across the globe, while failing to adequately address Europe's colonial legacies and actually undermining democratic values abroad. We theorize the normative contours and incoherences of this paradox as the EU's 'Messiah complex'. This refers to the Eurocentric discursive and symbolic commitment to 'lead' democratization efforts internationally, yet simultaneously often contributing to the support of authoritarian governments abroad. Beyond this normative incoherence, a failure to address Europe's colonial legacies in how to approach democracy support internationally ignores the historical roots of political domination and can overshadow local efforts, expertise, and preferences, such as when a liberal model of economic organization is promoted as a prerequisite for, or coextensive with, liberal democratic institutions (Theuns 2017). This chapter develops a normative critique of EU 'democracy promotion' policies in the international arena.

This analysis opens an opportunity to develop a 'decolonial project for Europe' as proposed by Bhambra (2022), which begins by acknowledging the material structures inherited from colonialism that are still present today:

> The peculiarity of colonialism and the end of empire is that the nations that were responsible are not required to account for those wider histories in discussions of their past. In contrast, the world that was subjugated by Europe cannot examine issues in its present without taking into account how their past of having been colonized has determined their present and futures. (Bhambra 2022: 232)

Largely overlooking the relevance of its colonial past, the way in which the EU has attempted to foster democracy outside the EU has been characterized by a 'one-size-fits-all' model, especially in the area of trade (Theuns 2019). Despite rhetoric to the contrary, partner countries have been expected to unilaterally adopt EU standards,

[1] Of course, this narrative of the history of European integration in the second half of the twentieth century is blinkered. For example, although these Southern European countries were ultimately and peacefully integrated in the European project, we cannot ignore that the Francoist dictatorship in Spain, which lasted until 1975, the far-right militarist Junta ruling Greece from 1967 to 1973, and the brutal Yugoslav wars of the 1990s coexisted with the evolving institutions of European integration. Even for the earliest participants in the EU project, a story of development and democratization that ignores the bloody aftershocks of colonialism is hagiographic. Consider for instance how the French army was using torture systematically in the Algerian war at the same time the French government signed the Treaty of Rome (Lazreg 2016; Brown 2022).

both in the cases of EU candidate countries negotiating accession as well as countries further afield engaging in trade negotiations with the EU. Yet a commitment to democracy and equal partnership demands a greater scope for differentiation in terms of policy choices and, more fundamentally, the inclusion of non-executive actors in the discussions (Theuns 2017). The net benefit of cooperation with the EU may be considerable, but using this as a conditional incentive requires a nuanced approach. It is important to recognize that demands of wide and deep economic reforms also come with significant costs to candidate countries. Such transformations come at considerable sacrifices for some and may even be detrimental to democratization when applied without sensitivity to the broader power dynamics at play. Such normative incoherences and paradoxes, which we theorize as the EU's 'Messiah complex' in democracy promotion, are thus tied in with Europe's colonial legacies.

The chapter is structured as follows. After this introduction, we first examine the EU's recent 'geopolitical turn' in international affairs, critically evaluating commitments to strategic autonomy and European sovereignty through a decolonial perspective. Next, we discuss a dominant perspective in EU democracy promotion; namely the idea that the EU may be able to spread democratic norms through its approach to trade. We consider why the implementation of a standardized trade model, whereby partner countries are not conceived of as democratic partners which determine their own economic and trade policies, undermines a democratic ethos. Third, the chapter argues that the EU has often empowered autocratic actors in partner countries, undermining a democracy-promotion agenda. We argue that the EU has applied the standards with which it rewards reform or sanctions regression on democratic governance ('conditionality') unequally. This undermines the expressive clarity of EU democracy promotion policy, in both its 'instructive' function, i.e. communicating which governance reforms would be taken to constitute democratic advances, and its 'declarative' function, articulating the normative ideal the EU is trying to defend (Poama and Theuns 2019: 797–799). Fourth, we argue that the EU often empowers authoritarian actors through its international agreements. In the fifth section, we articulate our notion of the EU's 'Messiah complex' in democratization. We argue that the EU must learn lessons from democratic backsliding within the European Union, orienting democratization efforts towards promoting democratic pluralism. We conclude with a wider perspective, suggesting that moving towards a decolonial paradigm may be a way to fulfil the EU's promises as a democratic actor in international affairs.

3.2 The EU's 'geopolitical turn' of 'strategic autonomy' and 'European sovereignty': a decolonial reading

The last few years have seen the rise of the securitization or 'geopoliticization' (Meunier and Nicolaïdis 2019) of 'Europe', with the discursive deployment of concepts such as 'strategic autonomy' and 'European sovereignty' (Jacobs et al. 2022).

Relatedly, the Von der Leyen European Commission (2019–24) defined itself as the 'geopolitical Commission', a narrative that has only grown stronger since the Russian invasion of Ukraine in February 2022. However, 'defending Europe' has not traditionally been part of EU institutional narratives (Biegoń 2013), as this field has rather been associated with defence policy and institutions such as NATO. This is changing, due partly to the ideational entrepreneurship of actors such as French President Emmanuel Macron, who has put forward a narrative conceptualized as 'Make Europe Great Again' (Bouza García and Oleart 2021). Yet, the way that the EU conceptualizes this internal–external relation remains paternalistic, even neo-colonial, in ways that undermine the possibility of the EU acting in line with democratic values as a positive force for democracy abroad.

It is important to acknowledge the complexity of external policy, given the difficulties of trying to shape outcomes in jurisdictions beyond one's direct control. Thus, foreign policy is liable to be accused of hypocrisy. However, the inconsistencies in terms of principles fit within a relatively coherent pattern of strengthening global hierarchies whereby the imbalance of power between the EU and (most of) the rest of the world is maintained. Thus, it prioritizes the agency and knowledge production of Eurocentric perspectives, sidelining the agency of actors contesting the status quo.

The EU's 'geopolitical turn' allows European actors both to offer a new form of more affirmative pro-Europeanism, and to address and challenge Europe's internal and external 'rivals'. In this way, the supposedly threatening role of external actors is crucial in conveying a coherent narrative that would unite all Europeans against foreign 'others' such as Russia or China. This idea of uniting the national sovereignties of the EU Member States into a European sovereignty is sometimes justified on the basis that citizens demand protection from an external enemy, while also connecting the internal and external dimension of sovereignty (see Roch and Oleart 2024). In a speech to the EU Parliament that was exemplary of this rhetorical strategy, French President Emmanuel Macron (2018) argued the following:

> Confronted with all the current tensions with certain neighbours such as Russia, Europe has shown a front of unity and sovereignty. We need to continue this work ... I want to belong to a generation which will defend European sovereignty because we fought for it, because it means something and because it is this sovereignty which will enable future generations to choose their own futures. I will not yield to any fascination for authoritarian sovereignties.

Such a muscular and combative approach to EU internal–external relations may be appealing for pro-Europeans, but as a foundation for EU democracy-promotion in international affairs it is blinkered. It is broadly unable to cope with post-colonial legacies that remain in place today, as 'colonialism never left Europe unaffected and is still part of European reality' (Kinnvall 2016: 153). The EU often references

Europe's past to make sense of European integration as a process of maintaining 'peace', yet sidelines colonialism from its collective memory (see Sierp 2020). However, on 13 October 2022 at a speech at the College of Europe, then High Representative and Vice President Josep Borrell broke the silence, arguing:

> Europe is a garden. We have built a garden. Everything works. It is the best combination of political freedom, economic prosperity and social cohesion that the humankind [*sic*] has been able to build—the three things together. . . . The rest of the world . . . is not exactly a garden. *Most of the rest of the world is a jungle, and the jungle could invade the garden.* The gardeners should take care of it, but they will not protect the garden by building walls. . . . *The gardeners have to go to the jungle.* Europeans have to be much more engaged with the rest of the world. Otherwise, the rest of the world will invade us, by different ways and means. Yes, this is my most important message: we have to be much more engaged with the rest of the world. (EEAS 2022, emphasis added)

This discourse illustrates how mainstream EU political discourse remains highly paternalistic in the way in which the relationship between the EU and third countries is conceived, sidestepping a decolonial commitment to mutuality, colonial reparations, and the dismantling of existing oppressive material structures. Referring to the world beyond Europe through the jungle metaphor is simply a problematic image that rests on a racist and colonial trope wherein Europeans are 'civilized' and non-Europeans 'wild'.

The idea that the EU should have 'strategic autonomy' becomes problematic when it ignores Europe's colonial past and present. Such claims are framed as a way to compete with other (imperial) 'powers', such as China or Russia, whose imperialist attitudes remain evident. This perspective of inter-imperial competition between imperial polities takes away the agency and indeed the autonomy of countries that have traditionally been subordinated to colonial relations. This is problematic when juxtaposed with the EU's supposed normative ambitions to promote democracy globally. Paradoxically, while denying the ways in which material relations between states today remain marked by the history of colonialism, much of the EU institutional discourse, illustrated by Borrell's speech, remains anchored in the idea of 'helping them to develop', which they are viewed as unable to do by themselves.

In fact, alongside a colonial narrative of the *mission civilisatrice*, EU institutional racism continues to racialize communities—for instance through the 'border protection' policies of Frontex that systematically put in danger thousands of people fleeing from war and looking for a better life (Léonard and Kaunert 2022). In this way 'Europe' is constructed as an 'imagined community' (Oleart and Van Weyenberg 2019), leaving out the colonial legacies of the EU (see Van Weyenberg 2019).

Conceiving global relations in a more egalitarian way is crucial to encourage transnational and decolonial democratization. As climate change and the Covid-19 pandemic have demonstrated, ours is a shared fate that cannot be summarized as a competition between imperial powers that leaves out of the picture the voices of often-excluded actors, such as indigenous peoples, the Global South, and citizens of poorer and less populous countries.

A decolonial project requires that the EU see itself not as a 'garden' that ought to be protected from 'the jungle' that it must seek to 'tame'. Instead, European actors in foreign policy should depart from the diagnosis that what is conceived by EU officials as the 'garden' was inseparably constructed through a history that includes widespread colonial exploitation. Such exploitative relations are antithetical to the kind of mutuality required of a relationship based on democratic principles, and therefore must be overcome. Yet, many aspects of this exploitative relationship remain in place today through various means (including migration, development, and trade).

It is telling that, even when discussing racism within the EU, it is rarely discussed in the context of the history and aftershocks of global European colonialism.[2] Migration is a case in point. When Margaritis Schinas was proposed as EU Commissioner for 'Protecting the European Way of Life' by Commission President-candidate Ursula von der Leyen with the portfolio of migration, a public outcry followed. This controversy centred on two elements: first, Schinas's portfolio would include migration, which would seem to imply conceding the far-right attack line that immigrants threaten the 'European way of life'; second, it is reductive in imagining that there is such a monolithic thing as 'the' European way of life instead of recognizing plural *ways* of life. Under pressure, Von der Leyen adjusted the job title to 'Promoting our European Way of Life', but the initial phrasing is a good indication of the way in which migration is conceived. The EU's internal conception of whom the 'we' refers to remains both racialized and inextricably connected to Europe's colonial past (see Fekete 2019; Oleart 2023).

In fact, as Hansen and Jonsson (2014: 31) have argued in their book *Eurafrica: The Untold History of European Integration and Colonialism*, the 'unification of Europe and a unified European effort to colonize Africa were two processes that presupposed one another. Africa could be developed only by Europe, and Europe could develop its fullest potential only through Africa' (see also more recently Kundnani 2023). If the EU is to promote democracy in Africa, it must first

[2] It is relevant to remember the 2012 commercial developed by the EU in which the EU portrayed itself as a white woman dressed as Uma Thurman's character 'The Bride' in the 2003 film *Kill Bill: vol. 1*, confronting, in an abandoned train station, an Asian man, an Arab man with a turban and a sword, and a bare-chested black man (see Allen Greene and Pérez Maestro 2012). The video was met with swift accusations of racism through stereotypical representations, and with completely sidelining Europe's colonial past, after which it was taken down.

come to terms with this history. Acknowledging the colonial origins of the EU, as well as its ongoing colonial legacies, is a first step towards democratizing European foreign policy.

3.3 Democracy promotion through trade: the development paradigm and a democratic ethos

As a powerful actor in economic terms, one of the major tools the EU claims to use in its pursuit of democracy abroad is trade. While the Union also makes use of other strategies, the main strategy of normative power Europe (NPE) to promote democracy abroad has been 'leverage': using economic conditionality to try to incentivize progress towards democratic reform (Theuns 2017). Evaluating the normative tensions of the EU's use of economic conditionality to promote democracy clarifies some of the more general normative concerns we wish to highlight regarding the EU's approach to democracy promotion.

The potential for using European wealth for pro-democratic ends is substantial. Making preferential access to the EU market conditional on democratic reforms could serve as a powerful incentive for elites in authoritarian states to democratize and could subsidize the costs of democratic transition. Such conditionality can be divided into 'positive' and 'negative' forms; positive conditionality revolves around the offer of some benefit (such as trade benefits) in exchange for progress, whereas negative conditionality imposes a sanction (such as freezing assets or rolling back trade) as a response to regression on democratic norms. The benefits or sanctions involved can be financial, political, or social.

While the primary arena of NPE was post-Cold War democratization (Börzel and Risse 2009), to understand the genealogy of EU democracy promotion we have to go back to EU development policies. The Lomé trade and aid agreements between the EU and African, Caribbean and Pacific group (ACP) countries would eventually formalize commitments to human rights and democratic principles. While Lomé I (1976) did not provide for any formal conditionality mechanisms, the EU suspended most aid to Uganda as a response to human rights violations by the regime of Idi Amin. Partly in response to this, Lomé III (1985) formalized abstract political commitments to human rights and human dignity in the trade and aid deal, but it was not until the fourth Lomé Convention (1990) that a specific commitment to democracy was included.

'Partner' countries from the African, Caribbean and Pacific group saw the normative goals of the Lomé agreements as dominated by the European side (Sampson and Theuns 2023). Both the unilateralism of suspension mechanisms and the absence of joint procedures for measuring violations led to strong opposition from ACP countries (Holland and Doidge 2012: 72). However, their opposition proved ineffective, and conditionality was introduced in a 1995 revision to

Lomé IV, which contained, for the first time, a suspension clause (Art 366a). This clause enabled the agreement to be suspended as a last resort response to violations of human rights, democracy, or the rule of law (Art 5). The suspension clause was consequently invoked by the EU against Burundi (1996), Niger (1996), Nigeria (1993), Rwanda (1995), and Sierra Leone (1997).

Conditionality as a leverage strategy for pursuing normative governance goals in EU foreign affairs therefore preceded the EU democratization programmes of the 1990s. In early versions, the type of conditionality was 'negative' and focused on suspension as a last resort response. A more gradated strategy, including elements of both positive and negative conditionality, developed in the 1990s with the first MEDA programme (running from 1995 to 1999, this programme covered Algeria, Egypt, Jordan, Lebanon, Morocco, Syria, Tunisia, Turkey, and the Palestinian Authority) and the European Initiative for Democracy and Human Rights (running from 1994 to 2007, this initiative was global in scope, extending to over 100 countries). This set the stage for the EU strategy of using trade deals to try to proactively pursue democratic reforms, though these tools have not always been used coherently (Theuns 2019: 12–14).

The idea that EU foreign policy is based on promoting democracy, the rule of law and respect for human rights has been widely echoed by EU institutions as one of the guiding discursive justifications of its policy choices. Academically, it has been reflected in concepts such as 'Normative Power Europe' (Manners 2002) or 'Ethical Power Europe' (Aggestam 2008). But, to examine the promise and pitfalls of EU democracy promotion in the international order, we must look beyond the lofty rhetoric to the substantive question of whether and, if so, how EU action in the international arena upholds or undermines democracies beyond the EU's borders (Alcazar III 2024). Moreover, despite a rhetoric of cooperation and coordination, the EU tends to apply a standard trade model and international cooperation to partner countries (see, e.g., Delcour 2013; Kostanyan 2015). While there is some differentiation, especially at the regional level, EU trade policy seems one-sided when we look beyond partners in Europe, North America, Latin America, and East Asia (Sampson and Theuns 2023). This undermines a democratic ethos whereby partner countries are perceived as potential democratic partners who determine their own economic and trade policies (Theuns 2017). Furthermore, the conception of democracy upon which such efforts are built fails to incorporate social justice, as illustrated by the marginalization of trade unions and demands for social and economic rights in the context of the EU's 'democracy assistance' during the Arab Spring (see Teti 2015).

Ultimately, the political underpinnings of the EU's standard trade model encourage countries in the Global South to develop export-led economies that benefit from having easy market entry points to the EU. This increases the political and economic dependency on the EU and consolidates the existing asymmetric power relations. The hierarchical relationship is consolidated by an imaginary that situates these countries as 'unable' to develop themselves (on the concept of 'failed states', see Woodward 2017). Less powerful countries are seen as in need of 'development'—hence the term 'developing countries' (see Orbie et al. 2022)—a process that requires the agency of (colonial) European actors that 'know better'. Overall, this dynamic reproduces a paternalistic relationship between actors of the Global North and the Global South (on how the identities constructed by European development aid workers shape their practices, see Baaz 2005). Such unequal relationships reflect the ongoing colonial legacies, which hinders EU 'democracy promotion'.

Recent changes in EU trade policy show a similar insensitivity for mutuality. As a response to the politicization of (particularly) the Transatlantic Trade and Investment Partnership (TTIP, EU–US) and the Comprehensive and Economic Trade Agreement (CETA, EU–Canada), the European Commission has introduced increasingly frequent references to 'European values' in trade documents (Oleart 2021b). For instance, the 2015 Trade for All strategic document reframed trade as a way to 'not only project our interests, but also our values' (European Commission 2015: 5), which remains within the post-colonial 'development' paradigm (Ziai 2013).

What could an alternative decolonial approach look like? To remain coherent with the democratic values that underpin the EU's ambition to be a normative power in international affairs, democracy promotion by the EU must follow a democratic ethos that sees democratizing partners as countries whose peoples ought to determine their *own* domestic affairs democratically, including in the domains of economics and trade. Perhaps a starting point would be holding accountable the private corporations—most of which are run out of the Global North and many of which are European—that most benefit from trade agreements, often at the expense of environmental concerns, labour standards, or human rights. For example, in 2014, after the initiative taken by the government of Ecuador (co-sponsored by the governments of Bolivia, Cuba, South Africa, and Venezuela), the United Nations Human Rights Council (UNHRC) adopted by a simple majority a resolution calling for a binding treaty on business and human rights (see European Parliamentary Research Service 2022). Yet all EU Member States (as well as the United States) sitting on the UNHRC voted against the resolution, on the grounds that such a process (which would operate in parallel to the EU Directive on corporate sustainability due diligence) could undermine the credibility of the EU and its Member States as promoters of democracy and human rights. Despite ongoing negotiations, the EU still lacks a formal mandate from the Council with regard to the binding treaty. Thus, one step towards a decolonial approach to democratizing foreign trade policy would be for the EU to democratize its approach to trade by supporting the binding treaty seeking to holding accountable the multinational corporations that benefit most from the unequal relations between the Global North and the Global South. This leads us to our next point: the role that EU external policies may have when empowering authoritarian governments abroad. Such empowerment can be an unwanted side-effect of EU trade and development policy, but it can also entail collusion between the EU's developmental perspective and domestic authoritarian actors.

3.4 Empowering foreign authoritarian actors via the EU's international agreements

'He may be a son of a bitch, but he's our son of a bitch' is a quote often attributed to Franklin Delano Roosevelt when referring to Anastasio Somoza García, Roosevelt's contemporary as the authoritarian President of Nicaragua and an anti-communist ally of the United States. While it is most likely apocryphal, it described well the asymmetric foreign policy of the United States government in this period, which often had the US supporting dictators in the name of 'freedom'. Similarly, the EU has sometimes (though perhaps more inadvertently) empowered autocratic actors in partner countries (Theuns 2019) by (1) externally legitimizing them through partnership and inconsistently applying the leverage tools it has at its disposal and (2) by accepting superficial or merely 'functional' reforms instead of real democracy reform.

One way the EU empowers authoritarian actors abroad is simply by externally legitimizing, and therefore inadvertently reinforcing, the domestic power of the political elite in an authoritarian country. The risk is contributing to a dynamic where pro-democratic opposition and civil society actors find their own position relatively worse off, as the EU provides some authoritarian governments with a significant economic and symbolic legitimacy. For instance, there is evidence that the EU's migration management aid strengthens security actors and authoritarian practices (see Norman and Micinski 2022), at the expense of local civil society. The recent 2023 EU–Tunisia deal is a case in point, whereby the EU committed to support the Tunisian economy (led by President Kais Saied, who has a highly problematic track record on democracy and human rights) in exchange for, among other things, halting migration to the EU. Several human rights groups critiqued the agreement. For instance, Lauren Seibert, refugee and migrant rights researcher at Human Rights Watch, argued that 'by funding security forces who commit abuses during migration control, the EU shares responsibility for the suffering of migrants, refugees, and asylum seekers in Tunisia' (Human Rights Watch 2023). Similarly, in March 2024 almost 200 civil society organizations called for the suspension of the EU–Israel Association Agreement (International Federation for Human Rights 2024), as the Agreement includes human rights and democratic principles as 'essential elements'. In spite of the human rights violations against Palestinians in Gaza[3] in the aftermath of the deadly Hamas-led attack on 7 October 2023, the EU maintained its support for the Netanyahu-led Israeli government, leaving the Association Agreement intact while 'othering' Palestine (Oleart and Roch 2025).

[3] South Africa put forward a case in December 2023 (pending at the time of writing in July 2025) in the International Court of Justice against Israel on the grounds that it is committing a genocide against Palestinians in Gaza. Amnesty International (2024) has also made that case.

These examples illustrate the inconsistency with which the EU applies negative conditionality mechanisms (Seeberg 2009; Pace 2009), and the continuity of colonial thinking. We can see that the EU often prioritizes other ends such as geopolitical concerns, strategic autonomy, and simple self-interest over democracy promotion and the consistent application of conditionality against authoritarian regimes that violate supposedly minimal conditions of democratic government and respect for human rights. This undermines the normative coherence of democracy promotion (Sampson and Theuns 2023). Coherence in how the European Union gives form to its commitment to democracy is not only a concern of normative theory; the core treaties of the EU make an explicit commitment to this kind of coherence. For instance, Article 7 of the Treaty of the Functioning of the EU (TFEU) states that the EU 'shall ensure consistency between its policies and activities, taking all of its objectives into account'. The link to the EU's fundamental values (listed in TEU, Art 2) is even clearer in Article 13 of the TEU, which insists that the entire institutional framework of the EU 'shall aim to promote its values, advance its objectives, serve its interests, those of its citizens and those of the Member States, and ensure the consistency, effectiveness and continuity of its policies and actions'. Thus, not only must EU policies and actions be *internally* coherent in that they do not undermine one another—what may be called 'weak coherence'—but they should also to an extent derive from ('aim to promote') the same core values.

Thus, it is crucial not to compromise efforts to democratize third countries simply because the governments of such countries are willing to adhere to the EU's negotiation proposals, as they may reinforce the dominant position of authoritarian actors vis-à-vis their own population. The negotiation and ratification of bilateral free trade agreements of the EU with certain governments, especially when negotiated on the basis of 'European values' as a 'force for good' (for the EU–Vietnam trade agreement, see Nessel and Verhaeghe 2022), may legitimize and whitewash those governments and complicate the democratization of those polities. For that reason, 'democracy promotion' via trade agreements or through other international negotiations may have a negative effect overall, and the main benefactors of these sorts of negotiations are multinational European export and import companies as well as authoritarian governments.

Another way in which EU efforts at democracy promotion can empower authoritarian actors is when the EU accepts superficial reforms, or reforms that merely liberalize policymaking in their outcomes, as progress towards democratic government. An example of this can be seen in the way the EU seeks to liberalize trade, immigration, and anti-corruption policies in Morocco. By avoiding sensitive 'red lines', while reinforcing the narrative that the Moroccan monarchy was liberalizing such policies, the EU played into the hands of those seeking to consolidate authoritarianism and legitimize the regime (Catalano and Graziano 2016; Natter 2021: 857). Such empowerment can be an unwanted side-effect of EU trade and development policy, but it can also entail collusion between the EU's developmental perspective and domestic authoritarian actors.

In this way, EU actors who are supposed to be working towards democracy promotion are often satisfied with securing minor policy reforms, rather than tackling deeper political problems such as corruption or the constitutional aspects of authoritarianism. Anna Khakee and Ragnar Weilandt (2022: 475) put this dynamic well in the context of their research on EU relations with Moroccan civil society actors in trade relations and anti-corruption policies: 'To seriously challenge nepotism and corruption involves challenging the very foundations of the Moroccan political establishment, an establishment that the EU has relatively good working relations with'. The agreements with Tunisia and Morocco illustrate how some of the EU's external policies are directly responsible for the strengthening of authoritarian governments and contribute to whitewashing them. In doing so, the EU is undermining democracy activists protesting against such governments.

3.5 Overcoming the EU's Messiah complex: from empowering autocrats to strengthening civil society and democratic pluralism

In an article on the legitimacy of European integration, Joseph Weiler defines political messianism as when 'the justification for action and its mobilizing force derive . . . from the ideal pursued, the destiny to be achieved, the "Promised Land" waiting at the end of the road' (2012: 832). In the way the EU has pursued democracy promotion activities, we identify a form of this sort of political messianism. The worthiness of the ideal—democratization—serves to obscure critical attention to the means used to pursue the ideal. Too often this leads to normative paradoxes and incoherences in EU democracy promotion, what we call the EU's 'Messiah complex'. Suggesting that European 'gardeners' need to tame the 'jungle' is the explicit dimension of the neo-colonialism that underlies the EU's Messiah complex.

Some of the pitfalls of the EU's 'democracy promotion' policies closely mirror the pitfalls around its response to democratic backsliding in EU Member States. By many accounts (e.g. Holesch and Kyriazi 2022), Hungary and Poland have slipped below minimum democratic and rule of law standards, and Hungary is no longer widely considered a democratic country. This democratic rot inside the EU corrodes the credibility of the EU to promote democracy abroad. The inaction of various EU institutional actors—especially the European Commission and the European Council—in the face of democratic backsliding in the EU undermines the message that democracy is really a core value of the European integration project. Combined with the discourse of authoritarian actors in the EU claiming they support alternative models of democracy, such as Viktor Orbán's 'illiberal democracy', this inaction further muddies the waters of what EU democracy promotion intends to promote, undermining the express coherence of EU policy in this area

(Theuns 2020; Theuns 2022). Thus, addressing democratic backsliding within the EU must be an urgent priority if the EU has the ambition of being a pro-democratic actor in international affairs.

As developed in a recent article (see Oleart and Theuns 2023), the EU in general, and the European Commission in particular, tends to have a rather depoliticized conceptualization of 'democracy' that is not suited to addressing democratic backsliding in a meaningful way. The normative import of democratic contestation, democratic opposition, and democratic pluralism are overlooked (Theuns 2021). Unsurprisingly, then, efforts to address democratic decay in EU Member States have been largely ineffective so far. The Commissioners' framing of democracy matches the policy choices made in responding to democratic backsliding. Support for pluralist civil society is ignored in favour of an approach that focuses largely on the rule of law. A less technocratic and more politicized approach would also stimulate and reinvigorate the EU as a more integrated and democratic polity, potentially leading towards an 'empowering dissensus' (Bouza and Oleart 2018; Oleart 2021a) for European integration.

The Commission has developed myriad legal monitoring tools to assess Member States' judicial systems and the rule of law. Yet, few of these mechanisms assess the ailing health of the public spheres of backsliding Member States (the case of Hungary is the most evident), the suppression (through death by regulation, co-option, and intimidation) of critical voices in academia, civil society, and the media, or the disadvantages stacked against opposition actors and parties to compete as equals in the public sphere. Sanctions mechanisms are focused on the eventual exclusion of backsliding parties from EU political decision-making, securing *de jure* concessions on the organization of the judiciary and anti-corruption, and cutting off EU funds to backsliding states. These may be important elements, not least to try to contain the influence of budding autocrats on EU legislation and to reduce the complicity of the EU in Member States' backsliding (Theuns 2020; Theuns 2025), but they do little in themselves to foster pluralist democracy and a healthy public sphere.

This approach can also be projected on international negotiations between the EU and third countries. Pluralist democracy should be promoted not through a series of checklists of legal-constitutional reforms, economic thresholds, and legislative alignment. Real commitment to democratic values requires fostering vibrant democratic contestation and acknowledging that the European project was built upon the colonial dispossession of millions of people around the world. This is especially urgent, given that authoritarian EU Member States may serve as an inspiration for other political elites across the world, and particularly in candidate countries whose political elites may be attracted by the benefits of EU membership but reluctant to give up control. Addressing democratic backsliding within EU Member States is thus vital for the credibility and coherence of the EU's actions internationally. Abandoning the 'Messiah complex' that the EU should advance its own technocratic standards of 'democracy'—which often lead to the empowering of autocrats within and beyond the EU—is the first step towards engaging in a commitment to democratic pluralism.

3.6 Conclusion: moving towards a decolonial perspective in EU 'democracy promotion' policy

The chapter has laid out a normative critique of the EU's philosophy and action when 'promoting democracy' in the international arena, and suggested ways to address the colonial legacies in EU foreign policy. Alternatives should begin by acknowledging the EU's colonial origins and adopting a logic of decoloniality, which entails striving 'to ethically prioritise situated and embodied knowledges from the global souths whose historical presence is often elided' (Alcazar III et al. 2023: 188). Rather than 'democracy', perceived geopolitical 'self-interest' (which is often accompanied by neoliberalism and free trade) is still often the driver of the EU's actions in the international arena, justified with the language of 'values' and 'democracy'. In contrast, a decolonial perspective is oriented towards challenging the undemocratic global hierarchies of political power that maintain the EU (and the Global North more broadly) in a structural position of dominance vis-à-vis the Global South. Such a perspective is antithetical to a Eurocentric commitment to 'lead' the world, which has often led to support for authoritarian governments abroad. Instead, the EU should support pro-democratic civil society, even if this is at the expense of benefits to European companies.

In practice, the EU's 'democracy promotion' efforts should be oriented towards acknowledging and strengthening the agency of democratic actors in third countries. Democratic legitimacy demands that political choices are made in the context of a vibrant public sphere, in which a plural set of political parties compete in free and fair elections, and where trade unions and civil society play a meaningful role in shaping public discourse and policymaking. Wide and deep reforms to partners' economies and their alignment with the EU's positions are fundamentally political choices that ought to be decided by democratic processes of the polities with which the EU negotiates in the international arena. This perspective breaks away from an 'administrative' understanding of democracy that emphasizes the legal dimension over the political one. For democracy to be vibrant, processes of representation and contestation must include the confrontation of real alternative visions of society, deliberated in an open way in civic spaces that facilitate such exchanges.

To be a pro-democratic actor in the international arena, the EU should reconceptualize its relations with third countries through a commitment to mutuality, including accepting that it may sometimes need to do 'less' in the international arena (Rutazibwa 2010). Furthermore, the EU must both acknowledge and materially address its colonial past and present and avoid empowering autocratic actors, however inadvertently. Finally, the EU should meaningfully address democratic backsliding within the EU over trying to 'export' democratic government abroad.

Our chapter has implications not only for the EU's actions in the international arena, but also for the way in which academics address it. We should aim to contribute not only to the democratization of the EU internally and externally, but also to the democratization and decolonization of the *study* of international relations. The academic field of European studies, including that oriented towards the EU's action in the international arena, remains largely anchored within the development paradigm. Furthermore, while there has been excellent work departing from a more critical perspective (Haastrup et al. 2020; Nessel 2021; Orbie 2021), some critical approaches have been oriented towards the symbolic dimension of the EU's relation to the rest of the world. Under the umbrella of 'decentring' Europe (see Fisher Onar and Nicolaïdis 2013; Keukeleire and Lecocq 2018; Wolff et al. 2022), the driving idea is to strengthen the 'voices' of non-European actors. Such a perspective falls short of calling for the dismantling of the colonial material structures that still remain in place today. The risk, in other words, is that the EU could 'decentre' without 'decolonizing' (see Orbie et al. 2023).

The EU ought to focus not only on prioritizing historically marginalized voices and 'reversing the gaze' to learn from democratic experiences around the world (Nicolaïdis and Youngs 2023), but also on dismantling existing material structures that reflect and perpetuate Europe's colonial character. The inherent paternalism and propensity to securitization and exploitation of the colonial framework is antithetical to the norms of mutualism and equality that a democratic ethos demands.

It is crucial for the EU to move away from developmental thinking and a colonial mindset if it is to operate meaningfully in a way that has a positive influence on democracy within and beyond the EU, two dimensions that are closely linked to each other. In other words, 'without a reckoning on how coloniality is part of the tapestry of the EU's identity, at least in Africa where many are no longer at ease with the status quo, the drive to improve relations will remain aspirational' (Haastrup et al. 2021: 553). The EU needs to reckon with its own past and present by abandoning its Messiah complex, dismantling existing colonial structures, and getting its own democratic house in order, if it is to become an actor for transnational and decolonial democratization.

References

Aggestam, L. (2008). Introduction: Ethical Power Europe? *International Affairs*, 84(1): 1–11.

Alcazar III, A. S. M. (2024). *Brussels's Burden: (Un)making the Global Souths in the European Union's Preferential Trade Policy, Doctoral Dissertation*, Vienna, Central European University.

Alcazar III, A. S. M., Nessel, C., and Orbie, J. (2023). Decolonising EU Trade Relations with the Global Souths? *Journal of Contemporary European Research*, 19(2): 181–205.

Allen Greene, R. and Pérez Maestro, L. (8 March 2012). EU Kills Kill Bill-Style Video Over Racism Complaints. CNN. https://edition.cnn.com/2012/03/08/world/europe/europe-racist-video/index.html. Accessed 2 June 2023.

Amnesty International (2024). Israel/Occupied Palestinian Territory: 'You Feel Like You Are Subhuman': Israel's Genocide Against Palestinians in Gaza. https://www.amnesty.org/en/documents/mde15/8668/2024/en/. Accessed 21 July 2025.

Baaz, M. E. (2005). *The Paternalism of Partnership: A Postcolonial Reading of Identity in Development Aid.* London/New York, Zed Books.

Bhambra, G. K. (2022). A Decolonial Project for Europe. *JCMS: Journal of Common Market Studies*, 60(2): 229–244.

Biegoń, D. (2013). Specifying the Arena of Possibilities: Post-structuralist Narrative Analysis and the European Commission's Legitimation Strategies. *JCMS: Journal of Common Market Studies*, 51(2): 194–211.

Börzel, T. and Risse, T. (2009). Venus Approaching Mars? The European Union's Approaches to Democracy Promotion in Comparative Perspective. In Magen, A., Risse, T., and McFaul M. A. (eds). *Promoting Democracy and the Rule of Law.* Basingstoke, Palgrave Macmillan: 34–60.

Bouza, L. and Oleart, A. (2018). From the 2005 Constitution's 'Permissive Consensus' to TTIP's 'Empowering Dissensus': The EU as a Playing Field for Spanish Civil Society. *Journal of Contemporary European Research*, 14(2): 87–104.

Bouza García, L. and Oleart, A. (2021). Make Europe Great Again: The Renewed Pro-European Narrative of Macron. In Haapala, T. and Oleart, A. (eds). *Tracing the Politicisation of the EU: The Future of Europe Debates Before and After the 2019 Elections.* Cham, Palgrave Macmillan: 271–293.

Brown, M. (2022). *The Seventh Member State: Algeria, France, and the European Community.* Cambridge, MA, Harvard University Press.

Catalano, S. L. and Graziano, P. R. (2016). Europeanization as a Democratization Tool? The Case of Morocco. *Mediterranean Politics*, 21(3): 364–386.

Delcour, L. (2013). The European Union: Shaping Migration Patterns in the Neighbourhood ... and Beyond? In Amtenbrink, F. and Kochenov, D. (eds). *The European Union's Shaping of the Legal International Order.* Cambridge, Cambridge University Press: 261–282.

Dudley, D. (2020). European Union Membership Conditionality: the Copenhagen Criteria and the Quality of Democracy. *Southeast European and Black Sea Studies*, 20(4): 525–545.

EEAS (13 October 2022). European Diplomatic Academy: Opening Remarks by High Representative Josep Borrell at the Inauguration of the Pilot Programme. https://https://www.eeas.europa.eu/eeas/european-diplomatic-academy-opening-remarks-high-representative-josep-borrell-inauguration_en. Accessed 21 October 2022.

European Commission (14 October 2015). Trade for All: European Commission Presents New Trade and Investment Strategy. http://trade.ec.europa.eu/doclib/press/index.cfm?id=1381. Accessed 13 June 2022.

European Parliamentary Research Service (2022). Towards a Binding Treaty on Business and Human Rights. https://www.europarl.europa.eu/RegData/etudes/BRIE/2022/729435/EPRS_BRI(2022)729435_EN.pdf. Accessed 12 December 2023.

Fekete, L. (2019). Colonial Continuities within Managed Migration. *Global Affairs*, 5(2): 163–170.

Fisher Onar, N. and Nicolaïdis, K. (2013). The Decentring Agenda: Europe as a Post-colonial Power. *Cooperation and Conflict*, 48(2): 283–303.

Haastrup, T., Duggan, N., and Mah, L. (2021). Navigating Ontological (In)security in EU–Africa Relations. *Global Affairs*, 7(4): 541–557.

Haastrup, T., Mah, L., and Duggan, N. (eds). (2020). *The Routledge Handbook of EU-Africa Relations.* London, Routledge.

Hansen, P. and Jonsson, S. (2014). *Eurafrica: The Untold History of European Integration and Colonialism.* London, Bloomsbury Publishing.

Holesch, A. and Kyriazi, A. (2022). Democratic Backsliding in the European Union: the Role of the Hungarian-Polish Coalition. *East European Politics*, 38(1): 1–20.

Holland, H. and Doidge, M. (2012). *Development Policy of the European Union*. Basingstoke, Palgrave Macmillan.

Human Rights Watch (2023). Tunisia: No Safe Haven for Black African Migrants, Refugees. https://www.hrw.org/news/2023/07/19/tunisia-no-safe-haven-black-african-migrants-refugees#:~:text=Though%20international%20human%20rights%20standards,assisting%20illegal%20entry%20or%20exit. Accessed 12 December 2023.

International Federation for Human Rights (2024). Suspend the EU–Israel Association Agreement. https://www.fidh.org/en/international-advocacy/european-union/suspend-the-eu-israel-association-agreement. Accessed 26 March 2024.

Jacobs, T., Gheyle, N., De Ville, F., and Orbie, J. (2022). The Hegemonic Politics of 'Strategic Autonomy' and 'Resilience': COVID-19 and the Dislocation of EU Trade Policy. *Journal of Common Market Studies*, 61(1): 3–19.

Keukeleire, S. and Lecocq, S. (2018). Operationalising the Decentring Agenda: Analysing European foreign policy in a Non-European and Post-Western World. *Cooperation and Conflict*, 53(2): 277–295.

Khakee, A. and Weilandt, R. (2022). Supporting Democratic Participation beyond Democracy Promotion? EU Relations with Moroccan and Tunisian Civil Society in the Areas of Trade and Anti-Corruption. *Mediterranean Politics*, 27(4): 456–482.

Kinnvall, C. (2016). The Postcolonial has Moved into Europe: Bordering, Security and Ethno-cultural Belonging. *Journal of Common Market Studies*, 54(1): 152–168.

Kostanyan, H. (2015). Neither Integrated nor Comprehensive in Substance: Armenia and Georgia. In Wetzel, A. and Orbie, J. (eds). *The Substance of EU Democracy Promotion*. London, Palgrave Macmillan: 134–48.

Kundnani, H. (2023). *Eurowhiteness: Culture, Empire and Race in the European Project*. London, Hurst Publishers.

Lazreg, M. (2016). *Torture and the Twilight of Empire: From Algiers to Baghdad*. Princeton, NJ, Princeton University Press.

Léonard, S. and Kaunert, C. (2022). The Securitisation of Migration in the European Union: Frontex and its Evolving Security Practices. *Journal of Ethnic and Migration Studies*, 48(6): 141–1429.

Macron, E. (20 April 2018). Speech in the EU Parliament. https://www.elysee.fr/en/emmanuel-macron/2018/04/17/speech-by-emmanuel-macron-president-of-the-republic-at-european-parliament. Accessed 21 July 2025.

Manners, I. (2002). Normative Power Europe: a Contradiction in Terms? *Journal of Common Market Studies*, 40(2): 235–258.

Meunier, S. and Nicolaïdis, K. (2019). The Geopoliticization of European Trade and Investment Policy. *Journal of Common Market Studies*, 57(1): 103–113.

Natter, K. (2021). Crafting a 'Liberal Monarchy': Regime Consolidation and Immigration Policy Reform in Morocco. *The Journal of North African Studies*, 26(5): 850–874.

Nessel, C. (2021). Colonialism in its Modern Dress: Post-Colonial Narratives in EUrope-Indonesia Relations. *Asia Europe Journal*, 19(1): 59–74.

Nessel, C. and Verhaeghe, E. (2022). 'A Force for Good': The Narrative Construction of Ethical EU–Vietnam Trade Relations. *Journal of Common Market Studies*, 60(3): 741–758.

Nicolaïdis, K. and Youngs, R. (2023). Reversing the Gaze: Can the EU Import Democracy from Others? *Journal of Common Market Studies*, 61(6): 1605–1621.

Norman, K. P. and Micinski, N. R. (2022). The European Union's Migration Management Aid: Developing Democracies or Supporting Authoritarianism? *International Migration*, 61(4): 57–71.

Oleart, A. (2021a). *Framing TTIP in the European Public Spheres: Towards an Empowering Dissensus for EU integration*. London, Palgrave Macmillan.

Oleart, A. (2021b). The Discursive Legitimisation of Market-oriented EU Trade Policy Through 'European Values' in a Post-permissive Consensus Era: From 2006 Global Europe to 2015 Trade for All. In Foret, F. and Vargovčíková, J. (eds). *Value Politics in the European Union: From Market to Culture and Back*. New York, Routledge: 78–95.

Oleart, A. (2023). *Democracy Without Politics in EU Citizen Participation: From European Demoi to Decolonial Multitude*. London, Palgrave.

Oleart, A. and Roch, J. (2025). The Colonial Imaginary of 'Europe' in the EU's Asymmetrical Response to the Russian and Israeli Aggressions: Ukraine as a Member of the 'Family' Whilst 'Othering' Palestine. *Journal of Common Market Studies*, 63(6): 1689–1709.

Oleart, A. and Theuns, T. (2023). 'Democracy Without Politics' in the European Commission's Response to Democratic Backsliding: From Technocratic Legalism to Democratic Pluralism. *Journal of Common Market Studies*, 61(4): 882–899.

Oleart, A. and Van Weyenberg, A. (2019). Introduction to the Special Issue Narrating 'Europe': a Contested Imagined Community, *Politique Européenne*, 66(4): 6–14. DOI: https://doi.org/10.3917/poeu.066.0006.

Orbie, J. (2021). The Graduation of EU Development Studies: Towards a Post-Colonial Turn? *Global Affairs*, 7(4): 597–613.

Orbie, J., Alcazar III, A. S. M., and Sioen, T. (2022). A Post-Development Perspective on the EU's Generalized Scheme of Preferences. *Politics and Governance*, 10(1): 68–78.

Orbie, J., Alcazar III, A. S. M., Bougrea, A., Nagy, S., Oleart, A., Paz, J. C., Sebhatu, R. W., Williams, T. G., and Wodzka, I. (2023). Decolonizing Rather than Decentring 'Europe'. *European Foreign Affairs Review*, 28(1): 1–8.

Pace, M. (2009). Paradoxes and Contradictions in EU Democracy Promotion in the Mediterranean: the Limits of EU Normative Power. *Democratization*, 16(1): 39–58.

Poama, A. and Theuns, T. (2019). Making Offenders Vote: Democratic Expressivism and Compulsory Criminal Voting. *American Political Science Review*, 113(3): 796–809.

Roch, J. and Oleart, A. (2024). How 'European Sovereignty' became Mainstream: the Geopoliticisation of the EU's 'Sovereign Turn' by Pro-EU Executive Actors. *Journal of European Integration*, 46(4): 545–565.

Rutazibwa, O. U. (2010). The Problematics of the EU's Ethical (Self)Image in Africa: The EU as an 'Ethical Intervener' and the 2007 Joint Africa–EU Strategy. *Journal of Contemporary European Studies*, 18(2): 209–228.

Sampson, M. and Theuns, T. (2023). Comparing Chinese and EU Trade Agreement Strategies: Lessons for Normative Power Europe? *International Relations*, 39(1): 101–124.

Seeberg, P. (2009). The EU as a Realist Actor in Normative Clothes: EU Democracy Promotion in Lebanon and the European Neighbourhood Policy. *Democratization*, 16(1): 81–99.

Sierp, A. (2020). EU Memory Politics and Europe's Forgotten Colonial Past. *Interventions*, 22(6): 686–702.

Staeger, U. (2016). Africa–EU Relations and Normative Power Europe: A Decolonial Pan-African Critique. *Journal of Common Market Studies*, 54(4): 981–998.

Teti, A. (2015). Democracy without Social Justice: Marginalization of Social and Economic Rights in EU Democracy Assistance Policy after the Arab Uprisings. *Middle East Critique*, 24(1): 9–25.

Theuns, T. (2017). Promoting Democracy through Economic Conditionality in the ENP: a Normative Critique. *Journal of European Integration*, 39(3): 287–302.

Theuns, T. (2019). The Legitimacy of Free Trade Agreements as Tools of EU Democracy Promotion. *Cambridge Review of International Affairs*, 32(1): 3–21.

Theuns, T. (2020). Containing Populism at the Cost of Democracy? Political vs. Economic Responses to Democratic Backsliding in the EU. *Global Justice: Theory Practice Rhetoric*, 12(02): 141–160.

Theuns, T. (2021). Pluralist Democracy and Non-Ideal Democratic Legitimacy: Against Functional and Global Solutions to the Boundary Problem in Democratic Theory. *Democratic Theory*, 8(1): 23–49.

Theuns, T. (2022). The Need for an EU Expulsion Mechanism: Democratic Backsliding and the Failure of Article 7. *Res Publica*, 28: 693–713.

Theuns, T. (2025). *Protecting Democracy in Europe: Pluralism, Autocracy and the Future of the EU*. New York, Oxford University Press.

Van Weyenberg, A. (2019). 'Europe' on Display: A Postcolonial Reading of the House of European History. *Politique Européenne*, 66(4): 44–71.
Weiler, J. H. (2012). In the Face of Crisis: Input Legitimacy, Output Legitimacy and the Political Messianism of European Integration. *Journal of European Integration*, 34(7): 825–841.
Wolff, S., Gazsi, D., Huber, D., and Fisher-Onar, N. (2022). How to Reflexively Decentre EU Foreign Policy: Dissonance and Contrapuntal Reconstruction in Migration, Religious and Neighbourhood Governance. *Journal of Common Market Studies*, 60(6): 1611–1628.
Woodward, S. L. (2017). *The Ideology of Failed States*. Cambridge, Cambridge University Press.
Ziai, A. (2013). The Discourse of 'Development' and why the Concept should be Abandoned. *Development in Practice*, 23(1): 123–136.

4
Ideas of EU Democracy Across Time and Space: The Contributions of the Commission and the Court of Justice

Lise Rye and Cristina Fasone

4.1 Introduction

The European Union (EU) has been described as the outcome of a process instrumental to economic and legal integration between the Member States (Cappelletti, Seccombe, and Weiler 1986; de Burca 2011). The Ventotene Manifesto made no clear commitment to the creation of a transnational democracy, beyond the promise to abolish the division of Europe into national, sovereign states responsible for the atrocities of the Second World War (see Chapter 2 in this volume).

However, not only were the founding Member States 'politically joined by an aversion to authoritarianism and a commitment to democracy' (Chapter 2, Section 2.2 in this volume), but the EU's institutions and decision-making procedures are increasingly invoked to protect democracy and the rule of law outside and within its borders (von Bogdandy et al. 2021). Which visions of democracy (if any) has the EU sought to channel over space and time and have they been consistent across EU institutions?

This chapter engages with the ideas of democracy promoted by the EU and their historical and spatial evolution. It does so under the assumption that there is no unique and monolithic understanding of democracy at the supranational level, but that there are slightly different visions depending on the institution at stake. While representative institutions like the European Parliament (EP), the Council of Ministers and the European Council have already been the object of in-depth investigations from the standpoint of both their democratic underpinnings and their impact on EU democratic decision-making (e.g. Rittberger 2005; Puetter 2014), other key actors within the EU institutional system, notably the European Commission and the Court of Justice of the European Union (CJEU or 'the Court'), have rarely been analysed from this perspective. The lack of specific

Lise Rye and Cristina Fasone, *Ideas of EU Democracy Across Time and Space: The Contributions of the Commission and the Court of Justice* In: *The Promise of EU Democracy*. Edited by: Jan Wouters, Julie Smith, Kolja Raube, and Ben Crum, Oxford University Press. © Lise Rye and Cristina Fasone 2026. DOI: 10.1093/9780191996191.003.0005 studies devoted to the Commission and the CJEU as institutions committed to enhancing democracy in the EU is not very surprising, as these two supranational institutions lack genuine democratic credentials themselves and their source of legitimacy is primarily grounded in the technical knowledge and the expertise of their members in various policy areas, starting with the internal market.

Only after the 2009 Treaty of Lisbon (Art 17(7) TEU) was an attempt made formally to link the appointment of the Commission to the results of EP elections (Crum 2023; Ceron, Christiansen, and Dimitrakopulos 2024). The 'life' of any Commission, anyway, has always been under the threat of a censure by the Parliament (Treaty of the Functioning of the EU (TFEU), Art 234), even when it was not directly elected. Moreover, the Commission exercises powers that are politically highly salient in agenda-setting, legislative initiative, and consultation of interested parties. Even the profile of Commissioners has become increasingly political over the last twenty years, with most of them being experienced politicians at EU and domestic levels, including former national ministers.

By contrast, due to the principle of judicial independence, the CJEU has tried to remain detached from democratic politics and national interests in its institutional design and operations (Tridimas 2018; but see critically, Kochenov and Butler 2021). Yet to improve the quality of the appointment procedure for the Court's judges and advocates-general against the influence of the Council of Ministers, under the Treaty of Lisbon, Article 255 TFEU established a link with the main symbol of EU democracy (Dumbrovsky, Petkova, and Van der Sluis 2014): the European Parliament proposes one of the members of the new panel set up to give an opinion on the candidates' suitability to perform the duties of judge and advocate general. However, by no means does this procedure make the Court a democratic body of the EU.

Despite being endowed with different powers, composition, and mandate, the Commission and the CJEU were both established at the outset of the founding Communities, entrusted to safeguard the enforcement of EU treaties, including the fundamental value of democracy, first enshrined in the 1999 Treaty of Amsterdam (TEU, Art 2). The Commission and the Court have acted as the engines of integration and, thus, as primary players in shaping the European trajectory. Thus, given their capacity to influence the evolution of the EU, their visions of EU democracy provide insights into the way the enforcement of EU law is combined with promoting democratic principles in the Union to push the legitimacy of the European integration process further, nurturing a transnational democracy in the making to supplement but not replace national democracies (Chapter 2 in this volume). At the same time, both the Commission and the Court of Justice's engagement with democracy depend on the need to entrench it as one of the Union's foundational values (again, under TEU, Art 2), cutting across the functioning of supranational as well as domestic institutions. Indeed, taking stock of their counter-majoritarian function vis-à-vis the national governments, they seem to firmly believe that the 'transnational interlocking of powers' at supranational level is meant to 'secure and strengthen [domestic] democracies' (Chapter 2 in this volume).

Our focus on the Commission and the CJEU allows us to consider whether, and if so how, two powerful EU institutions, devoid of strong democratic credentials, unlike the Parliament and the Council of Ministers, which embody the idea of representative democracy in the EU (TEU, Art 10), channel and promote democracy in the EU. The research draws on archival work regarding the Commission and on textual analysis of judgments and other official documents as well as academic publications by judges in its analysis of the Court. It aims to unpack and compare the visions of democracy portrayed by the two institutions. Additionally, attention is devoted to ascertaining whether the EU enlargement process has triggered a shift in the democratic visions of the Commission and the Court and their roles in portraying a certain idea of democracy to the candidate countries.

The analysis shows that the vision of democracy channelled by the two institutions has grown incrementally and to a large extent consistently with one another, as this comparison demonstrates throughout this chapter. This common idea encompasses strengthening representative democracy through the EP, the guarantee of pluralism, and the insistence on transparency, access to documents and citizens' participation. However, there are some inevitable differences. Interestingly, while the Commission has concentrated on facilitating citizens' participation in EU democracy, the CJEU has built a vision of democracy broader than that of the Commission, also insisting on fundamental rights' protection. The target of this democratic vision has expanded in scope and refers not only to the EU institutional system but also to the democratic systems of the Member States in the context of backsliding in the rule of law.

Finally, it appears that this more compelling vision of democracy has not been conveyed clearly to acceding countries in the framework of the enlargement process. While the Court does have a clear view on democracy in the European context, it has not made it sufficiently explicit in the guidance provided to candidate states since the big enlargement of 2004, as the priority back then was smoothing the integration of the Member States into the internal market. Less attention was paid—retrospectively by mistake, as the rule of law backsliding highlights—to integrating them into the realm of liberal democracies, in light of judicial standards that had already been developed at supranational level.

4.2 The vision of the European Commission on democracy

4.2.1 The 1950s and 1960s: an instrumental view of democracy

The European Commission was established with the 1957 Treaty of Rome. Like the High Authority of the European Coal and Steel Community (ECSC) in operation since 1952, this executive body of the European Economic Community (EEC) was a manifestation of Jean Monnet's original vision of technocratic policy leadership (Featherstone 1994: 150). The Rome Treaty granted the Commission important powers while establishing its complete independence, making it clear that its appointed members, 'chosen on the ground of their general competence and European commitment from persons whose independence is beyond doubts', should 'neither seek nor take instructions from any Government or other institution, body, office or entity' (Treaty of Rome establishing the EEC, Art 157). The perception of the EU as being disconnected from its citizens and hence undemocratic has since been closely connected with the Commission's powerful but independent position in the EU system (Harcourt and Radaelli 1999: 107; Wille 2012: 387; Fiedlschuster 2018: 82). Research on the recent history of the Commission indicates that little has changed. A study of the European Commissioners' speeches in the period 2018–21 concludes that the Commission promotes a depoliticized idea of democracy that prioritizes a technocratic, legalistic perspective of democracy over a democratic pluralist one (Oleart and Theuns 2023). The Treaty of Rome gave the Commission the task of ensuring the functioning and development of the Common Market (Treaty of Rome, Art 155). While we see the Commission's instrumental view of democracy in the light of this mandate, the aim of this part of the chapter is to show how the Commission's ideas on transnational democracy have evolved, from an instrumental view on democracy to increasingly substantive ideas, as well as why this has been the case. This part of the chapter further shows that over time, the Commission has gone from regarding EU democracy as something that was safeguarded by the European Parliament, to taking a more active role in facilitating transnational democracy.

Before reviewing Commission ideas of democracy, it is useful to recall why supranational institutions were established in the first place. The overriding challenge that the European countries were facing at the beginning of the 1950s was to avoid a return to devastating war and realize their economic potential (Spierenburg and Poidevin 1994). The willingness of the ECSC founding members to share authority over two commodities, coal and steel, that had been central to the war industry reflected this greater challenge of securing the peace. The introduction of supranational institutions also reflected the experience that actors of the time had with totalitarian regimes and the failed attempts to keep these in check via intergovernmental cooperation. This was not least the case for Monnet himself, who had served as deputy secretary-general of the League of Nations from 1919 to 1923 (Duchene 1994; Gillingham 2003). For Jean Monnet, the solution to Europe's problems was a European federation. He consistently presented common rules enforced by supranational institutions as the first step on the way there. Shifting power from elected but short-sighted politicians to independent experts who, disconnected from citizens and national interests, would practise joint rules for the purpose of a joint cause, was a means to bring Europe's history of self-inflicted disasters to an end.[1]

Monnet never made it his business to discuss the democratic implications of the transfer of authority from the participating states to supranational institutions. The many speeches he gave both before and after his time as president of the High Authority rather suggest that he saw it as his task to explain and defend the creation of supranational institutions. These speeches do, however, give some insight into how Monnet thought about democracy within the framework of supranational European cooperation. The impression they leave is that he saw no contradiction between technocracy and democracy. Monnet's message throughout was that the Community's institutional architecture was in accordance with basic principles of democratic governance. In an address to the Coal and Steel Community's Common Assembly in autumn 1952, he emphasized that the ECSC was based on the principle of the separation of powers, that the Assembly was the first European assembly to be endowed with decision-making powers, and that the High Authority was responsible to the Common Assembly (Monnet 1952b: 17–18). In other contexts, Monnet highlighted that the ECSC included a 'series of checks and balances, ensuring democratic control over all decisions' (Monnet 1953), that the Common Assembly was 'elected by the national Parliaments' (Monnet 1952a), and that the Treaty of Paris included provisions for the introduction of the Assembly's direct election by the people (Monnet 1952a). Monnet's emphasis on the democratic credentials of the ECSC in his external discourse must nevertheless be interpreted as strategic and instrumental. Research on the creation of the Coal and Steel Community has documented that the institutions that were created to balance and keep the High Authority in check were not included in Monnet's original proposal, and that they were only established as a result of pressure from other delegations (Boerger-de-Smedt 2012).

Contrary to the High Authority, the European Commission was from the beginning concerned that European integration needed public support. Historical research hails its first president, Walter Hallstein, for 'his clear perception of the institutional arrangements which need to be made if the European Union is to overcome its shortfall of democratic legitimacy and political effectiveness' (Loth 2014: 90). Already in 1959, Hallstein pointed to the importance of introducing direct elections to the Common Assembly, which he referred to as his 'most profound wish' (Hallstein 1959). Still, he presented the strengthening of democratic procedures primarily as a means of achieving the goal of a European federation. 'In the grandiose enterprise on which we are irrevocably embarked', Hallstein stated at an event at Belgium's Royal Institute of International Relations in November that year, 'the support of the peoples, communities and individuals is a conditio sine

[1] For a selection of Monnet's speeches in the period, see Monnet (1955).

qua non of success' (Hallstein 1959). There is thus reason to claim that Hallstein primarily continued the instrumental approach to democracy that Monnet had introduced.

As with Monnet, there is nothing in Hallstein's public discourse to suggest that he regarded the Commission's independent role as a democratic challenge. On the contrary, Hallstein was careful to emphasize that the Commission was accountable only for the interests of the Community (Hallstein 1959). Hallstein's statements both before and after his time as President of the European Commission show that, in the same way as Monnet had done with the ECSC, he presented the EEC as a community on the way to becoming a federal state, where the Commission represented the common European interest and the Council the Member States, and where the Parliament, which was appointed but composed of politicians that had been elected to their national parliaments, fulfilled the role of 'the democratic organ' (Hallstein 1969).

Hallstein argued that the members of the European Parliament should be elected directly. He emphasized that the treaties foresaw the need for direct elections, and he was clear that the responsibility for this not yet happening lay with the Member States (Hallstein 1969). At the same time, he conveyed the idea of the European Communities (EC) as an unorthodox but democratically legitimate collaboration, that derived its legitimacy from the participating states:

> All the variations described of the standard of parliamentary democracy are, naturally, covered and legitimized by the initial treaty and its parliamentary ratification in the six member countries in accordance with their constitutions. (Hallstein 1969.)

Following the 1974 decision finally to introduce direct elections, the demand for more power for the European Parliament grew stronger. This happened in tandem with the prospect of an enlargement of the Community and more extensive Community powers and not least as a result of the European Parliament's own efforts (Kelbel and Navarro 2020). The Commission had previously advanced the idea that democracy in the ECSC/EEC/EC was safeguarded by the European Parliament. During the 1970s the preoccupation with the need to strengthen the EC's democratic legitimacy became more pronounced. Following the 1974 decision to introduce direct elections to the European Parliament, François-Xavier Ortoli, who presided over the Commission in the period 1973–77, highlighted, for instance, how this would strengthen the legitimacy of European integration. Ortoli's public discourse also suggests that he was sceptical about too technocratic an approach to the construction of Europe, which he claimed ignored, or at least underestimated, the basic requirements of democracy:

> For the first time the objective of European Union has been broached in terms of European suffrage. This has a symbolic value and, at the same time, considerable

practical implications, in that it represents a commitment to build up the new institutional system in accordance with democratic principles. This in itself is something very precious, since one could easily imagine (not without foreboding) how an unduly technical approach to the work of preparing for the Europe of tomorrow might have disregarded, or at the very least underestimated, the fundamental requirements of democracy (Commission 1975).

4.2.2 The 1970s and beyond: democracy by integration and the turn to conditions for democracy

In the 1970s, the idea of integration as a *source* of democracy gained ground. At the 1973 Copenhagen Summit, the EC Member States adopted the Declaration on European Identity in which they identified representative democracy as one of the fundamental elements of this identity, together with the rule of law, social justice and respect for human rights (European Communities 1973). In its opinion on the Greek application for membership of the European Communities three years later, the Commission justified its recommendation to open negotiations with Greece with the desire to consolidate Greek democracy, which it described as a fundamental concern not only of the Greek people, but also of the Community and its Member States (Commission, 1976). Integration had initially been portrayed as something that would democratize relations *between* states. The 1976 opinion ushered in a new phase, characterized by the idea that membership would have a democratizing effect *on* states. By referring to the founding treaties, the Commission also presented the idea of democracy by integration as an original and fundamental idea. In its 1978 opinion on the Portuguese application, the Commission referred to the 'clear intention' of the Treaties of Rome and Paris 'that other European states sharing the democratic ideal of the European Community's Member States should be able to accede to the Community' (Commission 1978a). In its opinion on the Spanish application from November of the same year, the Commission highlighted King Juan Carlos I's engagement 'in restoring a pluralist democracy and providing guarantees for individual liberties' (Commission 1978b: 8).

In parallel with its promotion of the idea of democracy by integration, the Jenkins Commission in 1979 recommended the accession of the Community to the European Convention on Human Rights (ECHR), which suggests that a more substantial idea of EC democracy was gaining ground. Three years earlier, the Commission had concluded that Community accession to the ECHR was superfluous, as the Community was already obliged to observe the human rights embodied in the ECHR on the basis of the decisions of the Court. Closer consideration had, however, 'revealed more clearly to the Commission the disadvantages which arise from the lack of a written catalogue both for the image of the Community in general and for the protection of the rights of the European citizen' (Commission 1979).

The Delors Commission also stressed the need for the Community to become more democratic before Denmark's 'no' to the Maastricht Treaty and France's 'petit oui'. When Delors presented the Commission's 1992 programme to the European Parliament in February that year, he highlighted the beginnings of European citizenship and increased powers for Parliament as steps in the right direction. The new co-decision procedure should, said Delors, 'be used above all for key texts that appeal directly to the man in the street' (Delors 1992: 8). Delors also believed that Parliament had to be involved in the development of common policies in the economic and monetary and foreign policy areas. Delors' address to the European Parliament also reads, however, as if more democracy was subordinate to the desire for more integration: 'To make a success of Maastricht', he told the European Parliament, 'we must also take into account firstly the Community's growing involvement in international affairs and the prospects opened up by the new Treaty on a common foreign and security policy and secondly the desire to make the Community more democratic, in particular by strengthening the powers of the European Parliament' (Delors 1992).

Events later that year made it obvious that European integration 'no longer could be taken for granted' (Delors 1993). The Delors Commission's discourse prior to the Danish and French referendums can be interpreted as if the Commission had been concerned about a democratic deficit in the Community, in the sense of a mismatch between the growing authority of the Community and the relative weakness of the Parliament, as well as about the lack of a democratic substructure, in the form of a European demos or identity. Faced with a new reality, the Commission turned its attention to conditions for democracy, in the form of more information about what the Community was doing and why: 'As the demand for democracy grows, we must explain, again and again, what we are doing and why. We must reassure the reluctant and encourage the enthusiastic', Delors told the European Parliament in February 1993 (Delors 1993).

Alongside a commonplace, almost cliché-ridden, emphasis on the need to connect with the citizens, Delors established that nothing would weaken the Commission's determination 'to prepare the ground for entry into force of the new Treaty'. Delors also emphasized that the Community had to accept the need to review its institutional structure and decision-making procedures in order to make it 'more successful than it has been at reconciling effectiveness, diversity and democracy'. In this context, he referred, as he had done previously, both to the practice of subsidiarity and the new co-decision procedure, which he described as 'central to the union's constitution and its democratic credentials'. Delors now announced nothing less than a 'crusade for democracy', based on the application of subsidiarity, on making Community action more transparent, and on the preparation of 'a pertinent communication Policy' (Delors 1993).

For subsequent Commissions, transparency and communication remained important priorities. The Santer Commission's 1996 Citizens First programme aimed to make European citizens more 'aware of their rights and opportunities from the Single Market and other Community policies, with a particular focus on their rights to live, work and study in other EU Member States (Commission 1996). With the Prodi Commission, focus shifted to the Commission itself. 'It is time for some glasnost here!' Romano Prodi declared when presenting his Commission designate to the European Parliament in September 1999. 'I want to bring Europe out from behind closed doors and into the light of public scrutiny. I want people to be able to look over my shoulder and check that the Commission is dealing with the issues that most concern them . . . Transparency is vital for the democratic health and accountability of the European Union' (Prodi 1999).

4.2.3 The new millennium: facilitating for deliberative democracy

In contrast to its predecessors, and as part of the debate triggered by Joschka Fischer's May 2000 speech on the future of Europe (see Chapter 2 of this volume), the Prodi Commission conveyed an idea of democracy where deliberation was central. In its July 2001 White Paper on European Governance, this Commission highlighted the democratic nature of EU cooperation, in the sense that it was built on the rule of law, that it could draw on the Charter of Fundamental Rights, and that it had 'a double democratic mandate through a Parliament representing EU citizens and a Council representing the elected governments of the Member States' (Commission 2001). At the same time, turnouts in European Parliament elections were decreasing and in Ireland a majority of the voters had just rejected the Treaty of Nice. Acknowledging that many people were 'losing confidence in a poorly understood and complex system to deliver the policies that they want', the Prodi Commission proposed a renewal of the Community method by following a less top-down approach. More people and organizations had to be involved in the shaping and delivery of EU policy, and such involvement would, in turn, depend on access to reliable information and improved communication on the part of EU institutions and Member States (Commission 2001).

To the Prodi Commission, access to information and better communication was about more than informing citizens about the benefits of integration. By highlighting access to information as a precondition for the creation of a common public sphere, this Commission expressed a more comprehensive idea of democracy, that focused not only on policy outcomes and input in the form of citizen participation and political procedures, but also on *throughput*, here understood as 'governance processes with the people' (Schmidt 2013: 2). The ambition was that participation in the form of deliberation would strengthen the ties between policy-makers and citizens, and enable more responsive governance:

> Providing more information and more effective communication is a pre-condition for generating a sense of belonging to Europe. The aim should be to create a trans-national 'space' where citizens from different countries can discuss what they perceive as being the important challenges for the Union. This should help policy makers to stay in touch with European public opinion and could guide them in identifying European projects which mobilise public support. (Commission 2001.)

Within the framework of enlargement policy, the Prodi Commission carried forward the idea of integration as a source of democracy. With the adoption of the Copenhagen criteria ten years earlier, the European Council had made EU accession conditional on the meeting of a set of economic and political standards that included the stability of institutions guaranteeing democracy. On the eve of the 2004 Eastern Enlargement, the Commission established that stable democracies were well established in Central and Eastern Europe. Although credit for this development primarily belonged to the candidate countries, it had also been 'aided by the prospect of EU membership' (Commission 2003).

The Barroso Commission (2004–13) continued the Prodi Commission's emphasis on deliberation as central to democracy. This Commission took office with the enhancing of dialogue and information as one of its priorities. With the French and Dutch rejections of the Constitutional Treaty the year after, communication moved up its political agenda—a development that was reflected in its renaming of the Directorate-General for Press and Communication to DG Communication. The Barroso Commission responded to the negative votes in the 2005 referendums as well as to a general decline in public trust in the EU with three closely linked initiatives. It presented these initiatives as 'a long-term plan to reinvigorate European democracy and help the emergence of a European public sphere where citizens are given the information and the tools to actively participate in the decision-making process and gain ownership of the European project' (Commission 2006: 2–3).

The July 2005 Action Plan established that Commissioners needed to devote more time to communication and that every member of the Commission staff had to be 'capable of informing the public or the press about the Commission's policies'. It also urged Directorates-General to draft their policies 'in clear, simple and precise terms'; to provide important proposals with 'layperson's summaries', and to unify the use of slogans and symbols (Commission 2005a). The October 2005 Plan D for Democracy, Dialogue and Debate was in turn presented as a means to 'stimulate a wider debate between the European Union's democratic institutions and citizens' (Commission 2005b). Finally, and as yet another means to close the gap between the EU and its citizens, an October 2006 White Paper on a European

Communication Policy set out to move communication 'away from one-way communication to reinforced dialogue, from an institution-centred to a citizen-centred communication, from a Brussels-based to a more decentralised approach' (Commission 2006: 4).

The Barroso Commission placed great weight on communication, presenting it as 'essential to a healthy democracy' (Commission 2006: 2) and arguing that it should 'become an EU policy in its own right, at the service of the citizens' (Commission 2006: 4). At the same time, this Commission's emphasis on communication was closely linked to its promotion of substantial democracy, marked by a concern with the need to strengthen democratic substructures, in the form of a European identity and the development of a European public sphere. The emphasis on deliberation remained a priority for this Commission, which presented its guidelines for its second term to the European Parliament in September 2009. José Manuel Barroso then declared that the process of shaping the European interest could not take place in a political vacuum, stating that 'it has to be the result of political debate in a true European public space' (Barroso 2009).

The Juncker Commission (2014–19) turned attention back to democratic procedures, in a way that highlighted the principle of accountability. Its focus reflected the EU's handling of the eurozone crisis as well as the new *Spitzenkandidat* process. When Jean-Claude Juncker came to Strasbourg to present his Commission's political guidelines, he established that the democratic legitimacy of EU cooperation had 'suffered as many new instruments had to be created outside the legal framework of the European Union' (Commission, 2014). Against this backdrop, the *Spitzenkandidat* process, which had formed a direct link between the outcome of the European Parliament elections and the proposal of the President of the European Commission, had the potential to strengthen the legitimacy of EU decision-making:

> This follows long-standing calls from the European Parliament echoed and repeated over several decades. It has the potential to insert a very necessary additional dose of democratic legitimacy into the European decision-making process, in line with the rules and practices of parliamentary democracy. (Commission 2014.)

Juncker presented the establishment of a link between the European Parliament elections and the proposal for a Commission President as an important first step in the effort to make the EU more democratic. He also expressed the expectation that the EU in the future should be able to replace the 'troika' with 'a more democratically legitimate and more accountable structure, based around European institutions with enhanced parliamentary control both at European and at national level'. The troika had been set up four years earlier to monitor the bailout programmes established to manage the eurozone crisis. It consisted of the European Commission representing the EU, the International Monetary Fund and the European Central Bank. As the troika worked at present, Juncker established, it lacked democratic substance, as it lacked a parliamentary dimension (Commission 2014).

It is difficult to get an overall picture of Juncker's idea of democracy in the EU. On the one hand, he stressed that he wanted a political, rather than a technocratic, dialogue between the Commission and the European Parliament, and he declared his intention always to send political representatives of the Commission to important trilogue negotiations, which suggests a political, rather than a technocratic, focus. On the other hand, Juncker did not voice concerns about the increasing use of trilogues, which had enabled faster, but also less democratic decision-making, in the form of less open and involving processes (Rasmussen 2011: 42). His emphasis on a more political role for a body that had been perceived as disconnected from the citizens and hence undemocratic may further suggest a narrow view on transnational democratic legitimacy. The statement can, however, also be seen in the context of the fact that Juncker was the first Commission President to have a mandate via the *Spitzenkandidat* process.

During the term of the Von der Leyen Commission (2019–24), and as a result of Russia's full-scale invasion of Ukraine, enlargement policy gained new centrality. Four months after the invasion, the Commission recommended candidate status for Ukraine. The opinion presented the aspiration to belong to the EU as 'an underlying motive for democratic changes over the past decade and a driver of a number of key reforms founded on European values' (Commission 2022). It thus continued the vision of the democratizing power of EU cooperation.

On the inside of the Union, the Von der Leyen Commission (2019–24) reinforced efforts to bring the EU closer to its citizens. The main move in this respect was the Conference on the future of Europe, which helped translate the idea of deliberative democracy into practice. Von der Leyen linked the new initiative to the 2019 elections to the European Parliament, which had seen the highest voter turnout since 1994. 'We must respond to that call by giving Europeans a stronger role in decision-making', she told the European Parliament when presenting her political guidelines, adding that her Commission would 'go further than ever before to make this happen' (Von der Leyen 2019: 19).

Alongside the new push for deliberative democracy, Von der Leyen also advocated a strengthening of the European Parliament. She made it clear that she supported a right of initiative for the Parliament and argued for the need to improve the *Spitzenkandidat* process.[2] The Conference on the Future of Europe that ran

[2] In 2019 the European Council nominated Ursula von der Leyen as President of the Commission despite the fact that she had not been the European People's Party (EPP) lead candidate. The European Parliament subsequently elected her with a narrow majority of nine votes (see Crum 2023). In 2024, by contrast, Ursula von der Leyen stood as the EPP lead candidate in the European elections and, following the European Council's nomination, was elected by the Parliament with a broad majority of 401 votes (at least 360 votes were needed).

from April 2021 to May 2022 enabled European citizens to debate what kind of Europe they would like to live in. One of its results was a final report with forty-nine specific proposals, which was handed over to the presidents of the European Parliament, the Council, and the European Commission. Although the Conference on the Future of Europe received mixed reviews (von Ondarza and Ålander 2022), the Commission later presented the conference as 'a major pan-European democratic exercise' that enabled 'the embedding of deliberative democracy in EU policymaking' (Commission 2023).

To sum up, the Commission has over time gone from expressing an instrumental view of democracy to emphasizing the necessity of participation and, subsequently, deliberation. At the same time, the Commission has also moved from a passive to an active role. In contrast to the Hallstein Commission's idea of democratic legitimacy as something that derived from the participating states and was safeguarded by the European Parliament, the Von der Leyen Commission sought through the Conference on the Future of Europe to facilitate a political culture of participation. This development has been neither straightforward nor unambiguous. Jean-Claude Juncker wanted to send political representatives to important trilogue meetings, but failed to point out that the use of trilogues has made the EU's legislative process less transparent and inclusive. Ursula von der Leyen wanted to strengthen the European Parliament, while at the same time allowing herself to be elected Commission President without having been the EPP group's lead candidate in 2019. Moreover, following her 're-election' as Commission President in 2024, von der Leyen's relationship with the European Parliament has deteriorated, as shown by the tabling and (unsuccessfully) voting of two motions of censure in 2025 alone.

The development from instrumental to increasingly sophisticated procedural ideas is still in line with the literature on democratic consolidation and its argument that in the course of such consolidation, instrumentalist ideas of democracy will give way to proceduralist ideas (Norris 2011). Research on the German reunification has shown that the transition from instrumentalist to proceduralist conceptions of democracy took a generation to complete (Landwehr and Leininger 2019). Against this background, and in light of the EU's size and complexity, it is not surprising that the work towards more democratic cooperation takes time.

4.3 The vision of the CJEU on democracy

4.3.1 From the origins to the post-Lisbon setting

As highlighted in the literature and by former CJEU judges, democracy was not in the DNA of the EU integration process (e.g. Mancini and Keeling 1994), particularly after the failure of the European Political Community project in 1954 (de

Burca 2011). For this reason, democracy was not intended to be a central target of the CJEU's case law at first. However, since the 1960s the Court has started to build a jurisprudence from which a broad definition of democracy emerges. Moreover, the CJEU has defined important democratic standards and thresholds also relevant for candidate countries in the EU enlargement processes, especially from the 1980s onward, as part of the *acquis communautaire.*

Indeed, the CJEU has gradually and incrementally developed the idea of liberal democracy grounded on the separation of powers—fine-tuned to the specificity of the EU institutional framework—and protection of human rights. In the late 1950s the Court came to devise the principle of inter-institutional balance as a surrogate of the fully-fledged principle of separation of powers at the national level, meaning that the then-EC institutions could not delegate their constitutional powers, as conferred by the treaties, to other bodies (notably executive agencies) thereby abdicating their functions. Nor could they act beyond the limits of their competences, neglecting the mandate of another supranational institution (Jacqué 2004). In the leading case, *Meroni*, the CJEU justified the recognition of the principle of inter-institutional balance as 'a fundamental guarantee granted by the Treaty in particular to the undertakings and associations of undertakings to which it applies' (Case 9/56 *Meroni v High Authority* 1958), thus as a constraint for the supranational authorities to protect legal certainty and the legitimate expectations of private parties (Patrin 2021). The European Parliament has successfully used this principle in its strategic litigation before the CJEU to strengthen its own authority (as in the *Isoglucose* case: Joined Cases 138/79 *Roquette Frères v Council* and 139/79, *Maizena v Council*), yet it represents a constraint on the Parliament too (Case 149/85 *Wybot v Faure* 1986, para 23).

The guarantee of fundamental rights started to resonate in the Court's case law in the late 1960s without any specific legal basis in the treaties beyond the four fundamental freedoms in the common market. Taking concrete steps toward deepening EU integration, the CJEU identified in both the protection of the individual and the Union as a community of people the bulwarks to build the doctrines of direct effect (Case 26/62, *van Gend & Loos v Netherlands Inland Revenue Administration* 1963) and primacy (Case 6/64*Costa v ENEL* 1964). The Court has been able to resort to the common constitutional traditions of the Member States to develop a certain vision of EU democracy, which is inherently connected to national constitutional democracies (Lenaerts 2013). Lacking a Community charter of fundamental rights in the 1960s, the Court started to develop its fundamental rights jurisprudence drawing on those national constitutional traditions and on the European Convention of Human Rights. It did so in an intense and sometimes heated exchange with national courts, in particular the German Federal Constitutional Court and the Italian Constitutional Court (see, in sequence, Case 29/69 *Stauder v City of Ulm* 1969; Case 11/70 *Internationale Handelsgesellschaft v Einfuhr- und Vorratsstelle* 1970; Case 4/73 *Nold v Commission* 1974; Case 44/79

Hauer v Land Rheinland-Pfalz 1970; and the commentary by Kumm 2010). In the 1970 ruling in *Internationale Handelsgesellschaft*, commonly considered a turning point in European case law, the CJEU affirmed that fundamental rights qualify as 'an integral part of the general principles' of Community law (Davies 2017: 157). The CJEU judges have emphasized the 'autonomisation' of fundamental rights in the Community from national or international legal sources (Pescatore 1970), possibly also with the intention of granting more legitimacy to the then European Community and its Court (Tridimas 2010).

Between the 1970s and the Maastricht Treaty, much of the CJEU's case law on the democratic principle, as for the Commission, revolved around the attempt to build a fully-fledged Parliament for Europe (Rittberger 2005). The gradual expansion of powers of the newly elected European Assembly has been driven through litigation before the CJEU (see, for example, the already mentioned *Isoglucose* case and *Chernobyl*, Case C-70/88 *European Parliament v Council* 1991). Not by chance, the first judicial qualification of the EU as a community anchored to the rule of law was proposed in a 1986 case revolving around the reimbursement of political parties in the aftermath of the European elections and the limits of the European Parliament's discretion (Case 294/83, *Parti écologiste 'Les Verts' v European Parliament*, on which see Jacqué 2010; Lenaerts 2010; Boerger and Davies 2017).

Since the Maastricht Treaty, we have witnessed further development of the Court's case law on democracy (Ninatti 2004). The largest share of this case law is still directed to strengthening representative democracy via empowerment of the European Parliament within and beyond the legislative process, such as in the comitology procedures and, now, on delegated acts (Case C-355/10 *European Parliament v Council* 2012; Case C-286/14 *European Parliament v Commission* 2016), on the EU budget process (e.g. Case 77/11 *Council of the European Union v European Parliament* 2013; C-73/17, *France v European Parliament* 2018, compared to the pre-Lisbon case law: Case 34/86 *Council of the European Communities v European Parliament* 1986; Case C-41/95, *Council v European Parliament* 1995), and on international agreements concluded by the Union (notably, Joined Cases C-317/04 and C-318/04, *European Parliament v Council and Commission* 2006). However, at times, as in the last case cited on the EU–US Passenger Name Records (PNR) Agreement, the 'victory' of the Parliament does not always correspond to a serious consideration of fundamental rights issues in the arguments of the Court or an advancement for democracy after all (Fahey 2017).

In fact, the Court has tried to provide a much richer vision of democracy than focusing only on the Parliament. On the one hand, the Court has stressed that, at the institutional level, representative democracy is not a monopoly of the Parliament. The Council, via the functioning of national democracies and domestic accountability procedures, can equally contribute to representative democracy in the EU (see e.g. Case C-130/10 *European Parliament v Council* 2012). Moreover, representative democracy does not mean that the Parliament has unlimited powers. Its decisions can be subject to judicial review even when they directly relate to parliamentary autonomy (Joined Cases T-222/99, T-327/99, and T-329/99 *Martinez and Others v European Parliament* 2001; Case C-486/01 P *Front National v European Parliament* 2004) and parliamentary privilege (Case C-163/10, *Criminal proceedings against Patrociello* 2011; Joined Cases C-393/07 and C-9/08 *Italy and Donnici v European Parliament* 2009) and have to be balanced against other rights and principles.

On the other hand, as the CJEU President Koen Lenaerts[3] clearly pointed out, the protection of EU democracy goes well beyond the composition and functioning of EU representative institutions (Lenaerts 2013). For example, elaborating on an important judgment issued by the Court on the disenfranchisement of prisoners' voting rights (Case C-650/13 *Delvigne v Commune de Lesparre Médoc and Préfet de la Gironde* 2015), Lenaerts expressly underscored the link established in the CJEU's decision between EU citizenship, first acknowledged by the Maastricht Treaty, and the democratic governance of the EU: 'the political dimension of EU citizenship is respectful of the constitutional allocation of powers sought by the authors of the Treaties' and 'is not only about rights, but also about ensuring that that representative democracy at EU level is effective and, most important, legitimate' (Lenaerts 2016: 165 and 174, respectively).[4]

Moreover, Lenaerts has argued that setting up EU independent agencies and protecting their independence through the Court's case law fulfils an important democratic function. They guarantee minority interests, which otherwise could be undermined by purely majoritarian decisions and by the 'tyranny of the majority' (Case C-518/07 *Commission v Germany* 2010). In addition, the Court has come to shape EU democracy under the umbrella of participatory democracy, both when looking at the involvement of social partners in EU decision-making (e.g. Case T-135/96 *UEAPME v Council* 1998) and at the leeway available to EU citizens to contribute to the policy-making, such as through the European Citizens' Initiative (contrast Case T-789/19 *Moerenhout and Others v Commission* 2021 and Case C-418/18 P *Puppinck and Others v Commission* 2019).

In this strand of post-Maastricht case law on democracy, a special place is occupied by its link with the principle of transparency. The Court has interpreted transparency both as a guarantee for access to documents (e.g. Case C-506/08 P *Sweden and Commission v My Travel* 2011) and as openness of legislative procedures, drawing on access to documents (e.g. Cases C-280/11 P *Council v Access Info Europe* 2013; Case T-540/15 *De Capitani v European Parliament* 2018; and Case T-163/21 *De Capitani v Council* 2023). In general, the Court has been keen to

[3] Appointed as a Judge at the Court of First Instance of the European Communities in 1989, Koen Lenaerts was then appointed as a Judge at the Court of Justice in 2003 and elected President of the Court on 8 October 2015.

[4] On the relationship between EU citizenship and democratic principles in the EU see also Case C-181/23 *Commission v Malta* 2025, paras 88–89.

develop a comprehensive understanding of democracy that includes fundamental rights protection, especially when the concerns about the lack of democratic, fair, and transparent procedures intersect problems in the enforcement of individual rights of third parties, such as the guarantees of non-discrimination and privacy (see Case C-362/14 *Schrems v Data Protection Commissioner* 2015 and Case C-311/18 *Data Protection Commissioner v Facebook Ireland and Schrems* 2020).

4.3.2 The influence of the CJEU's case law on the accession processes 2004–13

The development and enrichment of the CJEU's case law on democracy in part anticipated and partly ran in parallel to the EU's eastward enlargement in the decade 2004–13, when the last acceding country to date, Croatia, joined. Liberal democracy being a flagship of the Union toward the outside world, especially after it was embedded in the TEU as one of its fundamental values (Art 2), it is important to understand whether and to what extent the advancement in the CJEU's case law on democracy has been conveyed to the candidate states in order to maintain the EU's internal standards. How much has the broad reading of democracy by the CJEU contributed to orienting the accession process or, better, to portraying to the candidate countries the vision of democracy channelled by the European Court? Very little, at first glance. In connection to the previous case law analysis, this section aims precisely to assess which CJEU rulings on EU democratic principles and procedures, if any, have been selected to inspire the acceding countries in their transition. This section is not primarily meant to explore why such a narrow portrait of the Court's case law on democracy has been provided to the future Member States, although tentatively it emerges from the case selection that the primary concern was the preparation to join the internal market rather than the paving the way for democratic consolidation according to EU standards.

As Sadl and Madsen (2016) effectively put forward, the CJEU tried to portray itself and its contribution to interpreting EU law in a narrow way to the future ten new Member States of the big enlargement in 2004 and to the further accessions completed since then. The Court was asked to make a selection of the most significant landmark decisions, in terms of representative and defining precedents, for the acceding countries to orient their preparation for joining the Union. Of the 948 judgments and orders initially selected as 'historic European case law' (from the Court of Justice and the Court of First Instance, 1956–April 2004)[5] for the 2004 accession countries, only fifty-seven judgments were made available and translated

[5] The CJEU as an institution fulfils its mandate through a General Court—called the Court of First Instance prior to the Lisbon Treaty—and the Court of Justice, before which decisions of the General Court can be appealed, but only on a point of law (Art 19 TEU).

in the countries' official languages directly at the Commission's expense.[6] The Court's language units, however, translated a second tranche of seventy-nine decisions covering the period 2001–April 2004. These translated judgments were made available ahead of Bulgaria's and Romania's accession in 2007 and Croatia's accession in 2013.

This selection and translation of judgments was part of a combined effort by the Commission and, even more so, the CJEU to expedite the transition of new countries into the European legal system in line with the EU standards as interpreted in the Union's practice. In 2002, the Commission set up the Technical Assistance and Information Exchange Instrument (TAIEX) to support translating the most significant judgments into the new languages. The Commission would have carried out the initial translation, which would then have been revised by the designated National Translation Centres. At the same time, the Court was involved in organizing several seminars and training sessions meant to establish cooperation between the Directorate-General for Translation at the CJEU and the National Translation Centres (Sadl and Madsen 2016).

What is interesting for our purpose are, first, the selection method and criteria adopted and, second, the proportion of the selected judgments that deal with democracy in the EU and its standards. On the first point, the Court has not disclosed information on the method and criteria used. Sadl and Madsen (2016) extensively analysed these judgments and accessed the Internal Memorandum of the Court from 17 September 2003 and other relevant documents by filing a request for access to documents (TFEU, Art 15(3) and Decision of the CJEU of 11 December 2012). Thanks to these documents, we know that the Research and Documentation Department of the Court (i.e. clerks and officials) drew up the list of cases, taking into account the nature of the decision as a leading judgment, its ability to structure the European legal system and its influence in the relevant area of law. The compilation of the list occurred after consulting the Presidents of the CJEU and of the Court of First Instance, which ultimately approved the list (Sadl and Madsen 2016).

On the second point, the translated judgments, which are meant to provide reliable information on the Court's main lines of case law, touch only marginally upon democratic issues. This is problematic, given the weight of political-democracy conditions in the hierarchy of the Copenhagen criteria, following the indications provided in the Conclusions of the Luxembourg European Council in 1997. Those political conditions gained pre-eminence over other conditions for the start of accession negotiations, but according to many scholars (see e.g. Kochenov 2008: 85 ff.; Pinelli 2004), they remained poorly defined and operationalized and were implemented in contradictory ways. Thus, the Court's selection of its case law could

[6] The list is available on the Court's website, available at: https://curia.europa.eu/jcms/jcms/Jo2_14955/en/, accessed 20 July 2025.

have offered more specific guidance on the vision of democracy the EU asks the candidate countries to follow.

Some foundational judgments on the EU democratic legal system were, of course, included. These deal with issues such as direct effect and primacy (again, *van Gend & Loos v Netherlands Inland Revenue Administration* and *Costa v ENEL*), the relationship between national courts and the CJEU (Case 106/77 *Amministrazione delle Finanze dello Stato v Simmenthal* 1978; Case 283/81 *CILFIT and di Gavardo v Ministry of Health* 1982; Case 314/85 *Foto-Frost v Hauptzollamt Lübeck-Ost* 1978), non-discrimination (Case 43/75 *Defrenne v Sabena* 1976), and the protection of EU citizens against the lack of or poor implementation of EU law (Joined Cases C-6/90 and C-9/90 *Francovich and Bonifaci v Italy* 1991), in line with the narrative already highlighted, of the enforcement and protection of the individual (and the undertakings). For the rest, only three judgments—the rulings in the *Les Verts*, *Isoglucose*, and *Chernobyl* cases—engage just with the institutional dimension of representative democracy and with the powers of the European Parliament in particular.

In contrast, the other far-reaching dimensions of the democratic principle developed in the Court's case law are absent (transparency and openness, involvement of social partners, participatory instruments), including major judgments on fundamental rights. Except for a couple of cases on citizenship (Case C-85/96 *Martínez Sala v Bayern* 1998), cases dealing with the principle of inter-institutional balance and the European Parliament, comitology, the budget process, and the prerogatives and immunities of MEPs, were not included.

From this analysis, it is clear that the CJEU's selected jurisprudence gives prospective Member States the impression of a Court that is much less committed to protecting democracy than in fact is the case. Moreover, the many aspects and nuances of democracy that the CJEU has taken on board in its jurisprudence regarding the EU legal and political system could have allowed the Court to set reliable democratic standards whose fulfilment the candidate countries would have considered crucial prior to the accession. Or, at least, they could have raised their expectations.

4.3.3 The idea of liberal democracy channelled against the rule of law backsliding in the Member States: the advent of reinforced democratic standards?

The gap between the (lack of) emphasis on democracy in the CJEU's selection of translated case law for candidate countries and the actual developments in the case law of the Court is even more striking if one looks at the EU jurisprudence of the last few years. Next to the case law on the Charter that has further strengthened fundamental rights protection in the EU, the Court has been presented with cases dealing with electoral rights and EU principles and values that had never previously been used as a standard for review by the CJEU either because of the circumstances or due to the context.

In a landmark judgment on immunities for the Members of the European Parliament (Case C-52/19 *Junqueras i Vies* 2019) and drawing on Article 39 of the Charter, the CJEU constructed the right of MEPs to participate in parliamentary activities as instrumental in preserving the right of the EU citizens to be represented in the EP according to the vote expressed in the European elections. The invocation of Article 2 TEU, which embeds the democracy as a fundamental value following the Lisbon Treaty's reform, together with Article 10 TEU on the principle of representative democracy and the Charter provisions on the right to political association and electoral rights, have already been invoked successfully in some cases (e.g. Case C-808/21 *Commission v Czech Republic* 2024, where the key provision was Article 22 TFEU on the right to stand as a candidate in municipal elections).

Since the start of the rule of law crisis in Eastern Europe in the previous decade, CJEU case law on fundamental values, including democracy, has evolved significantly, further reinforcing its constitutional tone. In particular, the CJEU has clearly portrayed a vision of liberal democracy anchored to protecting access to justice and judicial independence as pillars for ensuring other fundamental rights, to protect minorities against discrimination, to safeguarding media pluralism as bulwarks against populist and anti-EU domestic governments taking advantage of electoral success to dismantle the rule of law from within. The CJEU has endorsed an idea of democracy that is about much more than free and competitive elections, encompassing the need for a constrained political power against the 'tyranny of the majority'.

Unlike what had happened in the past, the target was not only the EU institutional system, but rather domestic institutions. Starting from the famous 2018 *Associação Sindical dos Juízes Portugueses v Tribunal de Contas* decision (Case C-64/16), the Court has used Article 19(1) of the TEU in connection with Article 47 of the Charter and Article 2 of the TEU to ground the guarantee of effective legal remedies against the violation of EU law to target domestic reforms undermining judicial independence (among the many, see Pech and Kochenov 2021; von Bogdandy and Spieker 2023). Drawing on this line of case law and on that regarding the European Arrest Warrant in the aftermath of the rule of law backsliding (Case C-216/18 PPU *LM* 2018), the General Court considered that for national competition authorities and likewise courts, the guarantee of independence is a precondition for their cooperation across the Member States to ensure the effective enforcement of competition law and complainants' rights (Case T-791/19 *Sped Pro v Commission* 2022; Cseres 2024).

Moreover, the CJEU has condemned Hungary for serious violations of the Charter of fundamental rights, such as infringing academic freedom (Art 13) and the freedom to finance higher education institutions (Art 14(3)) with regard to the so-called 'anti-CEU law' (Case C-66/18 *Commission v Hungary* 2020). At the time of writing, infringement actions are pending before the Court against Hungary and its anti-LGBTI + law (Case C-769/22 *Commission v Hungary*, pending) for alleged violations of several Charter provisions, from protecting human dignity (Art 1) and respect for private and family life (Art 7) to prohibiting discrimination (Art 21) and guaranteeing the freedom of expression (Art 11). Moreover, Article 2 of the TEU, which includes democracy and the rule of law as the fundamental values, was invoked for the first time as a 'self-standing plea' (Von Bogdandy and Spieker 2023: 75). While the CJEU has not delivered its judgment yet, some 'precedents', if applied here, may further reinforce the democratic standards set for the Member States.

Indeed, in the 'twin judgments' on the 'rule of law conditionality Regulation' (Regulation 2020/2092) triggered by the actions for annulment by Hungary and Poland (Case C-156/21 *Hungary v Parliament and Council* 2022 and Case C-157/21 *Poland v Parliament and Council* 2022), the Court stated that Article 2 of the TEU does not contain programmatic guidelines but instead enforceable provisions forming an integral part of the 'European identity' and creating binding obligations on the EU countries. Furthermore, the Court had already established a continuum between the freedom of expression under Article 11 of the Charter and the value of democracy under Article 2 of the TEU (Joined Cases C-203/15 *Tele2 Sverige v Post- och telestyrelsen* and C-698/15 *Home Secretary v Watson and Others* 2016; Joined Cases C-511/18, 512/18, and 520/18 *La Quadrature du Net v Premier minister and Others* 2020 para 114; Case C-623/17 *Privacy International v Foreign Secretary and Others* 2020 para 62). This could orient the CJEU's expected ruling on the lack of media pluralism in Hungary, following the Commission's decision to refer the country to the CJEU for failure to comply with EU electronic communications rules (Case C-92/23 *Commission v Hungary* 2025, pending). As stressed in the Hungarian country chapter of the 2023 Rule of Law Report (Commission 2023b), the national Media Council refused 'to renew the broadcasting license of independent radio station Klubrádió, which resulted in the radio being taken off air'.

As Spieker (2023) highlighted on Hungary and its democratic decay, the CJEU may soon exploit the potential of Article 2 of the TEU on the value of democracy—after the consolidated line of case law on the value of the rule of law and judicial independence—to be 'operationalized' under Article 10 of the TEU enshrining the principle of representative democracy. It may also do so under Article 11 of the TEU on participatory democracy, whenever NGOs or minority groups are excluded from the public and political and debate on EU measures.

All in all, the CJEU now seems ready to set more demanding democratic standards to be guaranteed by EU institutions and Member States. It would be another significant step forward compared to the EU situation pre-Maastricht and after the enlargement when the EU had been accused of having double standards in democratic commitments, less demanding for Member States than for third countries. It remains to be seen whether, and to what extent, higher democratic thresholds set by the CJEU will inform the accession process of the countries of the Western Balkans, Georgia, Moldova, and Ukraine. Related to this, it is important to evaluate whether the CJEU will be able to portray a more reliable and accurate representation of its case law on democracy to candidate countries, taking stock of the many aspects of the democratic principle that permeate the Court's jurisprudence, especially in the light of the developments following the rule of law backsliding in Eastern Europe. Indeed, it could be convenient for the EU to spell out clearly, including through a better selection of the translated case law, what minimum democratic core the Union requires candidate countries to guarantee to respect the European identity and, thus, to become Member States.

4.4 Conclusion

Our analysis of the Commission and the CJEU suggests that both institutions have been significantly concerned about the value of democracy throughout the history of integration—thus, well before its codification in Article 2 TEU—despite their own lack of an original democratic mandate. They have tried to support an idea of transnational democracy that supplements national democracies, taking stock of the weaknesses of democratic legitimation at supranational level. Albeit in different ways, the vision of democracy they have endorsed revolves fundamentally around the principles of representative democracy, seconding the reinforcement of the EP, highlighting the democratic credentials of the Council being grounded in responsible domestic governments (especially for the CJEU), and valuing the principle of inter-institutional balance as the EU's specific understanding of separation of powers. Moreover, both institutions have also considered EU democracy as being shaped by the openness and transparency of the European institutions to the public, by the participation of citizens and interest groups in the EU decision-making. As such they see representative democracy as necessarily complemented by participatory democracy in the EU. Due to their enforcement role, the idea of democracy the CJEU and the Commission portray is quite pragmatic and incremental, i.e. gradually increasing the standards set, while they refrain from dealing with a forward-looking vision of democracy entailing bottom-up collective self-government or enhancing the democratic will-formation underpinning Treaty reform (as argued in the Introduction to this volume).

All in all, comparing the Commission's and the Court's ideas of democracy in the EU reveals several similarities, including the cited insistence on representative democracy, particularly through the European Parliament, as a vehicle of democratization of the Community. It has subsequently broadened to further dimensions such as access to documents, transparency and citizens' participation. Of course, the vision of democracy endorsed reflects the mandate and role of the institution, and clear differences can be detected. For example, unlike the CJEU, the Commission has become concerned by the public support it enjoys and its own democratic accountability. Lately, the Commission has also become particularly concerned about protecting the supranational and national democracies against foreign interferences, as shown by the 'European Democracy Shield' (Commission 2025). The CJEU, by contrast, due to its jurisdiction, has promoted democracy through its case law as strongly connected to protecting fundamental rights, to pluralism, and to the idea of limited government. It appears that the Commission and CJEU's visions of democracy nurtured within the EU have not been properly channelled to candidate countries for EU accession, to provide a common ground for democratic integration into the Union. Nevertheless, over the last decade both institutions have become increasingly engaged in the implementation of rule of law and democratic standards in their own remit *in concreto*, in particular against illiberal trends in Eastern Europe.

References

Barroso, J. M. (3 September 2009). *Political Guidelines for the Next Commission*. Brussels. https://sbe.org.gr/newsletters/eflashnews/2009_21/Barroso_Political_Guidelines_2009.pdf. Accessed 20 July 2025.

Boerger-de-Smedt, A. (2012). Negotiating the Foundations of European Law, 1950–57: The Legal History of the Treaties of Paris and Rome. *Contemporary European History*, 21(3): 339–356.

Boerger, A. and Davies, B. (2017). Imagining the Course of European Law?. Parti Ecologiste 'Les Verts' v. Parliament as a Constitutional Milestone in EU Law. In Nicola, F. and Davies, B. (eds). *EU Law Stories*. Cambridge, Cambridge University Press: 83–102.

Cappelletti, M., Seccombe, M., and Weiler J. H. H. (1986). *Integration through Law. Methods, Tools and Institutions*. Berlin-New York, De Gruyter, Vol. I.

Ceron, M., Christiansen, T., and Dimitrakopoulos, D. G. (eds) (2024). *The Politicisation of the European Commission's Presidency. Spitzenkandidaten and Beyond*. London, Palgrave.

Commission (1975). Excerpts from President Ortoli's Speech to the European Parliament. Luxemburg/Brussels, 14 January 1975: 2. https://aei.pitt.edu/. Accessed 20 July 2025.

Commission (1976). Commission Opinion on Greece's Application for Membership, 29 January 1976. *Bulletin of the European Communities Supplement* 2/76: 42.

Commission (1978a). Opinion on Portuguese Application for Membership, 19 May 1978. *Bulletin of the European Communities Supplement* 5/78.

Commission (29 November 1978b). Opinion on Spain's Application for Membership, 29 November 1978. *Bulletin of the European Communities Supplement* 9/78.

Commission (1979). Accession of the Communities to the European Convention on Human Rights. *Bulletin of the European Communities Supplement* 2/79.

Commission (1996). *Citizens First - European Community awareness campaign*, 26 November 1996. https://cordis.europa.eu/. Accessed 20 July 2025.

Commission (2001). European Governance – A White Paper, 12 October 2001. *Official Journal of the European Communities* C 287/1.

Commission (2003). Strategy paper and Report for the European Commission on the progress towards accession by Bulgaria, Romania and Turkey. https://enlargement.ec.europa.eu. Accessed 30 October 2025.

Commission (2005a). Action Plan to Improve Communicating Europe by the Commission. Communication to the Commission of 20 July 2005. https://eur-lex.europa.eu/. Accessed 20 July 2025.
Commission (2005b). *The Commission's Contribution to the Period of Reflection and Beyond: Plan-D for Democracy, Dialogue and Debate.* Brussels, 13 October 2005.
Commission (2006). *White Paper on a European Communication Policy.* Brussels, 1 February 2006. Available at: https://eur-lex.europa.eu/. Accessed 20 July 2025.
Commission (2014). *Juncker, J.-C., A New Start for Europe: My Agenda for Jobs, Growth, Fairness and Democratic Change. Political Guidelines for the next European Commission Opening Statement in the European Parliament Plenary Session.* Strasbourg, 15 July 2014.
Commission (2022). Commission Opinion on Ukraine's application for membership of the European Union. https://eur-lex.europa.eu/. Accessed 30 October 2025.
Commission (2023a). *Conference on the Future of Europe, 2023.* https://commission.europa.eu/. Accessed 20 July 2025.
Commission (2023b). *2023 Rule of Law Report,* 5 July 2023. https://commission.europa.eu/publications/2023-rule-law-report-communication-and-country-chapters_en. Accessed 20 July 2025.
Commission (2025). *Communication on the European Democracy Shield. Brussels,* 12 November 2025.
Court of Justice of the European Union, Decision of 11 December 2012 concerning public access to documents held by the Court of Justice of the European Union in the exercise of its administrative functions [2012] OJ C 38/2–4.
Crum, B. (2023). Why the European Parliament lost the Spitzenkandidaten-process. *Journal of European Public Policy,* 30(2): 193–213.
Cseres, K. (2024). The Role of Competition Law in Defending Rule of Law Values in the EU. In Fasone, C., Dirri, A., and Guerra, Y. (eds). *EU Rule of Law Procedures at the Test Bench. Managing Dissensus in the European Constitutional Landscape.* London, Palgrave: 261–279.
Davies, B. (2017). Internationale Handelsgesellschaft and the Miscalculation at the Inception of the ECJ's Human Rights Jurisprudence. In Nicola, F. and Davies, B. (eds). *EU Law Stories.* Cambridge, Cambridge University Press: 157–177.
De Burca, G. (2011). The Road Not Taken: The European Union as a Global Human Rights Actor. *The American Journal of International Law,* 105(4): 649–693.
Delors, J. (1992). From the Single Act to Maastricht and Beyond: The Means to Match our Ambitions, Strasbourg, 12 February 1992, *Bulletin of the European Communities Supplement* 1/92. Archive of European Integration. https://aei.pitt.edu/8564/1/8564.pdf. Accessed 20 July 2025.
Delors, J. (1993). Address by Jacques Delors, President of the Commission, to the European Parliament on the occasion of the investiture debate of the new Commission, Strasbourg, 10 February 1993. *Bulletin of the European Communities Supplement* 1/93: 5–13.
Duchene, J. (1994). *Jean Monnet: the First Statesman of Independence.* New York/London, WW Norton.
Dumbrovsky, T., Petkova, B., and Van der Sluis, M. (2014). Judicial Appointments: The Article 255 TFEU Advisory Panel and Selection Procedures in the Member States. *Common Market Law Review,* 51(2): 455–482.
European Communities (1973). *Document on The European Identity published by the Nine Foreign Ministers on 14 December 1973, in Copenhagen.* www.cvce.eu. Accessed 20 July 2025.
Fahey, E. (2017). Of 'One Shotters' and 'Repeat Hitters'. A Retrospective on the Role of the European Parliament in the EU-US PNR Litigation. In Nicola, F. and Davies, B. (eds). *EU Law Stories.* Cambridge, Cambridge University Press: 528–550.
Featherstone, K. (1994). Jean Monnet and the democratic deficit in the European Union. *Journal of Common Market Studies,* 32(2): 149–170.
Fiedlschuster, M. (2018). EU Concepts of Democracy and Civil Society. In: Fiedlschuster, M. (ed.). *Globalization, EU Democracy Assistance and the World Social Forum.* London, Palgrave Macmillan, Cham. https://doi.org/10.1007/978-3-319-70739-6_3.

Gillingham, J. (2003). *European Integration 1950–2003. Superstate or New Market Economy.* Cambridge, Cambridge University Press.
Hallstein, W. (1959). *Speech to the Royal Institute of International Relations*, Brussels, 10 November 1959. Archive of European Integration. https://aei.pitt.edu/14932/. Accessed 20 July 2025.
Hallstein, W. (1969). Speech Delivered to the European Luncheon Club, London, 5 May 1969. Archive of European Integration. https://aei.pitt.edu/12859. Accessed 20 July 2025.
Harcourt, A. and Radaelli, C. M. (1999). Limits to EU Technocratic Regulation? *European Journal of Political Research*, 35: 107–122.
Jacqué, J.-P. (2004). The Principle of Institutional Balance. *Common Market Law Review*, 41: 383–391.
Jacqué, J.-P. (2010). Les Verts v The European Parliament. In Azoulai, L. and Poiares Maduro, M. (eds). *The Past and Future of EU Law.* Oxford, Hart Publishing: 178–201.
Kelbel, C. and Navarro, J. (eds.) (2020). *Interinstitutional relations in the EU.* RECONNECT Working Paper Series.
Kochenov, D. (2008). *EU Enlargement and the Failure of Conditionality: Pre-accession Conditionality in the Fields of Democracy and the Rule of Law.* Alphen aan den Rijn, Kluwer.
Kochenov, D. and Butler, G. (2021). Independence of the Court of Justice of the European Union: Unchecked Member States Power after the Sharpston Affair. *European Law Journal*, 27: 262–296.
Kumm, M. (2010). Internationale Handelsgesellschaft, Nold and the New Human Rights Paradigm. In Azoulai, L. and Poiares Maduro, M. (eds). *The Past and Future of EU Law.* Oxford, Hart Publishing: 106–118.
Landwehr, C. and Leininger, A. (2019). Instrumental or Procedural Democrats? The Evolution of Procedural Preferences after Democratization. *Political Research Exchange*, 1(1): 1–19.
Lenaerts, K. (2010). The Basic Constitutional Charter of a Community Based on the Rule of Law. In Azoulai, L. and Poiares Maduro, M. (eds). *The Past and Future of EU Law.* Oxford, Hart Publishing: 295–315.
Lenaerts, K. (2013). The Principle of Democracy in the Case Law of the European Court of Justice. *The International and Comparative Law Quarterly*, 62(2): 271–315.
Lenaerts, K. (2016). EU Citizenship and Democracy, *New Journal of European Criminal Law*, 7(2): 164–174.
Loth, W. (2014). Walter Hallstein, a Committed European. In Dumoulin, M. (ed.). *The European Commission 1958–72. History and Memories of an Institution.* Luxembourg. Publications Office of the European Union.
Mancini, F. and Keeling, D. T. (1994). Democracy and the European Court of Justice. *Modern Law Review*, 57(2): 175–190.
Monnet, J. (1952a). Address to the Council of Ministers, Luxembourg, 8 September 1952.
Monnet, J. (1952b). Speech Delivered at the Opening Session of the Common Assembly, Strasbourg, 11 September 1952.
Monnet, J. (1953). Statement Before the 'Randall Committee' Investigating United States Foreign Trade Policy, Paris, 11 November 1953.
Monnet, J. (1955). *The United States of Europe has Begun. The European Coal and Steel Community—Speeches and Addresses by Jean Monnet, 1952–1954.* Archive of European Integration. https://aei.pitt.edu/14365/. Accessed 20 July 2025.
Ninatti, S. (2004). *Giudicare la democrazia?.* Milan, Giuffrè.
Norris, P. (2011). *Democratic Deficit. Critical Citizens Revisited.* Cambridge, Cambridge University Press.
Oleart, A. and Theuns, T. (2023). 'Democracy without Politics' in the European Commission's Response to Democratic Backsliding: From Technocratic Legalism to Democratic Pluralism. *Journal of Common Market Studies*, 61: 882–899.
Patrin, M. (2021). Meroni Behind the Scenes: Uncovering the Actors and Context of a Landmark Judgment. *European Papers*, 6(1): 539–551.

Pech, L. and Kochenov, D. (2021). *Respect for the Rule of Law in the Case Law of the European Court of Justice: A Casebook Overview of Key Judgments since the Portuguese Judges Case*, SIEPS, Report no. 3.
Pescatore, P. (1970). Fundamental Rights and Freedoms in the System of the European Communities. *The American Journal of Comparative Law*, 18(2): 343–351.
Pinelli, C. (2004). Conditionality and Enlargement in Light of EU Constitutional Developments. *European Law Journal*, 10(3), 354–362.
Prodi. R. (1999). Speech by Romano Prodi President-designate of the European Commission to the European Parliament, 19 September 1999. https://ec.europa.eu/commission/presscorner/detail/en/SPEECH_99_114. Accessed 20 July 2025.
Puetter, U. (2014). *The European Council and the Council. New Intergovernmentalism and Institutional Change*. Oxford, Oxford University Press.
Regulation (EU, Euratom) 2020/2092 of the European Parliament and of the Council of 16 December 2020 on a general regime of conditionality for the protection of the Union budget [2020] OJ L 433I/1–10.
Rasmussen, A. (2011). Early conclusion in bicameral bargaining: Evidence from the co-decision legislative procedure of the European Union. *European Union Politics*, 12(1): 41–64.
Rittberger, B. (2005). *Building Europe's Parliament*. Oxford, Oxford University Press.
Sadl, U. and Madsen, M. R. (2016). A 'Selfie' from Luxembourg: The Court of Justice and the Fabrication of Pre-Accession Case-Law Dossiers. *The Columbia Journal of European Law*, 22(2): 327–354.
Schmidt, V. A. (2013). Democracy and Legitimacy in the European Union Revisited: Input, Output and 'Throughput'. *Political Studies*, 61(1): 2–22.
Spieker, L. D. (2023). Beyond the Rule of Law: How the Court of Justice Can Protect Conditions for Democratic Change in the Member States. In Södersten, A. and Hercock, E. (eds.), *The Rule of Law in the EU: Crisis and Solutions*. SIEPS, 72–78.
Spierenburg, D. and Poidevin, R. (1994). *The History of the High Authority of the European Coal and Steel Community*. London, Weidenfeld and Nicolson.
Tridimas, T. (2010). Primacy, Fundamental Rights and the Search for Legitimacy. In Azoulai, L. and Poiares Maduro, M. (eds). *The Past and Future of EU Law*. Oxford, Hart Publishing: 179–202.
Tridimas, T. (2018). The Court of Justice of the European Union. In R. Schütze and T. Tridimas (eds). *Oxford Principles of European Union Law*, Vol. I. Cambridge, Cambridge University Press: 581–609.
Von Bogdandy, A. et al. (2021). *Defending Checks and Balances in EU Member States*: Nomos Verlag, Springer.
Von Bogdandy, A. and Spieker, L. D. (2023). Transformative Constitutionalism in Luxembourg: How the Court Can Support Democratic Transitions. *Columbia Journal of European Law*, 29: 65–92.
Von der Leyen, U. (2019). *A Union that Strives for More. My Agenda for Europe: Political Guidelines for the Next European Commission 2019-2024*. Brussels, Directorate-General for Communication.
Von Ondarza, N. and Ålander, M. (2022). *After the Conference on the Future of Europe: Time to Make Reforms Happen*. SWP Comment. No. 49.
Wille, A. (2012). The Politicization of the EU Commission: Democratic Control and the Dynamics of Executive Selection. *International Review of Administrative Sciences*, 78(3): 383–402.

Cases cited

Case 9/56 *Meroni & Co., Industrie Metallurgiche, SpA v High Authority of the European Coal and Steel Community* [1958] ECR 00133 [EU:C:1958:7].
Case 26/62, *NV Algemene Transport- en Expeditie Onderneming van Gend & Loos v Netherlands Inland Revenue Administration* [1963] ECR 00001 [EU:C:1963:1].
Case 6/64 *Flaminio Cost v E.N.E.L.* [1964] ECR 00585 [EU:C:1964:66].

Case 29/69 *Erich Stauder v City of Ulm – Sozialamt* [1969] ECR 00419 [EU:C:1969:57].
Case 11/70 *Internationale Handelsgesellschaft mbH v Einfuhr- und Vorratsstelle für Getreide und Futtermittel* [1970] ECR 01125 [EU:C:1970:114].
Case 4/73 *J. Nold, Kohlen- und Baustoffgroßhandlung v Commission of the European Communities* [1974] ECR 00491 [EU:C:1974:51].
Case 43/75 *Defrenne v Sabena* [1976] ECR 00455 [EU:C:1976:56].
Case 106/77 *Amministrazione delle Finanze dello Stato v Simmenthal* [1978] ECR 00629 [EU:C:1978:49].
Case 44/79 *Liselotte Hauer v Land Rheinland-Pfalz* [1979] ECR 03727 [EU:C:1979:290].
Joined Cases 138/79 *SA Roquette Frères v Council of the European Communities* and 139/79 *Maizena GmbH v Council of the European Communities* [1980] ECR 03333 [EU:C:1980:213].
Case 283/81 *CILFIT and di Gavardo v Ministry of Health* [1982] ECR 03415 [EU:C:1982:335].
Case 34/86 *Council of the European Communities v European Parliament* [1986] ECR 02155 [EU:C:1986:291].
Case 294/83 *Parti écologiste "Les Verts" v European Parliament* [1986] ECR 01339 [EU:C:1986:166].
Case 149/85 *Roger Wybot v Edgar Faure and Others* [1986] ECR 02391 [EU:C:1986:310].
Case 314/85 *Foto-Frost v Hauptzollamt Lübeck-Ost* [1987] ECR 04199 [EU:C:1987:452].
Case C-70/88 *European Parliament v Council of the European Communities* [1991] ECR I-04529 [EU:C:1991:373].
Joined Cases C-6/90 and C-9/90 *Francovich and Bonifaci v Italy* [1991] ECR I-05357 [EU:C:1991:428].
Case C-41/95 *Council v European Parliament* [1995] ECR I-04411 [EU:C:1995:431].
Case C-85/96 *Martínez Sala v Bayern* [1998] ECR I-02691 [EU:C:1998:217].
Case C-486/01 *Front National v European Parliament* [2004] ECR I-06289 [EU:C:2004:394].
Joined Cases C-317/04 and C-318/04 *European Parliament v Council and Commission* [2006] ECR I-04721 [EU:C:2006:346].
Joined Cases C-393/07 and C-9/08 *Italy and Donnici v European Parliament* [2009] ECR I-03679 [EU:C:2009:275].
Case C-518/07 *Commission v Germany* [2010] [EU:C:2010:125].
Case C-506/08 P *Sweden v Commission and MyTravel* [2011] ECR I-06237 [EU:C:2011:496].
Case C-163/10 *Criminal proceedings against Aldo Patriciello* [2011] ECR I/07565 [EU:C:2011:543].
Case C-355/10 *European Parliament v Council* [2012] [EU:C:2012:516].
Case C-77/11 *Council v European Parliament* [2013] OJ C325, 9.11.2014: 2.
Case C-280/11 P *Council v Access Info Europe* [2013] [EU:C:2013:671].
Case C-650/13 *Delvigne v Commune de Lesparre Médoc and Préfet de la Gironde* [2015] [EU:C:2015:648].
Case C-362/14 *Schrems v Data Protection Commissioner* [2015] [EU:C:2015:650].
Case C-286/14 *European Parliament v Commission* [2016] [EU:C:2016:183].
Joined Cases C-203/15 *Tele2 Sverige v Post- och telestyrelsen* and C-698/15 *Home Secretary v Watson and Others* [2016] [EU:C:2016:970].
Case C-64/16 *Associação Sindical dos Juízes Portugueses v Tribunal de Contas* [2018] [EU:C:2018:117].
Case C-73/17 *France v European Parliament* [2018] OJ C 436, 3.12.2018: 8–9.
Case C-216/18 PPU *LM* [2018] [EU:C:2018:586].
Case C-418/18 P *Puppinck and Others v Commission* [2019] [EU:C:2019:1113].
Case C-502/19 *Junqueras i Vies* [2019] [EU:C:2019:1115].
Case C-623/17 *Privacy International v Foreign Secretary and Others* [2020] [EU:C:2020:790].
Case C-66/18 *Commission v Hungary* [2020] [EU:C:2020:792].
Case C-311/18 *Data Protection Commissioner v Facebook Ireland and Schrems* [2020] [EU:C:2020:559].
Joined Cases C-511/18, 512/18, and 520/18 *La Quadrature du Net v Premier minister and Others* [2020] [EU:C:2020:791].

Case C-156/21 *Hungary v European Parliament and Council* [2022] [EU:C:2022:97].
Case C-157/21 *Poland v Parliament and Council* [2022] [EU:C:2022:98].
Case C-769/22 *Commission v Hungary* [2022] OJ C54, 13.2.2023: 16–17 (pending).
Case C-92/23 *Commission v Hungary* [2023] OJ C189, 30.5.2023: 12–13 (pending).
Case C-808/21 *Commission v Czech Republic* [2024] [EU:C:2024:962].
Case C-181/23 *Commission v Malta* [2025] [EU:C:2025:283].
Case T-135/96 *UEAPME v Council of Europe* [1998] ECR II-02335 [EU:T:1998:128].
Joined Cases T-222/99, T-327/99 and T-329/99 *Martinez and Others v European Parliament* [2001] ECR II-02823 [EU:T:2001:242].
Case T-540/15 *De Capitani v European Parliament* [2018] [EU:T:2018:167].
Case T-789/19 *Moerenhout and Others v Commission* [2021] [EU:T:2021:260].
Case T-791/19 *Sped Pro v Commission* [2022] [EU:T:2022:67].
Case T-163/21 *De Capitani v Council* [2023] [EU:T:2023:15].

5

The National Foundations of Europe's Promised Democracy

Anna Gora and Pieter de Wilde

5.1 Introduction

The promise of European democracy requires strong national foundations.[1] Healthy democracy within its Member States is necessary if the European Union (EU) is to defend its fundamental values for all its citizens. While the powers of Member States in EU decision-making differ from policy area to policy area, they are always involved in one way or the other and they collectively have the final word in many key decisions. Democratic deficiencies in one Member State indirectly affect all EU citizens (Müller 2015; Theuns 2022). Hence, the democratic credentials of the EU stand or fall with the democratic credentials of its Member States. Two decades since the first and largest of its eastern enlargements, the EU is witnessing concerning trends in the application of its founding principles in several of its Central and Eastern European (CEE) Member States.

In emphasizing the need to defend individual liberties[2] alongside procedural democracy, the EU's founding principles, laid out in Article 2 of the Treaty on European Union (TEU 1992), formalize its commitment to liberal democracy, the dominant democratic regime type in the world today. Here the rule of law has particular importance in that the defence of individual liberties and adherence to the conventions of procedural democracy depend on the rule of law being upheld. What is more, the functioning of the Single Market—arguably the EU's biggest achievement as a political project—is dependent on the rule of law to guarantee consumers and producers across the EU that products and services are produced in accordance with EU laws on a level playing field. It is then unsurprising that a particular focus for political and legal scholars has been directed at problems specifically within the rule of law in certain Member States (Kochenov 2008; Pech and Scheppele 2017; Sedelmeier 2014). One of the EU's fundamental values and a core

[1] This chapter is an extensively reworked and updated version of the Working Paper 'Mapping Democratic Systems in EU Member States', which was published as Deliverable 5.1. of the Horizon Europe project RECONNECT.

[2] These include respect for human dignity, freedom, democracy, equality, the rule of law, and respect for human rights, including the rights of persons belonging to minorities.

Anna Gora and Pieter de Wilde, *The National Foundations of Europe's Promised Democracy* In: *The Promise of EU Democracy*. Edited by: Jan Wouters, Julie Smith, Kolja Raube, and Ben Crum, Oxford University Press.
 DOI: 10.1093/9780191996191.003.0006

feature of liberal democracy, namely the rule of law, has likewise been the main issue targeted by the EU's response. In response to rising concerns, the European Commission invoked Article 7 of the TEU against Poland in 2017, citing serious breaches of the rule of law. Article 7, which outlines the procedure that the EU must follow in the event of a serious breach of one of its founding principles,[3] was triggered again in 2018, this time against Hungary. Just two years later, judges from all over Europe participated in the '1000 Robes March' in Warsaw to protest against infringements of the independence of the judiciary. Finally, in February 2022 the Court of Justice of the European Union (CJEU) ruled in favour of the 2021 conditionality mechanism tying EU funds to respect for the rule of law. At the same time, these events suggest that liberal democracy as reflected in Article 2 of the TEU places greater weight on the protection of individual liberties and the rule of law to sustain the procedural integrity of representative democracy than on more representative or discursive democratic qualities.

This chapter tests whether such a narrow focus on concerns with the rule of law is empirically warranted. The rule of law is one of many components of a thriving liberal democracy. Some assessments conceptualize rule of law problems as an indicator of democratic backsliding along a one-dimensional scale (e.g. Pech and Scheppele 2017). If this is the case, empirically the deterioration of any one of these components would serve as an accurate indicator of the overall deterioration of the others as well and warrant a holistic toolkit targeting all potential components of a democratic regime, and not just the rule of law. Other assessments conceptualize measurements of the quality of democracy as multidimensional, whereby separate indicators may improve or slide backwards independently on individual scales, not limited to the core components of liberal democracy but possibly also including additional participatory or discursive democratic components (Gora and De Wilde 2022; Greskovits 2015). If democratic backsliding unfolds along one or a few indicators of democracy only, this would justify a narrower, more targeted reaction by the EU. Likewise, if democracy is, in fact, multidimensional, democratic backsliding could also be multidimensional. In other words, some Member States could see a deterioration on one dimension of democracy, while others see deterioration on another. In that scenario, the EU needs a diverse toolkit to address the various forms of democratic backsliding.

In this chapter, we thus explore whether a narrow focus on concerns with the rule of law in backsliding Member States is indeed warranted, or whether rule of law backsliding is at the centre of a more encompassing process of democratic backsliding. First, we investigate whether democracy at the national level in Europe is uni- or multidimensional. We then proceed to ask how the dimensionality of

[3] Article 7 of the TEU refers specifically to a breach of one or more of the founding values outlined in Article 2 of the TEU: 'respect for human dignity, freedom, democracy, equality, the rule of law and respect for human rights, including the rights of persons belonging to minorities' (TEU Art 2).

democracy in the EU has developed over time. Finally, we explore in which democratic components backsliding has been most manifest.

5.2 The backsliding and hollowing of European democracy

The dominant scholarly discourse on democratic backsliding in the EU revolves around the notion of backsliding on a continuous one-dimensional scale of stronger and weaker democracies that differ in their levels of commitment to a shared set of democratic features (Diamond 2015: 143; see also Sedelmeier 2014). For example, Poland and Hungary, two cases of democratic backsliding that have received significant attention from the EU, have been characterized as 'semi-authoritarian regimes' (Dawson and Hanley 2016), 'diffusely defective democracies' (Bogaards 2018), and 'hybrid regimes' falling somewhere on the continuum between full democracies and autocracy (Bozóki and Hegedűs 2018; Krekó and Enyedi 2018). On a similar continuum, Hungary has also been labelled an 'elected autocracy' (Ágh 2015). Applying its own one-dimensional measures, the Economist Intelligence Unit's Democracy Index for 2022 evaluates both states as flawed democracies, while Freedom House's freedom index for 2023 continues to characterize Poland as free but situates Hungary within the partly-free position on the continuum.[4]

The labels that scholars have used to characterize regimes vary, but they all have in common that they map countries along a continuum between democratic and non-democratic regimes where backsliding on any one indicator will signify general backsliding towards a less democratic regime type away from a democratic benchmark which, in most cases, is an interpretation of liberal democracy. Backsliding is thus often tied to the observed decay of the liberal values, especially the rule of law, that are also enshrined in the EU's promised form of democratic regime in Article 2 of the TEU (e.g. Gibler and Randazzo 2011; Kochenov 2008; Pech and Scheppele 2017).

Liberal democracy has been the dominant variant of consolidated democracy across much of the contemporary world. The operationalization of liberal democracy has varied. However, it is consistently characterized by an emphasis on the protection of civil liberties, the separation of power, the rule of law, and a preference for representation over participation (for examples, see Diamond 1999, 2008; Lührmann et al. 2018; Møller and Skanning 2013; Zakaria 1997). Despite being almost universally accepted as the normative benchmark to which real-world

[4] Our data were gathered before the 2023 general elections in Poland, which saw a coalition defeat the Law and Justice Party that had ruled Poland since 2015 and had been a driving force behind democratic backsliding and rule of law problems there. At the time of writing, the implications of the 2023 elections in Poland had yet to emerge.

democracies are held, the liberal variant is certainly not the only one and it has not been without criticism. For example, proponents of more participatory or direct forms of democracy have argued that liberalism's emphasis on individual liberties and representation exists in conflict and contradiction to participation and popular sovereignty (Mouffe 2000; Schmitter 2018; Schmitt 1988), whereby the emphasis on representation limits opportunities for participation to regularly held elections and, in some instances, occasional referendums.

Despite the popularity of envisaging democracy and non-democracy as two ends of a single, generally liberal democratic, continuum, in a review of literature on democratic backsliding, Waldner and Lust (2018) warn researchers of the possibility of overestimating the degree of backsliding when using continuous one-dimensional indicators. They point out that such indices, in failing to distinguish movement on individual components of democracy, run the risk of an over-interpretation of small changes. Others are also cautious of the degree of progress or change that is implied by the term 'backsliding'. They argue that what we are witnessing is not the backsliding of healthy democracies but rather the consequences of the instability of democracies that never fully consolidated (Dawson and Hanley 2016; Dimitrova 2018; Levitsky and Way 2015; Van Beek 2019). Antoaneta Dimitrova suggests that leading up to EU membership, democratic institutions and the rules of the EU's acquis communautaire were adopted and implemented in CEE as 'empty shells' while informally coexisting alongside a parallel non-democratic system (Dimitrova 2010). Empirical analysis seems to back these assessments as it shows that the 2004 and 2007 EU accession states have been converging with the rest of the EU on the quality of governance over the last twenty years, but not necessarily on democratic indicators (Börzel and Schimmelfennig 2017: 283).

While the emerging consensus amongst democracy scholars is that the EU is facing a backsliding of democracy in some of its members, there is variation in the identification of what is going wrong. As mentioned above, the dominant focus of EU policymakers and legal scholars is on rule of law problems, which fits in a broader legal-institutional perspective that also emphasizes individual liberties and institutional features of democracy within a single indicator. Contrary to this legal-institutional perspective, a cultural-discursive perspective on democracy and democratic backsliding focuses on norms and discourse as decisive factors, particularly on deliberative and participatory democracy, which are omitted from the conventionally emphasized features of liberal democracy. Ever since Almond and Verba ([1963] 2015), authors have argued that for democracy to thrive, a supportive 'civic culture' needs to be in place amongst citizens to support otherwise fragile institutions. Recent studies confirm the importance of public support for democracy for its survival (Claassen 2020).

Beyond citizens, norms and discourse among elites matter too. Levitsky and Ziblatt (2018) identify mutual toleration and institutional forbearance as the essential 'guardrails' of democracy. Mutual toleration refers to the norm amongst elites that competing elites are not an enemy to be destroyed but rivals to be defeated. Institutional forbearance implies restraint by those in power not to use all legal means available to play 'constitutional hardball' against their opponents. Combined, they form a live-and-let-live mentality amongst political elites. These dynamics are not easily captured by the indicators of liberal democracy mentioned earlier. Yet, rising populism within the EU, for example, is often characterized by claims that domestic rivals are traitors and are 'betraying the people' (Dawson and Hanley 2019; Enyedi 2016). In Romania, mainstream political parties increasingly refer to each other as 'criminals' (Mungiu-Pippidi 2018). Thus, we face the question of what is at the core of democratic backsliding. Is it a change in the constitution and other institutions that we should worry about, or rather changes in norms and elite discourse? If democracy does indeed exist as a multidimensional space, then these changes are not necessarily correlated.

A decline in the deliberative and participatory components of democracy is a dominant theme in the literature on crises of consolidated, mostly 'old' Western democracies (see Macedo et al. 2005; McCaffrie and Akram 2014; Putnam 2000; Stoker 2006). Mair characterized what he called *hollowing* as a two-sided process, defined by a withdrawal of both citizens and governments from participatory politics. Rather than engaging in solutions that foster political engagement, he argued that governments react with further depoliticization and 'shielding' of political decisions from participation (Mair 2006: 45) whilst turning to '"technical" (or "technocratic") solutions' (Cianetti 2018: 321). The most dramatic assessments claim to witness a transition to 'post-democracy', whereby the institutions are in place and functioning as they should but are devoid of any democratic substance (e.g. Crouch 2004; Heartfield 2013). The notion of democratic hollowing therefore considers the possibility that the integrity of a democratic regime may be conditional on its participatory, cultural and discursive qualities rather than, or in addition to, the protection of individual liberties and the rule of law that have been so strongly the focus of the EU's promised democracy.

Bringing together these notions of democratic hollowing and backsliding in the context of the CEE Member States, Béla Greskovits posits that challenges to democracy are not one-dimensional but instead appear on two dimensions as varying combinations of different degrees of hollowing and backsliding (Greskovits 2015: 32). This opens the possibility that movement along one dimension might not necessarily be correlated to movement along the other. This study indicates that this may in fact be the case.

Therefore, in this chapter, we investigate the dimensionality of European democracy at the national level. We first test whether democracy in Europe is one- or multidimensional and then illustrate the specific features—in other words, 'components'—that any dimensions discovered are composed of. If liberal democracy indeed dominates, then we would see a single dimension characterized by the rule of law, protection of individual liberties and procedural democracy. If it is indeed multidimensional, real existing democracy may not be the kind of liberal democracy that the values listed in Article 2 TEU promise. We ask whether and if so, how the dimensionality of democracy in the EU has evolved between the 2004 enlargement and 2022, which allows us to see whether Europe's promised democracy is becoming more dominant over time. Finally, we test whether a toolbox focused on the rule of law is sufficient. To do this, we take a closer look at the dimensions identified in order to examine which components, rule of law or other, have been driving the democratic decline observed, particularly in some Central and Eastern European member countries.

5.3 Five components of democracy

To explore the dimensionality of democracy in Europe, we first need to unpack procedural democracy from liberalism and other possibly coexisting non-procedural and supplemental procedural features. For the analysis that follows, we draw on one of the most renowned and elaborate comparative databases on democracy: V-Dem (Coppedge et al. 2019). V-Dem contains a range of indicators on democracy which are measured annually in over 200 countries. We use five of V-Dem's mid-level indices for components of democracy: polyarchy, liberalism, participation, deliberation, and egalitarianism.

We treat the concept of polyarchy, which Dahl (1971) developed as a realistic normative measure of existing democratic regimes, as the minimum procedural bar for democracy. Polyarchy has been widely used as a minimum benchmark by institutionally focused literature on democratic consolidation (Herman 2016: 254) and forms the democratic foundation of V-Dem's high-level democratic indices. We propose that the addition of the other four components, in different combinations and to varying degrees, builds separate democratic typologies supplementing polyarchy's institutional procedural minimum. Conceptually we treat each component as existing along its own one-dimensional continuum. Some, like participation, can theoretically exist without polyarchic democracy, while others such as egalitarianism largely exist as a normative addition to it when combined with liberalism.

Polyarchic democracy then stands for the most minimal operationalizations of democracy as an electoral regime with a set of institutions deemed necessary for it to operate as a genuine democracy: freedoms of the press, speech, and assembly, and the requirement that governments and parties are both responsive and accountable to voters. Secondly, the *liberal* component reflects the key features of the twentieth century understanding of representative democracy that is backed by the protection of civil liberties including human rights, limited government and the rule of law. This is the component that we expect to see perform strongly across EU Member States if the EU's understanding of democracy as enshrined in Article

2 of the TEU is upheld in practice. We do not break liberalism down further into its individual parts, as we consider them a package. A decline in any one of them (for example, human rights, rule of law, etc.) represents an overall decline on the liberal continuum. Thirdly, *egalitarianism* is concerned with the equal distribution of resources, both material and immaterial, to the extent that this ensures equal opportunity for all citizens to participate in democratic life and the civil liberties that liberalism guarantees. It is one of the core values heralded by proponents of the welfare state and social democracy.

The final two components pick up on conceptualizations of democracy held by proponents of the hollowing thesis (for example Greskovits 2015; Mair 2006). The *deliberative* component relates to the quality of decision-making processes in democracy. It values public reasoning concerned with the common good that is inclusive of competing interests and diverse opinions. Transparency of these processes is essential for deliberation to be effective. The highly deliberative models of democracy characteristic of the work of Jürgen Habermas (1991; 1998) and Hannah Arendt (1958) sit at the normative high end of this continuum. Finally, the *participatory* component reflects the degree to which citizens can directly engage in democratic decision-making through citizens' initiatives, plebiscites, and referendums. Models envisaging citizens' direct participation in policy decisions, such as that advocated by Carole Pateman (1970), sit at the upper end of the participatory continuum.

These five components, which together form the basis of V-Dem's 'varieties of democracy', summarize a consensus on the central distinguishing features of the various conceptions of democracy that exist today (Coppedge et al. 2011; Lindberg et al. 2014). They also cover the varying foci that are characteristic of the hollowing (i.e. participation and deliberation) and backsliding (i.e. polyarchy and liberalism) debates. Echoing Diamond's (2015) remarks on the consequence of disagreements in defining democracy over assessments of its quality, we accept that if various types of democracy are found to exist, then the core democratic features of these already established conceptualizations will likely form their components. Heeding Morlino's warnings that participatory and discursive tools do not necessarily indicate a healthy democracy (Morlino 2009), we assume the empirical possibility that the remaining four components can also exist in the absence of polyarchic democracy.

Disentangling a minimalist idea of democracy from the possible democratic components ultimately starts with a normative choice regarding the minimally accepted parameters for democracy, which are aligned with V-Dem's operationalization of polyarchy. The conceptualization of what actual democracy in Europe looks like is determined by the degree to which these five components are present comparably across the EU. It is against this background that the divergence of any of its Member States is assessed and the possibility of a one-dimensional, two-dimensional, or even multidimensional democratic space is explored. We seek to assess the dimensionality of democracy in the EU rather than to measure Member States' democratic regimes against a single liberal democratic benchmark. In other words, while we explore the empirical possibility of multiple democratic regimes in the EU, of which liberal democracy may be just one, this chapter does not claim to contribute to the theoretical debate on the normative desirability of these regimes.

5.4 Method

The debate between the democratic divergence thesis and the backsliding thesis becomes empirically assessable through the analysis of the dimensionality of democracy in the EU. We proceed to conduct a principal component analysis of a range of V-Dem democracy indicators. Beyond its elaborate and comparative measurement of democracy, V-Dem's key strength lies in being coded by national experts, who draw on all kinds of sources for their assessment, ranging from formal legal documents to interpretations of media and parliamentary discourse.

In our analysis, we focus only on EU Member States in order to contribute to the current debate about democratic backsliding and possible counter actions on behalf of the EU. The limited number of countries involved means that a full factorial analysis on all indicators of democracy contained in the V-Dem dataset would lead to unstable measurements. As a rule of thumb, we employ the standard of having four times as many cases as variables contained in the principal component analysis. Our findings for the period 2004–23—when the EU had more than twenty Member States—are thus more reliable than our findings for the 1990–2004 period, when it had fewer. Besides the basic indicators, V-Dem also contains high-level indices and mid-level indices. We make the empirical assumption that polyarchy may coexist both in combination with other democratic components or without them and that changes in each do not necessarily need to move in the same direction. However, V-Dem's five high-level indices all contain polyarchy components, meaning they are not independent measurements. This also violates a key assumption of principal component analysis. Hence, we resort to the mid-level indices. Of the twenty-one mid-level indices, several are again not independent from each other. Others, like the share of the population with suffrage (v2x_suffr), are excluded due to a lack of variation or due to advice from the V-Dem team not to include it in such analyses (i.e. v2x_elecoff). We end up with five key indicators for democracy to include in the principal component analysis which measure the five core components of democracy described above: 1) the multiplicative polyarchy index (v2x_mpi)[5]; 2) the liberal component index (v2x_

[5] The multiplicative polyarchy index and the additive polyarchy index are so highly correlated that the results are not affected by including either one or the other.

liberal); 3) the participatory component index (v2x_partip); 4) the deliberative component index (v2xdl_delib); and 5) the egalitarian component index (v2x_egal).[6] This makes no difference for our principal component analysis regarding the underpinning dimensionality of democracy in the EU, but it is important to consider when studying absolute trends in the indices.

Staying loyal to Dahl's definition, V-Dem's multiplicative *polyarchy* index is built from indicators measuring the freedoms of association and expression, the share of the population with universal suffrage, the degree to which elections are free and fair, and whether the heads of state and government are popularly elected. The *liberal* component index is calculated based on indicators of the presence of individual liberties and equality before the law, and judicial and legislative constraints on the executive. V-Dem operationalizes *participation* into four sub-variables: availability and ease of access to direct popular vote; citizen participation in civil society paired with its degree of access to policymaking; whether local governments are elected and operate independently from unelected bodies; and whether regional governments are elected and operate independently from unelected bodies. The extent to which citizens choose to partake in opportunities for participation diverges from how it is understood in earlier research on democratic hollowing (see Mair 2006; Greskovits 2015; Cianetti 2018), which was more focused on actual participation than on opportunities for participation. The *deliberative* component index considers whether political elites defend their positions on public policy issues by offering reasoned justifications, as well as justifications based on the common good. It also considers the range of parties that are consulted, the degree to which counterarguments are respected, and the breadth and depth of deliberation in the public sphere (e.g. media). Finally, V-Dem's *egalitarian* component is constructed from indicators on the protection of rights and freedoms equally across all groups, equal opportunity for all groups to participate in politics, and the equal distribution of resources such as wealth, education, and healthcare.

Principal component analysis (PCA) is the method of choice to identify whether multiple, independently measured scales are empirically related to such an extent that they jointly form fewer, or perhaps just one, underpinning dimension. Not only will it indicate how many dimensions exist empirically, but also how the various original scales load onto them. The latter facilitates the interpretation of what the core of empirically observed dimensions is.[7] To assess the dimensionality of democracy in the EU, we look at the total components identified that satisfy the criteria specified in footnote 7. In addition, we plot the explained variance

[6] It should be noted, that the MPI polyarchy index inherently generates greater spread than the other indexes because of its multiplicative, as opposed to averaging, nature of construction.

[7] We conduct standard principal component analysis with varimax rotation for the period 1990–2022 per year, using V-Dem version 13. We report components with either >1.00 Eigenvalue or that combined reach standard acceptable norms of a total of at least 60% explained variance. In some cases, the latter norm means the inclusion of a component with Eigenvalues slightly below the 1.00 threshold.

of the first component by year. This is because, in a multidimensional democracy space, the variance explained by the dominant dimension may vary. The higher the explained variance of the first component, the more the empirical variation in democracy within the EU approximates a one-dimensional space. So, if we were to find an increase in the explained variance of the first component over time, we would conclude that democracy in the EU is becoming more one-dimensional, which we interpret as evidence that the rule of law indeed forms part and parcel of a single dimension of democracy and that problems with rule of law are thus indicative of democratic backsliding more generally. On the other hand, if the explained variance of the first component is decreasing over time, then rule of law backsliding only forms one piece of the puzzle of democratic backsliding and too much focus on rule of law alone would lead to a misunderstanding of the broader problems related to the promise of democracy in the European Union.

5.5 Findings

The principal component analysis reveals a two-dimensional space of democracy in the EU (Tables 5.1 and 5.2). While there is variation from year to year, the polyarchy, liberalism, deliberation, and egalitarianism indices constitute the core of the first component, while participation constitutes the second component. Given the fact that multiple indicators load on the first dimension, it would be inaccurate to label this dimension the liberal part of liberal democracy. Rather, it is much more encompassing. Deterioration along this dimension can thus be considered general democratic backsliding. The core of the second dimension is formed by the component index of participation. Deterioration along this dimension is thus essentially a restriction in opportunities for citizens to engage with politics.

The dominant focus on rule of law problems in EU Member States that we find among EU officials and legal scholars is thus in a sense warranted, as a deterioration of rule of law can be seen as an indication of a broader decline in democracy. Free and fair elections, the quality of public discourse and minimizing inequality

Table 5.1 Principal component analysis

Component	Initial Eigenvalues		
	Total	**% of Variance**	**Cumulative %**
1	3.271	65.425	65.425
2	.971	19.426	84.851
3	.351		

Table 5.2 Rotated component matrix[a]

	Component	
	1	2
Multiplicative polyarchy index	.912	
Liberal component index	.872	
Participatory component index		.996
Deliberative component index	.906	
Egalitarian component index	.897	

Notes: Extraction Method: Principal Component Analysis. Loadings reported >.299.

Rotation Method: Varimax with Kaiser Normalization.

[a] Rotation converged in three iterations

to keep the opportunities of democratic citizenship open to all go hand in hand with the rule of law. However, an exclusive focus on the rule of law also restricts the ability of EU officials and legal scholars to grasp fully the much more encompassing process of democratic backsliding and—more importantly—overlooks the key participatory dimension of democracy. To put it bluntly, Europe's democracies might be hollowing out without the rule of law observers ever noticing it.

Figure 5.1 shows the development of explained variance of the main democracy dimension in the EU over time. In other words, it shows how meaningful it is to think of all EU Member States as located somewhere along a single continuum from least to most democratic. Given the relatively low number of observations per year—identical to the number of Member States—our analysis contains significant uncertainties, as modelled in Figure 5.1. That said, in the 1990s, the variance explained hovered around 52 per cent, indicating the differences among Member States clearly defied a logic of more to less democratic. The 2004 and 2007 Eastern enlargement had a clear effect on the dimensionality of democracy in the EU. The explained variance of the main democracy dimension increased to around 62–63 per cent. It further increased to around 68 per cent in 2016 and then stabilized. In other words, since 2000, it makes more and more sense to think of EU Member States as located on a single dimension from more to less democratic. The difference between Member States that are overall more democratic and those that are overall less democratic increased with Eastern enlargement and continued to increase afterwards, up until around the year 2018, after which it stabilized (Figure 5.1). This means that since 2018, rule of law problems in any Member State are more indicative of broader problems related to democracy in that Member State than they were before. Still, the dominant dimension of democracy does not explain all variance. Thirty to 35 per cent of variance remains unanswered for. This

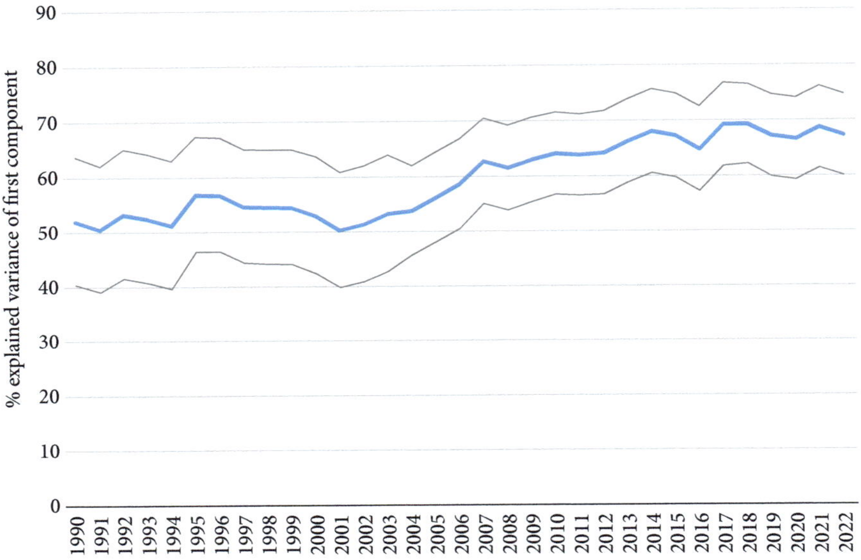

Figure 5.1 Explained variance of the main democracy dimension in the EU over time, with 68% confidence interval, captured between the upper and lower grey lines

means that an exclusive focus on rule of law would overlook important differences between how EU Member States fulfil the promise of democracy.

Figure 5.2 plots EU Member States on factor loadings resulting from the principal component analysis. In other words, it portrays the result of the PCA and depicts how high each Member State scores on the main democracy and participatory democracy dimensions. Lines are drawn through the mean on both dimensions, dividing the EU democratic space into four quadrants. Note that these are relative, rather than absolute, quadrants. In the top-right corner, we see full democracies that perform comparatively highly on both the main and secondary democracy dimensions. In the bottom-left corner are hollow states that score comparatively low on both dimensions. Countries in the bottom-left quadrant are not necessarily undemocratic, but they are not as democratic as the ones in the top-right quadrant.

Figure 5.2 clearly reveals the democratic problems of Poland, Romania, and Hungary compared to most of their West European fellow Member States. It also reveals that the countries that have received the most attention within the EU when it comes to rule of law problems—Hungary and Poland—are certainly not alone. Attention to Romania and Cyprus is warranted and many other Member States have problems, albeit less pressing ones.

Yet, importantly, Figure 5.2 also reveals that if we focus on rule of law only, we miss important differences between EU Member States. The difference between

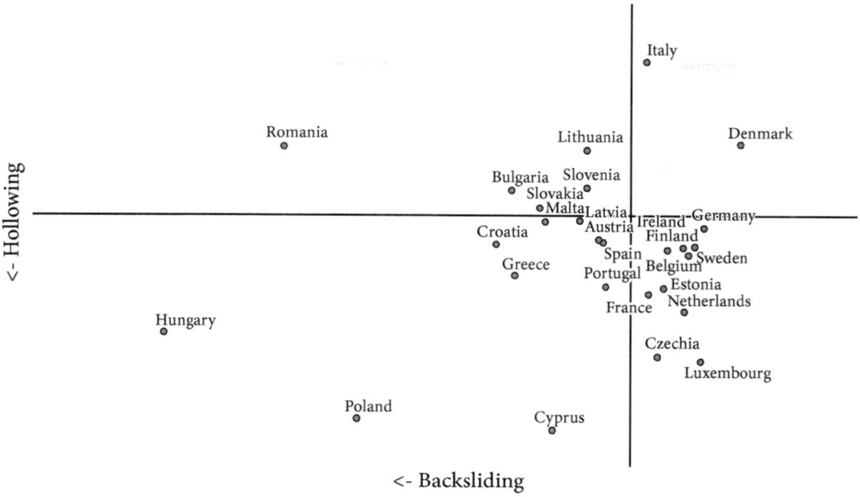

Figure 5.2 Two-dimensional democracy in the EU 27 in 2022

Poland on the one hand and Romania on the other would be overlooked. Also, it would miss the differences between the Czech Republic, Cyprus, and Luxembourg on the one hand and Italy, Denmark, and Lithuania on the other, with the latter three featuring more opportunities for participation. If we are to grasp fully the potential obstacles facing EU Member States to fulfil the promise of democracy, then we should look beyond rule of law issues. In particular, we should keep an eye on the opportunities for participation that EU citizens have and the extent to which they make use of them.

When studying the five components of democracy separately, the largest divergences within the EU—the areas where EU Member States differ from each other—are in the polyarchy and deliberation indexes (see Table 5.3). The minima of these indicators, at .20 and .37 respectively, are considerably lower than for the other indicators. Divergence within the EU is also indicated by the standard deviations of these indicators which are about twice as high as those of the other three indicators. In other words, when mapping the degree of democracy in EU Member States, the biggest differences between them can be found when it comes to free and fair elections and healthy public debates, much more so than independence of the judiciary or other rule of law issues on which many in Brussels circles are fixated. The quality of deliberation especially receives a lot less attention in EU policy circles than the empirical problems surrounding it warrant.

Taking a closer look at developments within the Central and Eastern European EU Member States, we see in yet another way how decreasing quality in deliberation stands at the heart of current democratic backsliding within the EU (Figure 5.3). Deterioration of democracy starts immediately after enlargement,

Table 5.3 Divergent democracy within the EU 27 in 2022[a]

	Minimum	Maximum	Mean	Std. Deviation
Multiplicative polyarchy index	.20	.87	.70	.153
Liberal democracy index	.69	.98	.89	.081
Participatory democracy index	.54	.76	.64	.048
Deliberative democracy index	.37	.98	.83	.156
Egalitarian democracy index	.66	.97	.86	.078

[a] The five mid-level V-Dem indexes discussed in the method section.

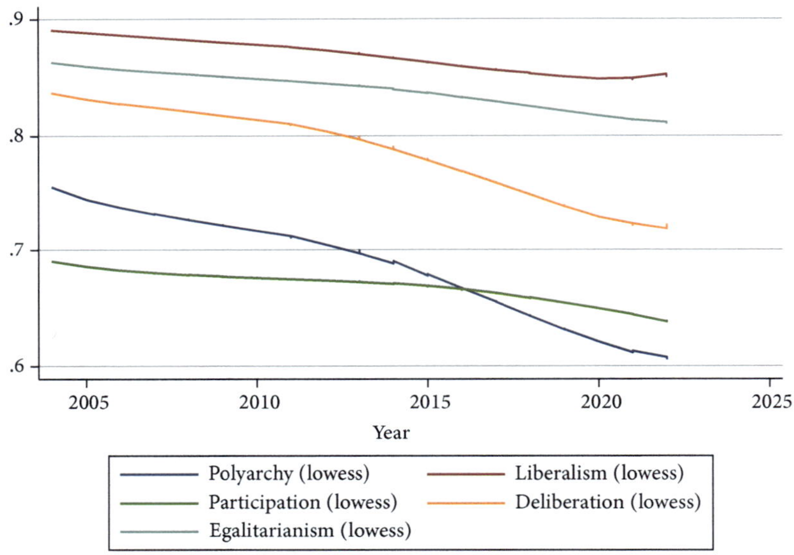

Figure 5.3 Developments in CEEC EU Member States along five key democracy dimensions since 2004

across all five indicators. Figure 5.3 shows Lowess lines of the five key democracy indicators for CEE EU Member States from 2004 to 2022. Lowess lines smooth out strong differences, thus revealing trend lines over time rather than short-term variation. Note that recent years, starting around 2013, show a rapid decrease in polyarchy and the quality of deliberation as the most noticeable developments. Moreover, rule of law indicators captured in the liberalism index actually show improvement—albeit marginally—since 2020.

To summarize, we have documented here that the EU's democratic space is structurally two-dimensional. The dominant democracy dimension and the secondary participation dimension are rather stable over time since the early 1990s, despite substantial changes in the EU, most notably enlargement from twelve to twenty-eight Member States (reduced to twenty-seven following Brexit in 2020). Following Eastern enlargement rounds in 2004, 2007, and 2013, the dominant dimension of democracy has become even more dominant, as seen in the increase in variance explained by this dimension from a little over 50 per cent to close to 70 per cent.

Where much attention in EU circles in recent years has been devoted to problems concerning rule of law and independence of the judiciary, our findings show that such a focus likely reveals more general patterns in democratic backsliding, more so since 2018 than before. At the same time, our analysis shows that we should be more concerned about the core democratic elements of free and fair elections (here captured in the polyarchy index) and the quality of public debate (here captured in the deliberation index) than the predominant rule of law focus allows for.

5.6 Conclusion

Developments in Central and Eastern Europe since 2010 have regularly been described as democratic backsliding. Responding to this, EU officials and legal scholars have pointed out problems and deterioration in the rule of law. This is important from a normative perspective as the rule of law is central to liberal democracy and enshrined in Article 2 of the TEU. At the same time, the rule of law is essential to the functioning of the EU and its flagship Single Market project in particular. Yet, a focus on the rule of law when discussing broader challenges of democracy implies an understanding of democracy as a single-dimensional continuum; a single space ranging from least to most democratic in which any change in the rule of law is indicative of a broader change along that continuum. Should the assumption that the rule of law and democracy are not fully aligned be true, that changes in one of them do not—or not fully—reveal changes in the other, then a singular focus on the rule of law would be problematic. It would overlook and maybe underestimate important developments in the extent to which EU Member States fulfil the promise of democracy. Our chapter therefore set out to investigate the extent to which rule of law backsliding is part and parcel of a broader development of democratic backsliding. Put in other words, if we focus on the rule of law in the EU, do we miss anything important related to democracy?

Through systematic analysis of the dimensionality of democracy within the EU, we found it to be consistently two-dimensional throughout the period 1990–2022. The first dimension contains a range of democratic indicators. It revolves primarily around the extent to which Member States allow free and fair elections and how deliberative and egalitarian they are. Together, the polyarchy and deliberative components capturing these elements of democracy are not only the most central to this primary democracy dimension, but they also feature the greatest difference between EU Member States. In other words, if we want to fully grasp the process of democratic backsliding or the status of democracy at any given point in time within EU Member States, we get the clearest picture if we focus on the extent to which there are free and fair elections and a vibrant, healthy public sphere.

How well liberal checks-and-balances, the rule of law and individual rights are protected also loads onto the main democracy dimension. Hence, a focus on the status of the rule of law or changes therein is likely to reveal important patterns in democracy more generally. Moreover, the extent to which a focus on the rule of law can capture important patterns in democracy within EU Member States has increased steadily during the first two decades of the twenty-first century and is thus now more warranted than ever.

Yet, the analysis also reveals a second dimension in democracy, which concerns participation. This includes the opportunities for citizens to engage in democratic politics at local and national levels. The fact that the EU democratic space is two-dimensional means there are theoretically four ideal types of democracy in the EU currently, in each of the corners of this two-dimensional space. The purest form of democracy would be one that is highly deliberative and egalitarian, with strong electoral freedom and fairness, robust liberal checks and balances, individual rights, and high participation. Denmark currently approximates this ideal type. A second form—'hollow democracy'—would see low participation potential while the other indicators of democracy remain strong. Finland and Portugal are the closest examples of this within the EU at the time of writing. The third ideal type is a 'participatory state', without the necessary institutions in place to call it a democracy. Bulgaria is a case in point. The final ideal type is a state scoring low on all five key components of democracy: a hollow, undemocratic state. Hungary and Poland are in this corner.

Our findings show that the promise of democracy remains elusive not only at the EU level. Ultimately, the democratic credentials of the Union depend on the credentials of its constituent Member States. To fully understand the extent to which the EU fulfils its promise of democracy thus also requires a closer look at the extent to which its Member States fulfil this promise and are reinforced to do so as integration proceeds.

Crucially, there are reasons to be concerned. Over the past decade or so, developments in several EU Member States—Hungary and Poland in particular—have led EU officials and legal scholars to raise concerns about the rule of law and to contemplate measures to counteract deterioration in the rule of law. We have argued in this chapter that such a predominant focus on the rule of law presumes that democracy is a single continuum, ranging from 'fully democratic' via 'somewhat democratic' to 'undemocratic'. We set out to find out how valid this single-dimensional assumption is. The main answer is: somewhat, and increasingly so over time. Yet, an exclusive focus on the rule of law does not capture the full variation in the extent to which EU Member States fulfil the promise of democracy. To grasp that, a focus on the extent to which there are free and fair elections, and a vibrant, healthy public sphere are more warranted. Moreover, an exclusive focus on the rule of law fails to reveal important differences between Member States in the extent to which they facilitate the participation of citizens in the democratic process.

References

Ágh, A. (2015). De-Europeanization and De-Democratization Trends in ECE: from Potemkin Democracy to the Elected Autocracy in Hungary. *Journal of Comparative Politics*, 8(2): 4–26.

Almond, G. A. and Verba, S. (2015). *The Civic Culture*. Princeton NJ, Princeton University Press (Original work published 1963).

Arendt, H. (1958). *The Origins of Totalitarianism*, 2nd edn. Cleveland, World Pub. Co.

Bogaards, M. (2018). De-democratization in Hungary: Diffusely Defective Democracy. *Democratization*, 25(8): 1481–1499.

Börzel, T. A. and Schimmelfennig, F. (2017). Coming Together or Drifting Apart? The EU's Political Integration Capacity in Eastern Europe. *Journal of European Public Policy*, 24(2): 278–296.

Bozóki, A. and Hegedűs, D. (2018). An Externally Constrained Hybrid Regime: Hungary in the European Union. *Democratization*, 25(7): 1173–1189.

Cianetti, L. (2018). Consolidated Technocratic and Ethnic Hollowness, But No Backsliding: Reassessing Europeanization in Estonia and Latvia. *East European Politics*, 34(3): 317–336.

Claassen, C. (2020). Does Public Support Help Democracy Survive? *American Journal of Political Science*, 64(1): 118–134.

Coppedge, M., et al. (2011). Conceptualizing and Measuring Democracy: A New Approach. *Perspectives on Politics*, 9(2): 247–267.

Coppedge, M., et al. (2019). V-Dem Codebook v9, Varieties of Democracy (V-Dem) Project.

Crouch, C. (2004). *Post-Democracy*. Malden MA, Polity Press.

Dahl, R. A. (1971). *Polyarchy: Participation and Opposition*. New Haven CT, Yale University Press.

Dawson, J. and Hanley, S. (2016). The Fading Mirage of the 'Liberal Consensus'. *Journal of Democracy*, 27(1): 20–34.

Dawson, J. and Hanley, S. (2019). Foreground Liberalism, Background Nationalism: A Discursive-Institutionalist Account of EU Leverage and 'Democratic Backsliding' in East Central Europe. *Journal of Common Market Studies*. 57(4): 710–728.

Diamond, L. (1999). *Developing Democracy: Towards Consolidation*. Baltimore MD, Johns Hopkins University Press.

Diamond, L. (2008). *The Spirit of Democracy: The Struggle to Build Free Societies Throughout the World*. New York, Henry Holt and Company.

Diamond, L. (2015). Facing up to the Democratic Recession. *Journal of Democracy*, 26(1): 141–155.

Dimitrova, A. L. (2010). The New Member States of the EU in the Aftermath of Enlargement: Do New European Rules Remain Empty Shells? *Journal of European Public Policy*, 17(1): 137–148.

Dimitrova, A. L. (2018). The Uncertain Road to Sustainable Democracy: Elite Coalitions, Citizen Protests and the Prospects of Democracy in Central and Eastern Europe. *East European Politics*, 34(3): 257–275.

Enyedi, Z. (2016). Populist Polarization and Party System Institutionalization. *Problems of Post-Communism*, 63(3): 210–220.

Gibler, D. M. and Randazzo, K. A. (2011). Testing the Effects of Independent Judiciaries on the Likelihood of Democratic Backsliding. *American Journal of Political Science*, 55: 696–709.
Gora, A. and De Wilde, P. (2022). The Essence of Democratic Backsliding in the European Union: Deliberation and Rule of Law. *Journal of European Public Policy*, 29 (3): 342–362.
Greskovits, B. (2015). The Hollowing and Backsliding of Democracy in East Central Europe. *Global Policy*, 6(1): 28–37.
Habermas, J. (1991). *The Structural Transformation of the Public Sphere: An Inquiry into a Category of Bourgeois Society*. Cambridge MA, MIT Press.
Habermas, J. (1998). *Between Facts and Norms: Contributions to a Discourse Theory of Law and Democracy*, William Rehg (trans.). Cambridge MA, MIT Press.
Heartfield, J. (2013). *The European Union and the End of Politics*. Alresford, Zero Books.
Herman, L. E. (2016). Re-evaluating the Post-Communist Success Story: Party Loyalty, Citizen Mobilization and the Erosion of Hungarian Democracy. *European Political Science Review*, 8(2): 251–284.
Kochenov, D. (2008). *EU Enlargement and the Failure of Conditionality: Pre-Accession Conditionality in the Fields of Democracy and the Rule of Law*. Alphen aan den Rijn, Kluwer Law International.
Krekó, P. and Enyedi, Z. (2018). Explaining Eastern Europe: Orbán's Laboratory of Illiberalism. *Journal of Democracy*, 29(3): 39–51.
Levitsky, S. and Way, L. (2015). The Myth of Democratic Recession. *Journal of Democracy*, 26(1): 45–58.
Levitsky, S. and Ziblatt, D. (2018). *How Democracies Die*. New York, Crown.
Lindberg, S. et al. (2014). V-Dem: A New Way to Measure Democracy. *Journal of Democracy*, 25(3): 159–169.
Lührmann, A., Tannenberg, M., and Lindberg, S. I. (2018). Regimes of the World (ROW): Opening New Avenues for the Comparative Study of Political Regimes. *Politics and Governance*, 6(1): 60–77.
Macedo, S. et al. (2005). *Democracy at Risk: How Political Choices Undermine Citizen Participation, and What We Can Do About It*. Washington DC, Brookings Institution Press.
Mair, P. (2006). Ruling the Void: The Hollowing of Western Democracy. *New Left Review*, 42: 25–51.
McCaffrie, B. and Akram, S. (2014). Crisis of Democracy? Recognizing the Democratic Potential of Alternative Forms of Political Participation. *Democratic Theory*, 1(2): 47–55.
Møller, J. and Skanning, S.-E. (2013). *Democracy and Democratization in Comparative Perspective: Democracy, Conjunctures, Causes, and Consequences*. London, Routledge.
Morlino, L. (2009). Legitimacy and the Quality of Democracy. *International Social Science Journal*, 60(196): 211–222.
Mouffe, C. (2000). *The Democratic Paradox*. London, Verso Books.
Müller, J.-W. (2015). Protection of Democracy and the Rule of Law. *European Law Journal*, 21: 141–160.
Mungiu-Pippidi, A. (2018). Explaining Eastern Europe: Romania's Italian-Style Anticorruption Populism. *Journal of Democracy*, 29: 104–116.
Pateman, C. (1970). *Participation and Democratic Theory*. Cambridge, Cambridge University Press.
Pech, L. and Scheppele, K. L. (2017). Illiberalism Within: Rule of Law Backsliding in the EU. *Cambridge Yearbook of European Legal Studies*, 19: 3–47.
Putnam, R. (2000). *Bowling Alone: The Collapse and Revival of American Community*. New York, Simon & Schuster.
Schmitt, C. (1988). *The Crisis of Parliamentary Democracy*, Ellen Kennedy (trans.). Boston MA, MIT Press (Original work published 1923).
Schmitter, P. C. (2018). A Sketch of What A 'Post-Liberal' Democracy Might Look Like, unpublished manuscript. European University Institute.
Sedelmeier, U. (2014). Anchoring Democracy from Above? The European Union and Democratic Backsliding in Hungary and Romania. *Journal of Common Market Studies*, 52(1): 105–121.

Stoker, G. (2006). *Why Politics Matters: Making Democracy Work.* Basingstoke, Palgrave.
Theuns, T. (2022). The Need for an EU Expulsion Mechanism: Democratic Backsliding and the Failure of Article 7. *Res Publica*, 28: 693–713.
Treaty on European Union (Maastricht Treaty) [1992] OJ C 191/1–112.
Van Beek, U. (2019). The Return of the Nationalist Ethos: The Loss of Liberal Democracy in Poland?. In Ursula van Beek (ed.), *Democracy Under Threat. A Crisis of Legitimacy?* Cham, Palgrave MacMillan: 93–120.
Waldner, D. and Lust, E. (2018). Unwelcome Change: Coming to Terms with Democratic Backsliding. *Annual Review of Political Science*, 21: 93–113.
Zakaria, F. (1997). The Rise of Illiberal Democracy. *Foreign Affairs*, 76(6): 22–43.

PART II

THE PROMISE OF EU DEMOCRACY AND DEMOCRATIC MECHANISMS: CONNECTING WITH EUROPEAN CITIZENS?

6

Why Do Voters Choose Badly? An Investigation of Citizen-Based Factors Explaining the Mass–Elite Preference Gap in European Parliament Elections

Julien Navarro and Camille Kelbel

6.1 Introduction

The alleged representation gap between citizens and their elected officials is one of the most vivid current democratic challenges, calling into question the very essence of representative democracy. In its wake many symptoms of the democratic deficit may be unveiled: growing mistrust of elites and of political parties, erosion of support for government parties; and the rise of more radical or populist forces. This chapter investigates the representation gap by examining the potential discrepancy between voters and representatives and their triggers at the European Union (EU) level. It looks at the level of agreement between voters and the party they cast their ballot for as the main indicator of whether elections effectively create a meaningful link between European citizens and their representatives in the European Parliament (EP). In other words, are voters choosing parties and candidates that best match their political preferences? If not, what factors are driving this misalignment?

There are in fact several reasons for voters to cast their ballot for specific parties and candidates, which contribute to the colossal literature on vote choice and electoral behaviour (Fisher et al. 2020). Voters may care for candidates' personal traits, identify with a party as part of a group, repeat past voting behaviour, want to sanction the incumbent government, or even be drawn to a choice that is not their first one by the electoral system or other considerations. However, the most appealing explanation of vote choices still resides in political preferences and issue-voting, which rest on rationality (Downs 1957). After all, the idea that voters make choices that maximize their goals (be they ideological or policy-based) is

Julien Navarro and Camille Kelbel, *Why Do Voters Choose Badly? An Investigation of Citizen-Based Factors Explaining the Mass–Elite Preference Gap in European Parliament Elections* In: *The Promise of EU Democracy*. Edited by: Jan Wouters, Julie Smith, Kolja Raube, and Ben Crum, Oxford University Press.
DOI: 10.1093/9780191996191.003.0008

nothing less than the backbone of electoral democracy. Yet, rational decisions are constrained by both the abilities of the decision-maker and the environment (see for instance Lee et al. 2016). There is growing evidence in the literature that voters do not necessarily make their choices by processing the information they receive, nor do they have access to such information. In other words, voters may simply fail to identify the right choice or there may be no such choice available (Steiner and Hillen 2021). Moreover, such choice is not purely rational, resting on the idea that voters enter a 'market' and base their choices only on policy preferences; choices may also be shaped by values and normative beliefs.

The EU electoral context undoubtedly appears as a distinct environment (Kritzinger et al. 2020). Within this setting, voters often cast their vote for a variety of reasons which are unrelated to their actual policy preferences at the EU level, including to express dissatisfaction with their national government (Schmitt et al. 2020; Viola 2015). As Follesdal and Hix (2006: 536) observe, European elections 'are not about the personalities and parties at the European level or the direction of the EU policy agenda. . . . European Parliament elections are also not about Europe, as parties and the media treat them as mid-term national contests'. The absence of linkage by media and parties is indeed frequently cited as a key reason for the absence of truly 'European' elections. Consequently, citizens may struggle to accurately identify the candidates and parties at the EU level, potentially contributing to a gap between voter preferences and election outcomes. This, in turn, is not only a problem for the individual parties but 'also implies dangers for the system as a whole' (Holmberg 1989: 29). A lack of policy congruence is indeed generally associated to an increase of political disaffection and anti-establishment politics (Bakker, Jolly, and Polk 2021), risking ultimately further undermining the legitimacy of the EU (Schmitt and Thomassen 1999: 19).

Shifting away from the dominant 'macro' analysis of congruence, this chapter thus asks how and why individual voters (mis)judge the policy positions of candidates and parties in European elections. It uses congruence analysis to examine the extent to which citizen-based factors such as political competence, information acquisition and electoral campaign contacts affect the alignment of preferences of voters and their representatives in the EP. Those preferences are measured along basic political positioning (left–right and pro–anti integration), as well as across key policy domains. The analysis is based firstly on the RECONNECT 2019 citizens' survey which covered seven EU Member States (Germany, France, Italy, Spain, Denmark, Poland, and Hungary) and 14,000 respondents (Plescia et al. 2020).[1] Secondly, the chapter makes use of the 2020 RECONNECT MEP survey, which collected data for 122 MEPs belonging to ninety-five parties in twenty-six

[1] This was a two-wave panel survey. The pre-election wave gathered 2,000 respondents per country and was conducted from 2 to 21 April 2019. The second—post-election—wave was down to between 900 and 1,300 re-interviewed respondents and ran from 27 May to 21 June 2019.

countries (Kelbel, Navarro, and Neihouser 2023). Ultimately, the aim is to address the question of how effectively voters are represented at the EU level, with the EP being the only direct representation link at this level of government.

6.2 Theory and hypotheses

A potential disconnect between citizens and their representatives concerning European integration and EU-level policies is not a new observation (Hooghe 2003; Mattila and Raunio 2006; Müller, Jenny, and Ecker 2012). It has however widened over recent years in the wake of the eurozone crisis (Freire, Teperoglou, and Moury 2014; Real-Dato 2017). The economic situation is in fact only one of the context-related 'macro' factors that have been shown to affect the level of mass–elite (in)congruence on EU matters. Other such factors found in the literature include, for instance, the geographic divide between old and new Member States (Casado-Asensio and Lefkofridi 2011; Mattila and Raunio 2012; Real-Dato 2017) as well as the type of electoral system (Golder and Ferland 2017). Another research strand emphasizes the importance of political parties' characteristics and their electoral strategies, notably party size (Mattila and Raunio 2012), their type (mainstream vs niche) (Costello et al. 2021) or their relative position in the political space (Kelbel, Navarro, and Neihouser 2023). Furthermore, the representatives' profile, in particular their political experience (Belchior 2013), degree of professionalization (Vogel 2023) or the representative style they adopt (Kelbel, Navarro, and Neihouser 2021), also feature prominently among the oft-cited explanations for the varying level of mass–elite congruence.

Compared to such systemic or structural factors, 'micro' explanations related to voters' characteristics have received much less attention (Belchior 2013). Yet, the growing mismatch between the masses and elites on EU matters is predominantly attributed to changes in public opinion, which has become more sceptical of integration in recent years, while the views of elites have remained more or less stable (Mattila and Raunio 2012; Vogel and Göncz 2018). This points to the need to examine individual-level models based on the assumption that voters take policy proximity to parties into account when deciding how to vote but may inaccurately assess the positions of the parties or their candidates. The ensuing incongruence may in fact come from two different sources: alienated citizens who fail to identify the right choice, and distant citizens who intentionally differentiate themselves from the political offer which they feel does not represent them. In other words, some people simply encounter difficulties in identifying the political offer that best suits them due to a lack of political competence (Fowler and Margolis 2014). Arguably, they will thus make 'wrong' choices. Others are forced *in fine* to choose among the parties, the one that is less repulsive to them without necessarily matching their preferences, a phenomenon known as negative identification.

Voters have typically been described as 'information misers' who lack time and resources to scrutinize candidates' and parties' specific policy positions (Kitschelt 2000: 851). The ability of individuals to assess candidates and parties (including party manifestos) and to identify those that best match one's own preferences may vary as it requires skills and knowledge that voters possess unequally. Higher levels of political sophistication, resulting in particular from higher levels of education (Ritchie, Bates, and Deary 2015), have been associated with higher levels of voter–party ideological congruence (Boonen, Pedersen, and Hooghe 2017; Rosset and Stecker 2019).[2] Empirical research at the EU level has so far resulted in mixed findings. While some studies of representation in the EP confirm that voters with higher levels of education and political knowledge are generally better represented (Walczak and Van der Brug 2013; Dolný and Baboš 2015), others only partially corroborate this relationship (McEvoy 2012), which should thus be further tested. Beyond general competences, political participation requires specific skills, which in the case of the EP elections might relate to knowledge of the EU. We thus anticipate that voters who are more acquainted with the functioning of the EU will be more apt to choose the 'right' representatives.

- *H.1a: More educated citizens are likely to be more congruent with their representatives in the EP.*
- *H.1.b: Citizens who are more knowledgeable about the EU are likely to be more congruent with their representatives in the EP.*

Knowledge, however, is not a given. In this respect, the academic literature is largely unanimous in recognizing that media outlets have the prime responsibility for conveying relevant political information to the electorate during campaigns (Kriesi 2004; Overholser and Jamieson 2005; Ohme 2019), thereby influencing voting behaviour (Beck et al. 2002). Although certain political actors might receive disproportionate media attention due to their populist communications styles (Koopmans and Muis 2009; Schmidt 2020), news consumption during election periods can generally be expected to foster greater congruence between voters' preferences and their choices at the ballot box. One mechanism through which this alignment occurs relates to the so-called 'echo chamber' effect: individuals tend to select media outlets that match their existing preferences, which in turn reinforces those views and influences their votes accordingly. In the EU context, research has shown that media coverage, by amplifying interest group mobilizations, can indeed foster closer congruence between voters' preferences and those

[2] Such a relationship may also result from the attitude of the representatives, who better represent the more educated, middle- and higher-class strata of society because of strategic reasons and a shared background (Walczak and Van der Brug 2013). Nevertheless, in this study, we focus exclusively on voters' individual-level factors.

of their representatives (De Bruycker and Rasmussen 2021). Citizens who consume more news are thus better positioned to align their choices with their political preferences. Yet, media consumption itself is unevenly distributed, potentially creating informational discrepancies between regular consumers and those who are less engaged with news media.

- *H.2: The more voters are exposed to political media content during an electoral campaign, the more they will be congruent with the candidates and parties they voted for.*

Still, building on the 'paradox of ignorance' (Aidt 2000), which posits that the rational voter may simply be uninformed about social, economic, and political issues and therefore unable to make proper choices, we expect political parties to provide relevant information to remedy this gap. Congruent attitudes may arise from relationships within groups or institutions, as these entities may socialize different actors (in this case, political elites and voters) into a shared vision. In this vein, 'political parties were historically the most important agents of political socialization' (Boas and Smith 2019: 310). In their seminal work, Przeworski and Sprague (1986) claim that parties have the ability to shape voter preferences, an idea already suggested by the party identification thesis (Campbell et al. 1960). But even when voters are 'apartisan' or lack clear party preferences, knowing party positions on key issues can help them navigate the process of understanding possible positions and identifying the one they feel closer to—a phenomenon the literature refers to as party-cueing (Brader et al. 2020). If such is the case, then taking cues from parties should increase congruence. More generally, from a theoretical viewpoint, the group-based approach in political sociology traces political attitudes to the influence of one's personal contacts. Putting it to a test, Smith and Zipp for instance provide evidence that those residing close to a party official are, among others, 'more likely to discuss politics and share partisan identifications with those officials, and more likely to vote' (1983: 975). We thus expect party contacts to lead to an increased similarity in political preferences and therefore of agreement between voters and their parties or representatives. At the same time, a common and documented criticism specifically addressed to the EU polity is that it has led mainstream political parties to adopt similar positions, blurring the distinction between them for the electorate (Nanou and Dorussen 2013). Such a convergence necessarily translates into a widening chasm between citizens (who did not change their positions in a spatial perspective) and representatives (who did), a situation which may moderate our expectation.

- *H.3: The more voters have been in contact with political parties during the electoral campaign, the more they will be congruent with the candidates and parties they voted for.*

Finally, recent scholarship has underscored the importance of analysing congruence across multiple dimensions (Pareschi, Giglioli, and Baldini 2023). This is due to evidence showing that the degree of alignment between MEPs and their constituents varies depending on the issue (Kelbel, Navarro, and Neihouser 2023; Vasilopoulou and Gattermann 2013). Political parties typically present voters with a 'package deal', forcing them to vote for the entire package even when they do not agree on every issue (Costello, Thomassen, and Rosema 2012). As a result, congruence between voters and their representatives is not guaranteed across all policy dimensions, even when voters cast their ballots based on policy preferences. Notably, congruence tends to be highest on issues that are the broadest or the most salient in the political debate (Esaiasson and Holmberg 1996: 88–89; Lax and Phillips 2012). At the EU level, this challenge is compounded by the fact that political competition is multidimensional, unlike at the national level. The left–right axis that dominates national politics has to be complemented by a pro/anti-integration dimension. Parties are generally more aligned with their voters on the left–right dimension than on the EU dimension (Mattila and Raunio 2006). Moreover, we anticipate that the factors influencing congruence will differ depending on the specific issue. Media coverage of EU-specific policies is often limited, suggesting that news consumption may be more effective in reducing the mass–elite gap on broader political dimensions than on specific issues. However, knowledge of the EU is expected to have a stronger effect on congruence regarding EU integration than on the left–right axis.

6.3 Data and methods

6.3.1 Measuring congruence

We measure congruence by comparing the views of voters with those of their elected representatives in the European elections across Member States that differ in ways that are relevant for citizens' preferences concerning the EU: Denmark, France, Germany, Hungary, Italy, Poland, and Spain (Kritzinger et al. 2021). While Denmark, France, Germany, Italy, and Spain are older Member States, having joined the EU before the 1990s, Hungary and Poland are more recent Member States having joined the EU in 2004. These countries also differ in terms eurozone status and levels of EU politicization, ranging from high in Germany and Hungary to lower levels in Denmark and Spain. Congruence on key political dimensions and issues is operationalized as a *one-to-one* relationship, corresponding to the absolute distance between individual voters and their preferred party as a whole (Golder and Stramski 2010). Importantly, congruence differs from responsiveness, in that we do not measure an adaptation of MEPs but a 'supply' that voters may choose or not (Beyer and Hänni 2018). To compile the data, we rely on the 'national parties' of the MEPs and their voters to match the former with the latter.

Regarding voters, the panel structure of the voter survey allows us to detect (in the second wave) those who declared having voted for one of the party lists on which the MEPs of our MEP survey ran. In terms of the operationalization of the MEPs' parties, we identify 'national parties' with their corresponding candidate lists in the 2019 EP elections (see Appendix 6.1). We are thus able to compare the preferences of MEPs to those of their voters empirically.[3]

Voter–MEP congruence is measured for six questions asked with the exact same wording to the voters and the MEPs (see Appendix 6.2). The design of the research produced a quasi-simultaneous measure, with the voters' data collected immediately before and after the election and the MEPs necessarily interviewed after the elections, but both surveys happening only a few weeks apart. We consider first congruence on the standard left–right dimension ('In politics people often talk of "left" and "right". Where would you place yourself on this scale from 0 to 10?'). We then look at the respondents' general attitude towards European integration ('Some say European unification should be pushed further. Others say it already has gone too far. What is your opinion?'). Beyond these two broad dimensions, we measure congruence on four major policy issues for which respondents were asked to locate themselves between two opposite views regarding (1) the environment (protection of the environment vs economic growth); (2) immigration (whether or not immigrants take away jobs from one's country); (3) economic inequalities (whether or not wealth should be redistributed from the rich to the poor); and (4) economic policy (whether or not unemployment needs to be fought, even at the expense of high national debt). For all these questions, the surveys capture the voters and the MEPs' self-placement on a 0–10 scale. The congruence is calculated as the absolute difference between the respondent's location and the median location of the MEPs belonging to the party the respondent voted for: its value therefore ranges from 0 to 10.

6.3.2 Independent variables

We use the respondents' education (more precisely the highest level of education achieved) as a proxy for political competence. Considering that educational duration has (positive) causal effects on cognitive capacity (Ritchie, Bates, and Deary 2015), voters with a higher level of education are generally expected to be more congruent with their representatives. To allow for meaningful cross-country analyses, the initial categories were recoded into three broad categories: low, medium, and high.

The 'knowledge of the EU' variable is a composite index based on four closed questions about the EU institutional setting, namely: the election of the EP; the

[3] More details about the datasets and the empirical strategy are presented in Kelbel, Navarro, and Neihouser (2023).

nomination process of the President of the Commission; the EU legislative procedure; and the composition of the Council of the EU. Each correct answer adds one unit to the respondent's score, resulting in a 0–4 scale.

The media consumption of political news ('media consumption') is also a composite index relying on the following question asked in the second wave of the citizens' survey: 'During the last week of the European Parliament election campaign, how often did you follow European politics news through the following various types of media?'. The respondents had to indicate with what frequency (never, on one day, on two days . . . up to seven days) they had consulted five major types of media (television, newspapers, radio, news websites/apps/blogs, and social media). The scores for each type of media were added, resulting in a single measurement, which was then recoded into a 0–4 scale.

As regards the contacts with political parties during the electoral campaign, we rely on two distinct indicators based on the second wave of the citizens survey. On the one hand, the respondents were asked whether they received a letter, flyer, phone call, text message, or an e-mail from parties or candidates during the electoral campaign. We computed how many such communications each respondent received. The variable 'received communication' was recoded into a 0–4 scale. On the other hand, the respondents were asked whether they talked to party workers or had been visited by politicians during the electoral campaign. Again, we computed the number of such contacts each respondent had and recoded the outcome into a 0–4 scale (variable 'direct contacts').

In addition to our variables of interest, we controlled for individual-level factors, which the literature has found to influence the distance between voters and their representatives, namely: voters' gender (Reher 2018), age (Stiers, Hooghe, and Goubin 2020), economic status (Flavin 2012; Rosset and Stecker 2019), and residential area (Best 2023). Gender is a dummy variable, with 1 indicating male and 2 indicating female. The respondents' age was recoded into the following five categories: 18–29 (coded 1), 30–39 (2), 40–49 (3), 50–59 (4), and 60+ (5). The economic status is based on a self-assessment of the respondents' current income situation, where they indicated whether they 'Get along very well' (coded 1), 'Get along well' (2), 'Get along with difficulty' (3) or 'Get along with great difficulty' (4). Similarly, the type of residential area is a self-reported ordinal variable, categorized as follows: village (coded 1), small town (2), mid-size town (3), suburbs of a large city (4) and centre of a large city (5).

6.4 Results

Are voters making 'wrong' vote choices? Before delving into the details of the empirical analysis, it is worth noting that the level of congruence between voters and their representatives somewhat varies depending on the country and the nature of

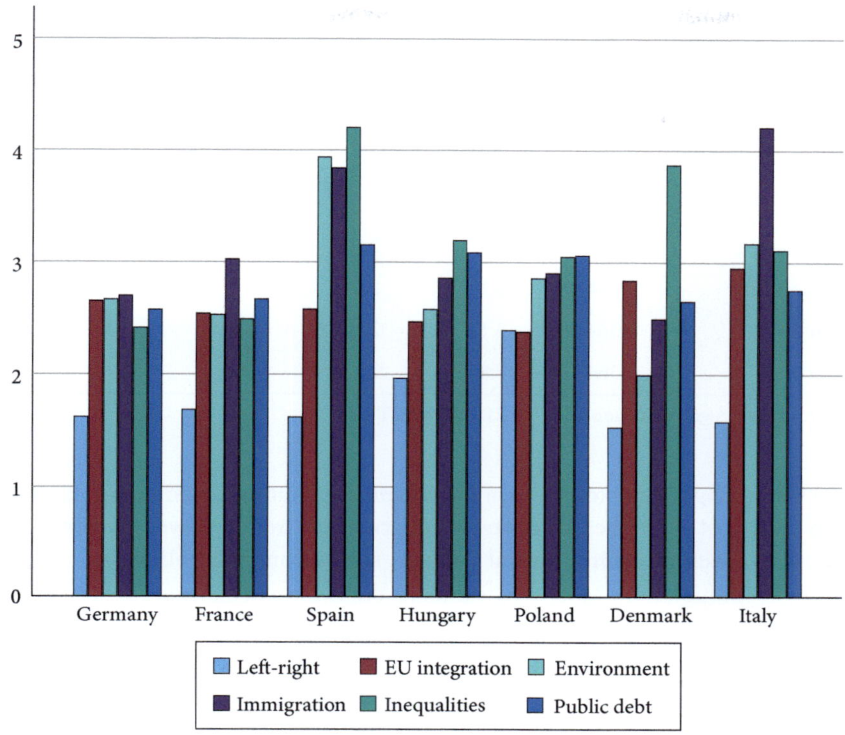

Figure 6.1 Level of congruence (mean) depending on the country and the issue
Source: authors' own elaboration based on RECONNECT data

the chosen indicator (Figure 6.1). Congruence being operationalized as the absolute difference between individual voters' position and that of their MEPs, a longer bar indicates that there is *less* congruence, and a shorter one means a better voter–representative alignment. The representation gap thus appears to be comparatively most pronounced in Spain on the issues of the environment, inequalities, and immigration, while it is also critical on the issue of inequalities in Denmark and on immigration in Italy. By contrast, French and German MEPs show the strongest alignment with their voters across various political dimensions. However, these trends should be interpreted with caution, as they may be driven by structural factors, such as the dynamics of electoral competition or party ideological positioning, which are beyond the scope of this chapter and have been explored elsewhere (Kelbel, Navarro, and Neihouser 2023).

When further examining differences across issues (Table 6.1), the alignment of voters and representatives is at its maximum on the left–right dimension, which is also the one around which party competition is traditionally thought to be organized. Voter–MEP agreement is also fairly high as regards the general attitudes towards European integration, although to a lesser extent. This suggests that MEPs

Table 6.1 Summary statistics for voter–representative congruence across political dimensions and issues

	N	Mean	SD	Min	Max
Left–right dimension	4307	1.79	1.44	0	9
EU integration	4241	2.61	2.23	0	10
Environment	4364	2.86	2.26	0	10
Immigration	4364	3.17	2.64	0	10
Inequalities	4364	3.12	2.46	0	10
Public debt	4364	2.85	2.15	0	10

Source: authors' own calculation using the RECONNECT data

are representing their voters well on the two most encompassing dimensions generally used in other studies. By contrast, congruence is notably lower on more specific issues, such as environmental policies, socio-economic policies and, most strikingly, immigration. Moreover, standard deviation coefficients reveal greater homogeneity on the left–right dimension compared to all others. These observations, which we are cautious not to over-interpret for the reasons mentioned above, support the broader argument that congruence is issue-specific and should be analysed across its various empirical dimensions.

Accordingly, Table 6.2 presents the results of regression analyses for six outcome variables: congruence on the left–right dimension, EU integration, environment, immigration, inequalities, and macroeconomic policy. All models analyse the data with the ordinary least squares (OLS) regression estimator and include country dummies to account for country-specific characteristics. While these models explain only a small proportion of the variance, they highlight several individual-level factors that significantly influence the distance between the views of the voters and those of their representatives.

The first hypothesis, which links voter–representative congruence to voters' competence, is supported across most political dimensions and issues. Voters with a higher education level are more aligned with their representatives in the EP than the rest of the sample, be it on the left–right dimension, EU integration, immigration, and, with a lower level of statistical significance, the environment. Similarly, voters' knowledge of the EU has the expected impact: the more knowledgeable voters are about the EU institutional setting, the more they agree with the MEPs they voted for on the four same dimensions. Strikingly, both predictors have a greater impact on the EU integration dimension than on the left–right dimension. This aligns with earlier research indicating that EU politics tends to widen the gap between the best-educated voters and the rest of society (Cautrès and Grunberg 2007). As regards the socio-economic domain, the coefficients do not reach the

Table 6.2 Determinants of MEP–voter congruence (OLS regressions)

Congruence on ...	Left–right	EU integration	Environment	Immigration	Inequalities	Public debt
Constant	1.662*** (.157)	3.275*** (.250)	3.949*** (.242)	4.230*** (.283)	4.727*** (.262)	2.926*** (.235)
Education (low)	.114 (.078)	.192 (.126)	–.258* (.119)	.117 (.139)	.032 (.129)	–.158 (.115)
Education (high)	–.178*** (.048)	–.322*** (.074)	–.154* (.074)	–.297*** (.087)	.015 (.080)	–.041 (.072)
Knowledge of the EU	–.071** (.022)	–.103** (.034)	–.075* (.034)	–.142*** (.039)	–.051 (.036)	–.044 (.032)
Media consumption	.029+ (.016)	–.038 (.026)	–.003 (.025)	–.010 (.029)	.034 (.027)	.019 (.024)
Received communication	–.031 (.019)	–.022 (.032)	–.037 (.030)	–.015 (.035)	–.073* (.033)	–.071* (.029)
Direct contact	–.053 (.038)	.001 (.059)	.035 (.059)	.081 (.069)	.170** (.063)	.092 (.057)
Gender	.040 (.045)	.044 (.070)	.036 (.069)	–.086 (.081)	–.095 (.075)	–.040 (.067)
Age	.003 (.017)	–.059* (.026)	.052* (.026)	–.004 (.030)	–.069* (.028)	.063* (.025)
Income situation	.065* (.032)	.035 (.051)	–.062 (.050)	.011 (.058)	–.090 +(.054)	.037 (.048)
Residential area	–.006 (.016)	–.045 +(.025)	–.040 (.024)	–.005 (.028)	–.011 (.026)	.024 (.024)
Adj. R2	.043	.016	.042	.042	.06	.009
N	4306	4240	4363	4363	4363	4363

Cell entries are coefficients. Standard errors in parentheses. All models also include country dummies (not shown).

+ $p < 0.10$, * $p < 0.05$, ** $p < 0.01$, *** $p < 0.001$.

Source: authors' own calculation using the RECONNECT data

standard levels of statistical significance even though, with one exception, they point to the expected direction.

In contrast, information acquisition does not yield the hypothesized outcomes. Contrary to our expectations, voters who consumed more political news in the week leading up to the European elections are not better ideologically aligned with the MEPs they voted for. The coefficients in most models are not significant. There is nevertheless one exception regarding the left–right dimension, where the coefficient is weakly significant and positive, suggesting that greater news consumption may lead, not to more, but to *less* voter representative congruence. These trends may relate to both the media offerings and citizens' news consumption habits. On the one hand, media coverage of European news, even during election periods, is notoriously weak (Boomgaarden et al. 2010). As a result, citizens may have limited exposure to the candidates running in the EP elections, even if they are attentive and faithful followers of the news. On the other hand, not all media outlets produce the same effects (Eveland and Scheufele 2000). Research has shown that when the content is more political (e.g. in TV news or mass-circulation newspapers), knowledge gains are significantly higher and so is the likelihood of voting (de Vreese and Boomgaarden 2006). A different research design could thus involve analysing how the type of media citizens engage with influences the level of congruence; however, that is beyond the scope of this chapter.

Similarly, contacts with parties, candidates and politicians during the EP election campaign have, at best, a limited effect on the congruence between voters and their representatives. We rely on two predictors to capture this effect: first, the receipt of communications from parties or candidates (e.g. a letter, flyer, phone call, text message, or email) and, second, direct contacts in the form of encounters and discussions with politicians and party workers. Neither predictor produces a consistently significant or strong impact. The 'received communication' coefficient is significant and in the expected direction for only two issues: attitudes toward inequalities and public debt. Likewise, the 'direct contact' coefficient is significant in the case of inequalities, but contrary to our hypothesis, it *reduces* the degree of voter–representative congruence. This suggests again that there may be 'biases' in whom voters actually meet and what political actors communicate, ultimately cancelling out the anticipated positive effect of personal contacts on the level of congruence.

Beyond the discrepancies across the various independent variables, noteworthy patterns emerge when comparing the distinct political dimensions used as outcome variables. The regression models measuring congruence based on attitudes toward inequalities and public debt yield markedly different results compared to those using other outcome variables. In these two specific policy domains, an increase in voters' competence (be it measured by the level of education or by the knowledge of the EU) does not improve the quality of representation in terms of voter–representative ideological proximity, whereas the 'received communication' predictor has the anticipated positive impact. In sharp contrast, for the other four measurements, competence contributes to explain voters' congruence with MEPs, while campaign contacts produce no significant effect. On the whole, these observations lend credence to our fourth hypothesis according to which causal patterns of congruence are, to some extent, issue specific. However, the expectation that knowledge of the EU would play a bigger part in explaining congruence on more directly EU-related questions (starting with the general attitude toward EU integration) is not entirely verified. Finally, with a few exceptions, the coefficients for control variables do not generally reach the standard levels of statistical significance.

In addition to the preceding analyses, we verified that our main model produces similar results when replicated at the national level, country by country.[4] These robustness checks largely support our key findings, although the coefficients rarely meet the standard threshold of significance likely due to smaller sample sizes compared to the main models. They also reveal some minor country-specific differences, with the models being slightly less effective for France and Denmark. Regarding the main variables of interest, the analyses confirm that education and EU knowledge generally have a significant, negative effect on the distance between MEPs and their constituents, while the impact of media consumption and political contacts is not substantiated. In other words, the most significant results of the main model remain consistent when the analysis is narrowed to each of the seven countries individually.

6.5 Conclusion

Although EP elections are often characterized as second-order national elections, this does not imply the absence of pan-European trends. On the contrary, this characterization helps to identify and explain common patterns observed across the continent, such as lower voter turnout compared to national first-order elections, weaker performances by parties in government and the success of smaller parties. Another notable trend that has spread across Europe over the last decades is the rise of parties advocating Euroscepticism or even calling for the dissolution of the EU. This phenomenon, particularly apparent in the 2019 and 2024 EP elections, is frequently cited as one of the most worrying signs of the growing disconnect between pro-European political elites and electorates who are becoming increasingly dubious about the European integration process (Vogel and Göncz 2018). It highlights the extent of the distrust—and even outright hostility—towards European integration among large shares of the electorate (Treib 2021). Against

[4] The detailed analyses, which are not shown here due to space constraints, are available upon request from the authors.

this backdrop, the objective of this chapter has been to explore processes determining the ideological distance between voters and their representatives. Given that the voters ultimately have the responsibility to choose their MEPs, the empirical analysis has focused on the relatively understudied aspect of voters' individual-level dynamics.

Our first finding is that, in line with results from earlier research, citizens with a higher education level vote for parties and candidates that better represent their views. Moreover, specific knowledge about the functioning and institutions of the EU also reduces the mass–elite gap, thus suggesting that, in addition to the role of education which constitutes undoubtedly a prerequisite for a well-functioning democracy, the diffusion of specialized information about the EU may contribute to enhance the quality of representation at the supranational level. All in all, these observations, which hold true across most political dimensions, in particular the most encompassing and salient ones, indicate that more educated and more knowledgeable citizens may be better equipped to identify those parties whose policies match their preferences. If, because they enhance voters' awareness of parties' positions and their ability to make sound judgements, education and specialized knowledge are conducive to a better representation, then one would expect voters' efforts to acquire more information before an election to improve their congruence with their elected representatives too. Yet, contrary to our hypothesis but in line with earlier empirical research (Walczak and Van der Brug 2013), we find that the media consumption of political news in the week leading up to the EP election does not result in a greater concordance between the voters and their representatives. This speaks to the literature, which has demonstrated the limited media coverage of EU level politics in general and that of European elections in particular (e.g. Maier and Maier 2009). In other words, the news media probably do not provide the necessary information about candidates and parties that would enable voters to vote for candidates who adequately represent their views

Our third major finding relates to the role of political parties during electoral campaigns. Do contacts with party workers or candidates result in a better alignment of voters' preferences and those of the candidates they vote for? Does receiving communication material from political parties help voters make a more enlightened vote choice? Here again our results are rather negative in the sense that, with very limited exceptions, neither the reception of communication material from the parties nor direct contacts with parties, candidates, or politicians during the EP election campaign contribute to bridging the chasm between voters and their representatives. We interpret these results as an indication that either parties' communications misrepresent their true policy preferences or, more probably, emphasize aspects that are not directly relevant to the mass–elite policy congruence (perhaps because they are not in fact about EU policies). All in all, it seems that, in the current state of European politics, one should not put too much faith in the capacity of the media and the political parties to reconcile voters with their representatives.

References

Aidt, T. S. (2000). Economic Voting and Information. *Electoral Studies*, 19(2): 349–362.

Bakker, R., Jolly, S., and Polk, J. (2021). Multidimensional Incongruence, Political Disaffection, and Support for Anti-Establishment Parties. In Hobolt, S. B. and Rodon, T. (eds). *Domestic Contestation of the European Union*. London, Routledge: 132–149.

Beck, P. A., Dalton, R. J., Greene, S., and Huckfeldt, R. (2002). The Social Calculus of Voting: Interpersonal, Media, and Organizational Influences on Presidential Choices. *American Political Science Review*, 96(1): 57–73.

Belchior, A. M. (2013). Explaining Left–Right Party Congruence Across European Party Systems: A Test of Micro-, Meso-, and Macro-Level Models. *Comparative Political Studies*, 46(3): 352–386.

Best, R. E. (2023). Are Leftist or Rightist Voters Better Substantively Represented? The Effects of Variance in District Magnitude on Party-Voter Ideological Congruence. *Electoral Studies*, 82: 102584.

Beyer, D. and Hänni, M. (2018). Two Sides of the Same Coin? Congruence and Responsiveness as Representative Democracy's Currencies. *Policy Studies Journal* 46(1): 13–47.

Boas, T. C. and Smith, A. E. (2019). Looks Like Me, Thinks Like Me: Descriptive Representation and Opinion Congruence in Brazil. *Latin American Research Review* 54(2): 310–328.

Boomgaarden, H. G., Vliegenthart, R., de Vreese, C. H., and Schuck, A. R. T. (2010). News on the Move: Exogenous Events and News Coverage of the European Union. *Journal of European Public Policy*, 17(4): 506–526.

Boonen, J., Pedersen, E. F., & Hooghe, M. (2017). The Effect of Political Sophistication and Party Identification on Voter–Party Congruence. A Comparative Analysis of 30 Countries. *Journal of Elections, Public Opinion and Parties*, 27(3): 311–329.

Brader, T., De Sio, L., Paparo, A., and Tucker, J. A. (2020). 'Where You Lead, I Will Follow': Partisan Cueing on High-Salience Issues in a Turbulent Multiparty System. *Political Psychology*, 41(4): 795–812.

Campbell, A., Converse, P. E., Miller, W. E., and Stokes, D. E. (1960). *The American Voter*. Chicago IL, University of Chicago Press.

Casado-Asensio, J. and Lefkofridi, Z. (2011). Representation in the European Union: Congruence Between Citizens and Elites in the European Parliament's Two-Level Setting. *Perspectives on European Politics and Society*, 12(2): 161–179.

Cautrès, B. and Grunberg, G. (2007). Position sociale, identité nationale et attitudes à l'égard de l'Europe: La construction européenne souffre-t-elle d'un biais élitiste? In Costa, O. and Magnette, P. (eds). *Une Europe des élites? Réflexions sur la fracture démocratique de l'Union européenne*. Bruxelles, Editions de l'Université de Bruxelles: 11–36.

Costello, R., Thomassen, J., and Rosema, M. (2012). European Parliament Elections and Political Representation: Policy Congruence between Voters and Parties. *West European Politics*, 35(6): 1226–1248.

Costello, R., Toshkov, D., Bos, B., and Krouwel, A. (2021). Congruence Between Voters and Parties: The Role of Party-Level Issue Salience. *European Journal of Political Research*, 60(1): 92–113.

De Bruycker, I. and Rasmussen, A. (2021). Blessing or Curse for Congruence? How Interest Mobilization Affects Congruence between Citizens and Elected Representatives. *JCMS: Journal of Common Market Studies*, 59(4): 909–928.

de Vreese, C. H. and Boomgaarden, H. G. (2006). How Content Moderates the Effects of Television News on Political Knowledge and Engagement. *Acta Politica*, 41: 317–341.

Dolný, B. and Baboš, P. (2015). Voter–Representative Congruence in Europe: A Loss of Institutional Influence? *West European Politics*, 38(6): 1274–1304.

Downs, A. (1957). *An Economic Theory of Democracy*. New York, Harper.

Esaiasson, P. and Holmberg, S. (1996). *Representation From Above: Members of Parliament and Representative Democracy in Sweden*. New York, Taylor and Francis.

Eveland, W. P. and Scheufele, D. A. (2000). Connecting News Media Use with Gaps in Knowledge and Participation. *Political Communication*, 17(3): 215–237.

Fisher, J. et al. (eds) (2020). *The Routledge Handbook of Elections, Voting Behaviour and Public Opinion*. London, Routledge.
Flavin, P. (2012). Income Inequality and Policy Representation in the American States. *American Politics Research*, 40(1): 29–59.
Follesdal, A. and Hix, S. (2006). Why there is a Democratic Deficit in the EU: A Response to Majone and Moravcsik. *Journal of Common Market Studies*, 44(3): 533–562.
Fowler, A. and Margolis, M. (2014). The Political Consequences of Uninformed Voters. *Electoral Studies*, 34: 100–110.
Freire, A., Teperoglou, E., and Moury, C. (2014). Awakening the Sleeping Giant in Greece and Portugal? Elites' and Voters' Attitudes towards EU Integration in Difficult Economic Times. *South European Society and Politics*, 19(4): 477–499.
Golder, M., and Ferland, B. (2017). Electoral Rules and Citizen–Elite Ideological Congruence. In Herron, E., Pekkanen, R., and Shugart, M. (eds). *The Oxford Handbook of Electoral Systems*. Oxford, Oxford University Press: 213–246.
Golder, M. and Stramski, J. (2010). Ideological Congruence and Electoral Institutions. *American Journal of Political Science*, 54(1): 90–106.
Holmberg, S. (1989). Political Representation in Sweden. *Scandinavian Political Studies*, 12(1): 1–36.
Hooghe, L. (2003). Europe Divided? Elites vs. Public Opinion on European Integration. *European Union Politics* 4: 281–304.
Kelbel, C., Navarro, J., and Neihouser, M. (2021). Report on Alternative Institutional Options to Democratise and Re-legitimate the EU Polity in the Eyes of its Citizens. An Analysis of the Congruence Between MEPs and Their Voters on the EU Political System. RECONNECT Deliverable 6.4.
Kelbel, C., Navarro, J., and Neihouser, M. (2023). Great Minds Think Alike? A New Measure of MEPs–Voters Congruence Following the 2019 European Parliament Elections. *European Political Science*, 22(4): 476–495.
Kitschelt, H. (2000). Linkages between Citizens and Politicians in Democratic Polities. *Comparative Political Studies*, 33(6–7): 845–879.
Koopmans, R. and Muis, J. (2009). The Rise of Right-Wing Populist Pim Fortuyn in the Netherlands: A Discursive Opportunity Approach. *European Journal of Political Research*, 48(5): 642–664.
Kriesi, H. (2004). Strategic Political Communication: Mobilizing Public Opinion in 'Audience Democracies'. In Pfetsch, B. and Esser, F. (eds). *Comparing Political Communication: Theories, Cases, and Challenges*. Cambridge, Cambridge University Press: 184–212.
Kritzinger, S. et al. (2021). Discussions About the European Union Among Its Citizens. RECONNECT Deliverable 9.1.
Kritzinger, S. et al. (eds) (2020). *Assessing the 2019 European Parliament Elections*. London, Routledge.
Lax, J. R. and Phillips, J. H. (2012). The Democratic Deficit in the States. *American Journal of Political Science*, 56(1): 148–166.
Lee, I. et al. (2016). Voting Intention and Choices: Are Voters Always Rational and Deliberative? *PLOS ONE* 11(2): e0148643.
McEvoy, C. (2012). Unequal Representation in the EU: A Multi-Level Analysis of Voter–Party Congruence in EP Elections. *Representation*, 48(1): 83–99.
Maier, M. and Maier, J. (2009). News Coverage of EU Parliamentary Elections. In Strömbäck, J. and Kaid, L. L. (eds). *The Handbook of Election News Coverage Around the World*. New York, Routledge: 403–442.
Mattila, M. and Raunio, T. (2006). Cautious Voters—Supportive Parties: Opinion Congruence between Voters and Parties on the EU Dimension. *European Union Politics*, 7(4): 427–449.
Mattila, M., and Raunio, T. (2012). Drifting Further Apart: National Parties and their Electorates on the EU Dimension. *West European Politics*, 35(3): 589–606.
Müller, W. C., Jenny, M., and Ecker, A. (2012). The Elites–Masses Gap in European Integration. In Best, H., Lengyel, G., and Verzichelli, L. (eds). *The Europe of Elites*. Oxford, Oxford University Press: 167–191.

Nanou, K. and Dorussen, H. (2013). European Integration and Electoral Democracy: How the European Union Constrains Party Competition in the Member States. *European Journal of Political Research*, 52(1): 71–93.

Ohme, J. (2019). Updating Citizenship? The Effects of Digital Media Use on Citizenship Understanding and Political Participation. *Information, Communication & Society*, 22(13): 1903–1928.

Overholser, G. and Jamieson, K. H. (eds) (2005). *The Press*. New York, Oxford University Press.

Pareschi, A., Giglioli, M. F. N., and Baldini, G. (2023). Caught Between Sovereignty and Solidarity? A Multidimensional Revisitation of EU Mass–Elite Congruence. *Italian Political Science Review/Rivista Italiana di Scienza Politica*, 53(1): 3–23.

Plescia, C., Wilhelm, J., Kritzinger, S., Schübert, T., and Partheymüller, J. (2020). RECONNECT 2019 European parliament election panel survey (SUF edition). https://doi.org/10.11587/MOV0EZ, last accessed 23 July 2025.

Przeworski, A. and Sprague, J. D. (1986). *Paper Stones: A History of Electoral Socialism*. Chicago IL, University of Chicago Press.

Real-Dato, J. (2017). Party-Voters Congruence Concerning the European Union: An Analysis of Its Evolution During the Eurozone Crisis Using Elite and Mass Surveys. *Corvinus Journal of Sociology and Social Policy*, 8(3): 85–112.

Reher, S. (2018). Gender and Opinion–Policy Congruence in Europe. *European Political Science Review*, 10(4), 613–635.

Ritchie, S. J., Bates, T. C., and Deary, I. J. (2015). Is Education Associated with Improvements in General Cognitive Ability, or in Specific Skills?. *Developmental Psychology*, 51(5): 573–582.

Rosset, J. and Stecker, C. (2019). How Well are Citizens Represented by their Governments? Issue Congruence and Inequality in Europe. *European Political Science Review*, 11(2): 145–160.

Schmidt, F. (2020). Party Populism and Media Access: The News Value of Populist Communication and How It Is Handled by the Mass Media. *International Journal of Communication*, 14: 2360–2382.

Schmitt, H., and Thomassen, J. (eds) (1999). *Political Representation and Legitimacy in the European Union*. New York, Oxford University Press.

Schmitt, H., Sanz, A., Braun, D., and Teperoglou, E. (2020). It All Happens at Once: Understanding Electoral Behaviour in Second-Order Elections. *Politics and Governance*, 8(1): 6–18.

Smith, J. and Zipp, J. F. (1983). The Party Official Next Door: Some Consequences of Friendship for Political Involvement. *The Journal of Politics*, 45(4): 958–978.

Steiner, N. D. and Hillen, S. (2021). Vote Choices of Left-Authoritarians: Misperceived Congruence and Issue Salience. *Electoral Studies*, 70: 102280.

Stiers, D., Hooghe, M., and Goubin, S. (2020). Are 16-year-olds Able to Cast a Congruent Vote? Evidence from a 'Voting at 16' Initiative in the City of Ghent (Belgium). *Electoral Studies*, 63: 102107.

Treib, O. (2021). Euroscepticism is Here To Stay: What Cleavage Theory Can Teach us about the 2019 European Parliament Elections. *Journal of European Public Policy*, 28(2): 174–189.

Vasilopoulou, S. and Gattermann, K. (2013). Matching Policy Preferences: The Linkage Between Voters and MEPs. *Journal of European Public Policy*, 20(4): 606–625.

Viola, D. M. (2015). European Parliament Elections Theories. In Viola, D. (ed.). *Routledge Handbook of European Elections*. London, Routledge: 39–48.

Vogel, L. (2023). The Impact of Political Professionalization on Legislators-Citizens Congruence in Policies and Process Preferences. *Revue Internationale de Politique Comparée*, 30(2): 177–213.

Vogel, L., and Göncz, B. (2018). European Integration in the View of Political Elites and Citizens – An Increasing Gap? In Conti, N., Göncz, B., and Real-Dato, J. (eds). *National Political Elites, European Integration and the Eurozone Crisis*. London, Routledge: 88–114.

Walczak, A. and Van Der Brug, W. (2013). Representation in the European Parliament: Factors Affecting the Attitude Congruence of Voters and Candidates in the EP Elections. *European Union Politics*, 14(1), 3–22.

APPENDIX 6.1

The matching of voters and their representatives in the EP

In order to analyse the opinion congruence between MEPs and their voters, we need to match the 'party' of the voters with those of the MEPs who responded to our survey. Regarding voters, we rely on responses to question W2_Q60a of the RECONNECT Voter Survey asking voters what was their vote choice among the candidate lists for the EP 2019 elections. We then matched these responses with the corresponding list on which each MEP was elected.

Table 6.A1 The 'matching' of MEPs and their voters

Country	MEP party group (according to the RECONNECT MEP survey)	Lists on which MEPs were elected (source: webpage of the EP)	RECONNECT Voter Survey Party lists (W2_Q60a)
Germany	EPP	CDU-CSU	101 'CDU/CSU'
Germany	S&D	SPD	102 'SPD'
Germany	Renew	FDP	103 'Freie Demokratische Partei (FDP)'
Germany	Greens-EFA	GRÜNE	104 'Bündnis 90/Die Grünen (Grüne)'
Germany	GUE/NGL	DIE LINKE	105 'Die Linke (Linke)'
Germany	I&D	AfD	106 'Alternative für Deutschland (AfD)'
Germany	Renew	FREIE WÄHLER	107 'Freie Wähler (FW)'
Germany	Greens-EFA	PIRATEN	109 'Piratenpartei Deutschland (PIRATEN)'
France	S&D	Coalition (PS + RDG + PP + ND)	202 'Parti socialiste (PS)'*
France	Renew	Coalition (LREM + MoDem + A + MRSL)	203 'LREM/MoDem'
France	Green	EELV	204 'Europe Écologie-Les-Verts (EELV)'
France	GUE/NGL	FI	205 'La France Insoumise (FI)'
France	I&D	RN	206 'Rassemblement National (RN)'
Spain	EPP	PP	301 'Partido Popular (PP)'
Spain	S&D	PSOE/PSC	302 'PSO'

Table 6.A1 Continued

Country	MEP party group (according to the RECONNECT MEP survey)	Lists on which MEPs were elected (source: webpage of the EP)	RECONNECT Voter Survey Party lists (W2_Q60a)
Spain	GUE/NGL	Coal (UP + IU + Catalunya en Comú + Barcelona enComú)	303 'Podemos-IU/Catalunya en Comú-Podem'
Spain	Renew	C's	304 'Ciudadanos (Cs)'
Spain	ECR	VOX	305 'VOX'
Spain	NI	Coalition (PdCat + JXCat)	312 'Junts per Catalunya (JxCat)'**
Spain	Renew	Coalition (EAJ-PNV + CC + CxG+ Atarrabia Taldea + El Pi+ Demòcrates Valencians)	313 EAJ/PNV***
Hungary	NI	JOBBIK	401 'JOBBIK'
Hungary	S&D	Coalition (MSZP + Párbeszéd)	402 'MSZP-PM'
Hungary	S&D	DK	403 'Demokratikus Koalíció(DK)'
Hungary	EPP	Coalition (FIDESZ + KDNP)	406 'FIDESZ-KNDP'
Poland	ECR	PiS	501 'PiS/Zjednoczsona Prawica'
Poland	EPP	Coalition KE (PO + PSL + SLD +N + Z)	502 'PSL-PO-N-SLD-Zielo'
Denmark	S&D	A (S)	602 'Socialdemokraterne (A)'
Denmark	Renew	V (V)	603 'Venstre (V)'
Denmark	Green	F (SF)	605 'Socialistisk Folkeparti(SF)'
Denmark	GUE/NGL	Ø (EL)	606 'Enhedsliste'
Italy	S&D	PD	702 'Partito Democratico (PD)'
Italy	NI	M5S	703 'Movimento 5 Stelle (M5S)'
Italy	ECR	FDI	705 'Fratelli d'Italia (FdI)'
Italy	I&D	LN	706 'Lega'

* The proposed lists in the Voter Survey did not exactly match the electoral offer in the EP elections: *Nouvelle Donne*, which was indicated as forming a coalition with *Génération.s* (207 'G.s/Nouvelle Donne'), should in fact have been listed as standing on the same list as the Socialist Party. We rely on this latter response as it is the most proximate to MEPs in our sample.

** In Spain, the proposed lists in the Voter Survey did not exactly match the electoral offer: several parties which formed a coalition in the EP elections were presented separately in the Voter Survey. Here we match the MEPs with the declared voters of their party (as distinct from the voters of their electoral list).

*** Same comment as above.

APPENDIX 6.2

The dimensions of congruence

Table 6.A2 List of questions asked in both the MEP survey and the citizen survey

Questions	Short name	Text	MEP Survey	Citizen Survey
Left–Right Position	Left–right	**In political matters, people talk of the 'Left' and the 'Right'. Where would you place each of the following on a scale from 0 to 10, where 0 means 'Left' and 10 means 'Right'? Choose one box per line.** - Yourself - Your national political party - Your party's voters - Your European political group	Q5.5	Q16
Pro-anti EU integration Position	EU integration	**Some say European integration should be pushed further. Others say it already has gone too far. Where would you place each of the following on the question of European integration? Choose one box per line.** - Yourself- Your national political party - Your party's voters - Your European political group	Q5.6	Q21, 22

Issues	Issues	**Now a few questions on your views on various issues. For each issue, please position yourself on a scale from 0 to 10, where 0 means you fully agree with the statement on the left, and 10 means you fully agree with the statement on the right. What number on the scale describes your position best?**	Q5.10	Q39
	Issue: environment	Item 1: Protection of the environment, even at the cost of economic growth—Support economic growth, even at the cost of damage to the environment		
	Issue: same sex marriage	Item 2: Same sex marriages should be forbidden—Same sex marriages should be allowed		
	Issue: customs	Item 3: Immigrants should adapt to your country's customs—Immigrants should be free to keep own customs		
	Issue: jobs	Item 4: Immigrants take away jobs from your country—Immigrants do not take away jobs from your country		
	Issue: redistribution	Item 5: Wealth should be redistributed from the rich to the poor in your country—Wealth should not be redistributed from the rich to the poor in your country		
	Issue: inequalities	Item 6: For a fair society differences in standards of living should be small—For a fair society differences in standards of living do not matter		
	Issue: taxes	Item 7: Taxes should be raised to increase public services—Taxes should be cut, even at the expense of public services		
	Issue: debt	Item 8: Unemployment needs to be fought, even at the expense of high national debt—Unemployment should not be fought if this means higher national debt		
	Issue: welfare	Item 9: Restrict welfare benefits for immigrants—Maintain welfare benefits access for immigrants		

7

Towards a Genuine European Political Space? Revisiting the Legal Architecture of European Parliament Elections

Jan Wouters[*]

7.1 Introduction

The direct election of the European Parliament (EP, or Parliament) was designed to serve as a cornerstone of democratic legitimacy in the evolving European integration process. Its introduction in 1979 marked an important step towards the EU's democratization, providing the Parliament with an electoral mandate from citizens and contributing to its transformation from a consultative to a co-legislative body (Piodi 2019; Costa 2016). Yet, despite successive Treaty amendments and institutional developments, European elections still fall short of delivering on their democratic promise (Chapter 2 of this volume).

Indeed, the electoral framework remains marked by legal fragmentation, institutional ambiguity, and a persistent 'second-order' character (Bardi and Cicchi 2015; Wouters 2020), which has led some to conclude that EP elections are a collection of national rather than 'European' elections (Nogaj and Poptcheva 2015), or are at most 'Euro-national' (Antonuzzi and Lupo 2020). EP elections are largely shaped by national political dynamics and media discourses, but also by legal rules. It is this legal framework on which the present chapter focuses.

While the Treaty on European Union (TEU) stipulates that Members of the European Parliament (MEPs) shall be elected by direct universal suffrage in a free and secret ballot (TEU, Art 14(3)), it leaves substantial discretion to EU Member States regarding the organization of the vote. Article 223(1) of the Treaty on the Functioning of the European Union (TFEU) instructs the Parliament to

* The present chapter builds on earlier work under the H2020 RECONNECT project, of which the author was the overall coordinator, in particular Wouters, J. (2020) The Long and Winding Road towards a European Electoral Law. In Plescia, C., Wilhelm, J., Kritzinger, S., Raube, K., and Wouters, J. (eds). *Assessing the 2019 European Parliament Elections*. London, Routledge: 9–18.

Jan Wouters, *Towards a Genuine European Political Space? Revisiting the Legal Architecture of European Parliament Elections* In: *The Promise of EU Democracy*. Edited by: Jan Wouters, Julie Smith, Kolja Raube, and Ben Crum, Oxford University Press. © Jan Wouters 2026. DOI: 10.1093/9780191996191.003.0009 propose a uniform procedure, or a set of common principles, but this mandate remains only partially fulfilled, as discussed in Section 7.2.1 below. The very fact that this was a task left to the EP shows that the Member States themselves could not agree on it. The Act concerning the election of the Members of the European Parliament by direct universal suffrage adopted on 20 September 1976 (Council 1976; Electoral Act) formalized the electoral basis of the Parliament but allowed for wide variations in national implementation. Despite amendments in 2002 and 2018, at the time of writing the Electoral Act still falls short of harmonizing essential aspects of the electoral process. Recent reform efforts, including the 2018 Council Decision (Council 2018) and the European Parliament's 2022 legislative proposal (European Parliament 2022a; Kurmayer 2022), have sought to address these limitations (see Sections 7.3.1 and 7.3.2 below). However, political and legal obstacles—especially the requirement of unanimous Council approval and national ratification by all twenty-seven Member States—have hindered effective implementation.

The continued reliance on national laws for core features of European elections gives rise to a fragmented electoral space, characterized by divergences in national rules concerning voting age, thresholds, candidate eligibility, electoral districts, and rules on campaigning (Mańko 2023). This diversity of electoral rules and systems—sometimes referred to as a 'polymorphic electoral system' (European Parliament 2019)—undermines the principle of electoral equality as discussed in Section 7.4.1 below, complicates the democratic representativeness of the Parliament, and more generally hampers the development of a European political sphere (Costa 2016).

This chapter examines the current state of European electoral law, identifies the key institutional and legal challenges to its standardization, and assesses recent reform proposals. Drawing on the existing legal framework and the practice of recent elections, it explores whether and how a more coherent and genuinely European electoral procedure might emerge. While Treaty change remains unlikely in the short term, meaningful progress may still be achieved through layered reforms, soft law processes, and the gradual strengthening of the European dimension of electoral practice.

7.2 A legal patchwork: the architecture of European electoral law

The legal framework governing EP elections is an evolving construct that reflects the tension between integration and sovereignty, between supranational aspiration and national prerogative. While there is broad agreement that elections to the Parliament should be democratic and transparent, the current legal architecture remains fragmented and in many respects inadequate to realizing these principles. The present section considers the legal framework, starting with primary

EU law, i.e., the EU Treaties and the Electoral Act, followed by a brief discussion of instruments of secondary EU law.

7.2.1 The Treaties

The foundational provisions of European electoral law are laid down in the EU Treaties. Article 14(3) of the TEU establishes the principle that MEPs 'shall be elected for a term of five years by direct universal suffrage in a free and secret ballot'. In terms of composition of the Parliament, Article 14(2) just sets the ceiling, currently not more than 750 members, plus the President, and the minimum (six) and maximum (ninety-six) threshold of members per Member State. That ceiling has evolved over time: the 1997 Treaty of Amsterdam introduced the first ceiling of 700, making clear that the Parliament, then composed of 626 MEPs in a Union of fifteen Member States, could not grow endlessly (Treaty of Amsterdam 1997). To soften the impact thereof, a new paragraph was inserted into the Electoral Act, stating that 'the number of representatives elected in each Member State must ensure appropriate representation of the peoples of the States brought together in the Community' (Wouters 1998).

Interestingly, since the 2007 Treaty of Lisbon MEPs are called 'representatives of the Union's citizens' (Art 14(2) TEU; Treaty of Lisbon 2007), whereas before they were referred to for nearly sixty years as representing 'the peoples of the States brought together in the Community' (Treaty establishing the European Coal and Steel Community 1951, Art 20; Treaty establishing the European Economic Community 1957, Art 137). This new language is consistent with the Lisbon Treaty's 'provisions on democratic principles', which are laid down in Articles 9 to 12 of the TEU. These provisions make clear that '[t]he functioning of the Union shall be founded on representative democracy' (Art 10(1) TEU), that 'citizens are directly represented at Union level in the European Parliament' (Art 10(2) TEU), and that '[p]olitical parties at European level contribute to forming European political awareness and to expressing the will of citizens of the Union' (Art 10(4) TEU). The latter provision had originally been inserted as Article 138a in the EC Treaty by the 1992 Treaty of Maastricht, as the first Treaty recognition of such political parties (Treaty of Maastricht 1992; Tsatsos 1994). It was complemented in the 2001 Treaty of Nice with a legal basis for the adoption of 'regulations governing political parties at European level . . . and in particular the rules regarding their funding' (originally Art 191, para 2, TEC, now Art 224 TFEU; Treaty of Nice 2001). On that basis, after a first Regulation was adopted in 2003 (European Parliament and Council 2003; Von Arnhim 2005), in 2014 a Regulation on the statute and funding of European political parties and European political foundations was adopted, later amended in 2018 and 2019 (European Parliament and Council 2014; Lightfoot 2006).

Article 14 of the TEU confirms an essential principle: the Parliament is based on 'direct universal suffrage in a free and secret ballot'. This is considered so important for the rights of citizens that it was confirmed in Article 39(2) of the EU's Charter of Fundamental Rights (Charter). The Explanations to the Charter indicate that this provision 'takes over the basic principles of the electoral system in a democratic State' (Explanations 2007; see also European Court of Justice 2015: para 41; Lenaerts, Van Nuffel, and Corthaut 2021: 150–151).

As to the *general or universal nature* of the suffrage, reference can also be made to Article 22(2) of the TFEU, according to which every citizen of the Union has 'the right to vote and to stand as a candidate in elections to the European Parliament in the Member State in which he resides, under the same conditions as nationals of that State'. This right, introduced together with the very concept of Union citizenship by the 1992 Treaty of Maastricht (Closa 1992; Devroe and Wouters 1996; O'Keeffe 1994), was operationalized through Council Directive 93/109/EC in 1993 (Council 1993), and confirmed in Article 39(1) of the Charter.

The *direct* nature of the suffrage makes clear that no third persons can become involved (unlike in the US system of electors and electoral college) and that the old system of indirect representation by members of national parliaments that was the norm from 1952 to 1979 cannot be reintroduced (Bieber 2015). The *free and secret ballot* points to the unhampered exercise of the right to vote. This presupposes the existence of an enabling environment for holding the elections, both for candidates running campaigns, and for citizens receiving proper information, without unlawful practices, such as abuse of personal data. The EU passed legislation to tackle such abuses in 2019 (Council 2019). It also implies that there should be no interference in the election process from outside and that there should be a free choice among multiple candidates. A system of compulsory voting, as exists in Belgium, Cyprus, Greece, and Luxembourg, is not incompatible with this provision.

Article 14(3) of the TEU does not mention *equality* of suffrage. That is remarkable, as the Venice Commission includes it among the five principles underlying Europe's electoral heritage (universal, equal, free, secret, and direct suffrage) (Venice Commission 2002). The principle is also firmly recognized in international human rights law (see Universal Declaration of Human Rights, Art 21(3); International Covenant on Civil and Political Rights, Art 25(b)). According to the Venice Commission, the principle entails in the first place equality of voting rights, meaning that each voter has in principle one vote. It also implies equal voting power, meaning that seats must be evenly distributed between constituencies. However, this is clearly not the case for European elections: Article 14(2) of the TEU confirms that, in the EP, '[r]epresentation of citizens shall be degressively proportional'. This was a contentious point in the German Constitutional Court's 2009 ruling on the Treaty of Lisbon, where it held that, whilst unequal apportionment of EP seats to population is not a reason for objecting to the Lisbon Treaty, such an arrangement would meet with fundamental objections were an independent government vested with competences that are usual in States to be formed from within the Parliament (Bundesverfassungsgericht 2009).

Against this view Lord and Pollack have argued that the apportionment of EP seats should not necessarily be based exclusively on population (Lord and Pollack 2013). It has also been observed that, as an absolute principle, equality of suffrage would not be suitable for the European integration process (Bieber 2015). Furthermore, Fabbrini has discarded the criticism of degressive proportionality, based on arguments drawn from comparative law, showing that the EU situation is less exceptional than is often thought (Fabbrini 2015). However this may be, one may wonder whether, given the current wide divergences between the electoral systems of the Member States, fostering more equality of suffrage for EP elections should not be a particular point of attention for the future (see also Oelbermann, Oelbermann, and Pukelsheim 2011): see also below, Section 7.4.1.

An important further Treaty provision is Article 223(1) of the TFEU. It stipulates in its first paragraph that the Parliament 'shall draw up a proposal to lay down the provisions necessary for the election of its Members by direct universal suffrage in accordance with a uniform procedure in all Member States or in accordance with principles common to all Member States'. It is interesting to compare this provision to the wording of the original Article 138 of the 1957 EEC Treaty. The latter provided that the Assembly (which was the original name of the Parliament in the Treaties) 'shall be composed of delegates whom the Parliaments shall be called upon to appoint from among their members in accordance with the procedure laid down by each Member State', while adding that '[t]he Assembly shall draw up proposals for elections by direct universal suffrage in accordance with a uniform procedure in all Member States'—at the time the only case in the Treaties where the Parliament had a right of legislative initiative (Bradley 2018: 459). The 1992 Maastricht Treaty added a second paragraph to Article 138 pursuant to which the Council, acting unanimously after obtaining the assent of the Parliament (which must act by a majority of its component members), had to lay down the appropriate provisions, which it then would have to recommend to Member States for adoption in accordance with their respective constitutional requirements (Devroe and Wouters 1996). The pragmatic addition in Article 223 of the words 'or in accordance with principles common to all Member States' was a change brought about by the 1997 Treaty of Amsterdam (Bradley 1999; Wouters 1998), as a minimalistic response to a German proposal of October 1996 on a uniform electoral procedure which was tabled at the Intergovernmental Conference (IGC) leading to the Amsterdam Treaty. That German proposal reproduced key aspects of an earlier resolution of the EP of 10 March 1993 (European Parliament 1993).

Last but not least, the second paragraph of Article 223(1) of the TFEU requires the Council to adopt this proposal unanimously, 'in accordance with a special legislative procedure and after obtaining the consent of the European Parliament', after which the provisions will 'enter into force following their approval by the Member

States in accordance with their respective constitutional requirements'. This cumbersome decision-making process reflects the hybrid nature of the Union—its reliance on intergovernmental consent for institutional reform—and explains, at least in part, the slow progress towards electoral uniformity.

Nearly fifty years since legislation was introduced for the first EP elections, no fully uniform procedure exists. Instead, Member States conduct European elections according to national rules that only adhere to a minimum set of common principles. The primary legal instrument designed to provide this framework is the Electoral Act.

7.2.2 The Electoral Act

The Electoral Act, adopted pursuant to the original Art 138(3) EEC Treaty, established a common legal basis for direct EP elections. It entered into force in 1978 and enabled the first European elections in 1979. As it had to be ratified by Member States according to their respective constitutional provisions, the Electoral Act has the status of primary EU law, at the level of the EU Treaties (Van Raepenbusch 2016: 384).

The Electoral Act does not lay down a 'uniform procedure' for EP elections. The European Court of Justice confirmed in its 2019 *Junqueras* judgment that, 'as EU law currently stands, the Member States remain competent, in principle, to regulate the electoral procedure and, following that procedure, to declare officially the election results' (European Court of Justice 2019, para 69). While the Electoral Act provides a framework for conducting EP elections, it deliberately leaves many aspects of the process—such as electoral thresholds, constituency boundaries, and voting methods—to the Member States (see Section 7.2.3 below). It may also be observed that no consolidated version of the Electoral Act is in force. The various amendments have been published separately and require cross-referencing, which undermines the clarity and accessibility of the legal framework. This patchwork structure reflects the broader tension between the Parliament's ambition to act as a co-legislator and its limited institutional competence in shaping its own electoral procedure.

The most significant amendment to the Act currently in force came in 2002, after the Anastassopoulos Report which the Parliament had adopted in 1998 and which, in line with the Amsterdam Treaty's reference to 'principles common to all Member States', had proposed a number of common principles, next to a first suggestion of electing 10 per cent of the MEPs on transnational lists (European Parliament 1998; Costa 2016; the initial proposal was for 20 per cent: Hoffmeister 2020; on transnational lists see further below, Section 7.3.2). While the Council rejected the latter suggestion, it agreed on the principle of proportional representation as a binding requirement for all Member States and abolished the 'dual' mandate, thereby excluding the possibility for an MEP to be also a member of a national or regional parliament. In addition, it decided that elections would take place over two days (instead of four), and would be organized in May (instead of June) with a view of favouring participation. The 2002 reform also left Member States free to impose a minimum threshold for representation, which could at most be set at 5 per cent of the votes, to opt for open or closed lists, to use single transferable voting or preferential voting, to create regional constituencies, and to decide on how to fill vacancies (Costa 2016). In other words, part of the 2002 reform meant that a lot of leeway was given to Member States rather than pursuing the objective of a uniform electoral procedure.

The most relevant provisions of the current Electoral Act are discussed below.

Pursuant to Article 1, '[i]n each Member State, members of the European Parliament shall be elected as representatives of the citizens of the Union on the basis of proportional representation, using the list system or the single transferable vote' (para 1). Furthermore, it is stipulated that 'Member States may authorise voting based on a preferential list system in accordance with the procedure they adopt' (para 2), and that '[e]lections 'shall be by direct universal suffrage and shall be free and secret' (para 3).

As indicated above, the reference to proportional representation dates from the 2002 reform. This modification largely codified what in the meantime had become a reality, especially after the United Kingdom had adopted proportional representation for the 1999 EP elections (Corbett et al. 2024). It also ensured that the ten Member States acceding in 2004 would be in line with the principle (Farrell 2005). Proportional representation was seen as preferable to a simple majority voting system, as 'the objective was to achieve fair representation of major currents of opinion rather than to form a stable government majority as in national parliaments' (Corbett et al. 2024). The option for voting based on preferential lists has been used by a majority of Member States, although the national systems differ greatly (ibid.).

Article 2 of the Electoral Act provides that, '[i]n accordance with its specific national situation, each Member State may establish constituencies for elections to the European Parliament or subdivide its electoral area in a different manner, without generally affecting the proportional nature of the voting system'. In spite of the aforementioned 1998 proposals from the EP (European Parliament 1998), the Council did not make regional constituencies compulsory in the 2002 reform (Corbett et al. 2024). Article 3 stipulates that 'Member States may set a minimum threshold for the allocation of seats' but that '[a]t national level this threshold may not exceed 5 per cent of votes cast' (para 1). Article 4 of the Electoral Act leaves each Member State free to 'set a ceiling for candidates' campaign expenses'. There are significant differences between national rules in this respect. Article 5 lays down the five-year term of MEPs, which begins at the opening of the first session following each election; each MEP's term of office must begin and end at the same time of that period. Article 9 stipulates that no one may vote more than once in any EP election. Article 10 of the Electoral Act lays down the timing of EP elections;

while they must be held on the date and at the times fixed by each Member State, for all Member States this date shall fall within the same period starting on a Thursday morning and ending on the following Sunday. Member States may not officially make public the results of their count until after the close of polling in the Member State whose electors are the last to vote. These rules respect the different national traditions regarding polling day (which, for instance, in the Netherlands is always on a working day, whereas in Belgium it is always on a Sunday), while maintaining the 'European' character of the elections (Bradley 2018). Last but not least, Article 7 of the Electoral Act provides that:

> [s]ubject to the provisions of this Act, the electoral procedure shall be governed in each Member State by its national provisions. These national provisions, which may if appropriate take account of the specific situation in the Member States, shall not affect the essentially proportional nature of the voting system.

While the reference to a 'specific situation' seemingly finds its origins in the special situation of the German-speaking community in Belgium (Corbett et al. 2024), it also found an application in secondary EU law, namely in Council Directive 93/109/EC. Under Article 14(1) of this Directive, where more than 20 per cent of the electors are not nationals of a particular Member State in which they are resident, the Member State may lay down minimum periods of residence for the right to vote and to stand as a candidate in EP elections—a situation which only arises in Luxembourg, which has availed itself of this possibility (Council 1993; Commission 2023a).

In line with what was indicated above, Article 7 makes clear that the electoral procedure for EP elections still remains largely governed by national regulations. It no longer refers to the prospect of this being changed through 'the entry into force of a uniform electoral procedure', as the original 1976 provisions of the Electoral Act did. That prospect was in essence removed by the 2002 reforms.

7.2.3 Diversity at national level

While the Treaties and the Electoral Act establish some common rules, the conduct of European elections remains governed in practice by national electoral laws. National rules still vary significantly on issues concerning the eligibility to stand as candidates and to vote. This applies to the required minimum age, the question whether candidates must be nominated by political parties or can stand as independents, whether a candidacy requires deposits or lists of signatures, the existence of minimum thresholds for the allocation of seats, whether a country has regional constituencies, and whether there are preferential lists (Corbett et al. 2024). More specifically, as to the minimum voting age, while most Member States set it at eighteen, Austria and Malta permit voting from the age of sixteen, and Greece from seventeen (Mańko 2023). Some Member States use a single national constituency, others subdivide their territory (e.g. Belgium, Ireland, Italy). Electoral thresholds differ widely, with some countries imposing none (Germany, until 2024), while others enforce thresholds of between 3 per cent and 5 per cent. Finally, rules on candidate eligibility, campaign financing, and voting modalities (e.g. postal or electronic voting) are inconsistent. These discrepancies create unequal voting conditions for Union citizens and contribute to the perception of European elections as a collection of twenty-seven parallel national contests. They also complicate the formation of a genuine European political space, in which parties and candidates can compete on equal footing across borders.

It could be, and from time to time has been, argued that different national electoral traditions can be beneficial as they reflect the unique historical, cultural, and political contexts of each Member State, and that EP elections gain legitimacy by staying as close as possible to the trusted norms and principles that inform national elections. Sometimes the United States is given as an example of how there can be 'a workable and generally acceptable harmony of electoral processes without a centrally imposed uniformity or identity', in other words, how there can be 'a good measure of diversity' (Yourow 1981: 398).

While the argument about electoral rules staying 'as closely as possible to the citizens' may appeal to a perception of legitimacy and even subsidiarity (compare the wording of Art 1, second paragraph, TEU about 'decisions are taken as openly as possible and as closely as possible to the citizen'), it downplays too easily the negative effects of the diversity of national electoral rules upon the equality of Union citizens and solidarity within the EU.

As to the former, it should be kept in mind that equality of citizens is a fundamental imperative for the Union. According to Article 9 of the TEU, the EU must 'observe the principle of the equality of its citizens ... [i]n all its activities'. The generality of this provision means that it also applies to EU electoral law. Because of the gaps left by current EU electoral rules, Union citizens face unequal voting conditions, depending on the Member State in which they are resident, which plainly goes against the equality principle. As to solidarity, it was already explained in the 1991 Bindi I report of the European Parliament that there is an intimate relationship between equality and solidarity in the field of citizenship and electoral rights:

> Citizens and others must be given a framework of equality and solidarity. Unless it is seriously distorted, this concept can no longer tolerate a legal and political framework which denies the full enjoyment of fundamental freedoms. In essence it is no longer possible today to dissociate the concepts of citizenship and democratic freedom. (European Parliament 1991: 6.)

The *Commission v Malta* judgment of the European Court of Justice of 29 April 2025 may also have an impact on this matter (European Court of Justice 2025). Apart from reconfirming that 'Union citizenship constitutes the fundamental status of nationals of the Member States' (para 92, with reference to earlier case law), the CJEU emphasized the link between Union citizenship and solidarity, holding that 'Union citizenship is thus one of the principal concrete expressions of the solidarity which forms the very basis of the process of integration . . . and which is an integral part of the identity of the European Union as a specific legal system, accepted by the Member States on a basis of reciprocity' (para 93). Importantly, the CJEU made clear that EU law imposes limits on national legislation which affects the exercise of EU citizens' political rights:

> [I]n exercising the political rights conferred on them by Articles 10 and 11 TEU, Union citizens participate directly in the democratic life of the European Union. Its functioning is founded on representative democracy, which gives concrete expression to democracy as a value, which is, under Article 2 TEU, one of the values on which the European Union is founded . . . It follows that the exercise by the Member States of their power to lay down the conditions for granting their nationality has consequences for the functioning of the European Union as a common legal order. (para 89)

One can argue in a similar manner with regard to Member States' exercise of their powers to lay down conditions for voting and standing of EU citizens as candidate for EP elections. In other words, both the EU and the Member States should tackle the inequalities for EU citizens resulting from the current gaps in EU electoral law and the divergence of national electoral rules.

7.3 Electoral reform and political resistance

Efforts to reform the legal framework governing European elections have encountered significant resistance, both political and institutional. While the EP has consistently called for greater uniformity and visibility of European electoral processes, its reform proposals have met with limited success. The institutional architecture of electoral law reform—relying on unanimous Council approval and national ratification—entails formidable hurdles to meaningful change. This will be illustrated below with reference to the most recent reforms of 2018 and 2022.

7.3.1 The 2018 reform: limited reach, stalled implementation

In February 2015, the EP's Conference of Presidents authorized the drawing up of a legislative initiative report on the reform of EU electoral law, based on Article 223(1) TFEU. On 11 November 2015, the EP adopted a resolution, based on the legislative initiative report prepared by the Committee on Constitutional Affairs, calling for substantial reforms to the Electoral Act, with the aim of enhancing the democratic legitimacy and transparency of European elections. The proposed amendments sought to address several weaknesses identified in previous elections, including the lack of visibility of European political parties, the proliferation of small parties, and the inconsistent application of electoral rules across Member States. The EP aimed at strengthening the democratic and transnational dimension of European elections by proposing a number of changes, including equal visibility of European and national political parties on ballot papers (the enormous diversity of ballot papers had been highlighted in studies for and by the Parliament: Bardi and Cicchi 2015; Baranik et al. 2024); establishment of a joint constituency in which lists are headed by lead candidates for the post of President of the Commission; a common deadline of twelve weeks before the vote for the establishment of electoral lists and the nomination of lead candidates; gender-balanced electoral lists; the right of Union citizens living outside the EU to vote in European elections; and the introduction of an obligatory minimum threshold of between 3 and 5 per cent for constituencies (including single-constituency Member States) with more than thirty-five seats. It took five successive Council presidencies before Council Decision 2018/994 of 13 July 2018 amending the Electoral Act could be adopted (Council 2018). Moreover, at the time of writing the amendment has not entered into force, as it has not been ratified by all Member States.

The amended text provides for six innovations. First of all, a mandatory electoral threshold is introduced for Member States with more than thirty-five seats, aimed at limiting fragmentation in the Parliament. The new Article 3(2) stipulates that 'Member States in which the list system is used shall set a minimum threshold for the allocation of seats for constituencies which comprise more than 35 seats. This threshold shall not be lower than 2 per cent, and shall not exceed 5 per cent, of the valid votes cast in the constituency concerned, including a single-constituency Member State'. Second, Member States are given the option to display the name or logo of the European political party to which the national political party or individual candidate is affiliated on ballot papers (new Article 3b). Third, '[i]n order to encourage voter participation in elections to the European Parliament and to fully take advantage of the possibilities offered by technological developments' (fifth recital of the preamble), the new Article 4a allows Member States to 'provide for the possibilities of advance voting, postal voting, and electronic and internet voting' in EP elections. Appropriate safeguards are required, though: '[w]here they do so, they shall adopt measures sufficient to ensure in particular the reliability of the result, the secrecy of the vote, and the protection of personal data in accordance with applicable Union law'. Fourth, Member States must take measures necessary to ensure that double voting in EP elections is subject to effective, proportionate, and dissuasive penalties (new Article 9(2)). Fifth, a new Article 9a is inserted pursuant to which Member States may take, in accordance with their national electoral procedures, the measures necessary to allow those of their citizens residing in third countries to vote in EP elections. Finally, a new Article 3a is introduced which spells out that, where national provisions set a deadline for the submission of candidacies for EP elections, that deadline shall be at least three weeks before election day—thereby harmonizing timelines.

The 2018 amendment cannot enter into force until the last remaining Member State—Spain—has ratified, following Germany's ratification in March 2024 (Goris 2024). Spain's reluctance has to do with the current Spanish government's reliance on the support of peripheral nationalist and regional parties, which would struggle to obtain MEPs if a 5 per cent threshold were introduced (European Parliament 2025: 7–8). This situation highlights the inherent tension between the EP's supranational ambitions and the intergovernmental nature of electoral law reform. While the EP can initiate proposals under Article 223(1) of the TFEU, it lacks the power to legislate unilaterally and remains dependent on the goodwill of national governments and constitutional systems.

7.3.2 The Parliament's 2022 proposal: institutional innovation meets political inertia

Following the stalled 2018 reform, the EP advanced a more ambitious proposal in May 2022, seeking to further europeanize the electoral process (European Parliament 2022a; Kurmayer 2022). The proposal, submitted as a draft regulation on the basis of Article 223(1) of the TFEU, includes the creation of a Union-wide constituency to elect twenty-eight MEPs from transnational lists; the establishment of a European Electoral Authority, tasked with administering the transnational vote and ensuring compliance with electoral rules; a uniform voting age of sixteen for all Union citizens; the introduction of zipped (gender-alternating) lists, to promote gender parity; and a mandatory indication of European political party affiliation on all ballots.

The reform initiative reflects an ambitious vision of an integrated electoral space. However, the Parliament proved rather divided over the draft regulation, which was adopted by 323 votes for, 262 against and 48 abstentions (European Parliament 2022b; Pascua Mateo 2022). Moreover, its political feasibility is low. While some Member States showed openness for transnational lists in an EU-wide constituency (Croatia, France, Germany, Romania, and Slovenia) (Freund 2023), others expressed constitutional concerns and objected to the establishment of a supranational electoral authority. Still others were sceptical of lowering the voting age or mandating gender quotas. As a result, the proposal has not yet been taken up by the Council, and its prospects remain uncertain.

Some further reflections may be made regarding the proposal for transnational lists. As indicated in Section 7.2.2, a proposal for transnational lists was already part of the 1998 Anastassopoulos Report. The 2011 Duff report proposed allocating twenty-five EP seats to an EU-wide constituency, elected from lists submitted by European political parties (European Parliament 2011). A similar proposal was included in the EP's 2015 resolution on the reform of electoral law. However, these initiatives did not advance beyond the proposal stage (European Parliament 2015).

The introduction of transnational lists raises several complex legal questions. First, some Member States would need to amend their constitutions to accommodate a supranational constituency. Second, the legal basis for such an innovation remains contested; while Article 223(1) of the TFEU allows for reform of the electoral procedure, it does not explicitly authorize—nor prohibit, it should be added—the creation of EU-wide lists. In addition, implementing transnational lists would require a level playing field (both between Member States and between European political parties) in terms of media access, campaign financing, and electoral regulations, none of which currently exists. European political parties remain relatively weak actors, with limited resources and visibility, and would require substantial support to compete effectively in a transnational constituency.

Interestingly, around the same time as the EP adopted its 2022 proposal, the Conference on the Future of Europe completed its activities (see Chapter 11 of this volume) and proposed the following reform of EU electoral law in its final recommendations:

> Amending EU electoral law to harmonise electoral conditions (voting age, election date, requirements for electoral districts, candidates, political parties and their financing) for the European Parliament elections, as well as moving towards voting for Union-wide lists, or 'transnational lists', with candidates from multiple Member States, having taken into account the views expressed among citizens across the EU Member States on this issue. (Conference on the Future of Europe 2022.)

These proposals have not been followed up either.

7.4 Addressing persistent democratic deficits: equality, fragmentation, and public perception

Despite the significant increases in the EP's formal powers over various Treaty reforms (Single European Act, Maastricht, Amsterdam, Nice, Lisbon), European elections continue to exhibit persistent democratic deficits. The fragmented legal framework, combined with the dominance of national dynamics in campaign narratives, undermines the democratic legitimacy of the electoral process and reinforces perceptions of a disconnect between citizens and Union institutions. This section addresses the persistent problems of electoral inequality, fragmentation, and the second-order character of EP elections. It also takes a look at the experiment with lead candidates.

7.4.1 Electoral inequality across the Union

As discussed in Section 7.2.1, the principle of electoral equality (or equality of suffrage) constitutes a cornerstone of democratic systems, is part of Europe's electoral heritage, and is firmly embedded in international human rights law. This means not only equality of voting rights (each voter has in principle one vote) but also equal voting power, meaning even distribution of seats between constituencies. However, the principle of degressive proportionality, enshrined in Article 14(2) of the TEU, complicates this picture for EP elections. While it aims to balance representation between larger and smaller Member States, it also leads to significant disparities in the weight of a vote. For example, an MEP from Luxembourg represents far fewer citizens than one from Germany, raising questions about the consistency of electoral representation across the Union (for a proposed solution in the form of double proportionality or 'tandem', see Leinen and Pukelsheim 2021; 2023). Here above (Section 7.2.3) it has been argued that, in light of the equality and solidarity principles embedded in the EU legal order, both the EU and the Member States should tackle the inequalities for EU citizens resulting from the current gaps in EU electoral law and the divergence of national electoral rules.

One could still add a third meaning to electoral equality: it presupposes sufficient comparability of the conditions and modalities of the vote. However, these vary substantially among Member States for European elections. There are substantive inequalities in voting conditions and eligibility requirements (Tailor and Véron 2014).

7.4.2 Fragmentation and thresholds

As noted, EP elections are conducted under proportional representation systems, which is required by the 2002 amendment to the Electoral Act. However, the degree of proportionality varies, especially in relation to electoral thresholds. In the 2019 and 2024 European elections the electoral thresholds applied ranged between 5 per cent in nine Member States (Czechia, France, Croatia, Latvia, Lithuania, Hungary, Poland, Romania, Slovakia), 4 per cent in Italy, Austria, and Sweden, 3 per cent in Greece, and 1.8 per cent in Cyprus, while fourteen Member States set no thresholds (Del Monte et al. 2024).

In response to the growing number of small parties, the 2018 reform would, if ratified, introduce a mandatory threshold of 25 per cent for constituencies with more than thirty-five seats. This provision aimed to ensure parliamentary functionality and avoid excessive fragmentation. Nevertheless, its implementation has been challenged, notably in Germany. The German Federal Constitutional Court (*Bundesverfassungsgericht*) struck down provisions in the *Europawahlgesetz* with national thresholds for European elections of 5 per cent in 2011 (Bundesverfassungsgericht 2011) and of 3 per cent in 2014 (Bundesverfassungsgericht 2014), arguing that such thresholds infringed the principle of electoral equality and were disproportionate in the context of the Parliament's specific role (Michel 2016). These rulings significantly constrained the implementation of harmonized thresholds and illustrate how national constitutional norms can obstruct Union-wide electoral reforms. Unlike the German Federal Constitutional Court, the Czech Constitutional Court in 2015 did not find the 5 per cent threshold in the Czech Act on Elections of the European Parliament to be unconstitutional in Czechia (Smekal and Vyhnánek 2016). Similarly, the Italian Constitutional Court in 2019 upheld the 4 per cent threshold for European elections under Italian law (Antonuzzi and Lupo 2020; Delledonne 2019).

7.4.3 The second-order character of European elections

Academic literature has long characterized European elections as 'second-order national elections' (Reif and Schmitt 1980; see more recently, inter alia, Corbett 2014; Kritzinger et al. 2020; Lasan 2020), in which voters focus on domestic rather than European issues, and turnout tends to be lower than in national contests. Although it has been convincingly argued that the traditional classification of first- and second-order elections is no longer well-equipped to depict the increasingly politicized and Europeanized dynamics of political parties (Rubio, Oleart and Raube 2021), it cannot be denied that a number of structural features still contribute to this second-order character, such as: the lack of European-level campaign visibility; the minimal presence of European political parties in public discourse; the absence of harmonized rules on campaign financing, media access, or electoral symbols; and last but not least, low voter turnout, which averaged 50.66 per cent in 2019 and 50.74 per cent in 2024—admittedly indicating a certain increase compared to previous elections (Oelbermann and Pukelsheim 2020; European Parliament 2024). In addition, a rather low number of mobile EU citizens exercise their electoral rights, and usually in their countries of origin (European Commission 2020; Lodge, Smith and Fotopoulos 2025).

7.4.4 The Spitzenkandidaten experiment

The 2014 European elections introduced the concept of lead candidates (*Spitzenkandidaten*) for the presidency of the European Commission, with

European political parties nominating their preferred candidates. This innovation aimed to increase the visibility of European political parties, personalize the elections, and strengthen the link between the outcome of the vote and the composition of the executive (for a critical assessment, see, inter alia, Crum 2022; Crum 2023; Goldoni 2016; Navarro, Sandri, and von Nostitz 2018).

While the 2014 process led to the appointment as Commission President of Jean-Claude Juncker, whose European People's Party won the most seats, the 2019 elections revealed the fragility of this mechanism (Fromage 2020), which is not anchored in law and limits the European Council's prerogative to propose a candidate for President of the Commission (Lenaerts, Van Nuffel, and Corthaut 2021, 399). The European Council indeed nominated Ursula von der Leyen, who had not been a lead candidate nor even a candidate on any European ballot paper, prompting criticism from the EP and civil society actors. This episode demonstrated that, in the absence of a clear legal framework and genuine political commitment from Member States, the *Spitzenkandidaten* process remains an informal and reversible practice. Moreover, public awareness of the process remains limited, and national parties have shown only sporadic engagement with the European dimension of electoral campaigns. It has been submitted that the *Spitzenkandidaten* system may in the long run weaken the Parliament and parliamentary control vis-à-vis the Commission, and that direct election of the Commission President may be a better way forward (Van Hecke, Wolfs, and Paulissen 2023).

7.5 Rethinking uniformity without denying diversity: instruments for electoral convergence

While the goal of a (more) uniform electoral procedure is enshrined in Article 223(1) of the TFEU, the institutional and political landscape of the Union renders this objective difficult to achieve. Member States retain a strong attachment to their national electoral systems, and attempts at harmonization have frequently encountered resistance. Nonetheless, various incremental measures could foster greater convergence without requiring full uniformity. These include soft law measures such as codes of conduct, the creation of a European Electoral Authority, harmonization of ballot design, and certain tools to enhance participation.

As to soft law measures, reference can be made, by way of example, to the Code of Conduct for the 2024 European Parliament elections, which International IDEA developed in collaboration with European political parties and the European Commission (International IDEA 2024) to support a follow-up to the latter's 2023 Recommendation on inclusive and resilient electoral processes in the Union and enhancing the European nature and efficient conduct of the elections to the European Parliament (European Commission 2023b). The Code of Conduct, signed by ten European political parties on 9 April 2024, contains a commitment to abide by various rules deemed to ensure fair campaigning and integrity of the 2024 EP elections, in particular key values such as truth and accuracy, election integrity, privacy, transparency and safety, fairness, and ethical campaigning (Fotopoulos 2025). One can also think of other soft law instruments, such as interinstitutional agreements and Commission recommendations or communications, to encourage voluntary alignment and best practices.

As indicated above, one of the most innovative proposals in the EP's 2022 legislative initiative is the creation of a European Electoral Authority. The proposed Authority would be responsible for managing the transnational constituency, overseeing compliance with electoral rules, and coordinating with national electoral bodies (European Parliament 2022a). While the idea of such an authority has precedent in other policy areas, its application to electoral governance is politically sensitive. National governments are cautious about any move that might be perceived as infringing on their sovereignty. Nonetheless, the increasing complexity of electoral processes—particularly with the rise of digital campaigning, disinformation, and cybersecurity threats—makes the case for enhanced coordination compelling. The proposed Authority could initially be established with a limited mandate, focusing on standard-setting, technical assistance, and information exchange. Over time, its role could expand in response to practical needs and political developments.

Even without fundamental legal change, harmonizing certain symbolic aspects of the electoral process could improve its European dimension. One such measure is harmonized ballot design and party logos. The inclusion of the European political party's name and logo on ballot papers, alongside that of the national affiliate is provided for in the 2018 reform. Although some authors doubt its effectiveness (Pascua Mateo 2022), this proposed reform could potentially enhance voter awareness of the European affiliation of national parties and could encourage parties to adopt more coherent EU-wide platforms. It would also provide a visual cue of the supranational nature of the elections, helping to distinguish them from purely national contests.

Finally, there is the potential of using certain tools to enhance participation. Free movement of persons is a cornerstone aspect of Union citizenship, yet as indicated above, mobile EU citizens often face administrative and legal obstacles when voting in their country of residence. Problems include difficulties in obtaining correct information on how to vote and stand as a candidate, burdensome registration processes, and the effect of deregistration from elections in the Member State of origin (Commission 2021). For these reasons, the Commission made a proposal in 2021 based on Article 22(2) of the TFEU to replace Council Directive 93/109/EC, which the Council adopted in June 2025 (Council 2025). The new rules aim to facilitate the supply of information to citizens when voting in European elections and strengthen their electoral rights, notably through providing proactive information on their electoral rights and conditions for registration, standardized registration templates, and safeguards to prevent citizens from being automatically removed from the electoral rolls of their country of origin when they register abroad. There will also be more exchange of relevant information among Member States, including to prevent both double or undue voting due to a criminal conviction. Nevertheless, further work could be contemplated, including the development of a centralized voter registration platform, allowing EU citizens to register or update their voting status online. In parallel, secure electronic or postal voting systems could be piloted in selected Member States, with technical support and auditing provided at EU level. While concerns over electoral integrity remain, these could be addressed through stringent standards, encryption protocols, and independent oversight (Lupiáñez-Villanueva and Devaux 2018).

7.6 Conclusion: toward an electoral Union?

The direct election of the Parliament was designed to anchor the Union's democratic legitimacy in the will of its citizens. However, today, after ten European elections, the process remains constrained by fragmented legal frameworks, uneven national practices, and limited political integration (de León 2017).

This chapter has shown that the current framework, based on the 1976 Electoral Act and its partial amendments, offers only a minimum set of common principles. Electoral law remains in many respects national in substance and scope. Despite the EP's repeated efforts to promote reform, including its 2018 and 2022 proposals, progress has been slow and uneven. The history of electoral reform in the EU reveals a pattern of incrementalism constrained by unanimity. The need for unanimous Council approval and national ratification by twenty-seven Member States creates structural obstacles to innovation, even when reforms enjoy wide support within the Parliament and among segments of civil society. This situation contrasts with other areas of European integration, where qualified majority voting or codecision mechanisms have allowed for significant legislative progress. In electoral law, by contrast, the EU Treaty design still privileges national sovereignty and renders systemic reform highly improbable without broader constitutional change. In 2023 the EP adopted proposals under Article 48 TEU (European Parliament 2023) in which it proposed inter alia that any future reform of EU electoral law should be decided by qualified majority rather than unanimity (Müller 2023). The proposals have not been taken up by the Member States.

Nonetheless, the emergence of a European electoral space is probably just a matter of time. The growing assertiveness of the Parliament, the normative appeal of electoral equality, and the gradual development of a European public sphere all point to potential for further convergence. Even if full uniformity is elusive, targeted reforms—such as harmonizing ballot design, facilitating cross-border voting, and enhancing the role of European political parties—could produce incremental gains in legitimacy and visibility. The challenge is not merely legal or technical; it is above all political and symbolic. Still, a European electoral procedure that makes citizens feel part of a shared democratic project would represent a significant step toward consolidating the Union's political identity. In the absence of such a development, the disconnect between the democratic promise of the Union and the experience of its citizens is likely to persist.

In this light, the path forward requires a layered approach, combining continued advocacy for Treaty-based reform with pragmatic steps toward convergence and harmonization through secondary law and a variety of soft law tools (Hrbek 2019). The aim should not be uniformity for its own sake, but a more coherent and equitable electoral framework that reflects the Union's supranational character. Only then can European elections evolve from second-order contests into a cornerstone of democratic governance at the Union level.

References

Antonuzzi, A. and Lupo, N. (2020). The Thresholds for the EP Elections: the EU Electoral Act, National Legislation and the Case-Law of Constitutional Courts. In Marguery, T., Platon, S., and van Eycken, H. (eds). *Les élections européennes 40 ans après: bilans, enjeux et perspectives / The European Elections, 40 Years Later: Assessment, Issues and Prospects*. Brussels, Bruylant: 55–67.

Baranik, K., Del Monte, M., Kotanidis, S., and Mildebrath, H. (2024). *'Europeanising' the Electoral Ballot*, EPRS, PE 762.310, May 2024.

Bardi, L. and Cicchi, L. (2015). *Electoral Rules and Electoral Participation in the European Elections: The Ballot Format and Structure*, Study for the AFCO Committee of the European Parliament.

Bieber, R. (2015). Artikel 14 EUV. In von der Groeben, H., Schwarze, J., and Hatje, A. (eds). *Nomos Kommentar Europäisches Unionsrecht*. 7th edn, Baden-Baden, Nomos: 218.

Bradley, K. (1999). The European Parliament and Treaty Reform: Building Blocks and Stumbling Blocks. In O'Keeffe, D. and Twomey, P. M. (eds). *Legal Issues of the Amsterdam Treaty*. Oxford, Hart Publishing: 123–139.

Bradley, K. (2018). The European Parliament. In Schütze, R. and Tridimas, T. (eds). *Oxford Principles of European Union Law. The European Union Legal Order* Volume I. Oxford, Oxford University Press: 457–489.

Closa, C. (1992). The Concept of Citizenship in the Treaty on European Union. *Common Market Law Review* 29(6): 1137–1169.

Conference on the Future of Europe (2022). *Report on the Final Outcome*, May 2022. https://www.europarl.europa.eu/resources/library/media/20220509RES29121/20220509RES29121.pdf. Accessed 13 August 2025.

Corbett, R. (2014). 'European Elections Are Second-Order Elections': Is Received Wisdom Changing? *Journal of Common Market Studies* 52(6): 1194–1198.

Corbett, R., Jacobs, F., Neville, D., and Černoch, P. (2024). *The European Parliament*. 10th edn, London, John Harper Publishing.

Costa, O. (2016). *The History of European Electoral Reform and the Electoral Act 1976. Issues of Democratisation and Political Legitimacy*, European Parliament History Series, October 2016, PE 563.516. Luxembourg, Publications Office of the European Union.

Crum, B. (2022). It is Time to Resolve the Spitzenkandidaten Conundrum. RECONNECT Blog, 17 February 2022. https://reconnect-europe.eu/blog/it-is-time-to-resolve-the-spitzenkandidaten-conundrum. Accessed 13 August 2025.

Crum, B. (2023). Why the European Parliament lost the Spitzenkandidaten-process. *Journal of European Public Policy*, 30(2): 193–213.

de León, S. A. (2017). Four Decades of the European Electoral Act: A Look Back and a Look Ahead to an Unfulfilled Ambition. *European Law Review*, 14: 353–368.

Delledonne, G. (2019). 'A Goal that Applies to the European Parliament No Differently from How It Applies to National Parliaments': The Italian Constitutional Court Vindicates the 4% Threshold for European Elections: Italian Constitutional Court, Judgment of 25 October 2018 no. 239/2018 *European Constitutional Law Review* 15: 376–389.

Del Monte, M., Diaz Crego, M., Kotanidis, S., and Mildebrath, H. (2024). Electoral Thresholds in European Parliament Elections. EPRS, PE 749.770, April 2024.

Devroe W. and Wouters, J. (1996). *De Europese Unie. Het Verdrag van Maastricht en zijn uitvoering: analyse en perspectieven*. Leuven, Peeters.

European Commission (2020). Report on the 2019 Elections to the European Parliament, Communication from the Commission to the European Parliament, the Council and the European Economic and Social Committee, 19 June 2020, COM(2020) 252 final.

European Commission (2023a). Report on granting a derogation under Article 22(2) on the Treaty on the Functioning of the European Union, presented under Article 14(3) of Directive 93/109/EC on the right to vote and to stand as a candidate in elections to the European Parliament, Report to the European Parliament and the Council, 7 November 2023, COM(2023) 688 final.

European Parliament (1991). Interim Report of the Committee on Institutional Affairs on Union Citizenship (Bindi I), 23 May 1991, A3–139/91, PE 150.034/fin.

European Parliament (2011). Report on a proposal for a modification of the Act concerning the election of the Members of the European Parliament by Direct Universal Suffrage of 20 September 1976, (2009/2134(INI)), A7–0176/2011, 28 April 2011 (Duff Report).

European Parliament (2019). The European Parliament: Electoral Procedures, Factsheets on the European Union. https://www.europarl.europa.eu/ftu/pdf/en/FTU_1.3.4.pdf. Accessed 13 August 2025.

European Parliament (2022a). European Parliament legislative resolution of 3 May 2022 on the proposal for a Council Regulation on the election of the members of the European Parliament by direct universal suffrage, repealing Council Decision (76/787/ECSC, EEC, Euratom) and the Act concerning the election of the members of the European Parliament by direct universal suffrage annexed to that Decision (2020/2220(INL)—2022/0902(APP)) OJ 2002 C465/171.

European Parliament (2022b). Press Release. MEPs begin revising rules on EU elections, calling for pan-European constituency, 3 May 2022, 20220429IPR28242.

European Parliament (2024). European Elections 2024. Election Results. European Results. https://results.elections.europa.eu/en/turnout/. Accessed 13 August 2025.

European Parliament (2025). Draft Report on the reform of the European Electoral Act – hurdles to ratification and implementation in the Member States, 10 June 2025, PE767.970v01-00, 2025/2028(INI).

Fabbrini, F. (2015). Representation in the European Parliament: Of False Problems and Real Challenges. *Zeitschrift für ausländisches Recht und Völkerrecht*, 75(4): 823–846.

Farrell, D. M. (2005). Electing the European Parliament: How Uniform are 'Uniform' Electoral Systems?. *Journal of Common Market Studies*, 43(5): 969–984.

Fotopoulos, S. (2025). Voter Mobilisation in the 2024 European Elections. In Lodge, J., Smith, J., and Fotopoulos, S. (2025). *Palgrave Handbook on the 2024 European Parliament Elections*. Cham, Palgrave Macmillan: 57–67.

Freund, D. (2023). Blocked by Member States: No Transnational Lists for the 2024 European Elections. https://danielfreund.eu/no-transnational-lists-for-2024-elections/?lang = en. Accessed 13 August 2025.

Fromage, D. (2020). The *Spitzenkandidaten* Procedure for the Election of the European Commission President: A Critical View In Marguery, T., Platon, S., and van Eycken, H. (eds). *Les élections européennes 40 ans après: bilans, enjeux et perspectives/The European Elections, 40 Years Later: Assessment, Issues and Prospects*. Brussels, Bruylant: 77–83.

Goldoni, M. (2016). Politicising EU Lawmaking? The Spitzenkandidaten Experiment as a Cautionary Tale. *European Law Journal*, 22: 279–295.

Goris, C. S. (2024). The Long Delay in the Application of the 2018 Reform of the European Electoral Act: is it all About the Thresholds?, EIPA Blog, 23 May 2024. https://www.eipa.eu/blog/delay-european-electoral-act/. Accessed 13 August 2025.

Hoffmeister, K. (2020). Transnational Lists in European Parliamentary Elections – a Fresh Proposal for European Democracy. ZEuS 1/2020: 129–157.

Hrbek, R. (2019). The Arduous Way Towards a Uniform Electoral System for the European Parliament. In Costa. O. (ed.), *The European Parliament in Times of EU Crisis*. Cham, Springer: 255–274.

International IDEA (2024). *Code of Conduct for the 2024 European Parliament Elections*. https://www.idea.int/european-code-of-conduct-2024. Accessed 13 August 2025.

Kritzinger, S., Plescia, C., Raube, K., Wilhelm, J., and Wouters, J. (2020). *Assessing the 2019 European Parliament Elections*. London, Routledge.

Kurmayer, N. J. (2022). European Parliament Agrees Position on EU Election Law Overhaul, *Euractiv*, 3 May 2022. https://www.euractiv.com/section/politics/news/european-parliament-agrees-position-on-eu-election-law-overhaul/. Accessed 13 August 2025.

Lasan, N. (2020). Testing the Second-Order Elections Model on the 2019 European Elections in Romania. *Studia Universitatis Babes-Bolyai. Studia Europaea*, 65(2): 359–374.

Leinen, J. and Pukelsheim, F. (2021). The Tandem System: A New Electoral Frame for the European Parliament. *Zeitschrift für Parteiwissenschaften*, 27: 115–124.

Leinen, J. and Pukelsheim, F. (2023). Double Proportionality for the European Parliament: The Tandem System. In Kurz, S., Maaser, N., and Mayer, A. (eds). *Advances in Collective Decision Making. Interdisciplinary Perspectives for the 21st Century*. Cham, Springer: 289–300.

Lenaerts, K., Van Nuffel, P., and Corthaut, T. (2021). *EU Constitutional Law*. Oxford, Oxford University Press.

Lightfoot, S. (2006). The Consolidation of Europarties? The 'Party Regulation' and the Development of Political Parties in the European Union. *Representation*, 42(4): 303–314.

Lodge, J., Smith, J., and Fotopoulos, S. (2025). *Palgrave Handbook on the 2024 European Parliament Elections*. Cham, Palgrave Macmillan.

Lord, C. and Pollak, J. (2013). Unequal but Democratic? Equality according to Karlsruhe. *Journal of European Public Policy*, 20(2): 190–205.

Lupiáñez-Villanueva, F. and Devaux, A. (2018). Study on the Benefits and Drawbacks of Remote Voting. https://commission.europa.eu/system/files/2020-06/20181121_remote_voting_final_report_final_clean.pdf. Accessed 13 August 2025.

Mańko, R. (2023). *Voting Age for the European Elections*. European Parliament Research Service. https://www.europarl.europa.eu/RegData/etudes/ATAG/2023/749767/EPRS_ATA(2023)749767_EN.pdf.

Michel, B. (2016). Thresholds for the European Parliament Elections in Germany Declared Unconstitutional Twice. *European Constitutional Law Review*, 12: 133–147.

Müller, M. (2023). Crisis Learning or Reform Backlog? The European Parliament's Treaty-Change Proposals During the Polycrisis. *Politics and Governance*, 11(4): 311–323.

Navarro, J., Sandri, G., and von Nostitz, F. (2018). The Spitzenkandidaten System: Democratic Innovation or Window Dressing?. RECONNECT Blog, 27 December 2018. https://reconnect-europe.eu/blog/spitzenkandidaten-system/. Accessed 13 August 2025.

Nogaj, M. and Poptcheva, E. M. (2015). The Reform of the Electoral Law of the European Union. European Added Value Assessment Accompanying the Legislative Own-Initiative Report (Co-Rapporteurs Danuta Hübner and Jo Leinen), EPRS, PE 558.775, September 2015.

Oelbermann K., Oelbermann, F., and Pukelsheim, F. (2011). Future European Parliament Elections: Ten Steps Towards Uniform Procedures. *Zeitschrift für Staats- und Europawissenschaften*, 9: 9–28.

Oelbermann, K. F. and Pukelsheim, F. (2020). The European Elections of May 2019. Electoral Systems and Outcomes. EPRS, PE 652.037, July 2020.

O'Keeffe, D. O. (1994). Union Citizenship. In O'Keeffe, D. and Twomey, P. (eds). *Legal Issues of the Maastricht Treaty*. London, Wiley Chancery Law: 87–107.

Pascua Mateo, F. (2022). European Parliament and Representation of the Union's Citizens: What Can Be Expected from Electoral Law from a Democratic Standpoint?. *European Law Journal* 28: 63–88.

Piodi, F. (2019). Towards Direct Elections to the European Parliament. *Cardoc Journals* 4: 6–39.

Reiff, K. and Schmitt, H. (1980). Nine Second-Order National Elections – A Conceptual Framework for the Analysis of European Election Results. *European Journal of Political Research*, 8(1): 3–44.

Rubio, R. V., Oleart, A., and Raube, K. (2021). Parties in the 'Twilight Zone': Beyond First and Second-Order Elections for the 2019 European Parliament Elections in Spain. *Journal of Contemporary European Research*, 17(3): 349–368.

Smekal, H. and Vyhnánek, L. (2016). Equal Voting Power under Scrutiny: Czech Constitutional Court on the 5% Threshold in the 2014 European Parliament Elections. *European Constitutional Law Review*, 12: 148–163.

Tailor, A. and Véron, N. (2014). How Unequal is the European Parliament's Representation?, 14 May 2014. https://cepr.org/voxeu/columns/how-unequal-european-parliaments-representation. Accessed 13 August 2025.

Tsatsos, S. (1994). Europäische politische Parteien? Erste Überlegungen zur Auslegung des Parteienartikelen des Maastrichter Vertrages – Art. 138a EGV. *Europäische Grundrechte-Zeitschrift*, 21(3): 45–53.

Van Hecke, S., Wolfs, W., and Paulissen, T. (2023). The Life and Death of the *Spitzenkandidaten:* What Role is Left for European Political Parties? In Costa, O. and Van Hecke, S. (eds). *The EU Political System After the 2019 European Elections*. Basingstoke, Palgrave: 83–99.

Van Raepenbusch, S. (2016). *Droit institutionnel de l'Union européenne*. Brussels, Larcier.

Venice Commission (2002). Code of Good Practice in Electoral Matters. https://www.venice.coe.int/images/SITE%20IMAGES/Publications/Code_conduite_PREMS%20026115%20GBR.pdf. Accessed 13 August 2025.

Von Arnhim, H. H. (2005). The New EU Party Financing Regulation. *European Law Review*, 30: 273–284.

Wouters, J. (1998). Institutionele aspecten van het Verdrag van Amsterdam. In *Europa na het Verdrag van Amsterdam. Institutioneel en Sociaal*. Leuven, Peeters: 1–104.

Wouters, J. (2020). The Long and Winding Road towards a European Electoral Law. In Plescia, C. et al. (eds). *Assessing the 2019 European Parliament Elections*. London, Routledge: 9–18.

Yourow, H. C. (1981). The Electoral System of the United States: A Unified Community Elections Procedure in Comparative Perspective. In Sasse, C. et al. (eds). *The European Parliament: Towards a Uniform Procedure for Direct Elections*. Florence, European University Institute: 337–402.

Legal documents

Bundesverfassungsgericht (2009). Judgment of 30 June 2009 (2 BvE 2/08). https://www.bundesverfassungsgericht.de/entscheidungen/es20090630_2bve000208en.html. Accessed 13 August 2025.

Bundesverfassungsgericht (2011). Judgment of 9 November 2011 (2 BvC 4/10). https://www.bundesverfassungsgericht.de/SharedDocs/Entscheidungen/DE/2011/11/cs20111109_2bvc000410.html. Accessed 13 August 2025.

Bundesverfassungsgericht (2014). Judgment of 26 February 2014 (2 BvE 2/13). https://www.bundesverfassungsgericht.de/SharedDocs/Entscheidungen/EN/2014/02/es20140226_2bve000213en.html. Accessed 13 August 2025.

Consolidated Version of the Treaty on European Union [2016] OJ C202/13–45.

Consolidated version of the Treaty on the Functioning of the European Union [2016] OJ C202/47–388.

Council (1976). Act concerning the election of the members of the European Parliament by direct universal suffrage, annexed to Council Decision 76/787/ECSC, EEC, Euratom of 20

September 1976 [1976] OJ L278/5 as amended by Decision 93/81/Euratom, ECSC, EEC amending the Act concerning the election of the representatives of the European Parliament by direct universal suffrage, annexed to Council Decision 76/787/ECSC, EEC, Euratom of 20 September 1976 [1993] OJ L33/15, and Council Decision 2002/772/EC, Euratom of 25 June 2002 and 23 September 2002 [2002] OJ L283/1.

Council (1993). Council Directive 93/109/EC of 6 December 1993 laying down detailed arrangements for the exercise of the right to vote and stand as a candidate in elections to the European Parliament for citizens of the Union residing in a Member State of which they are not nationals [1993] OJ L329/34, as last amended by Council Directive 2013/1/EU of 20 December 2012; [2013] OJ L26/27.

Council (2018). Council Decision (EU, Euratom) 2018/994 of 13 July 2018 amending the Act concerning the election of the members of the European Parliament by direct universal suffrage, annexed to Council Decision 76/787/ECSC, EEC, Euratom of 20 September 1976 [2018] OJ L178/1.

Council (2019). Regulation (EU, Euratom) 2019/493 of the European Parliament and of the Council of 25 March 2019 amending Regulation (EU, Euratom) No 1141/2014 as regards a verification procedure related to infringements of rules on the protection of personal data in the context of elections to the European Parliament [2019] OJ L85 I/7.

Council (2025). Council Directive of 24 June 2025 laying down detailed arrangements for the exercise of the right to vote and to stand as a candidate in elections to the European Parliament for Union citizens residing in a Member State of which they are not nationals. https://data.consilium.europa.eu/doc/document/ST-9789–2024-REV-1/en/pdf. Accessed 13 August 2025.

Council of Europe. (1952) Protocol to the Convention for the Protection of Human Rights and Fundamental Freedoms. Paris, Council of Europe.

European Commission (2021). Proposal for a Council Directive laying down detailed arrangements for the exercise of the right to vote and stand as a candidate in elections to the European Parliament for Union citizens residing in a Member State of which they are not nationals. COM(2021) 732 final.

European Commission (2023b). Commission Recommendation (EU) 2023/2829 of 12 December 2023 on inclusive and resilient electoral processes in the Union and enhancing the European nature and efficient conduct of the elections to the European Parliament [2023] OJ L2023/2829.

European Council (2023). European Council Decision (EU) 2023/2061 of 22 September 2023 establishing the composition of the European Parliament [2023] OJ L238/114.

European Court of Justice (2015). Judgment of 6 October 2015, Case C-650/13, *Thierry Delvigne*, ECLI:EU:C:2015:648.

European Court of Justice (2019). Judgment of 19 December 2019, Case C-502/19, *Junqueras*, ECLI:EU:C:2019:1115.

European Court of Justice (2025). Judgment of 29 April 2025, Case C-181/23, *Commission v Malta*, ECLI:EU:C:2025:283.

European Parliament (1993). Resolution A3–0381/92 of 10 March 1993 on the draft uniform electoral procedure for the election of Members of the European Parliament [1993] OJ C115/121.

European Parliament (1998). European Parliament Resolution of 15 July 1998 on a draft electoral procedure incorporating common principles for the election of Members of the European Parliament [1998] OJ C292/66.

European Parliament (1998). Resolution of the European Parliament of 15 July 1998 on a draft electoral procedure incorporating common principles for the election of Members of the European Parliament (A4–0212/98), *OJ* 1998, C292/66.

European Parliament (2015). Resolution of the European Parliament of 11 November 2015 on the reform of the electoral law of the European Union. *OJ* 2015, C366/7.

European Parliament (2023). Resolution of the European Parliament of 22 November 2023 on proposals of the European Parliament for the amendment of the Treaties, 2022/2051(INL), P9_TA(2023)0427.

European Parliament and Council (2003). Regulation (EC) No 2004/2003 of the European Parliament and of the Council of 4 November 2003 on the regulations governing political parties at European level and the rules regarding their funding [2014] OJ L297/1, repealed.

European Parliament and Council (2014). Regulation (EU, Euratom) No 1141/2014 of the European Parliament and of the Council of 22 October 2014 on the statute and funding of European political parties and European political foundations [2014] OJ L317/1, as amended by Regulation (EU, Euratom) 2018/673 of the European Parliament and of the Council of 3 May 2018 [2018] OJ L114I/1 and by Regulation (EU, Euratom) 2019/493 of the European Parliament and of the Council of 25 March 2019 [2019] OJ L85I/7.

Explanations (2007). Explanations to the Charter of Fundamental Rights of the European Union [2007] OJ C303/17.

Treaty Establishing the European Coal and Steel Community (1951). Treaty establishing the European Coal and Steel Community, signed at Paris, 18 April 1951.

Treaty Establishing the European Economic Community (1957). Treaty establishing the European Economic Community, signed at Rome, 25 March 1957.

Treaty of Amsterdam (1997). Treaty of Amsterdam amending the Treaty on European Union, the Treaties establishing the European Communities and certain related acts [1997] OJ C340.

Treaty of Lisbon (2007). Treaty of Lisbon amending the Treaty on European Union and the Treaty establishing the European Community, signed at Lisbon, 13 December 2007 [2007] OJ C306/1; most recent consolidated version of Treaty texts in [2016] OJ C202/1.

Treaty of Maastricht (1992). Treaty on European Union, signed at Maastricht, 7 February 1992 [1992] OJ C19/1.

Treaty of Nice (2001). Treaty of Nice amending the Treaty on European Union, the Treaties establishing the European Communities and certain related acts [2001] OJ C80/1.

United Nations (1948). Universal Declaration of Human Rights. Paris, United Nations General Assembly.

8

Democratizing the Politicization of the EU: Channelling Pluralism through New Arenas

Ben Crum and Alvaro Oleart

8.1 Introduction: politicization, pluralism, and democracy in the EU

The relationship between European integration and politicization is a complex one. As the academic consensus has it, until the early 1990s, European integration proceeded as an elite-driven process; the general public's 'permissive consensus' allowed the political elites to build new political competences at the European level when they considered it expedient (Lindberg and Scheingold 1970). This 'permissive consensus' about European integration implied a general lack of popular participation, as intergovernmental actors dominated European Union (EU) decision-making and only a very limited range of societal actors was engaged. However, from the hard-fought referendums in Denmark and France on the ratification of the Treaty of Maastricht in the early 1990s onwards, European integration has increasingly become the object of politicization, in the sense that 'making collectively binding decisions [became] a matter or an object of public discussion' (Zürn et al. 2012: 74).

Politicization persisted in the mid-2000s when the European Constitutional Treaty was rejected in popular referendums in France and the Netherlands. Hooghe and Marks (2009) interpreted the ensuing situation as one in which European integration had become subject to a 'constraining dissensus', leaving European politicians a choice between halting European integration in the face of popular resistance and disagreement or seeking to proceed with European integration by downplaying its politicization. In light of this development, politicization has become an important focus of research in EU studies (De Wilde and Lord 2016; Haapala and Oleart 2022), and increasing attention is given not only to measuring the phenomenon but also to analysing the way in which it unfolds in narrative terms (Bouza García 2017). Arguably, however, portraying the relation between European integration and politicization as a trade-off reifies the defensive attitude of many politicians (Bartolini 2006). Thus, it fails to explore the possibility that EU politicization can also operate as a democratizing force. Instead of

Ben Crum and Alvaro Oleart, *Democratizing the Politicization of the EU: Channelling Pluralism through New Arenas*
In: *The Promise of EU Democracy*. Edited by: Jan Wouters, Julie Smith, Kolja Raube, and Ben Crum, Oxford University Press. DOI: 10.1093/9780191996191.003.0010

only acting like a 'constraint', politicization may also offer opportunities to build an 'empowering dissensus' for European integration (Bouza García and Oleart 2018; Oleart 2021). Such an argument suggests that politicization can empower integration by bringing new actors into European politics, thereby enlarging the political arena beyond the national level, connecting transnational struggles, and potentially contributing to the democratization of the EU (Rone 2020; Oleart 2023a).

A complicating factor in the case of the politicization of European integration is that the politicization of concrete EU policy decisions immediately spills over into politicizing and challenging the very existence of the Union. Famously, in his classical work on the legitimacy of political systems, David Easton (1953) made a systematic distinction between the legitimacy of the polity, the regime (or the government-in-office), and specific policies. These distinctions are important in a democratic system because they imply that citizens are able to disapprove of a specific policy without such negative sentiments necessarily undermining their belief in the legitimacy of the incumbent government; and even if they challenge the legitimacy of the government-in-office, this need not discredit the political system (or constitution) as a whole.

In the EU, citizens and analysts seem to have a hard time maintaining these distinctions between policies, regime, and polity. Objections against a particular EU policy quickly spill over into objections against the EU as a whole. Part of the explanation of this may have to do with the fact that the EU lacks a distinct executive that can be recognized as the (contingent) agent of its policies; something that in turn leads to an 'opposition deficit' (Mair 2007; Rauh and De Wilde 2018). Instead, many EU policies are perceived as being ingrained in the very structure of the Union. According to this logic, European integration is mainly governed by rules that have been enshrined in the treaties; these rules condition the decisions that the Member States can make, and they programme, as it were, the courts and the Commission as guardians of these rules (Grimm 2015). Such a rules-based logic is easily projected on Single Market decision-making where the foundational principles of competition, non-discrimination and the freedoms of goods, services, capital and workers appear to commit the EU to a neoliberal course. However, it can also be said of EU migration policy and the expansion of Frontex, the European Border and Coast Guard Agency, which can be seen as functionally inclined towards the construction of a 'fortress Europe' that reproduces racism and colonial relations (Sachseder et al. 2022).

The fact that politicization in the EU tends to directly challenge its character as a polity is not something that can be wished away or considered a transitional matter. To the contrary, EU polity contestation is an inherent ingredient of a union that is built on top of long-existing and historically embedded nation states that all offer their own, distinct understandings of what a legitimate polity looks like (Jachtenfuchs et al. 1998; Crum 2003). The inherently contested polity character of the EU creates a particular challenge for democratic deliberation and its ability to accommodate political diversity. In particular, it raises the risk that voices will be muted because they depart from an alternative understanding of the nature of the EU polity. For this reason, we have argued in a previous article (Wolthuis et al. 2025) that the EU should embrace and facilitate the politicization of its polity character as an expression of its full democratic nature rather than succumb to the inclination to suppress such contestation. At the same time, however, the inherently contested polity character of the EU also raises the risk that political actors invoke alternative polity understandings that are in fact beyond the pale of what can be justified in democratic terms. The bottom line in this respect is whether the polity conceptions invoked still meet the test of pluralism or whether they are actually premised on the suppression of the plurality of societal voices, either within or between the different Member States that constitute the EU.

This chapter addresses the interaction between politicization, pluralism and democracy in the EU (see also Crum and Oleart 2023a). In the next section, we develop an analytical framework that identifies the key desiderata, or preconditions, for a meaningful debate on the constitutional and democratic identity of the EU. We then zoom in on four arenas that might facilitate such a debate, some of which rely on existing EU institutions while others would require the establishment of new institutions: an EU Constitutional Council, the European Council, a permanent Constitutional Assembly, and a 'Popular Conference'. For each arena, we analyse how it could be optimized to facilitate the politicization of the EU polity; the kind of debates that it could host; and how it would be able to accommodate critical voices. We conclude by arguing that, by offering platforms to both accommodate as well as respond to criticism of the EU polity, such arenas can foster politicization in a constructive way and contribute to the democratization of the EU.

8.2 Analytical framework: the stakes of EU politicization

Previous research has emphasized the absence of 'politics' when discussing EU 'policies', something that is well captured by Vivien Schmidt's (2006) characterization of the EU as involving 'policy without politics'. The mismatch between 'policy' and 'politics' lies at the centre of our puzzle, in that in the EU 'major political decisions are made in executive networks relatively detached from democratic control' (Kauppi 2018: 20). From this perspective, the politicization of the EU can be understood as an attempt to match policy *with* politics. Indeed, as Trenz and Eder (2004: 7) argue, 'criticising the democratic deficit means initiating the process of democratising the EU'. Rather than 'constraining' European integration, EU politicization may in fact revitalize and empower European democracy.

Pluralism—understood as the free and fair competition between political actors that embody and mobilize contrasting political ideologies (Theuns 2021)—should be at the core of any analysis of democracy. In the case of the EU, this not only means the recognition of competing (and often mutually exclusive) interests on many issues, but also that the very polity structure of the EU within which such contestation is played out remains the object of legitimate political contestation. Hence, given the absence of a shared understanding of the nature of the EU as a polity, we suggest that concerns about the full scope of democratic pluralism deserve a more central place in analyses of democratic backsliding, (as well as of the resilience of democracy) in the EU than they are generally assigned (Gora and De Wilde 2022).

Crucially, EU institutions tend to be geared towards narrowing rather than broadening the political debate (McNamara 2019), and they particularly show limited openness towards thematizing the very polity nature of the EU. Political debates on EU legislation take place in the Council of the EU and the European Parliament (EP). These debates focus on concrete policy issues and tend to be framed in the divisions that characterize these institutions: the differences between national governments in the Council and the differences between party groups in the EP. Actors who want to thematize and challenge the polity character of the EU (like deviant Member State governments in the Council or Eurosceptic party groups in the EP) quickly place themselves outside the debate. The tendency to restrict the scope of politicization is even stronger in the European Commission, which prefers to approach politically sensitive questions as legal issues in a narrow sense rather than to recognize that they involve questions about the nature of the EU polity (Oleart and Theuns 2023). Hence, we argue for a greater recognition and awareness of the pluralism of EU conceptions in the Union, its Member States, and among its citizens, because conflicts between them are bound to resurface time and again. It follows that the EU needs to recognize its deeply pluralistic character and do more to accommodate processes of politicization that (also) concern its own identity. The recognition of the EU's pluralistic character is a necessary step to strengthen its democratic legitimacy.

In our previous analysis, we concluded that democratic debate on some of the most high-profile issues that the EU has faced since the entry into force of the Treaty of Lisbon in 2009 has been stymied because of the exclusion of the deeper polity-level concerns at stake (Wolthuis et al. 2025: 1154–1155). The most notable example is the way that the sovereign debt crisis in the eurozone became reduced to defining the terms under which bailouts could be offered, leaving little to no space for a wider debate about the rights and duties of countries in an economic, monetary, and political union (Crum 2013; Merlo 2023). In a similar way, the withdrawal of the United Kingdom from the EU was reduced to setting the specific terms of the new trade relationship, rather than causing serious soul-searching on the part of the EU. A democratic processing of these issues, taking all relevant positions into account, would have required a broader acknowledgement that these fundamental challenges to European integration are in fact debates invited by the very character of the EU itself (Bickerton et al. 2022). If we assume that the very nature of the EU remains contested, then the EU faces a democratic imperative to facilitate politicized debates in which the diversity of EU conceptions can be expressed.

If it is accepted that the EU should indeed facilitate the ongoing (and never-ending) debate about its nature as a polity, the question is how such a debate might be envisaged in organizational and procedural terms and what kind of arenas it would require. The *first* precondition, then, is the recognition that there is a need for a place (or places) for such polity-focused debate in the EU. This implies the acknowledgement that the question of the nature of the EU is bound to remain an open question that requires continuous attention. As a *second* precondition, one may want to make sure that this polity-focused debate remains at some distance from the everyday policy debate. As it is, EU decision-making is complex already as it involves the hearing and consent of different groups and majorities across multiple institutions. Those policy debates are unlikely to gain in effectiveness from the direct and integral problematization of the EU's polity character; although they may well benefit in the longer run from the polity debate being addressed in an open and engaging way in a parallel format. At the same time, as a *third* precondition, wherever an arena is created to debate the polity character of the EU, it remains important that there are informal and formal connections through which this debate and its (preliminary) outcomes can be channelled to the day-to-day decision-making in the EU.

As a *fourth* precondition, it is essential that any institutionalization of the EU polity debate be susceptible to opinions at the grassroots level and from within national politics in particular. Any appropriate new political arena has to be built on the recognition of (but also as a counterweight to) the lack of a unified European public sphere (Koopmans and Statham 2010), beyond some specific episodes of contention, such as the contestation surrounding the negotiations on the Transatlantic Trade and Investment Partnership (Oleart 2021). The lack of a common European language and mass media means that political interaction takes place primarily through the mediation of national political actors that address their national publics in national languages. The outcome is a set of fragmented public spheres, that nevertheless progressively evolve towards a European 'community of communities' (Risse 2010). Hence, the national public spheres are the central location in which EU politicization unfolds, and thus a key arena in which discussions surrounding the pluralism of the EU should take place. If the EU is to transition towards an 'empowering dissensus' for European integration, it will be through making a closer connection between national and EU politics.

The *fifth* and final precondition builds on the fourth by underlining that, under conditions of a fragmented public sphere, any democratic discussion of the EU as a polity cannot be settled in a top-down way but inevitably needs to be of a horizontal, deliberative character. In other words, this precondition recognizes that the EU order does not offer a supreme arbitrator to settle the question of its own identity, but instead constitutes a common political arena in which fundamentally different conceptions regularly confront each other and European policymakers have to find collectively acceptable arrangements. In line with the very idea of democratic deliberation under conditions of pluralism, the primary aim of any debate on the EU's polity character should be to come to an understanding of the full range of positions held among the participants. It should also allow for the suspension of a consensus and, in cases where consensus remains out of reach, to allow political representatives in the EU 'to agree to (reasonably) disagree'.

8.3 Four potential arenas to democratize the politicization of the EU

Having defined these five preconditions, we can think of different institutional arrangements that might serve as appropriate arenas for such a debate on the character of the EU polity. Concretely, we suggest four potential arenas. The first one builds on an earlier proposal by Joseph Weiler (1996) for an EU 'Constitutional Council': a judicial forum meant to facilitate 'horizontal' exchanges between the Court of Justice of the EU and national (supreme) courts. Secondly, moving to the political institutions of the EU, the European Council offers itself as a fitting arena in which to thematize the debate on the nature of the EU polity. Composed of the Heads of State and Government of the Member States, the European Council appears as the supreme arena where different understandings of the EU polity as they originate from the national public spheres can be expressed and find a hearing. A third option for locating the debate about the EU's identity would be to think of it more as a Constitutional Assembly that acts on a direct mandate of the people (Patberg 2020). Fourth and finally, building upon the experience of the 2021–22 Conference on the Future of Europe, we want to suggest the possibility of thinking beyond formal institutions and rather establishing a kind of 'Popular Conference' that would offer a platform for all kinds of individual and organized actors to engage with the question of the EU's character.

In the remaining subsections, we discuss the promise and limitations of each of these options in light of the five preconditions formulated before, and whether these arenas hold the potential for fostering EU politicization and, in turn, contribute to its democratization.

8.3.1 An EU Constitutional Council

Joseph Weiler (1996) proposed an EU Constitutional Council to address questions about the limits of EU competences. Characteristically, given the EU's contested polity character, it is not self-evident where (what the Germans call) the

Kompetenz-Kompetenz lies, that is, the ultimate authority to decide which institutions or level of government gets to exercise power over which issues (Schütze 2015). Formally, the scope of the EU's competences is subject to the principle of conferral (TEU, Art 5), which provides that the competences of the EU are delineated by the EU Member State governments and what they have conferred on it through the treaties that they have agreed. However, it is less clear where authority lies when there is disagreement about the exact scope and interpretation of these competences, especially if these disagreements touch upon principles that have been enshrined in national constitutions.

Against this background, Weiler (1996: 533) recognizes that there remains 'a built-in indeterminacy' in questions about the competences of the EU and their limits. Critically, he emphasizes that the question of EU competences is not one that can be decided 'internally' by EU institutions but that it 'is fundamentally also one of national constitutional norms [but still subject to a Union solution by a Union institution]'. Hence, Weiler proposes the establishment of an EU Constitutional Council that would offer a more 'horizontal' arena in which, instead of handing out judgments top-down from the apex of the EU legal system, different views of the nature of the EU and its legal system could be exchanged. Accordingly, although it would be chaired by the President of the Court of Justice of the EU, the Constitutional Council would be composed of delegated members from the constitutional courts (or their equivalents) in the EU Member States. The Constitutional Council would have the power to review EU laws for their compliance with the (limits of) EU competence after their adoption and before they would come into force, when requested to do so 'by any Community institution, by any Member State or national parliament, or by the European Parliament acting on a majority of its members' (Weiler 1996: 532). At the same time, Weiler also emphatically presents his proposal as a counterweight to the extreme intergovernmentalization of the EU legal order in which national (constitutional) courts, like the *Bundesverfassungsgericht*, can just adopt a unilateral stance on the limits of EU law. Essentially, the institution of an EU Constitutional Council would foster co-ownership of the shared EU order by creating a common arena to deliberate and adjudicate issues of EU competence.

Weiler's proposal for an EU Constitutional Council meets many of our preconditions. It is a forceful and institutional way to recognize that the question of the nature and the limits of the EU is inherently open-ended. It also creates a special arena for this debate, which is closely linked to, but also detached from, the actual policymaking debate. Most fundamentally, by fully integrating members from national (constitutional) courts it creates a 'horizontal' setting, which invites the deliberative exchange of different understandings of the EU.

However, the proposal also has some limitations. These mostly follow from it being a judicial rather than a political proposal. As a consequence, its proceedings would still be seen as rather technical and steered by the logic of adjudication, which would limit their public resonance. Relatedly, although Weiler lists an extensive list of actors that could invoke the EU Constitutional Council, these remain very institutional in character, and while one can well imagine national parliaments (which Weiler emphatically includes) to be spurred into action by societal actors, the public accessibility of an EU Constitutional Council is bound to remain constrained. While an EU Constitutional Council is an appealing proposal to recognize the pluralism within the EU, an effective exchange of the full diversity of views on the EU probably (also) needs a more political forum. For this reason, the remaining three arenas that we examine are indeed more political in character.

8.3.2 Politicizing the European Council

When turning to existing EU institutions to identify an arena where the ongoing debate on the nature of the EU might best be staged, the European Council emerges in many respects as the most appropriate place. The European Council sits at the summit of EU decision-making as it is composed of the Heads of State and Government of the EU Member States under the chairmanship of the President of the European Council. Also, its role essentially transcends the other EU institutions, as the European Council is meant to 'provide the Union with the necessary impetus for its development and [to] define the general political directions and priorities thereof' (TEU, Art 15.1). In fact, the treaty emphatically adds that the European Council 'shall not exercise legislative functions'.

As Heads of State and Government, the members of the European Council represent their national people at the highest level. They can articulate the views and sentiments about European integration that circulate in their national public spheres. Most of the debate about European integration remains encapsulated in national public spheres (Koopmans and Erbe 2004) and very much framed by national experiences and benchmarks (de Vries 2018). In that sense, the members of the European Council are likely to be able to articulate the main range of the most salient views on European integration, and to articulate them with the full weight of their national constituency behind them.

Notably, the European Council regularly does engage in high-level debates on the nature of the EU. Ultimately, it is the Heads of State and Government that have to agree to any changes to the EU treaties, the EU's basic structure. Hence, any round of treaty revisions is concluded by the members of the European Council—albeit convening as an 'Intergovernmental Conference' rather than as the European Council. Also, with some frequency, debates on the nature or the future of the EU are tabled in the European Council. A notable example was the informal European Council that took place on 9 May 2019 (just ahead of the European elections later that month) in the Romanian city of Sibiu. Such a practice could be institutionalized, for instance by obliging the European Council to debate the nature and the future of the EU at the beginning and mid-way of each five-year EU electoral cycle.

European Council summits are probably the most publicized meetings of any EU institution. However, in one aspect the current summits fall fundamentally short of acting as a credible public forum for the politicization of the EU's identity, and that is in the fact that they follow the classic diplomatic format of taking place behind closed doors. The members of the European Council report on their positions and the dynamics of the exchanges in so-called 'doorstep interviews' when they talk to the press on their way into a summit and in press conferences afterwards. However, the public does not get to see or hear what actually goes on in the room or the diversity of positions that are articulated. Moreover, any reports by its members are bound to be stylized or even sanitized. To allow for the identification and recognition of the diversity of views on European integration, it is essential for these debates to take place in public.

This logic certainly does not imply that all proceedings of the European Council should be in public. However, if the European Council were to serve as an arena in which the diversity of views of the nature of European integration becomes visible, then it is essential that those debates are open. Public debates will put on full display the position that each Head of Government represents. On the one hand, it will allow people to actually see their preferences being represented and to identify with national leaders and the positions they represent. On the other hand, public deliberation also invites public scrutiny, critique and accountability. Popular constituencies or the representatives that they have elected (like national parliamentarians, see Crum and Oleart 2023b) can then question and challenge the positions adopted by their Head of Government.

Ideally, public European Council debates would be complemented by national debates *before* the European Council meeting, to inform Heads of Government and provide them with a formal or informal mandate, and also *after* the summit, as a form of debriefing and accountability. So far, the extent and the ways in which national parliaments hold their Heads of State and Government to account over their participation in the European Council vary quite significantly (Wessels et al. 2013). Having institutionalized debates on the nature and future of the EU in the European Council may help these practices converge and also facilitate more transnational exchanges across parliaments (see Kinski and Crum 2020). In this way, one would institutionalize a form of two-level democratic deliberation (Savage and Weale 2009) in which well-deliberated national positions enter into the EU-level debate and EU-level dynamics feed back again into the national debates.

To sum up, the European Council scores very high on some of the five preconditions that we have formulated for an effective forum for discussing the diversity of EU conceptions. It is an extremely visible and high-profile EU institution that at the same time operates at some distance from the day-to-day legislative work in the EU. Due to its standing, any conclusions that it reaches can feed into the organization and the outcomes of EU decision-making. However, there are also some serious shortcomings to the European Council fulfilling such a role. One is that the composition of the European Council is bound to frame any debate, and the division lines that it highlights, in national terms. In principle, the Heads of State and Government may also invoke other identities and interests—for instance, in terms of party affiliation, personal characteristics, or values that they hold. In practice, however, the national representative role is bound to prevail. Regardless of how salient other (transnational) affiliations and identities may be among the peoples of Europe, the Heads of State and Government are ill-positioned to represent these. A second shortcoming is that the European Council in many respects is the most vertical EU institution at the apex of the EU's institutional architecture. For that reason, it is ill-positioned to facilitate debate between societal groups and interests that operate across borders. Finally, the heavily intergovernmental and institutionalized structure of the European Council and its members makes it a somewhat impermeable fortress for many societal groups and grassroots interests. In that respect, one rather would want a more open forum with more direct linkages to the peoples of Europe.

8.3.3 A 'Permanent Constitutional Assembly'

One way a potential EU institution could more directly link the debate on the nature of the EU polity with the people is the proposal by Markus Patberg (2020: 208–214) to establish a 'Permanent Constitutional Assembly'. Patberg's proposal is very much driven by his overarching normative concern that the political institutions involved in day-to-day EU decision-making should have no power over the way decision-making powers and processes are defined in the first place, given their own stake in these powers and processes. Patberg holds that the present EU set-up is fundamentally flawed because the 'constituent power' is controlled by the same actors that dominate the day-to-day decision-making process (the 'constituted power'), most notably the Member State governments.

Hence, inspired by the classical work of Sieyès (1982), Patberg's proposal is geared towards establishing a strict divide between 'constituted powers' (like the EU's institutions and procedures) and the 'constituent power' that defines the constitution. Concretely, he proposes the establishment of a 'Permanent Constitutional Assembly' as an on-going forum to reflect on the foundations of the EU and to deliberate and decide on any amendments to its constitutional structure as it is currently enshrined in the EU treaties. The way that Patberg envisages such an assembly remains very much predicated on electoral institutions, as it involves two 'chambers': one composed on the basis of pan-European lists and reflecting the principle of 'one person, one vote', the other composed by an equal number of representatives for each Member State elected on national lists. In that way, the constitutional assembly would mirror the dual character of the EU as a Union of peoples and of states at the level of constitutional decision-making in a similar way to how it is embodied in the EU legislative process in the division of tasks between the EP and the Council of Ministers.

By singling out and foregrounding the constitutional question in the EU, Patberg's aim very much aligns with our own. A Permanent Constitutional Assembly would establish a permanent forum to reflect on the nature of European integration and the diversity of views and choices involved in that. Compared to the European Council, a Permanent Constitutional Assembly would have a much more direct link to the people, while the bicameral set-up that Patberg proposes also allows him to calibrate between the national and the pan-European identities and affiliations of EU citizens. In fact, the members of the constitutional assembly would be elected specifically with their constitutional task in mind and the distinct views on European integration that they would bring to such deliberations. Also, by definition, the Permanent Constitutional Assembly would be precluded from being involved in day-to-day EU decision-making, as that is the domain of the 'constituted powers'. At the same time, given its exclusive competence over the EU's constitutional structure, it would hold far-reaching powers over the way decision-making is organized.

The most obvious objection to a Permanent Constitutional Assembly is a practical one: how can we expect the present constituent power-holders, specifically the Member States, to agree to establishing it in the first place? Short of a major popular uprising, it is difficult to imagine the Member States voluntarily relinquishing their gatekeeping power over the EU. Another practical question is whether there is a really a need for a constitutional assembly to be a permanent institution. Patberg's insistence on permanency is partly informed by the fact that it prevents constituted powers from holding any control over the initiation and timing of constitutional debates. However, one might question whether there is a need to have this forum active all the time. Is there enough work for it? Would it not foster a permanent state of constitutional uncertainty? Would its very institutionalization not take away the sense of engagement and opportunity that has historically accompanied *incidental* constitutional moments?

At a more principled level, reservations against the Permanent Constitutional Assembly mostly follow from the way its organization very much still mimics existing political institutions. One risk is that—despite the strict division between constituted and constituent power—the constitutional assembly would still be captured by the political parties that populate the existing constituted institutions. In that case, the political dynamics in the constitutional assembly might simply come to echo the well-established party dynamics in the European Parliament and other EU institutions. Patberg (2020: 213) dismisses this objection since he expects the elections and the internal dynamics of the constitutional assembly to develop a distinctive logic of their own. Still, one wonders whether constituent power as a collective constitution-making force necessarily needs to rely on the institution of elections and whether it might not be better served by an approach that more proactively appeals to the diversity of social identities and grassroots activism in Europe.

8.3.4 Towards a Popular Conference

Indeed, going beyond existing EU institutions, the debate about the nature of the EU polity potentially lends itself as a vehicle for new forms of bottom-up societal mobilization in Europe. In this spirit, in addition to the three arenas outlined above, we can imagine the establishment of a 'Popular Conference' with the explicit aim to channel societal actors into the fundamental debates about the nature of the EU polity. Notably, so far, the EU has tended to organize revisions of its constitutional powers as an extension of its existing institutions. Rather than introducing genuinely new forms of popular authorization, the strategy to 'democratize' these processes has been to extend the number of institutions from which members are involved (Crum 2023). This is well illustrated by the way that the 2009 Treaty of Lisbon amended the traditional EU treaty revision process in so-called Intergovernmental Conferences (IGCs). Building upon the EU Constitutional Treaty that had been prepared by the Convention on the Future of Europe between 2002 and 2004 (Crum 2012), the Lisbon Treaty (TEU, Art 48.3) basically added a preparatory stage of a European Convention, ensuring the involvement of parliamentarians from the national and the European level as well as members of the European Commission besides the government representatives that traditionally make up the membership of the IGCs.

This logic was taken even further in the plenary of the 2021–22 Conference on the Future of Europe (Alemanno and Nicolaïdis 2021; Oleart 2023a). On this occasion, institutional representatives of Member State and EU-level political institutions were joined by representatives from civil society organizations, trade unions and 'citizen ambassadors' from both EU-level and national citizen panels. Strikingly, however, despite its broad-based composition, the Conference on the Future of Europe very much ended up operating as a 'disintermediated and depoliticized' exercise, reproducing the depoliticized ways in which EU politics tends to operate (see Oleart 2023b). Bypassing any fundamental debates about the nature of the EU, the Conference became quickly oriented towards concrete policy solutions.

A genuine 'Popular Conference' would radicalize the logic of ever wider inclusion in fundamental EU debates. It would recognize that there is a limit to what institutional reforms can accomplish, as ultimately democracy depends on mass membership organizations (and also on single issue groups that are part of a broader movement, such as environmental NGOs) that are able to mediate between institutions and citizens. Thus, the hollowing out of democracies (Mair, 2013) is a central dimension that is particularly relevant in the EU context, given the weak mass membership organizations at the EU level. For that reason, a Popular Conference would have to focus on the responsiveness between public debates and 'politics' on the one hand and EU institutional processes on the other. To allow for such debates, a Popular Conference should not become yet another EU institution that reproduces the depoliticized dynamics but rather be structurally anchored in societal actors, like civil society groups, trade unions, and also political parties. It would have to reinforce local and national organizations as mass organizations to counter the decades-long trend of the hollowing out of trade unions and political parties, while at the same time constructing a space of permanent dialogue between movements across borders.

The mediation of collective societal actors is crucial to politicize the EU in the European public spheres. Mediating organizations can contribute to the political socialization with EU politics, offering an open door for people not previously socialized with EU politics in a way that makes them realize that their political concerns are inherently intertwined with those of others across the EU and beyond. Further, mediating organizations have a key role in channelling that societal energy towards the EU institutions. Intermediation is particularly required for those actors that are structurally marginalized from politics in general, and EU politics in particular. For instance, bankers have a structurally powerful position that sees their ideas circulating in the mainstream media (e.g. via the *Financial Times* or *The Economist*), through political parties that tend to be sympathetic to their points of view, and through interest groups that play a relevant role both in terms of policy and the public sphere. This does not mean that the participation of bankers in democracy is illegitimate, but rather that their political weight is much bigger than it should be, insofar it outweighs larger communities that hold a structurally less prominent political position, such as racialized groups, the poor, or immigrants. This perspective paves the way for an intersectional outlook for politics, in which mediation contributes to bringing together systemically discriminated groups (based on class, gender, or race). Mediating organizations can act as brokers who bring issues of local and national concern into the arena of EU politics as well as bringing European issues into the more grounded realms of social movement activity.

The 'Popular Conference' should operate as a platform to bring mediating organizations together transnationally. The Conference could amount to a regular series of gatherings across EU Member States (it would be important that the sessions do not take place uniquely in Brussels) in which a rolling number of activists, civil society, and trade union representatives (who are heavily underrepresented in the Brussels bubble in comparison to business lobbyists) exchange views among themselves and with representatives of EU institutions regarding their political priorities. The purpose of such a Popular Conference would be to pave the way for the construction of a transnational political field in which different national political debates and actors become increasingly intertwined. Anchoring the Popular Conference away from actors that prioritize technical and expert knowledge rather than political capital, and integrating EU-critical activists and organizations, it has the potential to transform the depoliticized Brussels arena into a more transnational and politicized one. This process does not entail erasing the differences between actors and movements but requires a commitment to engage in relational thinking and to embrace the tensions that might arise as being intrinsic to any genuinely democratic process.

8.4 Conclusion: towards a politicized conception of EU democracy

The chapter has sought to open new avenues for rethinking the relationship between politicization, pluralism and democracy in the EU. We have argued that there remains a void at the heart of EU democracy as there remain many competing conceptions of what the EU is and should be. However, these disagreements are marginalized in the EU's day-to-day decision-making and there is no functioning arena where they can be articulated and discussed. Hence, we advocate for the democratization of the EU's politicization. By accommodating and responding to EU critics, such an open approach can embolden the EU's democratic character and turn its inherent pluralism from a challenge to a virtue.

To elaborate this idea, we formulated and justified five preconditions that solutions to the existing void should ideally meet:

1) The question of the nature of the EU is bound to remain an open question and hence needs an arena where it can be addressed.
2) This polity-focused debate has to remain at some distance from the everyday policy debate.
3) At the same time, informal and formal connections are needed that connect the polity-focused debate to the day-to-day decision-making in the EU.
4) Any institutionalization of the EU polity debate should be susceptible to opinions at the grassroots level and from within national politics in particular.
5) Any democratic discussion of the EU's polity cannot be settled in a top-down way but needs to be of a horizontal, deliberative character.

These five preconditions emphasize that any attempt to democratize the EU requires the articulation of politicization, pluralism and democracy. Technocratic top-down institutional reforms are unlikely to make a meaningful difference. That is why we have imagined new arenas that can precisely foster the politicization of the EU in a constructive way, linking policy-related debate again to more fundamental polity discussions. These arenas may not only contribute to politicizing the EU, but also to strengthening collective actors (political parties, trade unions, civil society) to reverse the hollowing out of democracy. In this way, EU politicization will be more inclusive and not uniquely dominated by executive actors.

Rather than presenting a fully-fledged blueprint, we have outlined four potential arenas that represent the type of spaces where fundamental debates on the nature of the EU could take place: an EU Constitutional Council, a politicized European Council, a Permanent Constitutional Assembly, and a Popular Conference. Each of these arrangements would facilitate the confrontation of different EU conceptions and the politicization of EU affairs more generally. Each of them has its strengths and limitations, as summarized in Table 8.1. Importantly, however, the four arenas are not mutually exclusive. They can complement each other. Also, one can imagine further arenas that combine elements of the ones suggested here.

To be sure, none of these proposals is likely to be implemented any time soon. However, thinking them through helps to reinforce and clarify the ways in which

Table 8.1 Four potential arenas for politicizing the nature of the EU

	Strengths for politicizing the EU polity	**Limitations for politicizing the EU polity**
EU Constitutional Council	- Horizontal, transnational and deliberative setting	- Adjudicative and legal proceedings, limited openness to societal actors
Politicized European Council	- Strong and strategic position in EU architecture - Main, authorized and visible representatives of national public opinion - Potential linking between EU-level and national debates	- Non-public proceedings, traditionally - Strong focus on national identities - Strong hierarchical and intergovernmental orientation, not very accessible for societal interests
Permanent Constitutional Assembly	- Strict division of constituent power from constituted powers, and clear focus on competences - Direct linking with citizen preferences	- Strong institutionalization and election basis may limit, and bias, citizen engagement - Is permanency needed?
Popular Conference	- Building upon, and fostering, spontaneous political engagement - Open to an infinite range of (transnational) political identities	- Dependent on the will and enthusiasm of societal actors and citizens - No guaranteed leverage over existing institutions

the democratic debate in the EU is currently stifled on some of the most fundamental questions. Since the entry into force of the Treaty of Lisbon in 2009, the EU has been extremely reluctant to engage in any full-fledged revision of its constitutional structure (see Chapter 2 in this volume). Yet, fundamental questions about its functioning and democratic character do not go away, and treaty change becomes unavoidable as the prospect of new rounds of enlargement becomes more concrete. Even if no fully new institutions are established for the purpose of democratizing and politicizing the debate on the EU's identity, it is important to think of ways to move from the EU's traditionally technocratic understanding of democracy towards a more open and politicized approach.

References

Alemanno, A. and Nicolaïdis, K. (2021). Citizen Power Europe: The Making of a European Citizens' Assembly. *Revue Européenne du Droit*, 2(3): 7–15.

Bartolini, S. (2006). *Should the Union Be 'Politicised'? Prospects and Risks.* Notre Europe, Policy Paper 19. https://institutdelors.eu/content/uploads/2025/04/policypaper19-en-1.pdf. Accessed 22 July 2025.

Bickerton, C., Brack, N., Coman, R., and Crespy, A. (2022). Conflicts of Sovereignty In Contemporary Europe: A Framework of Analysis. *Comparative European Politics*, 20(3): 257–274.

Bouza Garcia, L. (2017). The 'New Narrative Project' and the Politicization of the EU. *Journal of Contemporary European Studies*, 25(3): 340–353.

Bouza Garcia, L. and Oleart, A. (2018). From the 2005 Constitution's 'Permissive Consensus' to TTIP's 'Empowering Dissensus': The EU as a Playing Field For Spanish Civil Society. *Journal of Contemporary European Research*, 14(2): 87–104.

Crum, B. (2003). Legislative–Executive Relations in the EU. *Journal of Common Market Studies*, 41(3): 375–395.

Crum, B. (2012). *Learning from the EU Constitutional Treaty*. London, Routledge.

Crum, B. (2013). Saving the Euro at the Cost of Democracy? *Journal of Common Market Studies*, 51(4): 614–630.

Crum, B. (2023). Models of EU Constitutional Reform: What do we Learn from the Conference on the Future of Europe? *Global Constitutionalism*, 13(2): 392–410.

Crum, B. and Oleart, A. (eds) (2023a). *Populist Parties and Democratic Resilience: A Cross-National Analysis of Populist Parties' Impact on Democratic Pluralism in Europe*. London, Routledge.

Crum, B. and Oleart, A. (2023b). Information or Accountability? A Research Agenda on European Commissioners in National Parliaments. *Journal of Common Market Studies*, 61(3): 853–864.

De Vries, C. E. (2018). *Euroscepticism and the Future of European Integration*. Oxford, Oxford University Press.

De Wilde, P. and Lord, C. (2016). Assessing Actually-Existing Trajectories of EU Politicization. *West European Politics*, 39(1): 145–163.

Easton, D. (1953). *The Political System: An Inquiry into the State of Political Science*. New York, Alfred A. Knopf.

Gora, A. and de Wilde, P. (2022). The Essence of Democratic Backsliding in the European Union: Deliberation and Rule of Law. *Journal of European Public Policy*, 29(3): 342–362.

Grimm, D. (2015). Democratic Costs of Constitutionalisation. *European Law Journal*, 21(4): 460–473.

Haapala, T. and Oleart, A. (eds) (2022). *Tracing the Politicization of the EU: The Future of Europe Debates Before and After the 2019 Elections*. London, Palgrave.
Hooghe, L. and Marks, G. (2009). A Postfunctionalist Theory of European Integration: From Permissive Consensus to Constraining Dissensus. *British Journal of Political Science*, 39(1): 1–23.
Jachtenfuchs, M., Diez, T., and Jung, S. (1998). Which Europe? Conflicting models of a Legitimate European Political Order. *European Journal of International Relations*, 4(4): 409–445.
Kauppi, N. (2018). *Toward a reflexive political sociology of the European Union: Fields, intellectuals and politicians*. Cham, Palgrave Macmillan.
Kinski, L. and Crum, B. (2020). Transnational Representation in EU National Parliaments: Concept, Case Study, Research Agenda. *Political Studies*, 68(2): 370–388.
Koopmans, R. and Erbe, J. (2004). Towards a European Public Sphere? Vertical and Horizontal Dimensions of Europeanized Political Communication. *Innovation: The European Journal of Social Science Research*, 17(2): 97–118.
Koopmans, R. and Statham, P. (eds) (2010). *The Making of a European Public Sphere: Media Discourse and Political Contention*. Cambridge, Cambridge University Press.
Lindberg, L. N. and Scheingold, S. A. (1970). *Europe's Would-Be Polity: Patterns of Change in the European Community*. Englewood Cliffs NJ, Prentice-Hall.
Mair, P. (2007). Political Opposition and the European Union. *Government and Opposition*, 42(1): 1–17.
Mair, P. (2013). *Ruling the Void: The Hollowing of Western Democracy*. London, Verso Books.
McNamara, K. (2019). When the Banal Becomes Political: The European Union in the Age of Populism. *Polity*, 51(4): 678–688.
Merlo, S. (2023). Self-fulfilling Crises in the Eurozone and the Institutional Preconditions Of Republican Sovereignty. *Review of Social Economy*, 81(1): 130–153.
Oleart, A. (2021). *Framing TTIP in the European Public Spheres: Towards an Empowering Dissensus for EU Integration*. Basingstoke, Palgrave Macmillan.
Oleart, A. (2023a). *Democracy Without Politics in EU Citizen Participation: From European Demoi to Decolonial Multitude*. Basingstoke, Palgrave Macmillan.
Oleart, A. (2023b). The Political Construction of the 'Citizen Turn' in the EU: Disintermediation and Depoliticization in the Conference on the Future of Europe. *Journal of Contemporary European Studies*: 1–15. DOI: https://doi.org/10.1080/14782804.2023.2177837.
Oleart, A. and Theuns, T. (2023). 'Democracy without Politics' in the European Commission's Response to Democratic Backsliding: From Technocratic Legalism to Democratic Pluralism. *Journal of Common Market Studies*, 61(4): 882–899.
Patberg, M. (2020). *Constituent Power in the European Union*. Oxford, Oxford University Press.
Rauh, C. and De Wilde, P. (2018). The Opposition Deficit in EU Accountability: Evidence from Over 20 Years of Plenary Debate in Four Member States. *European Journal of Political Research*, 57(1): 194–216.
Risse, T. (2010). *A Community of Europeans? Transnational Identities and Public Spheres?* Ithaca, Cornell University Press.
Rone, J. (2020). *Contesting Austerity and Free Trade in the EU: Protest Diffusion in Complex Media and Political Arenas*. London, Routledge.
Sachseder, J., Stachowitsch, S., and Binder, C. (2022). Gender, Race, and Crisis-Driven Institutional Growth: Discourses of 'Migration Crisis' and the Expansion of Frontex. *Journal of Ethnic and Migration Studies*, 48(19): 4670–4693.
Savage, D. and Weale, A. (2009). Political Representation and the Normative Logic of Two-Level Games. *European Political Science Review*, 1(1): 63–81.
Schmidt, V. A. (2006). *Democracy in Europe: The EU and National Polities*. Oxford, Oxford University Press.
Schütze, R. (2015). EU Competences: Existence and Exercise. In Chalmers, D. and Arnull, A. (eds). *The Oxford Handbook of European Union Law*. Oxford, Oxford University Press: 75–102.
Sieyès, E. (1982) [1789]. *Qu'est-ce que le tiers État?* Paris, Presses Universitaires de France.

Theuns, T. (2021). Pluralist Democracy and Non-Ideal Democratic Legitimacy: Against Functional and Global Solutions to Boundary Problem in Democratic Theory. *Democratic Theory*, 8(1): 23–49.

Trenz, H.-J. and Eder, K. (2004). The Democratizing Dynamics of a European Public Sphere: Towards a Theory of Democratic Functionalism. *European Journal of Social Theory*, 7(1): 5–25.

Weiler, J. (1996). European Neo-Constitutionalism: in Search of Foundations for the European Constitutional Order. *Political Studies*, 44(3): 517–533.

Wessels, W., Rozenberg, O., Van Den Berge, M., Hefftler, C., Kreilinger, V., and Ventura, L. (2013) *Democratic Control in the Member States of the European Council and the Euro zone summits.* PE 474.392. Brussels, European Parliament, Directorate-General for Internal Policies.

Wolthuis, B., Crum, B., Oleart, A., and Overeem, P. (2025). Democracy and Pluralism After European Integration: Incorporating the Contested Character of the EU. *Critical Review of International Social and Political Philosophy*, 28(6): 1136–1160.

Zürn, M., Binder, M., and Ecker-Ehrhardt, M. (2012). International Authority and its Politicization. *International Theory*, 4(1): 69–106.

9

Who is Misinformed About the EU?

Sylvia Kritzinger, Julia Partheymüller, Valentin Voith, and Carolina Plescia

9.1 Introduction

With the increasing politicization of the European Union (EU), public opinion about the EU has become less and less quiescent (Hooghe and Marks 2009; Hutter, Grande, and Kriesi 2016). Attacks on the legitimacy of the EU are first and foremost attacks on a supranational institution, about which many citizens lack knowledge (Rapeli 2014). In particular, the events surrounding Brexit have demonstrated that the complexity of the power-sharing arrangement at the EU level can accidentally be misperceived or even intentionally instrumentalized to frame EU politics in terms of unjust agendas pursued by unaccountable elites. To counteract the widespread prevalence of Eurosceptic attitudes, scholars have linked these problems to citizens' limited knowledge of the EU and called for efforts to activate the participation of ordinary citizens in EU policy processes (Habermas 2012). Indeed, knowledge is the pre-condition *sine qua non* in order to be able to fairly evaluate EU institutions and eventually appreciate the democratic nature of elected institutions. Previous findings suggest, however, that the 'active misinformed' (Hochschild and Einstein 2015) might pose an even bigger challenge to European democracy than the uninformed and apathetic citizens. Specifically, holding inaccurate information about the EU with a high degree of confidence may not only lead to a wrong evaluation of the European institutions, its actors, and the integration process per se, but may also fuel the 'blame portrayal' of the EU that national political stakeholders often resort to. Indeed, recent research has demonstrated that the misinformed, who lack understanding of the EU but are nevertheless firmly convinced they 'know it all', are most likely to hold a preference for leaving the EU and to engage in Eurosceptic contestation, while uninformed citizens, lacking such confidence, tend to remain indifferent about the EU and lack engagement (Partheymüller et al. 2022). While making EU processes more democratic seems worthwhile in itself, 'the promise of democracy' that this will lead to an informed citizenry may find its limits in citizens' motivations to process the available information.

With this in mind, this chapter aims to characterize *the misinformed* by describing their social and political profile as well as their information

Sylvia Kritzinger, Julia Partheymüller, Valentin Voith, and Carolina Plescia, *Who is Misinformed About the EU?*
In: *The Promise of EU Democracy*. Edited by: Jan Wouters, Julie Smith, Kolja Raube, and Ben Crum,
Oxford University Press. © Sylvia Kritzinger, Julia Partheymüller, Valentin Voith, and Carolina Plescia 2026.
DOI: 10.1093/9780191996191.003.0011

environment. For this purpose, we rely on survey data collected in eight EU Member States (Austria, Denmark, France, Germany, Hungary, Italy, Poland, and Spain) gathered in the context of the 2019 European Parliamentary election—an election which saw a rise in turnout but also a rise in voting for Eurosceptic parties. The survey included a newly designed item battery (including new questions) capturing two dimensions of EU knowledge—accuracy and confidence—which facilitates distinguishing the uninformed and misinformed from each other. The survey also included measures of socio-demographics, political predispositions, patterns of media use, and characteristics of political discussions, and thus allows examining the links of these factors with the propensity of being misinformed.

By investigating those links, the chapter aims to contribute to the existing literature on political knowledge as well as to the public debates on democratic governance in the EU. Our findings show that older and less educated citizens in particular tend to be misinformed. Most importantly, being misinformed appears to be particularly prevalent among highly politically interested citizens with extreme ideological positions (in particular, far-right positions), hinting at ideologically driven 'motivated reasoning' as one of the main underlying mechanisms. Interestingly, and to some extent unexpectedly, the misinformed do not appear to be living in isolated 'filter bubbles' or 'echo chambers', not 'hearing the other side', but instead use both traditional and new media fairly often and experience frequent disagreement in personal discussions. These findings give some clear indications about which groups of citizens are most likely to become misinformed about the EU, but also which mechanisms may be at work in the EU information processing of the misinformed. While recognizing that being misinformed may be difficult to fight off, these results can thus be useful to inform the design of policies and possible interventions to counteract the potentially detrimental effects of being misinformed. In fact, even if the promise of pluralistic democracies is that everybody has the right to actively participate in decision-making, there is a danger that misinformed but active citizens may contribute substantially to societal polarization, reducing consensus-seeking and imposing their will over less confident but better-informed citizens.

9.2 Previous research and hypotheses

9.2.1 What does it mean to be misinformed?

Previous research has distinguished between two dimensions of knowledge—accuracy and confidence (Kuklinski et al. 1998; 2000). Accuracy refers to the degree to which the mentally stored pieces of information are factually correct. Confidence refers to the subjective feeling that the stored information is correct. Although previous research has demonstrated that accuracy and confidence tend

Table 9.1 Types of informedness

	Low confidence	High confidence
Low accuracy	Uninformed	Misinformed
High accuracy	Partially informed	Well-informed

to correlate mildly positively in survey populations (Lee and Matsuo 2018), the two dimensions can be separated fairly well, not only analytically but also empirically.

Based on the two dimensions of knowledge, four types of citizens can be distinguished: the uninformed; the well-informed; the partially informed; and the misinformed (see Table 9.1). The latter group can be characterized as low on factual accuracy, but high in confidence. Previous research has sketched three underlying cognitive mechanisms of how people become misinformed (Kuklinski et al. 2000: 794–795): (1) drawing inferences based on limited information, (2) avoiding cognitive dissonance, and (3) a tendency to treat inferences as 'hard data' upon recall, leading people to become overconfident, i.e. overrating the accuracy of their own beliefs.

9.2.2 Who is misinformed about the EU?

While existing research has studied the accuracy dimension of EU knowledge (e.g. Rapeli 2014; Karp et al. 2003), research focusing specifically on those who are misinformed about the EU is lacking so far. For this reason, we rely upon the general literature on political knowledge and being misinformed to derive some testable hypotheses about the social and political profile as well as the information environment of those who are misinformed about the EU. This allows us to evaluate whether *being misinformed about the EU* is rooted in the same factors as *being misinformed in other domains of knowledge*, leading to the 'usual suspects', or whether the patterns diverge from what we already know based on the literature.

Starting with socio-demographic characteristics, we focus on age, gender, and education. Turning first to age, the scholarly literature explicitly addressing the association between age and being misinformed is relatively sparse. Nevertheless, two studies using similar models of political knowledge (Ortoleva and Snowberg 2015; Li and Wagner 2020) find a clear positive correlation between age and overconfidence.[1] Based on an argument put forward by Ortoleva and Snowberg

[1] The misinformed can be said to be 'overconfident' in the sense that their level of confidence exceeds their level of accuracy. We therefore use the two terms interchangeably.

(2015: 505) and assuming that overconfidence emerges from the false extrapolation of personal experience on factual reality, one could argue that the elderly are more inclined to overconfidence because they have unarguably collected the most experience and, thus, tend to think that, after all those years, they 'know how the world works'. Considering that, the elderly appear to be particularly prone to overconfidence, as they are highly confident with regards to their knowledge due to their long-standing experience, which is precisely what predisposes them to drawing wrong conclusions by substituting factual knowledge with personal experience.

Second, a persistent gap between men and women in levels of confidence in their abilities and knowledge can be regarded as a well-documented phenomenon within social science research. While men show higher degrees of self-esteem and tend to overestimate their abilities, women display lower levels of self-esteem and tend to underestimate their abilities (Kling et al. 1999; Soll and Klayman 2004; Niederle and Vesterlund 2011). Even when dealing with political knowledge, a domain where (on average) men are found to perform 'better' than women (e.g. Jerit and Barabas 2017), we still expect a pattern of systematic overconfidence among men. Here, it seems important to stress that the same determinant that is positively associated with being misinformed can also be positively associated with being well-informed, which, given the empirical evidence, is likely to be the case for male gender. Accordingly, the assumed outcome that men are indeed more often well-informed about the EU (see Fraile 2014) does not contradict our prediction that, compared to women, men's overall higher levels of confidence also more frequently translate into overconfidence, i.e., being convinced that one is right when one is objectively wrong.

Third, since two of the core tasks of education are to provide people with accurate knowledge and to equip them with critical thinking skills that make them less susceptible to being misinformed, we almost naturally expect education to decrease the likelihood of being misinformed. Elaborating on this notion in more detail, the advantage of higher levels of formal education generally manifests itself in two main aspects: first, the more formal years of schooling, the more sophisticated knowledge one is confronted with; second, there is a vast amount of empirical support indicating that highly educated individuals are better at extracting and retaining relevant information from news exposure (Price and Zaller 1993; Jerit et al. 2006). Additionally, taking into account the specificity of examining political knowledge *about the EU*, we note that an accurate understanding of the functioning of the EU, often being perceived as an abstract and remote institutional framework, demands high levels of *cognitive mobilization* (Inglehart 1970), which again privileges the higher educated. Indeed, Lee and Matsuo (2018) show that higher levels of education do not correlate with greater confidence, but *only* with accuracy, suggesting that the highly educated are indeed less frequently misinformed. From this research, we can derive the following hypothesis:

Hypothesis 1: Older citizens, men and less educated citizens are more likely to be misinformed than younger citizens, women, and highly educated citizens.

Further hypotheses can be deducted from the theory of motivated reasoning. Lodge and Taber (2013) suggest that there are two forms of motivations underlying information-gathering and processing. Specifically, we can distinguish between accuracy goals and directional goals. While citizens following accuracy motivations are keen to hold accurate beliefs, ideologically extreme voters often are more interested in seeking out attitudinally congruent information reaffirming their prior beliefs. Previous research has shown that general interest in politics typically correlates with higher levels of accuracy (e.g. Delli Carpini and Keeter 1996; Rapeli 2014; Lee and Matsuo 2018), whereas ideologically motivated reasoning—at both ends of the left–right political spectrum—tends to correlate with more inaccurate beliefs and more biased perceptions (Kraft et al. 2015; Harper and Baguley 2019). Therefore, the highly politically involved motivated reasoners at the ideological extremes might be the most misinformed of all, applying 'hot cognition' rather than 'cool consideration' when processing political information (Redlawsk 2002). Therefore, we expect:

Hypothesis 2: Ideological extremity in conjunction with strong political interest leads to citizens becoming misinformed.

Another aspect that may affect why some citizens are misinformed is the information environment. In particular, social media have been considered as a source responsible for the rapid spread of false and unsubstantiated claims (Lazer et al. 2018; Vosoughi et al. 2018). In contrast, the frequent use of traditional news media has often been shown to be conducive to learning and knowledge gains (Norris and Holtz-Bach 2001). Thus, we expect:

Hypothesis 3: Frequent users of traditional mass media are less likely to be misinformed than frequent users of social media.

Finally, we also explore the role of interpersonal discussions. Some have argued that interpersonal discussions provide a deliberative space, where pluralism of opinions ('hearing the other side') can lead to better-formed opinions (Mutz 2006). Exposure to heterogeneous viewpoints seems to have a positive effect on political knowledge, since it facilitates learning processes about politics (McLeod et al. 1999; Scheufele 2013). In particular, the existing literature has highlighted that exposure to disagreement in interpersonal discussions produces greater cognitive activity (Levine and Russo 1995) since it forces individuals to learn about alternative perspectives and reflect upon what they already know, thereby enhancing political knowledge and understanding (McPhee 1963). In contrast, those insulated from the opinions of others are said to be particularly prone to holding distorted and false beliefs. Therefore, our final hypothesis reads as follows:

Hypothesis 4: The less disagreement citizens experience in interpersonal political discussions, the more likely it is that they will be misinformed.

9.3 Data and methods

To examine these hypotheses, we use the pre-election survey gathered by the RECONNECT and AUTNES project[2] in the context of the 2019 European Parliamentary election (Plescia et al. 2020; Aichholzer et al. 2020). Together the surveys cover eight EU Member States: Austria, Germany, Denmark, France, Italy, Spain, Hungary, and Poland. The selection of countries includes Member States from different regions within the EU (East, West, North, South), among them the five largest nations by population. In each country, the participants were recruited from online access panels based on nationally representative quotas for the voting age population (aged older than sixteen years for Austria, or eighteen years for the other countries), with a sample size of 1,500 participants for the RECONNECT surveys and a sample size of 3,000 in the case of the AUTNES survey. To account for smaller deviations in the marginal distributions, post-stratification weights are included in all data sets that allow matching of the socio-demographic characteristics (gender, age, education, region) of the sample with population targets. To calculate country-averages using the pooled sample, these weights were combined with a country weight, giving each country the same weight, irrespective of sample size.

The survey included questions measuring the two dimensions of EU knowledge—accuracy and confidence. To measure accuracy, the module included five single-choice questions, with four response options each, capturing factual knowledge about the EU. The questions included one question about the European Parliament, one about the Council of the European Union, one about the European Commission, one about the President of the European Commission, and one about the EU budget (for the full question wording, see Appendix 9.1). Respondents were instructed to give their 'best guess' if they were uncertain about the correct answer, to avoid any bias stemming from the unequal propensities to opt for a 'don't know' response (Fraile 2014).

[2] RECONNECT was a four-year multidisciplinary Horizon Europe research project on 'Reconciling Europe with its Citizens through Democracy and the Rule of Law', aimed at understanding and providing solutions to the recent challenges faced by the European Union (EU). AUTNES stands for 'Austrian National Election Study'—more information can be found at www.autnes.at.

Table 9.2 Share of correct answers and average levels of confidence

Question	Correct answers (%)	Confidence (mean(sd))
Members of EP elected by citizens	69.1	5.6 (3.5)
EC President approved by EP majority vote	52.4	4.6 (3.0)
Administration not the largest item in the EU budget	40.5	5.0 (3.1)
National ministers represented in the Council of the EU	32.3	4.4 (3.0)
EC initiates new laws	29.2	4.4 (2.9)

Note: Pooled data for Austria, Denmark, France, Germany, Hungary, Italy, Poland, and Spain (N = 16.523, weighted). For the full question wording, see Appendix 9.1.

To capture uncertainty instead, each of those single-choice questions was followed by a question to measure confidence. For this purpose, respondents were asked to rate how sure they were that their answer was correct on an eleven-point scale, ranging from zero to ten. Table 9.2 provides an overview of the share of correct answers and average levels of confidence for each of the items.

Scaling techniques were applied to calculate summary measures of accuracy and confidence based on these items. For the measure of accuracy, we first recoded the answers to dummy variables, capturing whether the answer given was correct (1) or incorrect (0). Then, using a two-parameter logistic IRT model, a latent score of overall accuracy was calculated. Next, to construct a summary measure of confidence, we examined the correlation structure among the items capturing the subjective level of certainty. Factor analysis revealed that these items loaded strongly on one dimension, and we predicted factor scores to create a measure of confidence. Both the scores from the IRT model and those from the factor analysis have by design a mean of zero and the values of the latent scales should be interpreted in relative terms, reflecting being more or less accurate or confident, rather than absolute terms (see also Partheymüller et al. 2022).

Based on these latent scales, we classify respondents as 'misinformed' when their accuracy score was below the mean (<0), but their level of confidence was equal or above average (>=0).[3] We use this dummy variable (1 = misinformed, 0 = not misinformed) as the dependent variable in our analysis. It should be noted that the reference category is somewhat heterogeneous in the sense that it includes well-informed, uninformed, as well as partially informed citizens, but this

[3] We are referring to the grand mean of the pooled sample. As with the underlying latent scales, also the dichotomized indicator should only be interpreted in a relative sense as by construction about a quarter of the respondents will be classified as rather misinformed by using the mean as a cut-off value.

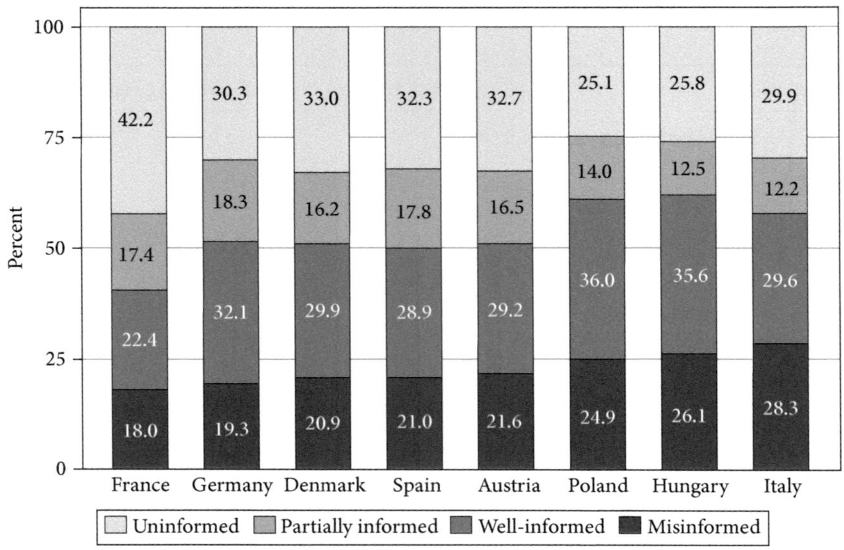

Figure 9.1 Share of misinformed citizens by country

coding has the advantage that it allows focusing on the group of the misinformed. In Figure 9.1, the darker portion of bars shows the share of misinformed voters by country in comparison to the other categories that result from applying these coding rules. The highest proportion of misinformed citizens can be found in Italy, Hungary, and Poland, with about one quarter of their citizens being misinformed. In the remaining countries, about one fifth are misinformed. Overall, though, in all countries the share of misinformed citizens is substantial and almost approaches the share of the well-informed, that typically hovers around 30 per cent across countries.

The independent variables include socio-demographic variables, political predispositions, news consumption and interpersonal political discussions. With respect to socio-demographic variables, we distinguish between five age groups (16–29, 30–39, 40–49, 50–59, 60+ years), two genders (male, female), and three levels of education (low, medium, high). Political predispositions include political interest and left–right self-placement. These variables were recoded as follows for ease of interpretation and to reduce the complexity of the analysis: political interest was measured on a four-point scale but recoded to a dummy variable (very/fairly low, fairly/very high. Left–right self-placement was measured on an eleven-point scale and recoded to a five-point scale ranging from 'far left' to 'far right', always combining two adjacent scale points, except for the category 'centre'. News consumption was measured by the weekly usage of traditional news sources (newspapers, television news) and news on social media. We combine newspapers and television, focusing on the medium most frequently used by the respondent.

We distinguish between citizens using these media 'ever', 'sometimes', or on a 'daily' basis. Finally, we also consider political conversations about the EU with a) family, b) friends, and c) co-workers. We created variables with three categories, setting apart respondents who (1) never discuss the EU, those who (2) have some EU discussions and never or only sometimes encounter disagreement in these discussions, and those who (3) have some EU discussions and often experience disagreement.

The analysis proceeds in two steps. First, we analyse the bivariate relationships between the independent variables and being misinformed using simple bar plots, alongside confidence intervals. This helps us to characterize the social and political profile of the misinformed as well as their information environment, without being conditional on other factors. It also allows for a preliminary assessment of our hypotheses. As mutual confounding of the various factors is likely, we next perform a logistic regression, including all of the independent variables simultaneously, including an interaction between left–right ideology and political interest, to test for the presence of ideologically motivated reasoning. In the regression model, we also include country-fixed effects to capture country differences in levels of being misinformed.

9.4 Bivariate analyses

Figure 9.2 shows the share of the misinformed for various socio-demographic groups. Regarding age, we see that the share of the misinformed is highest among the oldest age group (sixty-plus years), while the share of misinformed among younger age groups is noticeably lower. For instance, the gap between the youngest and oldest age group amounts to six percentage points. Among the younger age

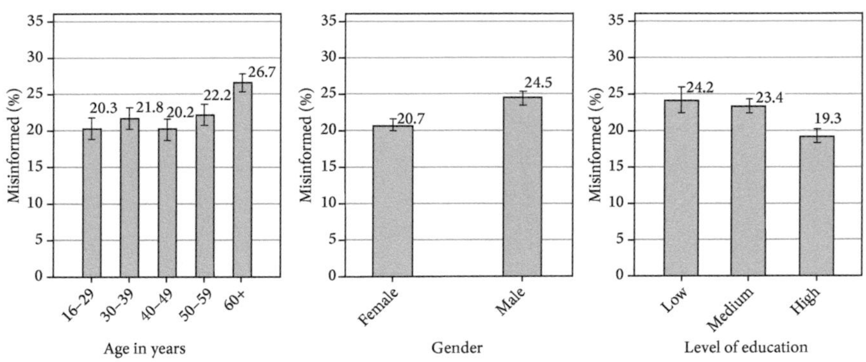

Figure 9.2 Age, gender, and education

Note: The Chi-Square Test yields significant results for the associations with age ($\chi^2(1) = 33.1$, p = .000, V = .06), gender ($\chi^2(4) = 62.4$, p = .000, V = .04) and education ($\chi^2(2) = 36.7$, p = .000, V = .05).

groups, there seem to be only rather minor differences or some random fluctuations. Although the pattern is overall in line with our expectations, the seemingly non-gradual nature of the observed pattern could point to the possible presence of a cohort effect in addition to or instead of the suspected life cycle effect.

Turning to gender, we notice that men seem to be only slightly more often misinformed than women. The proportion of men being misinformed is about four percentage points higher than that for women. Thus, there is overall only a small difference, which could possibly be related to differences in other background factors. For example, men and women are known to differ significantly with regard to political predispositions, such as political interest (Verba, Burns, and Schlozman 1997; Fraile and Sanchez-Vitores 2020) and ideological positions (Inglehart and Norris 2000). Therefore, we are not able to make a clear judgment whether gender yields any decisive explanatory power for being misinformed regarding the EU.

Next, we see that the highly educated are indeed less often misinformed than those with low and medium levels of formal education. Since the proportion of misinformed people is almost equally high among the latter two groups, it seems that the beneficial effect of education is limited to those having received at least some tertiary education. This corroborates the notion that an adequate understanding of the EU demands high levels of cognitive mobilization (Inglehart 1970). Overall, however, the differences across educational groups should not be overstated; as they amount to only five percentage points, they suggest that even the higher educated are by no means 'immune' from being misinformed.

For political interest, we note a substantive gap of nine percentage points in the proportion of being misinformed between those with high interest and those with low interest in politics (Figure 9.3). The politically interested are thus more likely to be misinformed than those who are politically uninterested. To give an accurate picture, we note that the politically interested are also more frequently well-informed, which points to a positive correlation between political interest

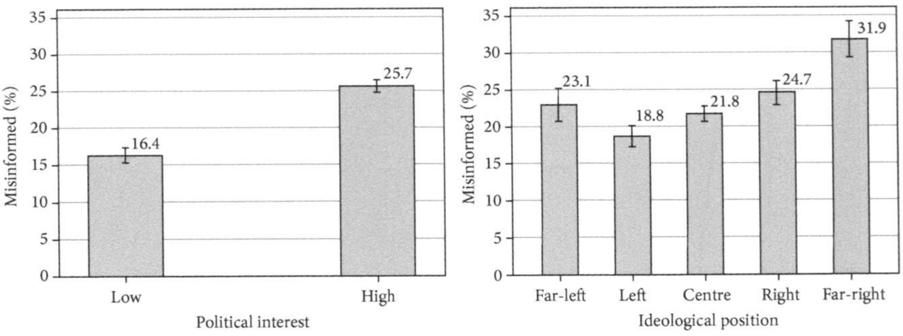

Figure 9.3 Political interest and ideological position

Note: The Chi-Square Test yields significant results for the associations with political interest ($\chi^2(1) = 182.2, p = .000, V = .11$) and ideology ($\chi^2(2) = 101.6, p = .000, V = .08$).

and confidence in one's perceived knowledge regardless of its accuracy, whereas the uninformed and partially informed usually are characterized by low interest. Overall, political interest thus seems to contribute to confidence in accurate knowledge, but also overconfidence and being misinformed.

Corroborating the importance of motivated reasoning, grouping individuals according to their ideological stance further reveals that the far-right section of the population displays by far the highest proportion of individuals who are misinformed about the EU. Contrary to our predictions, we do not find the same pattern for people with far-left attitudes, who are hardly more frequently misinformed than those in the ideological centre. Apart from the general tendency towards overconfidence among people with ideological extreme positions (Ortoleva and Snowberg 2015), there seem to be other crucial factors in play for far-right individuals. Since far-right stances usually go hand in hand with Euroscepticism (e.g. Szöcsik and Polyakova 2019), people holding such far-right attitudes might be inclined to project their strong rejection of the EU onto its institutional structure, of which they consequently have a certain, rather negative, idea that frequently does not correspond to reality. In the case of ideologically far-left individuals, it might be precisely this consistent position on the EU that is lacking, since their assessment of the EU appears to be more mixed (Lubbers and Scheepers 2007). On the one hand, the EU is criticized as a neoliberal free trade alliance or even as an imperialistic federation of states; on the other hand, it is seen as an opportunity to overcome petty nationalisms and to implement high social standards on a supranational level (Beaudonnet and Gomez 2017). While the far right has been quite successful in capitalizing on Eurosceptic positions, far-left parties have so far been more divided on how to position themselves on European issues (Wagner 2021).

Turning to the information environment (Figure 9.4), one immediately notices the remarkable similarity between the use of traditional and new media in terms of their relationship with being misinformed. Notwithstanding our hypothesis that

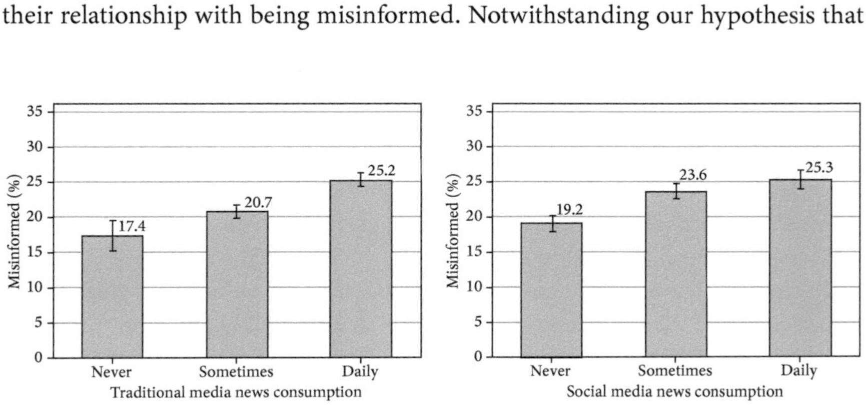

Figure 9.4 Use of traditional and social media

Note: The Chi-Square Test yields significant results for the associations with the consumption of traditional news media ($\chi^2(2) = 66.7$, p = .000, V = .06) and social media ($\chi^2(2) = 59.0$, p = .000, V = .06).

heavy users of social media as a news source are more likely to be misinformed than those consuming newspapers or television, both media types show the same pattern of a gradual increase in their relative frequency of misinformed individuals with higher levels of consumption, while the proportions themselves are also of almost equal size. Thus, contrary to the common notion in public debate, social media news consumption is not per se more strongly associated with being misinformed than traditional media news consumption, which reflects the inconclusive state of the literature on the role of echo chambers, filter bubbles, and the like as being the alleged driving forces of polarization and misinformation (compare for example Dylko 2016 with Dubois and Blank 2018). However, this comparison of traditional and social media news consumption should not convey the impression that we deal with two distinct communities who exclusively consume only one type of news media. Although 31.4 per cent of people who read newspapers and/or watch TV news on a daily basis never consume news on social media, only 3.6 per cent of those who use social media as a news source never consume traditional news outlets. Thus, rather than being an alternative, it seems that social media outlets function as a complement for most people's news media diet.

This finding of a positive correlation between general media news consumption and being misinformed may seem odd at first, but several explanations can be given.[4] First, the two-dimensional model of political knowledge covers not only the accuracy of, but also confidence in, one's knowledge. Since content on the EU is rather scarce in traditional news media, due to its abstractness (De Vreese 2001; Peter et al. 2003) and so-called 'soft news' formats are on the rise (Curran et al. 2009; 2010), heavy consumers of news programmes might be given the illusion of being well-informed, i.e., they develop confidence in their ability to answer questions on politics, even though their factual knowledge on the actual functioning of the EU remains limited. Second, our analysis does not distinguish between high-quality and low-quality news outlets. As low-quality news outlets might be more prevalent in the media landscape, it is possible that a part of the differences between light and heavy news consumers can be attributed to misinformation filter bubbles in social media and/or inaccurate information in tabloid newspapers. Finally, however, this pattern is in line with our previous findings on political interest, underlying once again that being misinformed is not the result of a lack of interest or information exposure, but rather related to the motivations underlying processing the available information.

In the last step of our descriptive analysis, we examine whether citizens who experience less disagreement in discussions about the EU are more frequently

[4] In accordance with our two-dimensional model of informedness covering four categories, the positive association between news consumption and being misinformed does not imply a negative one between news consumption and being well-informed. In fact, as our data show, heavy news consumers are also more frequently well-informed about the EU.

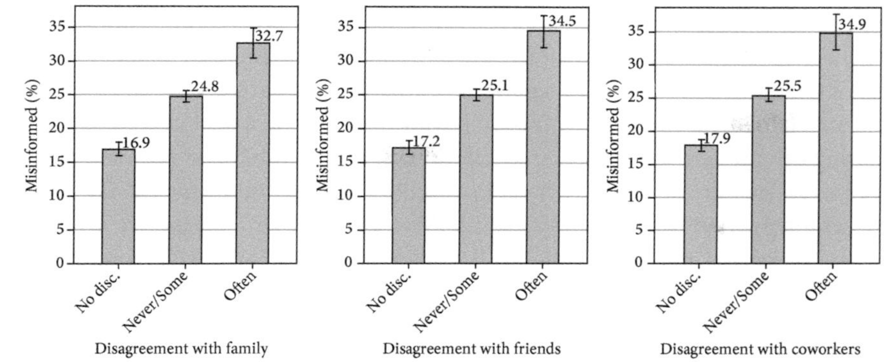

Figure 9.5 Political discussions and disagreement with family, friends, and co-workers

Note: The Chi-Square Test yields significant results for the associations with the level of disagreement with family ($\chi^2(2) = 241.2$, p = .000, V = .12), friends ($\chi^2(2) = 266.3$, p = .000, V = .13), and coworkers ($\chi^2(2) = 251.7$, p = .000, V = .12).

The first bar in each plot gives the proportion of the misinformed given that no discussion about the EU ('No disc.') takes place with the respective social environment, while the second and third bar display the frequency of disagreement ('Never/Some', 'Often') in discussions of this kind.

misinformed. Figure 9.5 distinguishes between discussions with family, friends, and co-workers. Since engaging in political discussions requires a certain level of confidence in one's knowledge and abilities, it is hardly surprising that those who do not discuss EU issues are less frequently misinformed but rather, as our data show, *uninformed*, meaning that, contrary to the misinformed, they are aware of their lack of knowledge. Hence, the information that is actually relevant for the hypothesis is to be found between those two groups that do not differ in their fundamental willingness to discuss EU issues, but in their self-perceived disagreement *within* these discussions. Here, we find more or less the same pattern for each of the possible interlocutors, indicating no substantive difference between strong (e.g. family) and weak (e.g. co-workers) tie relationships. Between those who never or only occasionally experience disagreement when discussing the EU and those indicating that they often experience disagreement in this context, there is a substantive gap of eight to nine percentage points. Thus, based on this preliminary assessment, it seems that the information environment of the misinformed is actually characterized by frequent disagreement, which contradicts the notion that the misinformed are living insulated from 'hearing the other side'.

There are several partly related explanations for this unexpected finding with various implications. Competing with the deliberative model (Mutz 2006) that predicts that people become more moderate in their opinions when confronted with dissimilar opinions (Sniderman 1981; Mutz 2002), the 'biased processing model' (Wojcieszak 2010), which can be understood as a concrete manifestation of motivated reasoning, predicts the exact opposite. Since misinformed individuals already hold a biased view of reality that they deem to be accurate, confronting them with contradicting and conflicting information will not make them question their own beliefs but instead even runs the risk of exacerbating their being misinformed (Prasad et al. 2009). This is due to the tendency of people already holding strong beliefs, such as misinformed individuals, to devote all their reasoning capacities to defending their prior views (Kunda 1990; Taber and Lodge 2006) instead of genuinely trying to 'hear the other side'. This leads to a strong adherence to factually wrong beliefs (Zollo et al. 2017), especially when they are congruent with one's prior ideological worldview (Lewandowsky et al. 2012). Another important aspect may be linked to the fact that there is only one way of being accurately informed, but multiple different ways of being misinformed. Therefore, if two people engage in a discussion on the basis of commonly shared knowledge, some reasons for disagreement almost naturally disappear. If there is, however, no commonly shared knowledge, there is a much higher potential for disagreement, which can occur not only between well-informed and misinformed individuals but also between two (differently) misinformed individuals. Our bivariate findings point in the direction that a lack of accurate knowledge about the EU could be a reason for disagreement in political discussions.

9.5 Multivariate analyses

After having examined the relevant bivariate associations, we now turn to the results of the multivariate logistic regression to assess their robustness. The left-hand graph in Figure 9.6 displays the average marginal effects of the independent variables on the probability of being misinformed. Regarding the social profile of the misinformed, we find that Hypothesis 1 is partially confirmed, even when controlling for other factors. We find, for instance, that there is a statistically significant age effect, showing that those over sixty years old are most at risk of being misinformed about the EU. Also, in line with expectations, having a high level of formal education significantly reduces the risk of being misinformed about the EU. Yet, no effect for gender can be detected, when controlling for other factors. Overall, most of our previous observations and remarks on socio-demographic factors are also reflected in the results from the multivariate analysis, although the picture is now somewhat more nuanced.

To test our second hypothesis, we included an interaction term between political interest and ideology in the model. The graph on the right of Figure 9.6 displays the average predictive margins with 95 per cent confidence intervals. We see that across the ideological spectrum the predicted probability of being misinformed tends to be higher for those high on political interest, although for most

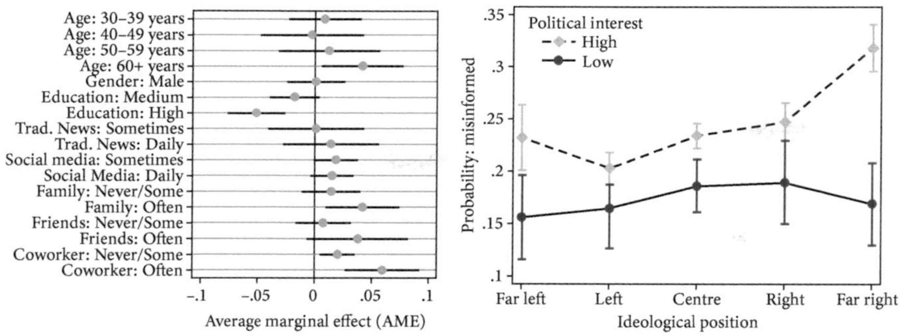

Figure 9.6 Average marginal effects and interaction plot

Note: Estimates based on logistic regression (see also Table A3.1 in the Appendix for further details); error bars show 95% confidence intervals.

groups only marginally. The gap is clearly largest among those with far-right positions (around 15 percentage points). Adding to what we have seen in the descriptive analysis, this means that the association between far-right stances and being misinformed depends on the presence of political interest or put differently, the role of political interest gets strongly amplified when the individual in question holds a far-right position. Ideological extremity seems to exert a conditional and asymmetric influence, restricted to those interested in politics. We find that with a probability of about 32 per cent the politically interested with far-right positions are most likely to be misinformed. For the politically interested on the far-left, levels of being misinformed are about the same as for those on the centre-right. Among those with little interest in politics, we see no significant differences across the ideological spectrum. Thus, the political profile of those misinformed about the EU mainly seems to be a story of ideologically driven motivated reasoning on the far-right, yielding overall partial confirmation for Hypothesis 2, with some qualifications.

Turning to the information environment, we find that when controlling for all other variables the positive bivariate association between media use and being misinformed disappears almost completely, suggesting that it was the result of confounding with other covariates such as political interest. We find no difference between social media news consumption and traditional media news consumption, nor does either of the respective variables have a significant substantive effect. Social media do not appear to be creating the misinformed, nor do traditional media reduce their numbers. Therefore, Hypothesis 3 is not supported.

Concerning the perceived disagreement in discussions about the EU, we observe that those who experience frequent disagreement are more likely to be misinformed, contrary to the common belief that the misinformed might be living isolated from 'hearing the other side' in discussions about the EU. Instead, we see a positive association for each of the three possible types of discussants, although the regression slopes are only significant at the 95 per cent confidence level for family and co-worker discussions. Therefore, we find no evidence that discussions in everyday life are conducive to becoming informed through deliberation, disconfirming Hypothesis 4. While discussions about the EU with family members increase the likelihood of being misinformed only when frequent disagreement takes place, discussions with co-workers about the EU are, all else being equal, generally associated with higher levels of being misinformed, albeit the regression results indicate a larger effect when disagreement is frequent. The particularly predictive power of co-worker discussion might emerge because discussing political issues with weak tie acquaintances requires high confidence in one's political knowledge in the first place. Conversely, the non-significance of discussions with friends in predicting being misinformed might be explained by the general rarity of friends with whom you disagree often. Regarding the causality between experiencing disagreement in discussions about the EU and being misinformed, it is important to bear in mind that we cannot infer from cross-sectional data the direction of a possible causal relationship. Consequently, instead of becoming misinformed through contentious discussions, it is equally plausible that misinformed individuals might be prone to experience frequent disagreement precisely due to being misinformed.

As a robustness check, we also conducted country-specific analyses to examine how predictors impact being misinformed across different countries. Despite wider confidence intervals due to the reduced sample size and some minor variations, the patterns are overall consistent with the results of the pooled analysis. In particular, we find in most countries a positive association for the sixty-plus age group, non-significant results for gender, a negative relationship for high education, mostly insignificant results for traditional and new media, and a positive association for disagreement. Regarding the interaction between political interest and far-Right ideology, we also find overall positive trends and convergent evidence. Only in Spain does political interest appear less relevant, and in Italy both the far-left and the far-right seem to be associated with a higher likelihood of being misinformed.[5]

On a final note, it should be mentioned that, even though we find several significant effects, helping us to broadly characterize the social and political profile as well as the information environment of the misinformed, the overall goodness of fit of the model is rather low (McFadden's $R^2 = 0.03$), which testifies to the complexity of the underlying reasons for being misinformed. Considering

[5] Country-specific analyses and results can be obtained by the authors upon request.

the potential detrimental effects of being misinformed, further research should seek to develop a more complete understanding of how and why people become misinformed.

9.6 Conclusion

The Brexit referendum has raised anxieties about the effects of being misinformed on support for the EU, and previous research has confirmed a link between being misinformed and a preference for voting to leave (Partheymüller et al. 2022). The problem since then has only grown bigger and concerns over the spread of misinformation have become the 'new normal' of elections in many democratic systems. In the EU context, the problem is exacerbated by a particularly low level of knowledge of this domain. Against this background, we asked who is misinformed about the EU and have explored the role of socio-demographics, political predispositions, media use, and interpersonal political discussions to characterize the social and political profile of the misinformed as well as their information environment.

Regarding the social profile of the misinformed, the results show that, in line with expectations, the elderly (sixty-plus years) and those with low or medium levels of education are most at risk of being misinformed. Gender, against expectations, plays less of a role, with the share of the misinformed being only slightly higher among women when not controlling for other factors. The political profile of the misinformed broadly matches with the expectations derived from the theory of motivated reasoning. We find, in particular, that being misinformed is associated with high levels of political interest in conjunction with far-right political ideology. The results for the far-left are less clear-cut, which may reflect that far-left parties are less unified in their response to European affairs.

The most unexpected results concern the information environment of the misinformed. The bivariate analysis showed a strong link between media use—both for traditional and social media sources—with being misinformed. The association vanished, however, when controlling for other factors such as political interest and ideology. These patterns suggest that media use is strongly driven by motivational factors. The misinformed do not seem to suffer from a lack of information and do not appear to be completely insulated in filter bubbles. Instead, it seems that their being misinformed comes from 'within', by interpreting messages in a way that fits their interests and selectively accepting messages matching with their ideological priors. This does not negate the possible detrimental influence of specific outlets, feeding false information to the public. Yet, our results suggest that at least it might not be the medium of social media per se, which is driving being misinformed. Regarding interpersonal political communication, we find that the misinformed citizens experience frequent disagreement within political discussions, in particular, in non-selective social relationships (family, co-workers), which is confirmed also by the multivariate analysis. These patterns show that, against common belief, the misinformed are not suffering from a lack of exposure to other opinions on EU matters. Instead, they seem to be confronted with other opinions quite regularly, resulting however in frequent disagreement instead of persuasion.

Overall, these results confirm theories according to which being misinformed is rooted in a tendency towards overconfidence in specific socio-demographic subgroups and amplified by motivated reasoning (e.g. Ortoleva and Snowberg 2015). Due to the logic of motivated reasoning, which media sources are being used seems to play less of a role, although future research should investigate more closely the role of media quality among various channels, to get a more fine-grained picture of how media supply matters. Our results to some extent also disappoint hopes that everyday communication in interpersonal discussions may provide a deliberative space whereby hearing the other side of the argument leads to a more comprehensive understanding of the nature of the EU. Instead, it seems that misinformed citizens provoke a lot of disagreement in their social networks, without this leading to greater 'enlightenment' or understanding. Hence, interpersonal political discussions may not be suitable to overcome being misinformed about the EU.

What does seem to reduce being misinformed is education. However, the link between formal education and being misinformed later in life deserves further investigation and theorizing. Specifically, it would be desirable to know whether educational interventions would be suitable to protect against the risk of becoming misinformed, how also elderly people could be reached by educational efforts, or whether ideology in the end 'overwrites' everything. While the theory of cognitive mobilization suggests the former, the theory of motivated reasoning points towards the latter. Our results show that both processes seem to be at work currently. In light of this, future research should investigate, in particular, how we can strengthen the former mechanism and reduce the latter, to minimize the potentially detrimental effects of being misinformed on political decision-making. Future research should also look into other domains of EU knowledge. The question battery used in this chapter mainly focused on knowledge about EU institutions, however there are many other aspects of EU politics and policies that may matter for (re-)connecting citizens with the EU.

It is often assumed that more information will solve the current challenges to EU democracy. Although making the EU more democratic and its citizens more informed is necessary, we show in this chapter that it might not be sufficient, as the fiercest opposition to the EU project stems from the misinformed and is driven by ideologically motivated reasoning. Therefore, in addition to disseminating more information, positive narratives on the future of EU integration that counter the nationalist Eurosceptic vision for the continent are required. The 2024 European Parliament elections did not live up to this idea. Instead, far-right narratives seeped into mainstream political discourse, and the rise of Eurosceptic parties continued. Fulfilling the 'promise of democracy' at the EU level from citizen perspective requires not only more information, but also a genuine political debate about Europe's collective future, without falling into (or simply copying) nationalistic rhetoric.

References

Aichholzer, J., Partheymüller, J., Wagner, M., Kritzinger, S., Plescia, C., Eberl, J.-M., Meyer, T., Berk, N., Büttner, N., Boomgaarden, H., and Müller, W. C. (2020). AUTNES Online Panel Study 2017–2019 (SUF Edition). https://doi.org/10.11587/QDETRI, AUSSDA, V1.

Beaudonnet, L. and Gomez, R. (2017). Red Europe versus no Europe? The Impact of Attitudes Towards the EU and the Economic Crisis on Radical-Left Voting. *West European Politics*, 40(2): 316–335.

Carpini, M. X. D. and Keeter, S. (1996). *What Americans Know about Politics and Why It Matters*. Yale University Press.

Curran, J., Iyengar, S., Lund, A. B., and Salovaara-Moring, I. (2009). Media System, Public Knowledge and Democracy: A Comparative Study. *European Journal of Communication*, 24(1): 5–26.

Curran, J., Salovaara-Moring, I., Cohen, S., and Iyengar, S. (2010). Crime, Foreigners and Hard News: A Cross-National Comparison of Reporting and Public Perception. *Journalism*, 11(1): 1–17.

De Vreese, C. H. (2001). Europe in the News: A Cross-National Comparative Study of the News Coverage of Key EU Events, *European Union Politics*, 2(3): 283–307.

Dubois, E. and Blank, G. (2018). The Echo Chamber is Overstated: The Moderating Effect of Political Interest and Diverse Media, *Information, Communication and Society*, 21(5): 729–745.

Dylko, I. B. (2016). How Technology Encourages Political Selective Exposure. *Communication Theory*, 26(4): 389–409.

Fraile, M. (2014). Do Women Know Less About Politics Than Men? The Gender Gap in Political Knowledge in Europe, *Social Politics: International Studies in Gender, State and Society*, 21(2): 261–289.

Fraile, M. and Sánchez-Vítores, I. (2020). Tracing the Gender Gap in Political Interest Over the Life Span: A Panel Analysis. *Political Psychology*, 41: 89–106.

Habermas, J. (2012). The Crisis of the European Union in the Light of a Constitutionalization of International Law. *European Journal of International Law*, 23(2): 335–348.

Harper, C. A. and Baguley, T. (2019). 'You are Fake News': Ideological (A)symmetries in Perceptions of Media Legitimacy. Working paper. https://psyarxiv.com/ym6t5/. Accessed March 2022.

Hochschild, J. L. and Einstein, K. L. (2015). Do Facts Matter? Information and Misinformation in American Politics. *Political Science Quarterly*, 130: 585–624. https://doi.org/10.1002/polq.12398.

Hooghe, L, and Marks, G. A. (2009). Postfunctionalist Theory of European Integration: From Permissive Consensus to Constraining Dissensus. *British Journal of Political Science*. 39(1): 1–23. doi:10.1017/S0007123408000409.

Hutter, S., Grande, E., and Kriesi, H. (eds) (2016). *Politicising Europe. Integration and Mass Politics*. Cambridge: Cambridge University Press.

Inglehart, R. (1970). Cognitive Mobilization and European Identity. *Comparative Politics*, 3(1): 45–70.

Inglehart, R. and Norris, P. (2000). The Developmental Theory of the Gender Gap: Women's and Men's Voting Behavior in Global Perspective. *International Political Science Review*, 21(4): 441–463.

Jerit, J. and Barabas, J. (2017). Revisiting the Gender Gap in Political Knowledge. *Political Behavior*, 39: 817–838.

Jerit, J., Barabas, J., and Bolsen, T. (2006). Citizens, Knowledge, and the Information Environment. *American Journal of Political Science*, 50(2): 266–282.

Karp, J. A., Banducci, S. A., and Bowler, S. (2003). To Know it is to Love it? Satisfaction with Democracy in the European Union, *Comparative Political Studies*, 36(3):271–292.

Kling, K. C., Hyde, J., Showers, C., and Buswell, B. N. (1999). Gender Differences in Self-Esteem: A Meta-Analysis. *Psychological Bulletin*, 125(4): 470–500.

Kraft, P. W., Lodge, M., and Taber, C. S. (2015). Why People 'Don't Trust The Evidence' Motivated Reasoning and Scientific Beliefs. *The Annals of the American Academy of Political and Social Science*, 658(1): 121–133.

Kuklinski, J. H., Quirk, P. J., Schwieder, D. W., and Rich, R. F. (1998). 'Just the Facts, Ma'am': Political Facts and Public Opinion. *The Annals of the American Academy of Political and Social Science*, 560(1): 143–154.

Kuklinski, J. H., Quirk, P. J., Jerit, J., Schwieder, D., and Rich, R. F. (2000). Misinformation and the Currency of Democratic Citizenship of Democratic Citizenship, *Journal of Politics*, 62(3): 790–816.

Kunda, Z. (1990). The Case for Motivated Reasoning. *Psychological Bulletin*, 108(3): 480–498.

Lazer, D. M. J., Baum, M. A., Benkler, Y., Berinsky, A. J., Greenhill, K. M., and Menczer, F. (2018).The Science of Fake News. *Science*, 359(6380): 1094–1096.

Lee, S. and Matsuo, A. (2018). Decomposing Political Knowledge: What Is Confidence in Knowledge and Why It Matters. *Electoral Studies*, 51: 1–13.

Levine, J. M. and Russo, E. M. (1995). Impact of Anticipated Interaction on Information Acquisition. *Social Cognition*, 13: 293–317.

Lewandowsky, S., Ecker, U. K. H., Seifert, C. M., Schwarz, N., and Cook, J. (2012). Misinformation and Its Correction: Continued Influence and Successful Debiasing. *Psychological Science in the Public Interest*, 13: 106–131.

Li, J. and Wagner, M. W. (2020). The Value of Not Knowing: Partisan Cue-Taking and Belief Updating of the Uninformed, the Ambiguous, and the Misinformed. *Journal of Communication*, 70(5): 646–669.

Lodge, M. and Taber, C. S. (2013). *The Rationalizing Voter*. New York, Cambridge University Press.

Lubbers, M. and Scheepers, P. (2007). Euro-Scepticism and Extreme Voting Patterns in Europe. In Loosveldt, G., Swyngedouw, M., and Cambré, B. (eds). *Measuring Meaningful Data in Social Research*. Leuven, Acco: 71–92.

McLeod, J. M., Scheufele, D. A., Moy, P., Horowitz, E. M., Holbert, R. L., Zhang, W., Zubric, S., and Zubric, J. (1999). Understanding Deliberation: The Effects of Discussion Networks on Participation in a Public Forum. *Communication Research*, 26(6): 743–774.

McPhee, W. N. (1963). *Formal Theories of Mass Behavior*. London, Free Press Glencoe.

Mutz, D. (2002). The Consequences of Cross-cutting Networks for Political Participation. *American Journal of Political Science*, 46(4): 838–855.

Mutz, D. (2006). *Hearing the Other Side: Deliberative versus Participatory Democracy.* New York, Cambridge University Press.

Niederle, M. and Vesterlund, L. (2011). Gender and Competition. *Annual Review of Economics*, 3: 601–630.

Norris, P. and Holtz-Bacha, C. (2001). 'To Entertain, Inform, and Educate': Still the Role of Public Television. *Political Communication*, 18(2): 123–140.

Ortoleva, P. and Snowberg, E. (2015). Overconfidence in Political Behavior, *The American Economic Review*, 105(2): 504–535.

Partheymüller, J., Kritzinger, S., and Plescia, C. (2022). Being Misinformed about the European Union and the Preference to Vote to Leave or Remain. *Journal of Common Market Studies*, 60(5): 1449–1469.

Peter, J., Semetko, H. A., and de Vreese, C. H. (2003). EU Politics on Television News: A Cross-National Comparative Study. *European Union Politics*, 4(3): 305–327.

Plescia, C., Wilhelm, J., Kritzinger, S., Schüberl, T., and Partheymüller, J. (2020). RECONNECT 2019 European Parliament Election Panel Survey (SUF edition)'. https://doi.org/10.1158 7MOV0EZ, AUSSDA, V2.

Prasad, M., Perrin, A. J., Bezila, K., Hoffman, S. G., Kindleberger, K., Manturuk, K., and Powers, A. S. (2009). There Must Be a Reason: Osama, Saddam, and Inferred Justification. *Sociological Inquiry*, 79: 142–162.

Price, V. and Zaller, J. (1993). Who Gets the News? Alternative Measures of News Reception and Their Implications for Research. *Public Opinion Quarterly*, 57: 133–164.

Rapeli, L. (2014). Comparing Local, National and EU Knowledge: The Ignorant Public Reassessed, *Scandinavian Political Studies*, 37(4): 428–446.

Redlawsk, D. P. (2002). Hot Cognition or Cool Consideration? Testing the Effects of Motivated Reasoning on Political Decision Making. *Journal of Politics*,64(4): 1021–1044.

Scheufele, D. A. (2013). Communicating Science in Social Settings. *Proceedings of the National Academy of Sciences*, 110, Supplement 3: 14040–14047.

Sniderman, P. (1981). *A Question of Loyalty*. Berkeley, University of California Press.

Soll, J. and Klayman, J. (2004). Overconfidence in Interval Estimates. *Journal of Experimental Psychology: Learning, Memory, and Cognition*, 30: 299–314.

Szöcsik, E. and Polyakova, A. (2019). Euroscepticism and the Electoral Success of the Far Right: The Role of the Strategic Interaction Between Center and Far Right. *European Political Science*, 18: 400–420.

Taber, C. S. and Lodge, M. (2006). Motivated Skepticism in the Evaluation of Political Beliefs. *American Journal of Political Science*, 50(3): 755–769.

Verba, S., Burns, N., and Schlozman, K. (1997). Knowing and Caring about Politics: Gender and Political Engagement. *The Journal of Politics*, 59(4): 1051–1072.

Vosoughi, S., Roy, D., and Aral, S. (2018). The Spread of True and False News Online. *Science*, 359(6380): 1146–1151.

Wagner, S. (2021). Euroscepticism as a Radical Left Party Strategy for Success. *Party Politics*, 28(6): 1069–1080.

Wojcieszak, M. (2010). 'Don't Talk To Me': Effects of Ideologically Homogeneous Online Groups and Politically Dissimilar Offline Ties on Extremism. *New Media and Society*, 12(4): 637–655.

Zollo, F., Bessi, A., Del Vicario, M., Scala, A., Caldarelli, G., Shekhtman, L., Havlin, S., and Quattrociocchi, W. (2017). Debunking in a World of Tribes. *PLOS ONE*, 2(7): e0181821.

APPENDIX 9.1

Question Wording and Estimation Tables

A1. Questions to measure the accuracy of knowledge

The order of the questions was randomized. Correct answers marked with an asterisk. Response options were all randomized where appropriate (exception: 'None/all of the above').

The members of which of the following EU institutions are directly elected by European citizens?

- The European Commission
- The European Parliament*
- The Council of the European Union
- None of the above

Jean-Claude Juncker is the current President of the European Commission. How did he become President?

- He was directly elected by EU citizens.
- He was selected on the basis of an internal vote within the European Commission.
- He was approved by a majority of the members of the European Parliament.*
- He was appointed without a vote taking place.

Which of the following EU institutions formally proposes new laws at the EU level?

- The European Commission*
- The European Parliament
- The Council of the European Union
- All of the above

Which of the following statements is <u>not</u> true?

- All EU citizens have the right to work in another EU country.
- Mobile phone roaming charges have decreased within the EU.
- Expenditure on the salaries of the EU officials is the largest item in the EU budget.*
- Individual EU countries cannot conclude their own trade agreements.

In which of the following EU institutions are the ministers of national governments represented?

- The European Commission
- The European Parliament
- The Council of the European Union*
- None of the above

A2. Questions to measure the confidence in knowledge

Each question above was followed by the following question.

How sure are you about the answer you have just given?

- 0 = Not at all sure
- …
- 10 = Completely sure

A3. Full estimation results

Table 9A.1 Logistic regression for being misinformed

	Full model	
	Estimate	**Std, Error**
Age (ref. <30 years):		
- 30–39	0.054	(0.100)
- 40–49	-0.017	(0.146)
- 50–59	0.077	(0.139)
- 60+	0.245*	(0.112)
Gender: Male	0.007	(0.078)
Education (ref. Low):		
- Medium	-0.100	(0.062)
- High	-0.304***	(0.075)
Political Interest: High	0.298**	(0.097)
Ideological position (ref. Centre):		
- Far Left	-0.215	(0.198)
- Left	-0.150	(0.169)
- Right	0.024	(0.182)
- Far Right	-0.115	(0.206)
Interaction terms:		
- Far Left X Political Interest: High	0.205	(0.163)
- Left X Political Interest: High	-0.034	(0.189)
- Right X Political Interest: High	0.052	(0.168)
- Far Right X Political Interest: High	0.550**	(0.206)
Traditional News Media (ref. Never):		
- Sometimes	0.006	(0.130)
- Daily	0.085	(0.122)
Social Media (ref. Never):		
- Sometimes	0.113*	(0.057)
- Daily	0.092	(0.058)
Disagreement: Family (ref. No Discussion):		
- Never/Some	0.089	(0.080)
- Often	0.245*	(0.096)
Disagreement: Friends (ref. No Discussion):		
- Never/Some	0.047	(0.076)
- Often	0.218	(0.129)

(continued)

Table 9A.1 Continued

	Full model	
	Estimate	**Std, Error**
Disagreement: Coworkers (ref. No Discussion):		
- Never/Some	0.124**	(0.047)
- Often	0.342***	(0.090)
Country (ref. Germany):		
- France	-0.089***	(0.013)
- Spain	0.113***	(0.021)
- Hungary	0.393***	(0.022)
- Poland	0.203***	(0.029)
- Denmark	0.100***	(0.020)
- Italy	0.339***	(0.024)
- Austria	-0.010	(0.012)
Constant	-1.889***	(0.245)
Observations	14872	
McFadden Pseudo R^2	0.030	
AIC	15325	
BIC	15378	

Note: Estimates are logit coefficients. Standard errors in parentheses. * $p < 0.05$, ** $p < 0.01$, *** $p < 0.001$

10

The Sweet Spot of EU Reform: How to Improve Citizens' Perceptions of EU Legitimacy

Oliver Treib, Constantin Schäfer, and Bernd Schlipphak

10.1 Introduction

The European Union (EU) is facing a profound 'crisis of legitimacy' (Schweiger 2016; Schmidt 2020). As the Union's authority has extended beyond creating a common market and has come to confront more controversial policy areas and core state powers, many citizens have turned towards Eurosceptic politicians who challenge the authority and legitimacy of the EU (Hooghe and Marks 2009). The rise of popular and party-based Euroscepticism has been reinforced by the EU's 'polycrisis' (Zeitlin et al. 2019); the eurozone crisis, the refugee crisis, the Covid crisis, and the energy crisis following Russia's invasion of Ukraine have all called into question the EU's ability to deliver on its promise of improving the living conditions of European citizens, thus boosting support for Eurosceptic parties in adversely affected countries and Eurosceptic sentiments among the wider public (Serricchio et al. 2013; Taggart and Szczerbiak 2018; Vasilopoulou 2018; Schäfer and Gross 2020).

As a result of this growing 'political conflict over Europe' (Schäfer et al. 2021), major integration projects such as the Constitutional Treaty foundered on public opposition in several national referendums (Hobolt 2009). Eurosceptic parties celebrated electoral victories at both national and European levels (Treib 2014, 2021), and public rejection of EU membership has even led to one former Member State leaving the Union altogether (Hobolt 2016). Moreover, the Union is increasingly under attack from authoritarian governments in some of its Member States, which seek to shield their national attacks on democracy and the rule of law from EU criticism by actively mobilizing their domestic audiences against what they consider to be illegitimate interference in domestic affairs (Schlipphak and Treib 2017; Schlipphak et al. 2023).

Although there is widespread agreement that the EU needs thorough reform to alleviate its legitimacy crisis, there is disagreement on the concrete reform path to

Oliver Treib, Constantin Schäfer, and Bernd Schlipphak, *The Sweet Spot of EU Reform: How to Improve Citizens' Perceptions of EU Legitimacy* In: *The Promise of EU Democracy*. Edited by: Jan Wouters, Julie Smith, Kolja Raube, and Ben Crum, Oxford University Press.
DOI: 10.1093/9780191996191.003.0012

be taken. The most recent attempt to develop reform options was the Conference on the Future of Europe of 2021–22 (CoFoE), a project of direct citizen involvement, which resulted in a diverse set of forty-nine proposals, ranging from very concrete policy measures to ambitious institutional reforms (Conference on the Future of Europe 2022). While pro-integration politicians such as Commission President von der Leyen supported proposals such as scrapping decision-making by unanimity in the Council or extending the EU's authority in areas such as defence or health, these proposals received a much more reluctant response from a coalition of thirteen Member State governments from Northern and Central and Eastern Europe (Euronews 2022; Sweden in EU 2022). More importantly, outright Eurosceptics such as the group of European Conservatives and Reformists (ECR) in the European Parliament not only rejected the outcomes but also questioned the legitimacy of the CoFoE, arguing that citizens in favour of deeper European integration were over-represented, since they were more likely to participate, and that expert hearings were dominated by pro-integrationist experts (European Conservatives and Reformists 2022).

Given these political controversies, sound empirical evidence on citizens' preferences concerning the future of European integration is crucial. However, there is surprisingly little research on the ideal configuration of the EU in the minds of European citizens. From previous studies, we know that EU attitudes are multidimensional (Boomgaarden et al. 2011) and are influenced by different individual and contextual determinants (Ejrnæs and Jensen 2019). The few existing studies on citizens' reform preferences have found, for example, that there is little appetite among citizens to follow the British example and leave the EU (Goldberg et al. 2021a). Confronted with different scenarios ranging from complete disintegration to the transformation of the EU into a fully-fledged state, only a small minority of citizens choose the two extreme options. The vast majority favour more moderate scenarios hovering around the status quo, ranging from an economic union to an EU with different speeds of deepening integration (Goldberg et al. 2021b). Studies that examined citizens' institutional preferences have revealed that citizens prefer a Union focused on peace and security, demand the use of referendums and support the current size of the EU (De Vries and Hoffmann 2015). Hahm et al. (2020) show that people reject the Commission's exclusive right of legislative initiative, support the existing bicameral legislative structure, and prefer majority voting to unanimity, while they disagree on who should decide on infringements.

Despite these initial findings, there is still a need for further research on which reforms could improve the EU's public legitimacy, i.e., citizens' support for the EU. Against this background, this chapter presents empirical evidence on citizens' preferences for EU-related reforms in response to three key questions. First, to what extent do citizens support further transfers of political authority to the European level? Second, in which policy areas do citizens most want the EU to take action?

Third, how do key reforms of EU decision-making affect citizens' acceptance of EU decisions in their most-preferred policy areas?

Moreover, we are interested in the factors that shape people's views on the ideal EU. As reforming the EU has proven to be a highly contentious affair in the past, it seems essential to gain insights into which types of reform are likely to be supported by a broad coalition of citizens and which are likely to fail due to deep rifts between different groups. Previous reform debates as well as research on general EU attitudes have shown that there are large cross-country differences in public opinion about the EU (for an overview, see Hobolt and De Vries 2016). In the first part of our empirical analysis, we explore the extent to which citizens' views on different aspects of EU reform vary across countries.

In the second part, we focus on differences between societal groups. The Brexit referendum revealed that the Eurosceptic leave vote was dominated by older, less educated, and poorer voters who felt marginalized by the process of increased international cooperation (Hobolt 2016). These findings tie in with a broader literature arguing that Western societies have seen the emergence of a new line of conflict between—often subjectively perceived rather than objectively defined—*winners* and *losers* of recent societal transformations such as modernization and globalization (Kriesi et al. 2006; 2012; Teney et al. 2014; Hooghe and Marks 2018; Ford and Jennings 2020). Following this line of argument, we analyse the degree to which the division between winners and losers, measured by two objective variables—age and education—and two subjective perceptions, namely citizens' self-reported socioeconomic status and their level of perceived societal marginalization (Bollwerk et al. 2022), influences citizens' perceptions toward European integration and the preferred policy area of EU decision-making. Furthermore, we investigate the extent to which citizens' EU-related reform preferences may be shaped by their general stances toward the European project.

We present data from the RECONNECT Citizen Survey, an online survey of 12,000 respondents in six EU Member States: Denmark, France, Germany, Hungary, Poland, and Spain. Based on several survey items and a conjoint experiment in which respondents were confronted with EU decision-making scenarios that systematically varied a set of institutional features, we show that citizens have a relatively strong status quo orientation, especially in areas that touch upon the distribution of powers between the EU and its Member States. Reforms that change this balance of power are thus likely to meet with public opposition, especially between more Eurosceptic losers and more Europhile winners of modernization and globalization.

However, there is still room to improve people's acceptance of EU decisions. The data show widespread support across the winner/loser divide for more direct citizen participation, more transparency in EU decision-making processes, and measures to improve the EU's ability to solve problems. Finally, citizens want the

EU to act primarily in policy areas with a clear transnational character. There are also indications that many of the policy areas favoured by citizens are related to perceptions of global threats, suggesting that EU action could be successfully framed along the lines of Emmanuel Macron's slogan 'Une Europe qui protège'.

10.2 The RECONNECT citizen survey

In the following, we present the dataset, the main variables, and the methods of our empirical analysis. We start by describing the collection of the data (10.2.1) before laying out the EU-specific questions (10.2.2) and the conjoint experiment (10.2.3), with which we provide answers to our research questions.

10.2.1 Data collection

As already mentioned, we conducted an online survey in the six EU Member States Denmark, France, Germany, Hungary, Poland, and Spain. The country selection reflects diversity in geography, population size, economic conditions, duration of EU membership, and level of democracy. In each country, respondents aged 18–89 years were sampled from an online access panel provided by the survey company KANTAR. We applied a random quota sampling regarding gender, age, and educational attainment based on 2019 Eurostat population data. The sample size per country was 2,000 respondents, yielding an overall sample size of n = 12,000. The interviews were conducted between 11 September and 23 October 2020. The dataset is freely available to the public.[1]

10.2.2 Measuring integration preferences and most preferred EU policy areas

As outlined in the introduction, we are mainly interested in three key aspects of European integration which, in combination, should provide us with a clearer image of what the ideal EU looks like to European citizens. First, we are interested in the *integration dimension*, i.e., the extent to which people wish to further concentrate political authority at the EU level or demand that EU competences be returned to the Member States. Therefore, we asked respondents, 'Some people say that the European Union should have more competences to take political decisions

[1] See https://doi.org/10.11587/D3PZEA for the dataset, the questionnaires, as well as the codebook and method report (accessed 22 July 2025).

in Europe. Others say that the nation states should regain competences that were transferred to the EU. What is your opinion on this topic?' Survey participants could then indicate their stance on a six-point scale ranging from 'Nation states should regain competences' (1) to 'The EU should have more competences' (6).

Second, we wanted to know what policy areas people would like to see dealt with at the European level. To measure this, we asked respondents to indicate their *most preferred EU policy area*. More specifically, the question reads: 'The European Union can take political decisions in several policy areas. However, other policy areas are reserved to the sole competence of the member states. In which of the following policy areas would you prefer most that the EU takes political decisions?' Respondents were asked to choose one out of twelve different policy fields that were randomly ordered to avoid order effects (see Figure 10.4 below for the list of policy fields).

10.2.3 Measuring institutional preferences: the conjoint experiment

The third and main objective of our analysis is to examine which institutional parameters of EU decision-making improve people's support for EU decisions. To investigate this, we have integrated a conjoint experiment into our survey. This technique, which has become a somewhat fashionable tool in political science, allows us to analyse 'situations in which a decision maker has to deal with options that simultaneously vary across two or more attributes' (Green et al. 2001: 57). The EU, with its complex institutional design, certainly represents such an attitudinal object with various features that can influence people's overall legitimacy beliefs. Therefore, we presented respondents with several hypothetical EU policy decisions, with each EU decision representing a profile that varies in six different (institutional) attributes. Importantly, we presented these profiles in pairs (see also Hainmueller et al. 2015) and asked respondents to choose their preferred profile.

From many potential institutional features, we selected six attributes that are likely to influence citizens' legitimacy beliefs on three dimensions: the EU's authority vis-à-vis its Member States, the procedures on the basis of which EU decisions are reached, and the performance of the EU's policy output (see Table 10.1). First, in the authority dimension, we included the extent to which EU decisions are binding or voluntary for all members ('bindingness') and the availability of veto powers for individual Member States, particularly visible in Council voting ('possibility of being outvoted'). Second, in the procedural dimension, the conjoint experiment covered two aspects highlighted by legitimacy research (Scharpf 1999; Schmidt 2013): the degree to which citizens can participate in the collective decision-making process ('citizen participation'), which is a key attribute of input legitimacy, and the transparency of decision-making processes ('public information'), which taps into throughput legitimacy. Third, in the performance dimension, we included a measure of output legitimacy, the ability of the political regime's policies to solve problems ('problem-solving'), which is tightly connected to the traditional functionalist and neo-functionalist narratives about the need for the EU to produce beneficial policies in order to elicit public support (Haas 1958; Mitrany 1966). We also explored the effect of the relative distribution of integration benefits between Member States, determined by the expected benefit of decisions for one's own country compared to others ('benefit for own country').

We undertook several steps to make the evaluation tasks as intelligible and realistic as possible. First, respondents were informed that the hypothetical EU decisions to be evaluated were taken in the policy area that they had previously chosen as most preferred to be dealt with at the EU level. Second, respondents were informed that 'each decision would have a substantial impact on people's lives', thereby enhancing the perceived importance of the following decision task. Third, respondents were provided with descriptions of the six attributes (see Table 10.1) before the actual conjoint experiment started. Each participant was presented eight distinct EU policy decisions ('profiles'), consisting of four pairs of two profiles. Within each pair, respondents were requested to indicate their preferred policy decision (see Figure 10.1 for an example).

In total, the 12,000 respondents evaluated 96,000 profiles (i.e. each respondent reviewed eight profiles displayed in four choice tasks). Using these individual choices, it is possible to statistically estimate the average marginal effect that each attribute level ('component') exerts on the choice for a given EU policy decision. The single profile represents the unit of analysis, making the dependent variable of this analysis binary (0 = profile not chosen, 1 = profile chosen). Therefore, we used logistic regression analysis as the estimation technique, and the regression outputs were computed as average marginal component effects (AMCEs), as per Hainmueller et al. (2014) and Bansak et al. (2023). The conjoint analysis thus provides insights into the relative explanatory power of each of the six institutional variables.

10.3 Citizens' attitudes toward EU reforms: mean levels and country differences

In the following, we first report results on respondents' preferences for more or less integration (10.3.1), followed by citizens' most preferred EU policy areas (10.3.2) and, finally, the effects of the six institutional attributes on people's willingness to accept an EU decision in their most-preferred policy area (10.3.3). For each of these steps, we demonstrate the mean levels of citizens' attitudes and explore any potential differences among the six countries.

Table 10.1 Conceptual dimensions, institutional attributes, attribute descriptions, and attribute levels of the conjoint survey experiment

Dimension	Attribute	Description	Levels
AUTHORITY	**Bindingness**	*'How binding or optional is the decision for the EU member countries, including [Country]?'*	(1) Every country must apply the decision (2) Single countries may deviate in exceptional circumstances (3) Each country may apply the decision voluntarily
	Possibility of being outvoted	*'If a country, including [Country], disagrees with the decision, can it be outvoted by other EU member countries?'*	(1) A country cannot be outvoted (veto power) (2) A country can be outvoted only by a large majority (75%) (3) A country can be outvoted by a small majority (50%)
PROCEDURE	**Citizen participation**	*'How can European citizens influence the decision-making process?'*	(1) Through parliamentary elections only (2) Through parliamentary elections and a citizen consultation (3) Through parliamentary elections and a referendum
	Public information	*'Is information about the decision-making process publicly available for all citizens?'*	(1) Not available (2) Available after the decision has been made (3) Available throughout the whole process
PERFORMANCE	**Benefit for own country**	*'What is the expected benefit of the decision for [Country]?'*	(1) Less than for other countries (2) The same as for other countries (3) More than for other countries
	Problem-solving	*'Based on previous experiences with comparable policy decisions, to what degree will the decision solve the underlying policy problem?*	(1) To a small degree (2) To a moderate degree (3) To a large degree

	Option A	Option B
Verbindlichkeit	Jedes Land **muss** die Entscheidung umsetzen	Einzelne Länder **können bei außergewöhnlichen Umständen von der Entscheidung abweichen**
Möglichkeit, überstimmt zu werden	Ein Land kann nur von einer **großen Mehrheit (75%)** überstimmt werden	Ein Land kann nur von einer **großen Mehrheit (75%)** überstimmt werden
Bürgerbeteiligung	**Nur** durch **Parlamentswahlen**	Durch **Parlamentswahlen** und **eine Bürgerbefragung**
Öffentliche Informationen	**Nicht** zugänglich	**Während des gesamten Prozesses** zugänglich
Nutzen für Deutschland	**Genauso** wie für andere Länder	**Geringer** als für andere Länder
Problemlösung	In **mittlerem** Ausmaß	In **starkem** Ausmaß
	Welche der beiden politischen EU-Entscheidungen würden Sie bevorzugen?	
	○	○
	Wie sehr wären Sie für oder gegen die jeweilige politische Entscheidung der EU?	
	○ ○ ○ ○ ○ ○ ○ ○ ○ ○ ○	○ ○ ○ ○ ○ ○ ○ ○ ○ ○ ○
	-5 -4 -3 -2 -1 0 1 2 3 4 5	-5 -4 -3 -2 -1 0 1 2 3 4 5
	Absolut dagegen … Absolut dafür	Absolut dagegen … Absolut dafür

Zur Erklärung der Merkmale können Sie einfach den Cursor über das entsprechende Merkmal bewegen.

Figure 10.1 Example of the conjoint experiment as seen by respondents (German language version)

10.3.1 Preferences for more or less integration

Starting with people's preferences on further European integration, we observe that the overall public opinion is rather ambivalent (see Figure 10.2). Most people locate themselves somewhere in the middle along the integration–disintegration

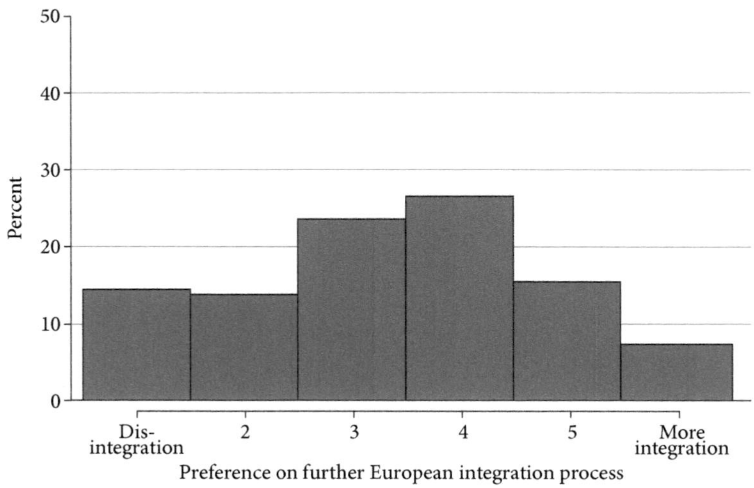

Figure 10.2 Distribution of preferences on further European integration among all survey respondents

Source: RECONNECT Citizen Survey

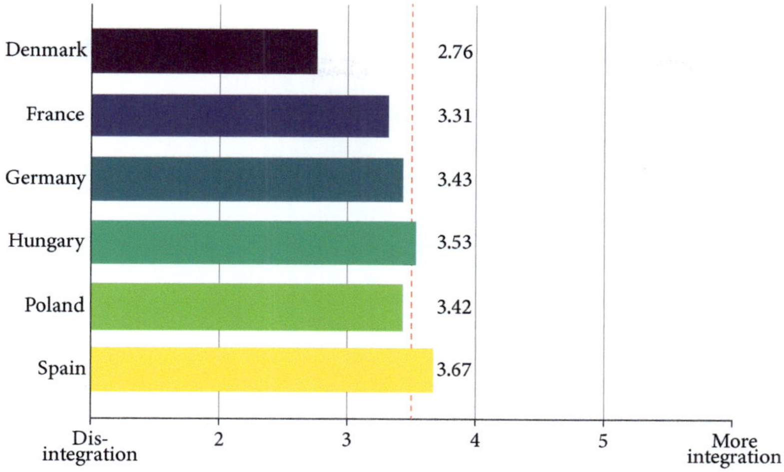

Figure 10.3 Mean preference on further European integration across the six survey countries

Notes: the dashed line represents the theoretical scale mean.

Source: RECONNECT Citizen Survey

dimension, meaning that 45.3 per cent of the respondents chose values 3 or 4. However, the 'disintegrationist camp' (1/2: 27.8 per cent of respondents) is larger than the integrationist camp (5/6: 20.4 per cent). Accordingly, the (weighted) mean value across the whole sample is 3.35 and, thus, slightly below the (theoretical) scale mean (3.5). Yet, the overall picture reveals a general preference for the status quo.

These overall results mask major differences between countries (see Figure 10.3). It shows that there is a group of countries whose average positions on further integration are close to the overall mean across all respondents. Two countries stand out, however. In line with well-known patterns of public opinion on the EU, Spanish respondents were significantly more supportive of further integration than the rest. Danish respondents, by contrast, showed by far the least appetite for a further transfer of competences to the European level. Instead, their comparably low mean (2.76) reveals that a relatively large part of Danish society would prefer political authority to be returned to the nation state. It can also be noted that in four out of the six countries, citizens lean slightly towards greater disintegration whereas only two countries have a slightly pro-integrationist tendency.

10.3.2 Most preferred EU policy areas

Which issues did respondents select as the policy areas in which they would most prefer that the EU take political decisions? Looking at the overall distribution of

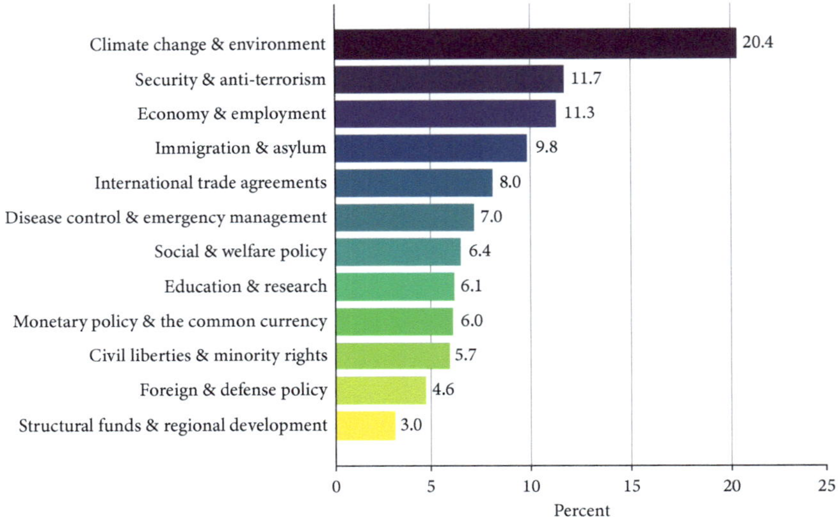

Figure 10.4 Most preferred EU policy areas among all survey respondents
Source: RECONNECT Citizen Survey

this variable, it is obvious that citizens' policy preferences are highly heterogeneous (see Figure 10.4). Yet, one key issue dominates regarding areas in which the EU is most preferred to act. About one-fifth of the respondents (20.4 per cent) prefer the policy field of climate change and environment, while two policy issues are in close race for second place: security and anti-terrorism (11.7 per cent) and economy and employment (11.3 per cent). The fiercely disputed areas of immigration and asylum (9.8 per cent) and international trade agreements (8.0 per cent) rank fourth and fifth. In contrast, policies that pro-integrationist social democratic and left-wing parties want to push further onto the EU agenda, such as social and welfare policy, education and research, or civil liberties and minority rights, rank much lower in citizens' priorities.

Comparing the top three most preferred EU policy areas across countries reveals that in overall terms, the differences are not very pronounced (see Table 10.2). Climate change and environment is the policy field in which EU action is most strongly demanded across countries. Only among Spanish citizens was environmental policy not the most preferred, although it was still in second place. In individual countries, we find additional policy fields to be significantly more important. This is the case for international trade agreements in Denmark or social and welfare policy in Hungary.

Taken together, European citizens seem to favour EU action in areas that have a clear transnational dimension (climate change and environment, security and anti-terrorism, immigration and asylum), suggesting that people value clear

Table 10.2 Most preferred EU policy areas across countries

	No. 1	No. 2	No. 3
Countries			
Denmark	Climate change and environment (23.5%)	International trade agreements (16.6%)	Security and anti-terrorism (13.9%)
France	Climate change and environment (21.9%)	Security and anti-terrorism (16.0%)	Economy and employment (13.0%)
Germany	Climate change and environment (25.2%)	Immigration and asylum (17.7%)	Security and anti-terrorism (12.0%)
Hungary	Climate change and environment (19.4%)	Social and welfare policy (11.9%)	Monetary policy and the common currency (11.2%)
Poland	Climate change and environment (17.4%)	Security and anti-terrorism (15.7%)	Economy and employment (9.8%)
Spain	Economy and employment (27.1%)	Climate change and environment (14.9%)	Immigration and asylum (9.9%)

Source: RECONNECT Citizen Survey

functional advantages of EU-wide collaboration. This observation is particularly evident in the case of climate change, which is by far the most frequently selected policy area. There is a plurality of reasons why respondents may have chosen this category. First, even though the survey was taken during the Covid-19 pandemic, the public salience of climate change remained high. Second, climate change is an issue for which coordinated action at the international level is recognized as essential to citizens. In contrast, policy areas without apparent transnational dimension (social and welfare policy, education and research, civil liberties and minority rights) rank much lower. Lastly, several of the most widely accepted EU policy areas seem instrumental in safeguarding EU citizens from (perceived) global threats such as climate change, terrorism, economic crises, and mass migration.[2] This result is in line with previous studies finding a public demand for a Union that provides security to its citizens (De Vries and Hoffmann 2015).

[2] If the pattern we observe here is correct, responses are likely to be influenced by current events that may move a particular policy area into the spotlight of people's threat perceptions. Had the survey been taken after the full-scale Russian invasion of Ukraine in 2022, for example, it is likely that the field of foreign and defence policy would have ranked significantly higher.

10.3.3 Institutional parameters and support of EU decision-making

After these insights into citizens' EU-related policy priorities, we now present the results of the conjoint analysis. Note that survey participants were asked to choose one out of two hypothetical EU policy decisions ('profiles') based on the six varying attributes: bindingness, possibility of being outvoted, citizen participation, public information, benefit for own country, and degree of problem-solving. Figure 10.5 displays the average marginal effects (AMCEs) of each attribute level on the predicted probability of choosing the profile. Each attribute contains three different levels, with the medium level of each attribute serving as reference category. An AMCE of 0.05, for example, means that this level (e.g. 'information always public') increases the probability that the profile is preferred (over the adjacent profile) by five percentage points compared to the medium level of the same attribute (e.g. 'information public ex post').

According to the AMCEs presented in Figure 10.5, the most preferred institutional setting is one in which EU decisions permit the possibility of opting out

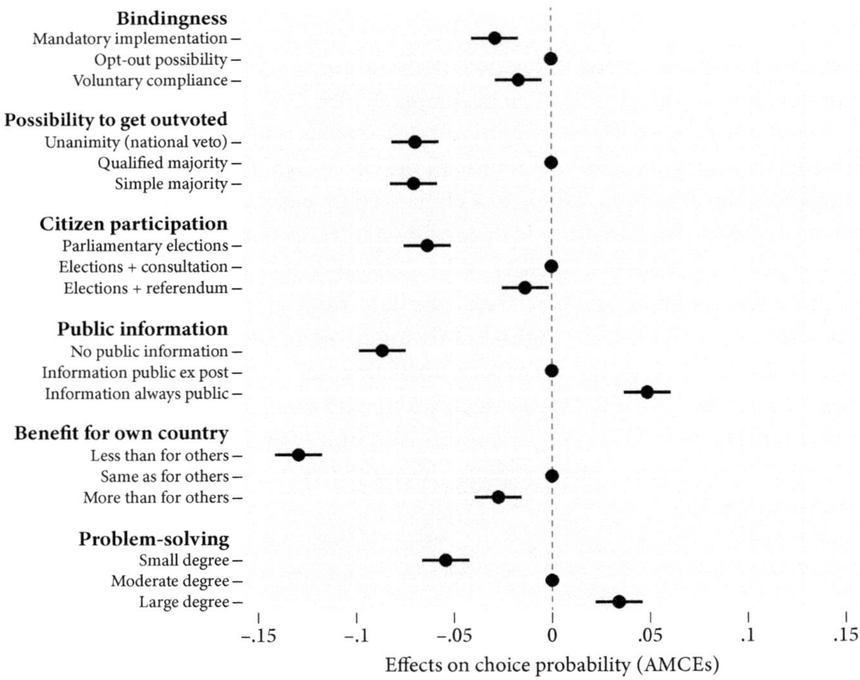

Figure 10.5 The effects of institutional attributes on the preference for EU level decisions

Notes: The figure shows AMCEs and 99% confidence intervals.

(bindingness) and where Member State governments can only be outvoted by a large, qualified majority (possibility to get outvoted). These two results imply that European citizens accept the political authority of the EU over political decisions, while insisting that national sovereignty should remain a consideration in decision-making at the supranational level. It is interesting to note that respondents display an intuitive preference for the fine balance between intergovernmental and supranational modes of decision-making that is already prevalent in the present-day EU. Conversely, the average respondent rejects both a strongly intergovernmental and a radically supranational decision-making mode over the status quo.

Furthermore, people demand additional avenues for effective participation beyond parliamentary elections (citizen participation), which is currently the status quo. Both citizen consultations and referendums seem to be desirable options for this purpose. The slight preference for deliberative democratic instruments reveals the public demand for 'people having their say' on EU matters. Citizens also seem to place a high value on transparency and accountability, as illustrated by the substantial effects exerted by the levels of public information (in either direction). We can infer from these results that Europeans demand greater input and throughput legitimacy regarding EU governance (Scharpf 1999; Schmidt 2013). Taken together, it shows that procedures matter to citizens and that positive outputs alone are not sufficient anymore for European integration support—if there ever was such a time.

Finally, the observation that outputs remain relevant to European citizens is affirmed by their demand for effective solutions to their problems through EU actions (problem-solving), even if the effect sizes are comparatively smaller than, say, the effects of information transparency. Hence, the traditional (neo-)functionalist argument about policies perceived to be beneficial by citizens generate public legitimacy still matters, albeit such performance considerations are not people's only concern. Interestingly, people do not seem to evaluate EU policy decisions solely through the lens of national self-interest, but also based on the interest in their neighbouring countries' benefits (benefit for own country). This conclusion stems from the evident preference for equal relative benefits amongst all EU Member States. However, as soon as people feel unfairly disadvantaged by EU policies, they tend to turn sharply against the Union.

Comparing the ideal institutional package across Member States largely confirms the overall picture, but also provides some notable additions (see Table 10.3). This is particularly true for Denmark and Spain, where people prefer referendums over consultations, possibly due to previous experiences with direct democratic instruments. Furthermore, citizens in France and, in particular, Hungary would prefer EU decisions to be even less binding to a degree where compliance is optional. These preferences displayed by Hungarian citizens could plausibly stem

Table 10.3 Most preferred institutional setting of the EU across countries

	Bindingness	Possibility to get outvoted	Citizen participation	Public information	Benefit for own country	Problem-solving
Countries						
Denmark	Opt-out possibility*	By qualified majority*	Elections + referendums	Always public*	Same as for others	Large degree*
France	Voluntary compliance	By qualified majority*	Elections + consultations	Always public*	Same as for others*	Large degree*
Germany	Opt-out possibility	By qualified majority*	Elections + consultations*	Always public*	Same as for others	Large degree*
Hungary	Voluntary compliance*	By qualified majority*	Elections + consultations	Always public*	Same as for others*	Large degree
Poland	Opt-out possibility*	By qualified majority*	Elections + consultations*	Always public*	Same as for others	Large degree*
Spain	Opt-out possibility	By qualified majority*	Elections + referendums	Always public	Same as for others	Large degree

Notes: Options in red represent deviations from the majority preferences, an asterisk means that the most preferred option is significantly different from the second-best option on a 99% level.

Source: RECONNECT Citizen Survey

from many EU decisions taken against the will and vote of the Hungarian government in the Council prior to our survey.

10.4 Citizens' attitudes toward EU reforms: the winner/loser divide

The findings presented in Section 10.3 suggest substantial agreement and consistency of EU policy and reform preferences among the public. This is in contrast to the debate about the increasing polarization of citizens' attitudes towards European integration, globalization and international cooperation. Essentially, the literature argues that divides between so-called 'winners' and 'losers' of recent societal transformations should not only influence how citizens evaluate international cooperation, but also—and in consequence—what avenues of EU reforms they should prefer. In this section, we therefore first describe which indicators we used to measure respondents'—objective and subjective—positions regarding the gulf between winners and losers of recent societal transformations as well as people's general stance on European cooperation (10.4.1.). Next, we examine whether citizens' attitudes towards European integration and their preferred EU policy areas differ based on their position on the societal division (10.4.2). Lastly, we present an analysis of the interactions between respondents' general stance on the EU and their responses in the conjoint analysis (10.4.3).

10.4.1 Indicators of societal and EU-specific divisions

Following empirical insights from previous research, we consider two socio-demographic variables as crucial objective indicators: age and education. Older and less educated individuals are likely to be rather on the losing side of modernization and globalization. Not only have these developments raised the societal status and the economic benefits of higher education,[3] they also come with a loss of traditional values and concepts of life more widely shared by the older generation. Older and less educated voters were also significantly over-represented among the 'Leave' voters in the Brexit referendum (Hobolt 2016).

To obtain the respondents' age, we asked survey participants for their birth year and subtracted it from the year in which the survey took place. Subsequently, we recoded the numeric age into five age groups: 18–24 years, 25–34 years, 35–44 years, 45–54 years, and 55 + years. We inquired about respondents' education by asking 'what is the highest level of education you have achieved?' and provided different educational attainments to choose from. These country-specific educational attainments were recoded into the education levels 'high', 'medium', and 'low' according to the International Standard Classification of Education (ISCED, UNESCO Institute for Statistics 2012).

As there may be a subjective side to being a winner or a loser of societal transformations, we include two more subjective measures: respondents' self-reported socioeconomic status (relative to the overall distribution in society) and their perception of being marginalized economically, culturally, and politically. These perceptions may differ from the more objective factors age and education, as these perceptions are dependent not only on people's living and working conditions but also on individual (psychological) predispositions.

The item used to measure perceived social class reads: 'Imagine a ladder with 11 steps, which reflects the social positions of the population in [COUNTRY]. Where would you place yourself and your own family on this ladder if 0 means "at the bottom" and 10 means "at the top"?' (Respondents were also shown an image of a ladder.) The second subjective indicator is perceived societal marginalization,

[3] As there always is a very strong correlation between reported education and reported income, and as the latter is more prone to biased answering behaviour, we focus on education rather than income here.

which has recently been introduced by Bollwerk et al. (2022). It includes perceptions of being marginalized economically, culturally, and politically, asking respondents to indicate on a scale ranging from 1 ('strongly disagree') to 6 ('strongly agree') their views on statements such as 'no matter how hard we work, people like me are not appreciated', 'the values of people like me are becoming less and less important in society', or 'problems of people like me are unimportant to most politicians'. The general level of a citizen's perceived societal marginalization (PSM) is measured as the average mean of a respondent's agreement with all statements across the economic, cultural, and political dimensions. For the analysis in this chapter, we recoded both continuous measures into ordinal variables with three values, representing groups of respondents who felt that they belonged to the lower, middle, or upper classes in society and groups with low, medium, or high levels of perceived societal marginalization.

Although it is reasonable to show the distribution of the European integration variable and the shares of policies that respondents want the EU to solve among these four societal subgroups, this is not the case for analysing the effect of the winner/loser divide in relation to our conjoint experiment. Hence, regarding the latter, we conducted a separate analysis addressing the relationship between respondents' answers to the conjoint experiment and their general EU-related attitudes. These attitudes were operationalized as supporting or opposing the EU membership of one's own country (Schäfer et al. 2023). We argue that this general EU-related attitude is strongly associated with the winner/loser divide, even though they should not be considered identical.

10.4.2 Attitudes toward EU integration and EU policy areas among societal winners and losers

Starting with attitudes toward more or less integration, our data show that there are major differences between societal winners and losers (see Figure 10.6), suggesting that the winner/loser divide and the conflict between Eurosceptics and Europhiles are closely related.

Even when controlling for the country differences discussed earlier, there is a clear split of attitudes along the winner/loser divide. Age seems to be almost linearly correlated to the integration–disintegration dimension. The younger European citizens are, the higher is the preference for deeper political integration. The only exception is the oldest cohort, where the peace-related benefits of European integration may outweigh the disadvantages associated with further European integration. Education is also a determining factor. The higher people's education level, the more they prefer further political integration. Perceived social class and perceived societal marginalization also show the expected effects. The higher people perceive themselves to be in their society's social order, the stronger is their

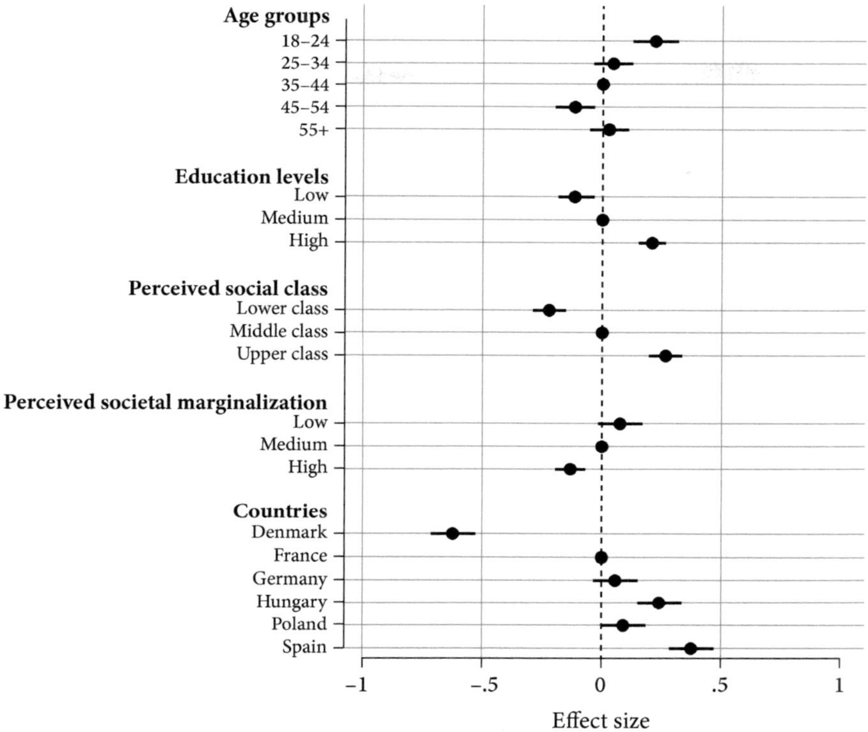

Figure 10.6 Predictors of the preference for more European integration

Notes: The figure shows the results of a linear regression estimating the effects of the depicted predictors on respondents' support of more integration.

Source: RECONNECT Citizen Survey

preference for further European integration. Conversely, individuals who consider themselves to be at the lower end of the socioeconomic ladder have the strongest preference for disintegration among all socio-demographic groups under observation. Respondents in the group with the highest level of perceived societal marginalization are significantly less inclined towards integration, while those perceiving low levels of marginalization are more supportive of further integration.

In sum, the aforementioned results are consistent with the expectations in the literature on the winner/loser divide. Promoting EU integration is supported by the winner side of this new divide, namely by younger, more highly educated citizens who consider themselves part of the higher echelons in society and do not feel marginalized. On the contrary, members of the loser side would oppose such a move. Older, less educated members of the lower class who feel marginalized in society instead favour repatriating competences from the EU to the national level.

When it comes to the most preferred EU policy areas the findings are more varied (see Table 10.4). Examining different socio-demographic groups, one can observe minor age differences. All age groups have the same top priority: climate

Table 10.4 Most preferred EU policy areas across different socio-demographic groups

	No 1	No 2	No 3
Age groups			
18-24	Climate change and environment (25.8%)	Economy and employment (12.6%)	Education and research (10.9%)
25-34	Climate change and environment (20.2%)	Economy and employment (15.1%)	Security and anti-terrorism (9.8%)
35-44	Climate change and environment (20.1)	Economy and employment (12.6%)	Security and anti-terrorism (11.0%)
45-54	Climate change and environment (18.9%)	Security and anti-terrorism (13.7%)	Immigration and asylum (10.7%)
55+	Climate change and environment (16.7%)	Security and anti-terrorism (16.2%)	Immigration and asylum (11.0%)
Education levels			
Low	Climate change and environment (17.6%)	Economy and employment (16.7%)	Security and anti-terrorism (12.8%)
Medium	Climate change and environment (20.3%)	Security and anti-terrorism (11.9%)	Economy and employment (10.4%)
High	Climate change and environment (22.8%)	Security and anti-terrorism (10.4%)	Economy and employment (10.3%)
Perceived social class			
Lower class	Climate change and environment (19.6%)	Economy and employment (13.2%)	Security and anti-terrorism (10.8%)
Middle class	Climate change and environment (21.0%)	Security and anti-terrorism (12.0%)	Economy and employment (11.6%)
Upper class	Climate change and environment (19.9%)	Immigration and asylum (11.8%)	Security and anti-terrorism (11.4%)
Perceived societal marginalization			
Low	Climate change and environment (27.3%)	International trade agreements (10.2%)	Security and anti-terrorism (9.7%)
Medium	Climate change and environment (20.9%)	Economy and employment (11.6%)	Security and anti-terrorism(10.5%)
High	Climate change and environment (19.0%)	Security and anti-terrorism (12.8%)	Economy and employment (12.6%)

Source: RECONNECT Citizen Survey

change. The younger citizens are, however, the more relevant EU action in this area becomes. Moreover, while younger age cohorts have economy and employment as their second priority, older cohorts have a stronger preference for joint action in the area of immigration and asylum. Different education groups also prioritize EU action on climate change, but higher education levels correlate with a stronger preference for EU action in this area. People with lower education rank economy and employment second, whereas this place is occupied by security and anti-terrorism among people with medium to high educational backgrounds.

Looking at the two subjective indicators of the winner/loser divide reveals a similar picture. For both perceived social class and perceived societal marginalization, all groups share the same top priority: climate change and environment. However, people not feeling marginalized are the group with the highest share of respondents mentioning climate change and environment as their preferred policy area (27.3 per cent).

Only the second and third most preferred options vary between the different class and marginalization groups; the lower class demands EU action in economy and employment, the middle class wishes more EU decisions in security and anti-terrorism, and the upper class has a stronger preference for immigration and asylum policies. People not feeling marginalized have a higher priority for international trade agreements as an area in which the EU should take action while the field of economy and employment seems to play a bigger role for those in the groups with medium and high levels of perceived societal marginalization. These findings support the previous impression that the economy matters most for those who are economically vulnerable, feel societally marginalized, or experience economic hardship (such as younger age cohorts, individuals with low education, and those who see themselves at the lower end of the socioeconomic hierarchy).

10.4.3 Citizens' attitudes toward EU reforms and the division between Europhiles and Eurosceptics

In the final step of our analysis, we address the degree of societal conflict over EU reforms. The empirical data from our conjoint experiment presented above revealed only minor country differences with regard to citizens' views on the ideal institutional setting of the EU. The results on the divergent preferences of citizens across the winner/loser divide when it comes to more or less EU integration suggest, however, that there should be more societal contestation about the two decision-making aspects in the authority dimension (bindingness and possibility of being outvoted). As this dimension directly relates to the question of more versus less integration, we can expect societal disagreement over these two attributes. In a separate analysis, we hence examined the interactions between citizens' general EU attitudes and their answers to the conjoint experiment (Schäfer et al. 2023). The results reveal that the general conflict over Europe indeed has an impact on the responses citizens gave in the conjoint experiment. General Euroscepticism or EU support moderate the two attributes in the authority dimension: Eurosceptics and Europhiles display widely diverging preferences when it comes to the bindingness of EU legislation and the decision-making rules in the Council. For Europhiles, the opt-out possibility and qualified majority voting increase their support for EU policy decisions. In stark contrast, Eurosceptics' support of EU policy decisions only increased when the implementation of the decision is left to voluntary compliance by each Member State.

However, general EU attitudes did not moderate the effect of all decision-making dimensions on people's support of EU decisions. In particular, both Europhiles and Eurosceptics agreed on having more direct citizen involvement (input), increasing the transparency of EU decision-making (throughput), and EU policies that actually solve the underlying problems (output). Therefore, it can be concluded that improving the input, throughput, and output legitimacy of the EU while at the same time steering clear of changes to the distribution of power between the EU and the Member States seems to be the sweet spot of EU reform.

10.5 Conclusions

What insights can we draw from our data about the ideal configuration of the EU in the minds of European citizens, and what are the implications of these findings for proposing reforms that could gain widespread support?

Overall, the majority of European citizens seem fairly content with the current distribution of power between the EU and its Member States. While there is a group of citizens that aims to transfer more power to Brussels, there is an equally large group that thinks integration has gone too far already. With regards to the authority dimension of EU reform, therefore, maintaining the status quo appears to be the best available option.

Our analyses show that attitudes towards further integration are related to a new societal divide between winners and losers of recent societal transformations, such as globalization and modernization (Kriesi et al. 2006; 2012; Teney et al. 2014; Hooghe and Marks 2018; Ford and Jennings 2020). The winner side is represented by younger, more highly educated, and more affluent groups who do not perceive themselves to be at the margins of society. These groups are attracted to European integration for both economic and cultural reasons. Economically, they are the main beneficiaries of European integration and globalization. Culturally, they are open-minded and cosmopolitan, which is why they endorse post-national projects like the European Union. On the other side, we find older, less educated, lower-class citizens who feel marginalized in society. They view the EU as a threat to their economic situation rather than an opportunity to advance their careers, and they react defensively to multiculturalism and open borders. For these reasons, they are opposed to pushing European integration forward and instead rather stick to the tried and tested context of their nation state.

In consequence, reforms that affect the balance of power between the EU and the Member States are likely to elicit deep rifts between those who benefit from globalization and modernization processes and those who do not. Therefore, policymakers should be cautious when calling for far-reaching additional powers for the EU. Such proposals are likely to evoke the type of unproductive zero-sum conflicts that have obstructed previous reform debates ever since the Single European Act in the 1980s. Some proposals for deepening integration that have come out of the Conference on the Future of Europe (2022), such as scrapping unanimous decision-making in the Council, need to be treated with caution. The reason is that it would lead to a major reduction of Member State autonomy in several contested policy areas where Member States currently still retain veto power, including taxation, social security and social protection, defence, and foreign affairs. Based on the results of our research, substantial conflicts are to be expected should these proposals be pursued—and the sceptical reactions by a relatively large number of governments to these proposals lend support to this expectation.

However, our findings indicate that not all reform trajectories are equally prone to societal conflicts. Our conjoint analysis has revealed what we call the 'sweet spot' of EU reform, namely changes to the way the EU reaches its decisions that are supported by a broad coalition of citizens bridging the gaps between winners and losers of societal transformations as well as between Eurosceptics and Europhiles. Three of these relatively uncontested areas of reform stand out.

First, our findings reveal significant demand for increasing input legitimacy by expanding direct citizen participation in EU decision-making. Citizens are not satisfied with the sole option of casting a ballot for the European Parliament every five years. They want to have more say in European affairs, not only in the form of referendums but even more so through citizen consultations. Although our results do not allow us to draw unequivocal conclusions about the exact institutional form such citizen consultations could take, our interpretation is that this finding supports calls to expand more direct citizen involvement. A potential option to be explored further is the format of randomly selected European Citizens' Panels, which was tested during the Conference on the Future of Europe and since then has been implemented by the European Commission for the preparation of several policy proposals. Other means of enhancing citizen involvement need to be explored as well. For example, the European Citizens' Initiative, which is currently hampered by relatively high hurdles regarding numbers of supporters and countries covered and unfavourable administrative barriers in some Member States, could be made more accessible.

Second, there is strong support for boosting throughput legitimacy by increasing the transparency of EU-level decision-making processes. This finding is also in line with CoFoE recommendations, which include calls for increasing transparency in general as well as in relation to specific policy issues. It is true that the EU has already achieved a comparatively high level of transparency if compared to many nation states. However, there are certainly still ways in which the EU could learn from the experience of open government frontrunners like the Nordic states. Potential avenues are shedding light on lobbying activities, on the workings of advisory committees that are involved in drawing up legislative proposals of the Commission, or on the comitology procedure. Recently, the latter sparked significant public attention when it transpired that the so-called 'EU taxonomy', which included controversial proposals to classify nuclear power and gas as climate-friendly energy sources, would be decided on the basis of a comitology procedure in which neither Member State governments nor the European Parliament have a major say.

Third, a broad coalition of citizens also supports strengthening the EU's output legitimacy. Many citizens want the EU to solve their problems. If they have the impression that the EU machinery is successful in doing so, their support of EU decisions rises significantly. Although considerations related to citizen participation, transparency, and decision-making procedures are important determinants of people's perceptions of the EU, the classical functionalist and neo-functionalist calculus that citizens would transfer their loyalties to the European level if Brussels produced beneficial policies still remains valid. This is noteworthy for at least two reasons. First, parts of the debate about the democratic deficit of the EU seemed to suggest that the focus of the legitimacy debate has completely shifted from outputs to inputs (see, for example, Føllesdal and Hix 2006; Habermas 2015). Although our findings support the idea that improving citizen participation and transparency could boost citizen support, they also show that we should not overlook traditional accounts on output legitimacy. This implication ties in with the results of previous research about the relevance of output considerations for EU attitudes (see, for example, Kritzinger 2005). Second, EU policymakers should carefully select issues that citizens consider pressing issues for the EU to tackle, while also considering the likelihood of decision-making impasses and thus the risk of failure of policy initiatives, which could negatively affect citizen support. In other words, EU policymakers should avoid promising solutions on which they cannot deliver.

In this context, a final piece of evidence from our analysis is worth mentioning: citizens' preferences for the policy areas that the EU should focus on in the future. The data suggest that the most popular policy areas are those with a clear transnational dimension, suggesting that people are aware of the benefits emerging from coordinated EU action in these areas. This is particularly striking for the most preferred EU policy area across the board: climate change and the environment. However, we have also seen demands for joint action in other international policy fields, such as security, anti-terrorism, or migration. By contrast, policy areas where the added value of EU action is less evident rank much lower in citizens' minds. Against this background, calls for more EU action in domestic policy areas like social policy or civil liberties and minority rights are likely to miss the mark in the eyes of many Europeans. The high priority given to EU action in areas related to perceptions of global threats suggests that Emmanuel Macron's narrative of *Une Europe qui protège* should resonate with many citizens. The debate on EU reforms could thus focus on the EU's role as a protective force against external threats. Taking into account the strong correlation between perceptions of (external) threats and Eurosceptic attitudes, which we know from previous research (McLaren 2002), the EU taking on such a role may even convince some of the Eurosceptics to become more favourable.

References

Bansak, K., Hainmueller, J., Hopkins, D. J., and Yamamoto, T. (2023). Using Conjoint Experiments to Analyze Elections: The Essential Role of the Average Marginal Component Effect. *Political Analysis*, 31(4): 500–518.

Bollwerk, M., Back, M., and Schlipphak, B. (2022). Development and Validation of the Perceived Societal Marginalization Scale. *European Journal of Psychological Assessment*, 38 (2): 137–149.

Boomgaarden, H. G., Schuck, A. R. T., Elenbaas, M., and De Vreese, C. H. (2011). Mapping EU attitudes: Conceptual and Empirical Dimensions of Euroscepticism and EU Support. *European Union Politics*, 12(2): 241–266.

Conference on the Future of Europe (2022). *Report on the Final Outcome.* Brussels, Publication Office of the European Union.

De Vries, C. and Hoffmann, I. (2015). What Do The People Want? Opinions, Moods and Preferences of European Citizens. *EUopinions* 2015/1, Bertelsmann Stiftung.

Ejrnaes, A. and Jensen, M. D. (2019). Divided but United: Explaining Nested Public Support For European Integration. *West European Politics*, 42(7): 1390–1419.

Euronews (9 May 2022). Von der Leyen Backs Ending Unanimous Voting in Some Areas of EU. https://www.euronews.com/my-europe/2022/05/09/von-der-leyen-backs-ending-unanimous-voting-in-some-areas-of-eu. Accessed 22 July 2025.

European Conservatives and Reformists (2022). ECR Group Delegation Withdrawal from the Conference on the Future of Europe. https://ecrgroup.eu/article/ecr_group_delegation_withdrawal_from_the_conference_on_the_future_of_europe. Accessed 22 July 2025.

Føllesdal, A. and Hix, S. (2006). Why There is a Democratic Deficit in the EU: A response to Majone and Moravcsik. *Journal of Common Market Studies*, 44(3): 533–562.

Ford, R. and Jennings, W. (2020). The Changing Cleavage Politics of Western Europe. *Annual Review of Political Science*, 23(1): 295–314.

Goldberg, A. C., van Elsas, E. J., and de Vreese, C. H. (2021a). Eurovisions: An Exploration and Explanation of Public Preferences for Future EU Scenarios. *Journal of Common Market Studies*, 59(2): 222–241.

Goldberg, A. C., van Elsas, E. J., and de Vreese, C. H. (2021b). One Union, Different Futures? Public Preferences for the EU's Future and their Explanations in 10 EU Countries. *European Union Politics*, 22(4): 721–740.

Green, P. E., Krieger, A. M., and Wind, Y. (2001). Thirty Years of Conjoint Analysis: Reflections and Prospects. *Interfaces*, 31(3): 56–73.

Haas, E. B., 1958. *The Uniting of Europe.* Stanford, Stanford University Press.

Habermas, J. (2015). Democracy in Europe: Why the Development of the EU into a Transnational Democracy is Necessary and How it is Possible. *European Law Journal*, 21(4): 546–557.

Hahm, H., Hilpert, D., and König, T. (2020). Institutional Reform and Public Attitudes Toward EU Decision Making. *European Journal of Political Research*, 59(3): 599–623.
Hainmueller, J., Hangartner D., and Yamamoto, T. (2015). Validating Vignette and Conjoint Survey Experiments Against Real-World Behavior. *Proceedings of the National Academy of Sciences*, 112 (8): 2395–2400.
Hainmueller, J., Hopkins, D. J., and Yamamoto, T. (2014). Causal Inference in Conjoint Analysis: Understanding Multidimensional Choices via Stated Preference Experiments. *Political Analysis*, 22(1): 1–30.
Hobolt, S. B. (2009). *Europe in Question: Referendums on European Integration*. Oxford, Oxford University Press.
Hobolt, S. B. (2016). The Brexit Vote: A Divided Nation, A Divided Continent. *Journal of European Public Policy*, 23(9): 1259–1277.
Hobolt, S. B. and De Vries, C. E (2016). Public Support for European Integration. *Annual Review of Political Science*, 19(1): 413–432.
Hooghe, L. and Marks, G. (2009). A Postfunctionalist Theory of European Integration: From Permissive Consensus to Constraining Dissensus. *British Journal of Political Science*, 39(1): 1–23.
Hooghe, L. and Marks, G. (2018). Cleavage Theory Meets Europe's Crises: Lipset, Rokkan, and the Transnational Cleavage. *Journal of European Public Policy*, 25(1): 109–135.
Kriesi, H. et al. (2006). Globalization and the Transformation of the National Political Space: Six European Countries Compared. *European Journal of Political Research*, 45(6): 921–956.
Kriesi, H., et al. (2012). *Political Conflict in Western Europe*. Cambridge, Cambridge University Press.
Kritzinger, S. (2005). European Identity Building from the Perspective of Efficiency. *Comparative European Politics*, 3(1): 50–75.
McLaren, L. M. (2002). Public Support for the European Union: Cost/Benefit Analysis or Perceived Cultural Threat? *Journal of Politics*, 64(2): 551–566.
Mitrany, D. (1966). *A Working Peace System*. Chicago, Quadrangle Books.
Schäfer, C. and Gross, M. (2020). Euroscepticism in Times of Crisis: A Macro-Level Analysis of the Euro Crisis' Effects on Public Opinion and Party Competition on European Integration. In Bladassari, M. et al. (eds). *Anti-Europeanism: Critical Perspectives Towards the European Union*. Cham, Springer Nature: 31–55.
Schäfer, C. et al. (2021). The Reshaping of Political Conflict Over Europe: From Pre-Maastricht to Post-'Euro Crisis'. *West European Politics*, 44(3): 531–557.
Schäfer, C., Treib, O., and Schlipphak, B. (2023). What Kind of EU do Citizens Want? Reform Preferences and the Conflict over Europe. *Journal of European Public Policy*, 30 (9): 1738–1761.
Scharpf, F. W. (1999). *Governing in Europe: Effective and Democratic?* Oxford, Oxford University Press.
Schlipphak, B. and Treib, O. (2017). Playing the Blame Game on Brussels: The Domestic Political Effects of EU Interventions Against Democratic Backsliding. *Journal of European Public Policy*, 24(3): 352–365.
Schlipphak, B. et al. (2023). When are Governmental Blaming Strategies Effective? How Blame, Source and Trust Effects Shape Citizens' Acceptance of EU Sanctions Against Democratic Backsliding. *Journal of European Public Policy* 30(9): 1715–1737.
Schmidt, V. A. (2013). Democracy and Legitimacy in the European Union Revisited: Input, Output and 'Throughput'. *Political Studies* 61(1): 2–22.
Schmidt, V. A. (2020). *Europe's Crisis of Legitimacy: Governing by Rules and Ruling by Numbers in the Eurozone*. Oxford, Oxford University Press.
Schweiger, C. (2016). *Exploring the EU's Legitimacy Crisis: The Dark Heart of Europe*. Cheltenham, Edward Elgar Publishing.
Serricchio, F., Tsakatika, M., and Quaglia, L. (2013). Euroscepticism and the Global Financial Crisis. *Journal of Common Market Studies*, 51(1): 51–64.

Sweden in EU (2022). Non-paper by Bulgaria, Croatia, the Czech Republic, Denmark, Estonia, Finland, Latvia, Lithuania, Malta, Poland, Romania, Slovenia, and Sweden on the Outcome of and Follow-up to the Conference on the Future of Europe. https://twitter.com/sfwedenineu/status/1523637827686531072. Accessed 22 July 2025.

Taggart, P. and Szczerbiak, A. (2018). Putting Brexit into Perspective: The Effect of the Eurozone and Migration Crises and Brexit on Euroscepticism in European States. *Journal of European Public Policy*, 25(8): 1194–1214.

Teney, C., Lacewell, O. P., and De Wilde, P. (2014). Winners and Losers of Globalization in Europe: Attitudes and Ideologies. *European Political Science Review*, 6(4): 575–595.

Treib, O. (2014). The Voter Says No, But Nobody Listens: Causes and Consequences of the Eurosceptic Vote in the 2014 European Elections. *Journal of European Public Policy*, 21(10): 1541–1554.

Treib, O. (2021). Euroscepticism is Here To Stay: What Cleavage Theory Can Teach Us about the 2019 European Parliament Elections. *Journal of European Public Policy*, 28(2): 174–189.

UNESCO Institute for Statistics (2012). *International Standard Classification of Education 2011*. Montreal, UNESCO Institute for Statistics.

Vasilopoulou, S. (2018). The Party Politics of Euroscepticism in Times of Crisis: The Case of Greece. *Politics*, 38(3): 311–326.

Zeitlin, J., Nicoli, F., and Laffan, B. (2019). Introduction: The European Union beyond the Polycrisis? Integration and Politicization in an Age of Shifting Cleavages. *Journal of European Public Policy*, 26(7): 963–976.

11

Citizen Participation without Democratization in the EU: From the European Citizens' Initiative to the Conference on the Future of Europe

Alvaro Oleart

11.1 Introduction: the relationship between citizen participation and EU democracy

There is a vast literature about the European Union (EU)'s 'democratic deficit', which is closely related to the lack of popular participation in the European project (and the low turnout in European elections) and the normative questions that arise from it in terms of democratic legitimacy (e.g. Kohler-Koch and Rittberger 2007). In response to these concerns, since the early 2000s the EU has developed an important emphasis on the participation of citizens, civil society, and on the construction of a European public sphere, which initially is conceived as part of the same process. The emergence of 'participatory democracy' as a 'norm' (Saurugger 2010) influenced not only the mainstream narratives of 'participation' in the EU, but also its practices. Since the Lisbon Treaty of 2009, there have been several innovations in the way in which 'participation' is conceived and practiced at the EU level. In addition to the pre-existing right of citizens to send petitions to the European Parliament, the Lisbon Treaty introduced the European Citizens' Initiative (ECI), in 2012 the European Commission created the citizens' dialogues, and in 2018 the Council organized the European Citizen Consultations (ECCs). All these participatory initiatives paved the way to the 2021–22 Conference on the Future of Europe (CoFoE), followed by a set of 'new generation' European Citizens' Panels (ECPs) organized by the European Commission.

While there are good reasons for expanding citizen participation in EU policy-making as a way to foster transnational democracy, the chapter questions whether these initiatives have actually contributed to democratizing the EU. After reviewing the different mechanisms, the chapter argues that, except for the ECI, most of these mechanisms have had a tendency to reproduce the pre-existing depoliticized EU

Alvaro Oleart, *Citizen Participation without Democratization in the EU: From the European Citizens' Initiative to the Conference on the Future of Europe* In: *The Promise of EU Democracy*. Edited by: Jan Wouters, Julie Smith, Kolja Raube, and Ben Crum, Oxford University Press. © Alvaro Oleart 2026. DOI: 10.1093/9780191996191.003.0013 political dynamics. Taking an agonistic perspective, the chapter argues that the depoliticization of participation is incompatible with EU democratization, and leads to a 'public relations' understanding of 'participation'. This dynamic has been conceived as 'citizenwashing' (Petit and Oleart 2025; Oleart 2025), an attempt by the EU to create the illusion of listening to 'everyday citizens' while in fact reproducing depoliticized institutional logics. In contrast, the chapter proposes that new mechanisms of citizen participation from a public sphere and mass politics perspective should be embedded more closely into the functioning of the EU, in such a way that they contribute to fostering EU debates in key spaces, such as national parliaments, the (national) media, and among civil society and social movements.

After this introduction, the chapter develops a conceptual framework of making sense of EU participatory instruments. Thirdly, the chapter introduces the ECI as a particularly relevant innovation of EU participatory instruments. Fourthly, the chapter dives into the citizen dialogues and the European Citizen Consultations. Next, the CoFoE and the post-CoFoE European Citizens' Panels are described. The chapter concludes with a comparative analysis of the different instruments, and argues that the latest innovations—the CoFoE and the ECPs—fail to deliver on their democracy promises, much like the previous democracy-enhancing participatory instruments.

11.2 The promise of participatory democracy in the EU: agonism or public relations?

The 'participatory turn' of the EU, conceptualized by Saurugger (2010), represents an attempt by the EU to tackle the existing gap between EU institutions and European citizens by encouraging debate through the participation of European 'civil society' actors. Many of these civil society actors became institutionalized and professionalized lobby organizations based in Brussels. EU institutions thus saw civil society actors as a sort of mediator between EU institutions and citizens. Civil society was seen as an integral component of EU democratization, with intermediary organizations expanding EU debates beyond the 'Brussels bubble' and contributing to the emergence of a European public sphere, while also shaping EU policies. However, the emergence of a Brussels-based network of European civil society actors has not necessarily facilitated the linkage between national and EU politics nor with 'citizens'. Brussels-based civil society actors have mostly adapted to the rather technical and depoliticized EU policy-making process, instead of bringing activist energy to EU institutions. In turn, the strong technocratic role of the Brussels-based organizations has meant that European civil society has mostly reinforced the 'field of Eurocracy' (Georgakakis and Rowell 2013) rather than expanding European debates onto national ones.

This system of 'elite pluralism' (Eising 2009) among strongly institutionalized actors (Greenwood 2003) structurally sidelines activist groups that aim to burst the Brussels bubble by taking EU debates to the European public spheres as a way to politicize the EU (Haapala and Oleart 2022). This structure of interest representation encourages a very technical (as opposed to 'politicized') process where actors must adapt to the Commission's framing of issues (Klüver, Mahoney, and Opper 2015). In Brussels, the majority of interest groups are business actors, which have a strong financial advantage vis-à-vis civil society actors in the EU lobbying contest (Baumgartner and Mahoney 2008). The European Commission has attempted to correct the imbalance among interest groups by providing funding for civil society umbrella organizations. These umbrella groups often represent other civil society actors at the national level (Sánchez Salgado 2014), in spite of the fact that they tend to operate more as lobbyists than activists. Therefore, the Commission has cultivated civil society 'partners' (Kutay 2012), rather than bottom-up contestatory organizations that may challenge its agenda not only in the corridors but also in the streets (Parks 2015).

In this context, a key element in normatively assessing the participatory democracy instruments that the EU has put forward is the extent to which they foster agonistic contestation in the European public sphere (Oleart 2021). If unable to politicize debates around EU policies and the EU as a polity, participatory instruments will mostly perform primarily a public relations role and reproduce the traditional consensus-oriented understanding of democracy in the EU context (Crespy 2014). The depoliticized approach to EU democracy is what has been conceptualized as 'democracy without politics' (Oleart and Theuns 2023; Oleart 2023a). The distinction between Schmidt's (2013) 'policy without politics' and the idea of 'democracy without politics' in this context is that there is no actual policy (or, rather, very limited) coming out of these exercises. Rather, they represent an effort to communicate that EU institutions are democratizing their relations with EU citizens, albeit following a depoliticized approach to democracy—hence 'without politics'.

This depoliticized approach to democracy discourages political parties, trade unions, and civil society actors from participating. The idea of *democracy without politics* reflects well how EU institutions may actually exacerbate the hollowing out (Mair 2013) of EU democracy. Rather than technical and consensus-oriented processes, pluralist democracy politics requires collective actors able to put forward their ideas in the public sphere and confront them with alternative ideas. As Chantal Mouffe has argued:

> Belief in the possibility of a universal rational consensus has put democratic thinking on the wrong track. Instead of trying to design the institutions which, through supposedly 'impartial' procedures, would reconcile all conflicting interests and values, the task for democratic theorists and politicians should be to

> envisage the creation of a vibrant 'agonistic' public sphere of contestation where different hegemonic political projects can be confronted. (Mouffe 2005: 3.)

While there are certainly reasons to complement EU representative democracy with participatory mechanisms, there are risks associated with cooptation of these instruments by EU institutions. If they cannot foster agonistic debates, such mechanisms can become elite-run participatory fora that reproduce EU jargon without any meaningful connection to grassroots activism, and in doing so reinforce technocratic dynamics rather than challenge them. It follows from this that the promises of participatory democracy in the EU can be conceived either as an attempt to bring agonism to EU debates in the European public spheres or, conversely, as an exercise of public relations by EU institutions.

11.3 The European Citizens' Initiative: connecting policy debates with the European public spheres

When the Lisbon Treaty came into effect in 2009, Article 11 of the Treaty of the European Union included references not only to organized civil society, but also to the ECI. This was the outcome of differentiated lobbying regarding direct participation (Bouza Garcia 2015), and an innovation in European politics based on the type of political participation that the EU rewards. Rather than 'technical expertise', the ECI emphasizes the capacity to mobilize large numbers of EU citizens for a particular cause; if at least one million signatures are collected, the EU institutions are obliged to 'respond'. Therefore, it has been argued that the ECI has the potential to modify the interaction between EU institutions and civil society (Bouza Garcia and Greenwood 2014), because a successful ECI requires the promoters to reach at least one million supporters and probably also requires them to cooperate with national civil society organizations, trade unions, and political parties to secure as many signatures as possible. In this process, the ECI transforms grassroots mobilization into a valuable resource (Oleart and Bouza 2018), an innovation considering that this type of participation was previously rarely mobilized beyond farmers and trade unions (Balme and Chabanet 2008). By using the ECI, its promoters need to frame their demands in such a way that they can reach different audiences simultaneously, both to the national publics (to secure the requisite number of signatures in multiple countries) and EU institutions (because they have to approve the demand and will also process it).

This is unprecedented in the EU context because previous mechanisms for interaction with civil society were based on organizations' responses to Commission proposals, which left EU institutions to frame the issues, traditionally in a relatively technocratic and depoliticized fashion (Radaelli 1999). Instead, the ECI allows actors to launch new initiatives, albeit within the limits of the existing Treaties. In doing so, the ECI provides incentives to use frames that resonate among the different national public spheres, and can be seen as a fertile ground for introducing new EU issues onto the national political agendas as well as EU-level discussions. The close connection between the policy process and public debates in the ECI is reflected in the way in which the mechanism is designed. Before starting to collect signatures, organizers must register their initiative with the European Commission and pass the test that the subject matter and the proposals are within the Commission's power to act in implementation of the EU treaties. Once the Commission accepts the proposal, a period of twelve months is given to the initiators to collect the necessary signatures. Finally, the ECI is also regulated as to the outcome. Initiators who successfully collect one million signatures (in addition to reaching a minimum threshold in at least a third of the Member States) are invited to a hearing in the European Parliament and the Commission must formally respond, indicating whether it will respond to the demands, and, if so, how. Only an issue that is widely discussed in the European public spheres can enter the EU policy agenda in this way.

Unfortunately, while the ECI may lead us to think that mass mobilization has become an important capital in the 'field of Eurocracy', the experience of successful ECIs demonstrates that the policy influence has been minimal. At the time of writing, ten initiatives had collected more than a million signatures: 'One of us' (on abortion); 'Water and sanitation are a human right! Water is a public good, not a commodity!'; 'Stop vivisection'; 'Minority SafePack – one million signatures for diversity in Europe'; 'Ban glyphosate and protect people and the environment from toxic pesticides'; 'End the Cage Age'; 'Save bees and farmers! Towards a bee-friendly agriculture for a healthy environment'; 'Stop Finning – Stop the Trade'; 'Save Cruelty Free Cosmetics – Commit to a Europe without Animal Testing'; and 'Fur Free Europe'. Furthermore, as of August 2025, one ECI was under examination by the Commission—'Cohesion policy for the equality of the regions and sustainability of the regional cultures'; and three more ECIs had reached the threshold but were still undergoing verification—'My Voice, My Choice: For Safe And Accessible Abortion'; 'Ban on conversion practices in the European Union'; and 'Stop Extremism' (see European Commission n.d.).

Additionally, the self-organized Stop TTIP ECI also reached the threshold in October 2015, although the Commission initially (incorrectly) denied its registration. All initiatives had received a 'response', but none of them had received a meaningful policy follow-up as demanded by the initiators, in spite of the claims by the Commission that there had been (this refers mostly to the two petitions on the right to water and banning glyphosate). Consequently, the incentives for future ECI initiators are rather low, in that overcoming the institutional hurdles of building an ECI campaign does not appear to be meaningfully rewarded in terms of policy and agenda-setting.

11.4 The citizen dialogues and the European Citizen Consultations

In parallel to the ECI, in 2012 the Commission initiated the 'citizen dialogues'. They were developed ahead of the 2013 'European Year of the Citizens', which commemorated the 20th anniversary of the Maastricht Treaty. Initially conceived as a communication exercise to demonstrate that the EU was 'closing the gap' with its citizens, they were expanded with the arrival of Jean-Claude Juncker as Commission President in 2014. The citizen dialogues mostly consisted in a questions and answers format in different cities across the EU, with at least one representative from the European Commission. They evolved progressively from a small-scale communication exercise during the final years of the Barroso Commission (2012–14) to become institutionalized during the Juncker and later Von der Leyen Commissions (see Hierlemann et al. 2022). The idea was to progressively expand them not only to promote what the Commission does, but also to get feedback on it.

The citizens' dialogues in this way ideationally facilitated the organization of the European Citizens' Consultations (ECC).[1] These were a one-off exercise carried out throughout 2018, pushed by French President Emmanuel Macron, who called for involving citizens in the debate about the future of Europe at a famous speech at the Sorbonne on 26 September 2017. This indicates a dialectic between the evolution of participatory democracy at the EU and national level. With the important influence of Ireland's experiences with citizens' assemblies (Farrell et al. 2019) and Macron's attempt to respond to the yellow vests movement (Ehs and Mokre 2021), the ECCs were part of a wider transnational trend towards 'listening to citizens directly' without intermediaries such as political parties, trade unions or civil society organizations.

The ECCs were an innovation in comparison to previous mechanisms at the EU level, providing a space in which citizens at the national level could participate in European democracy and the future of European integration. Unlike the citizen dialogues and public consultations, the ECCs were organized by the Member States in partnership with national and local organizations, and the results would be reported back to the European Council. However, Member States were given flexibility in terms of how they were carried out. Consequently, they followed very different procedures (Stratulat and Butcher 2018). The lack of common processes and concrete goals made the consultations a mainly symbolic mechanism that lacked coherence, and its biggest innovation was to put the future of Europe debate onto the national agendas of the Member States (Butcher and Pronckutė 2019), doing so in a disintermediated way from a 'citizen' perspective.

[1] EU institutions did not agree on a common title for this exercise. Following the European Policy Centre and particularly Butcher and Pronckutė (2019), I use the term European Citizens' Consultations in this chapter.

The ECCs were not followed by any concrete changes. The main formal outcome of it came in the form of the 13–14 December 2018 European Council summit conclusions, which included a vague hint towards following them up with another process: 'The European Council welcomes the holding of Citizens' Dialogues and Citizens' Consultations, which was an unprecedented opportunity to engage with European citizens and which could serve as an inspiration for further consultations and dialogues' (European Council 2018). In this way, the ECCs paved the way for the Conference on the Future of Europe.

11.5 The Conference on the Future of Europe

[2] Following Macron's emphasis on listening 'directly' to citizens at the EU level with the ECCs and at the national level through *Le Grand Débat* and the French Citizens' Convention for Climate in 2019 and 2020, European Commission presidential candidate Von der Leyen proposed the CoFoE to the European Parliament in order to gain political support for parliamentary approval of her Commission in July 2019. Von der Leyen promised the CoFoE as a two-year participatory democracy exercise that would give recommendations by 'citizens' about what the future of Europe should be. In her speech as President-elect of the European Commission, Von der Leyen suggested that the CoFoE 'should be inclusive for all institutions and citizens and the European Parliament should have a leading role' (European Commission 2019).

On Europe Day—9 May—2021, EU leaders finally launched the CoFoE, albeit following a year-long delay caused by the Covid-19 pandemic as well as by a lack of agreement among EU institutions on its governance. It was an attempt by EU institutions to reach out beyond the usual suspects and interest groups, by putting 'citizens at the centre'. The CoFoE was politically led by a joint presidency and an executive board composed by members of the three main EU institutions (European Commission, Council, and Parliament), and organizationally by a Common Secretariat that comprised officials from all three institutions. The CoFoE leadership divided the initiative in four main spaces: the Multilingual Digital platform, Decentralized Events, the European Citizens' Panels (and national citizens' panels), and the Conference Plenary.

The multilingual digital platform was a space in which any citizen could put forward their proposals. However, as an initial entry point for the Conference, it was unclear how it would connect to the other spaces that constituted the architecture of the Conference. The CoFoE encouraged the self-organization of events related to the future of Europe. As of 20 April 2022, there had been 6,465 events

[2] This section draws on Oleart (2023b).

and 652,532 event participants reported in the Conference platform (CoFoE 2022a: 13), considerably less than the million signatures required for a successful ECI, which illustrates the lack of popular appeal of the CoFoE. Furthermore, these events were organized by mediators such as civil society organizations, yet were not integrated substantively into the plenary. The events were meant to foster debate on the future of Europe, and were conceived as 'public outreach' rather than an attempt to meaningfully integrate ideas into the plenary (on the national and regional participation on the CoFoE, see Abels 2023). The institutional backing of the CoFoE sent a message to EU citizens that there was willingness on the part of the institutions to democratize the EU, but the lack of popular participation and the strong control of the process exerted by EU institutions made it very difficult for democratization to actually happen.

The most innovative dimension of the CoFoE was the creation of the European Citizens' Panels (and also the national citizens' panels, which were organized by some Member States, but had to follow particular criteria set by the CoFoE in order to be officially considered as such[3]): a set of four panels, the methodology of which was constructed by a number of deliberative democracy consultancies[4] (in constant cooperation with the CoFoE Secretariat), that touched upon different policy areas. Panel 1 covered Stronger economy, social justice, and jobs/youth, sport, culture, and education/digital transformation; panel 2 EU democracy, values, rights, rule of law, security; panel 3 Climate change, environment, health; and panel 4, EU in the world, migration. In each of the four panels, 200 randomly selected citizens from across EU Member States deliberated and made recommendations about the public policies the EU could take.

Each of the four panels had three three-day sessions (Friday, Saturday, and Sunday): the first one in Strasbourg at the European Parliament in September–October 2021, the second online in November 2021, and the third one in a different host city between December 2021 and February 2022 (panel 1 in Dublin, panel 2 in Florence, panel 3 in Warsaw, and panel 4 in Maastricht). During the first session, citizens deliberated in order to define the agenda, prioritizing a set of concrete issues within the policy area at stake. During the second session they undertook a thematic deepening of those issues prioritized in the first weekend, constructing a set of 'orientations', and the third session transitioned from these orientations towards concrete recommendations. The deliberation within the panels was moderated by 'neutral' facilitators, informed throughout the sessions

[3] Six EU Member States organized national citizens' panels that followed the CoFoE criteria: Belgium, Germany, France, Italy, Lithuania, and the Netherlands.

[4] The leading organization of the deliberative democracy consortium was Missions Publiques (France), in cooperation with the Danish Board of Technology (Denmark), ifok (Germany), and Deliberativa (Spain). The company Kantar Public was in charge of the selection of the European citizen panel participants, and the communication agency VO Europe also played a relevant role in the practical organization and implementation of the panels.

by 'neutral' experts that were selected by the CoFoE institutional leadership. The input provided by the 'experts' diverged widely, in spite of the fact that they were asked by the organizers to provide 'neutral' input. While the majority of 'experts' were academics, there were also former politicians, civil society representatives, think tank members, trade unionists, or current and former EU officials. In this way, political conflict was largely neutralized, as the randomly selected citizens were not confronted with the pre-existing conflicting views (for instance, the existing proposals by the different EU political groups) regarding the political issue they were deliberating upon.

The constant emphasis on the 'neutrality' of the process is likely to have been the outcome of a fragile equilibrium between the three leading EU institutions (Oleart 2023a). The three main EU institutions were in constant disagreement over the purpose of the CoFoE as a whole and the topics it should cover. The compromise was to cover every policy area, hence the thematic broadness of the four ECPs. The sensitivities of EU institutions also led the CoFoE Secretariat towards 'protecting' the participants of the European citizen panels from what they understood to be 'undue influence'. Thus, by design, the ECPs were meant to be insulated from the wider societal and political debate (see also Crum 2022), and the all-encompassing policy scope of the CoFoE complicated zooming in on particular dilemmas facing the future of European integration, and sidelined the voices of relevant mediators such as political parties, civil society organizations or trade unions. In fact, throughout the Conference plenary sessions there were repeated complaints in the public interventions of civil society and trade union representatives on the basis of their lack of involvement. In a public interview, Alexandrina Najmowicz, the Secretary General of the European Civic Forum and a member of the CoFoE plenary, argued the following vis-à-vis the role of civil society in the CoFoE:

> This lack of recognition has become even more visible and problematic when it comes to the Conference on the Future of Europe, its decision-making process and its functioning. The intergovernmental conference preparing the constitutional treaty in 2000 involved European networks of civil society organizations through a Civil Society Forum, and representatives of the latter were regularly invited to the conference. Twenty years later, *the role of intermediary civic organizations has taken a back seat*, as the EU plans to engage in a deliberative exercise by addressing European citizens directly and individually. This exercise is necessary, but *it must not be limited to institutional populism and public relations*, which will ultimately lead to an inevitable increase in mistrust of European and national institutions. (European Civic Forum 2022, emphasis added.)

The Conference Plenary was the most important component of the CoFoE. It was composed mainly of MEPs, Council representatives, the European Commission, and MPs from national parliaments; but also by ambassadors from

Table 11.1 Members of the CoFoE plenary by institution

Institution	Number of plenary members
European Parliament	108
National MPs	108
Council	54
European Commission	3
Citizen ambassadors (EU + National + EYF)	80 + 27 + 1
Committee of the Regions	18
European Economic and Social Committee	18
Elected regional authorities	6
Elected local authorities	6
Social Partners	12
Civil Society	8
Total	449

Source: CoFoE (n.d.)

the European and national citizens' panels, as well as members of civil society, social partners, and regional authorities (see Table 11.1). The Plenary was the main decision-making institutional actor of CoFoE, as it was the space where all the input gathered through the three spaces described above was discussed and deliberated upon. The Plenary was itself divided into nine 'Working Groups', each dedicated to a different policy area/cluster. The Working Groups covered the following themes: Climate change and the environment; Health; A stronger economy, social justice, and jobs; EU in the world; Values and rights, rule of law, security; Digital transformation; European democracy; Migration; and Education, culture, Youth, Sport.

The Working Groups were composed of a subset of members from among the different actors that composed the plenary. They introduced all the input on the particular policy cluster in common, and each of the Working Groups delivered a concrete set of recommendations to the wider plenary. Each working group had a 'chair', whose task was to gather and order the input from the members of the group. However, while the Working Groups were more thematically targeted, the functioning of the working groups was heterogeneous, as each chair put forward different 'rules' and methods for their working group. As for the voting, four institutional 'components' were required to vote formally—European Parliament, European Commission, national parliaments, and the Council. There was also a 'citizen component', formed by the 'citizen ambassadors' of the European and national citizens' panel, which gave support to the final report, even if it was not formally binding.

The CoFoE formally ended with a set of forty-nine proposals endorsed by the plenary and the component parts, all of which are available in the 'Report on the Final Outcome' of the CoFoE (2022b). The recommendations were developed and negotiated within the nine working groups, and each of them was constructed upon three dimensions: proposal, objective and measures. The 'proposal' indicates the main subject matter, the objective indicates the goals of the recommendation, and the measures include the specific ways in which those objectives are to be accomplished and how the subject matter is addressed (each recommendation includes multiple measures related to it). A selected set of democracy-related examples are included in Table 11.2.

Interestingly, one of the final CoFoE proposals advocated further citizens' assemblies, which was heavily supported by the 'citizen ambassadors'. Other proposals, such as the 'transnational lists' came from MEPs, using the CoFoE arena to promote and advocate ideas that have long been in the EU institutions corridors.

Table 11.2 Selected democracy-related final proposals from the CoFoE

N.	Proposal	Objective	(Selected) Measures
36	Citizens' information, participation and youth	Increase citizens' participation and youth involvement in democracy at the European Union level to develop a 'full civic experience' for Europeans, ensure that their voice is heard also in between elections, and that the participation is effective. That is why the most appropriate form of participation should be considered for each topic, for example by:	7. Holding Citizens' assemblies periodically, on the basis of legally binding EU law. Participants must be selected randomly, with representativeness criteria, and participation should be incentivized.
38	Democracy and elections	Strengthen European democracy by bolstering its foundations, boosting participation in European Parliament elections, fostering transnational debate on European issues and ensuring a strong link between citizens and their elected representatives, in particular by:	3. Amending EU electoral law to harmonize electoral conditions (voting age, election date, requirements for electoral districts, candidates, political parties and their financing) for the European Parliament elections, as well as moving towards voting for Union-wide lists, or 'transnational lists'...

Source: Own elaboration with text from the final report of the CoFoE (2022b)

In terms of the follow-up, the most relevant has been the European Parliament's push to open the discussion surrounding Treaty change. On 9 June 2022, only one month after the CoFoE official conclusion, the European Parliament adopted a plenary resolution that called on the European Council to kick off an open process to amend the EU Treaties, in accordance with Article 48 of the TEU. The EP's ambitious resolution included the right of legislative initiative for the EP, the abolition of veto powers in the Council and the strengthening of the European Pillar of Social Rights, among other things (European Parliament 2022). Furthermore, the CoFoE has contributed to normalizing the idea of citizens' panels within the EP. In fact, the EP adopted the report 'Parliamentarism, European citizenship and democracy' with a broad parliamentary majority in September 2023. The Resolution included 'the institutionalisation of representative deliberative participation processes based on the model of the CoFE's European Citizens Panels' (European Parliament 2023). However, while the EP is approving reports on citizen participation, the Commission is already organizing them.

11.6 The 'new generation' of European citizens' panels: technocratic 'citizen participation'

The main focus of EU institutions when attempting to demonstrate that they had taken into account the discussions of the CoFoE was twofold. First, the 'policy follow up'. Representatives from the Commission claimed that 80 per cent of their 2023 work programme was based on the CoFoE. Even if it were true, it probably reflects the fact that the recommendations reproduced pre-existing hegemonic ideas in the EU rather than illustrating how the Commission responded to the CoFoE. Second, and most importantly for this chapter, the Commission launched a series of 'new generation' of citizens' panels on specific topics. The new generation of citizen panels post-CoFoE is led by the European Commission, who has attempted to 'embed' participatory democracy within their own policy-making, following the methodology of the CoFoE's citizen panels. I personally observed the first six panels[5] dedicated to the narrower topics included in Table 11.3.

While the criteria used by the Commission to select these set of topics was never made explicit, based on conversations with actors involved in the organization of the panels, the topics were pragmatically chosen on the basis of (1) the handful of ongoing policy dossiers that were advanced enough to integrate input from a

[5] As of November 2025, at the time of finishing the chapter, there were two ongoing ECPs organized by the Commission, which I did not observe. The thematic focus of the first one was Intergenerational Fairness, and was largely based on the same methodology as the previous ECPs. The second one was the Young Citizens Assembly on Pollinators, which had some specificities in comparison to the other post-CoFoE ECPs, as it had a smaller number of participants (100 instead of 150) and they were all aged 18 to 19 years old.

Table 11.3 Dates of the three sessions of the seven 'new generation' panels

Topic of the panel	Session 1 (Brussels)	Session 2 (online)	Session 3 (Brussels)
Food Waste	16–18 December 2022	20–22 January 2023	10–12 February 2023
Virtual Worlds	24–26 February 2023	10–12 March 2023	21–23 April 2023
Learning mobility	3–5 March 2023	24–26 March 2023	28–30 April 2023
Energy efficiency	23–25 February 2024	15–17 March 2024	12–14 April 2024
Tackling hatred in society	5–7 April 2024	26–28 April 2024	17–19 May 2024
A new European budget	28–30 March 2025	25–27 April 2025	16–18 May 2025
Intergenerational Fairness	12–14 September 2025	17–19 October 2025	14–16 November 2025
Young Citizens Assembly on Pollinators	26–28 September 2025	5–7 December 2025 (in Brussels, not online)	6–8 March 2026

panel, and (2) topics that were not perceived as 'controversial'. Pragmatism was also at the core of the decision to hold the panels so quickly after the end of the CoFoE. There was a sense within the European Commission that if this step were not to be taken quickly, the momentum for integrating citizen participation might be lost, and the new President of the Commission in 2024 might not be supportive of citizen panels.

In terms of organization and its politics, the 'new generation' panels to a large extent reproduced the European citizen panels' model of the CoFoE: three weekends, the first and third taking place in person in Brussels and the second online, and a mostly deductive logic from a more informative first session towards specific recommendations. However, there were a number of differences. First, the number of citizens slightly changed, from 200 to a reduced 150 participants. Second, unlike in the CoFoE, the citizen panel set up a 'knowledge committee' that would be in charge of coordinating the substantive content provided to the participants, including the selection of experts. However, a backdrop of this way of functioning is that the 'knowledge committee' was set up by the Commission. This meant that the same executive institution that was running the policy and the panel was also responsible for deciding who ought to be provide input. Additionally, the very idea of a 'knowledge' committee, rather than a political one, hints towards a bureaucratization of the exercise rather than prioritizing political pluralism.

A relevant illustration of the lack of independence of the knowledge committee emerged in the 2025 ECP on a new European budget (which I attended as an observer). During the second session of this panel, one of the citizen groups suggested to 'Develop ways to empower elected representatives of citizens (EU Parliament) to have more influence in EU internal functioning, so that citizens can have a stronger voice in EU institutions'. Two members of the knowledge committee (one of them working for the European Commission) responded in written feedback ahead of the third and final session that such action 'cannot be connected to the EU budget in any way, neither directly nor indirectly. Its implementation would require major changes to the law, most likely the EU treaty. It is outside the remit of the Panel'. This example shows how citizen panel deliberations can be constrained by the organizing institutions. In this case, the knowledge committee undermined the possibility for citizens to recommend more political power to the European Parliament, reinforcing the Commission's own role.

Similarly, there is evidence that the EU has mobilized citizen panels as a way to build legitimacy for its tech policies without opening up the possibility to contest them. This refers not only to the Commission ECP on 'virtual worlds', but also to the Citizen Panel on Artificial Intelligence (AI) organized by the Belgian Presidency of the Council of the EU (see Petit and Oleart 2025). This is not entirely surprising, given that recent literature has shown the 'ideational business power' in the EU context; big tech corporations are perceived by EU institutions as 'partners' because their profit-seeking enterprise is not conceived as being in contradiction with public policy goals (see Obendiek and Seidl 2023; Griffin 2023; Kausche and Weiss, 2025; Oleart and Bouza García 2025).

Overall, this type of political process is gaining ground not only in the EU, but also globally, and is conceived by some political theorists as a 'new paradigm of democracy' (Landemore 2020). In the EU, Kalypso Nicolaidis has proposed a European Citizens' Assembly that would complement the European Parliament (see Bauböck and Nicolaidis 2025). However, the same political pluralism and conflictual politics that were absent in the CoFoE's citizen panels because of the use of 'neutral' experts was also missing in the post-CoFoE citizens' panels. Mediators such as political parties (both at national and EU level) or activist political groups were broadly absent from the process. Unsurprisingly, much of the focus of the final recommendations in all the post-CoFoE citizens' panels was in line with the pre-existing ideological position of the Commission regarding the topics (see Oleart 2023a). In consequence, this type of 'citizen participation' does not hold the potential for a real democratization of the EU.

11.7 Conclusion: disentangling democracy from mass politics in EU citizen participation

The chapter has described the EU's innovations in regards to participatory democracy during the last decade. Beginning from the EU's promises of reconnecting EU institutions with EU citizens, the chapter questions whether such promises

Table 11.4 Potential of EU participatory instruments along two axes: politicization and policy impact

EU Participatory Instruments	Potential for Politicization/ Mass Politics	Policy impact
ECI	High	Medium
Citizen Dialogues	Low	Low
ECCs	Low	Low
CoFoE	Low	Medium
ECPs	Low	Low

are based on an agonistic understanding of participation, or rather a public relations logic conceptualized as 'citizenwashing' (Petit and Oleart 2025). Whereas the former would aim to confront the traditional consensus-oriented understanding of democracy in the EU context, the latter focuses instead on reproducing a 'democracy without politics' approach accompanied by appeals to 'everyday citizens'. The chapter then outlined and analysed several participatory instruments: the ECI, the citizen dialogues, the ECCs, the CoFoE and the post-CoFoE ECPs. Table 11.4 summarizes the potential for politicization and mass politics of these mechanisms, as well as their policy impact.

As Table 11.4 illustrates, other than the ECI, the other 'citizen participation' mechanisms described are consistent with the conceptualization of 'democracy without politics' as they disentangle democracy from mass politics. Similarly, none of the participatory democracy instruments appears to have a strong policy impact, at least directly. However, there is some evidence that some ECIs had a policy follow up in line with the campaigners' demands. Nevertheless, the policy impact did not come from the institutional 'hearings', but rather from the pressure through the public sphere, mass politics and the mass media. Moreover, while a definitive evaluation would be premature, the CoFoE final recommendations are regularly cited by EU institutions as a way to legitimize their proposals. While certainly there is an element of cherry-picking, it is likely that the CoFoE will have some relevant policy impact—even if it in most cases such impact will relate to proposals that were already on the table prior to the CoFoE. On the contrary, the citizen dialogues, the ECCs and the ECPs have a very low potential for politicization, and no meaningful policy impact.

Out of these participatory instruments, it appears that deliberative minipublics are increasingly popular within EU institutions. Such a 'citizen turn' (Oleart 2023b) may be understood as a political attempt to build a new source of legitimacy that presents an alternative to the traditional conception of the European public sphere, replacing it with 'neutral' minipublics such as the ECPs that touch directly only several hundred citizens. The insulation of European citizen panels from the European public spheres and broader debates reminds us that 'the linkages between democracy and deliberation are contingent rather than necessary' (He and Warren 2011: 270). Hence, not all forms of deliberation have a democratizing potential, particularly when conceived in such a narrow and minimalistic way.

The European Commission has come out as the dominant institution when it comes to institutionalized 'citizen participation' within the EU: they implemented the ECI, the citizen dialogues, as well as the post-CoFoE set of European citizens' panels. However, as an institution the Commission has difficulties introducing mechanisms of 'citizen participation' within its policy-making process, given that the dominant practices are mostly technocratic. When implementing these participatory processes, the Commission tends to reproduce its own institutional self-understanding as a 'technical' institution that operates mostly through consensus. The emphasis on 'embedding' citizen participation within the consensus-oriented policy-making process of the Commission complicates the possibility of putting forward a more conflict-oriented approach. In turn, such processes fail to connect the ECPs with the broader public sphere, depoliticize political participation and transform 'citizen participation' into a public relations exercise. EU citizen participation mechanisms implemented have therefore not necessarily been accompanied with an actual democratization of EU politics. The actual democratization of the EU requires connecting 'democratic innovations' with vibrant agonistic debates in spaces such as parliaments (both the European and the national ones), the (national) media, and among civil society, trade unions and social movements.

References

Abels, G. (2023). *The Conference on the Future of Europe: National and Regional Participation in an Innovative Reform Process*. Baden-Baden, Nomos.

Balme, R. and Chabanet, D. (2008). *European Governance and Democracy: Power and Protest in the EU*. Plymouth, Rowman & Littlefield Publishers.

Bauböck, R. and Nicolaidis, K. (eds.) (2025). *Should a Citizens' Assembly Complement the European Parliament?* Florence, European University Institute. DOI: https://doi.org/10.2870/9250462.

Baumgartner, F. R. and Mahoney, C. (2008). The Two Faces of Framing: Individual-Level Framing and Collective Issue-Definition in the EU. *European Union Politics*, 9(3): 435–449.

Bouza Garcia, L. (2015). *Participatory Democracy and Civil Society in the EU: Agenda-Setting and Institutionalisation*. London, Springer.

Bouza Garcia, L. and Greenwood, J. (2014). The European Citizens' Initiative: A New Sphere of EU Politics? *Interest Groups & Advocacy*, 3: 246–267.

Butcher, P. and Pronckutė, S. (2019). European Citizens' Consultations: Consultation Begins at Home. *European View*, 18(1): 80–88.

Conference on the Future of Europe (2022a). Multilingual Digital Platform of the Conference on the Future of Europe. https://futureu.europa.eu/pages/reporting?format = html&locale = en. Accessed 25 July 2022.

Conference on the Future of Europe (2022b). Conference on the Future of Europe: Report on the Final Outcome. https://www.europarl.europa.eu/resources/library/media/20220509RES29121/20220509RES29121.pdf. Accessed 25 July 2022.

Conference on the Future of Europe (n.d.). Conference Plenary. https://futureu.europa.eu/en/pages/plenary?format = html&locale = en. Accessed 3 January 2023.

Crespy, A. (2014). Deliberative Democracy and the Legitimacy of the European Union: A Reappraisal of Conflict. *Political Studies*, 62: 81–98.

Crum, B. (2022). EU Democracy Beyond Participation: Building an EU Political Space. In von Sydow, G. and Kreilinger, V. (eds). *Making EU Representative Democracy Fit for the Future.* Stockholm, SIEPS: 18–32.

Ehs, T. and Mokre, M. (2021). Deliberation Against Participation? Yellow Vests and Grand Débat: A Perspective From Deliberative Theory. *Political Studies Review*, 19(2): 186–192.

Eising, R. (2009). *The Political Economy of State-Business Relations in Europe: Interest Mediation, Capitalism and EU Policy Making.* London, Routledge.

European Civic Forum (2022). Missions Publiques interviews Alexandrina Najmowicz: 'To rehabilitate European democracy, we must build on the bonds that bring us together'. https://civic-forum.eu/campaign/future-of-europe/missions-publiques-interview. Accessed 5 August 2025.

European Commission (2019). Speech by President-elect von der Leyen in the European Parliament Plenary on the occasion of the presentation of her College of Commissioners and their programme. https://ec.europa.eu/commission/presscorner/detail/en/SPEECH_19_6408. Accessed 22 March 2023.

European Commission (n.d.). The European Citizens' Initiative in key figures. https://citizens-initiative.europa.eu/find-initiative/eci-lifecycle-statistics_en. Accessed 8 August 2025.

European Council (2018). European Council Conclusions, 13–14 December 2018. https://www.consilium.europa.eu/en/press/press-releases/2018/12/14/european-council-conclusions-13-14-december-2018/. Accessed 5 August 2025.

European Parliament (2022). Parliament Activates Process to Change EU Treaties. https://www.europarl.europa.eu/news/en/press-room/20220603I PR32122/parliament-activates-process-to-change-eu-treaties. Accessed 12 January 2023.

European Parliament (2023). Parliamentarism, European Citizenship and Democracy. https://www.europarl.europa.eu/doceo/document/TA-9–2023-0330_EN.pdf. Accessed 22 September 2023.

Farrell, D. M., Suiter, J., and Harris, C. (2019). Systematizing' Constitutional Deliberation: The 2016–18 Citizens' Assembly in Ireland. *Irish Political Studies*, 34(1): 113–123.

Georgakakis, D. and Rowell, J. (eds) (2013). *The Field of Eurocracy: Mapping EU Actors and Professionals.* London, Springer.

Greenwood, J. (2003). *Interest Representation in the European Union.* London, Palgrave.

Griffin, R. (2023). Public and Private Power in Social Media Governance: Multistakeholderism, the Rule of Law and Democratic Accountability. *Transnational Legal Theory*, 14(1): 46–89.

Haapala, T. and Oleart, Á. (2022). *Tracing the Politicisation of the EU.* Cham, Palgrave.

He, B. and Warren, M. E. (2011). Authoritarian Deliberation: The Deliberative Turn in Chinese Political Development. *Perspectives on Politics*, 9(2): 269–289.

Hierlemann, D., Roch, S., Butcher, P., Emmanouilidis, J. A., Stratulat, C., and de Groot, M. (2022). Under Construction. Citizen Participation in the European Union. European Policy Centre. https://www.epc.eu/content/PDF/2022/Study_Under_construction.pdf. Accessed 14 May 2022.

Kausche, K. and Weiss, M. (2025). Platform Power and Regulatory Capture in Digital Governance. *Business and Politics*, 27(2): 284–308.

Klüver, H., Mahoney, C., and Opper, M. (2015). Framing in Context: How Interest Groups Employ Framing to Lobby the European Commission. *Journal of European Public Policy*, 22(4): 481–498.

Kohler-Koch, B. and Rittberger, B. (eds) (2007). *Debating the Democratic Legitimacy of the European Union.* Lanham, Rowman & Littlefield.

Kutay, A. (2012). Europeanisation of Civil Society through the Sponsored European Publics. *Javnost-the Public*, 19(1): 19–34.
Landemore, H. (2020). *Open Democracy: Reinventing Popular Rule for the Twenty-First Century*. Princeton NJ, Princeton University Press.
Mair, P. (2013). *Ruling the Void: The Hollowing of Western Democracy*. London, Verso books.
Mouffe, C. (2005). *On the Political*. London and New York, Routledge.
Obendiek, A. S. and Seidl, T. (2023). The (False) Promise of Solutionism: Ideational Business Power and the Construction of Epistemic Authority in Digital Security Governance. *Journal of European Public Policy*, 30(7): 1305–1329.
Oleart, A. (2021). *Framing TTIP in the European Public Spheres*. London, Palgrave Macmillan.
Oleart, A. (2023a). *Democracy Without Politics in EU Citizen Participation: From European Demoi to Decolonial Multitude*. London, Palgrave.
Oleart, A. (2023b). The Political Construction of the 'Citizen Turn' in the EU: Disintermediation and Depoliticisation in the Conference on the Future of Europe. *Journal of Contemporary European Studies*: 1–15. DOI: https://doi.org/10.1080/14782804.2023.2177837.
Oleart, A. (2025). The Citizenwashing of von der Leyen's 'New Push for European Democracy': The Conference on the Future of Europe and the Commission's European Citizens' Panels. In Abels, G., Kantola, J., Lombardo, E., and Müller, H. (eds). *The First Von der Leyen Commission 2019–24*. Oxford, Oxford University Press. DOI: https://doi.org/10.1093/9780198953692.003.0014.
Oleart, A. and Bouza, L. (2018). Democracy at Stake: Multipositional Actors and Politicization in the EU Civil Society Field. *Journal of Common Market Studies*, 56(4): 870–887.
Oleart, A. and Bouza García, L. (2025). From Self to Co-Regulation in the EU's Approach to Disinformation: The Framing Power of Big Tech Business Lobbies in the Lead to the Digital Services Act. *International Review of Public Policy*. DOI: https://doi.org/10.4000/14rse.
Oleart, A. and Theuns, T. (2023). 'Democracy Without Politics' in the European Commission's Response to Democratic Backsliding: from Technocratic Legalism to Democratic Pluralism. *Journal of Common Market Studies*, 61(4): 882–899.
Parks, L. (2015). *Social Movement Campaigns on EU Policy: in the Corridors and in the Streets*. London, Palgrave.
Petit, P. and Oleart, A. (2025). Citizenwashing EU Tech Policy: EU Deliberative Mini-Publics on Virtual Worlds and Artificial Intelligence. *Politics and Governance*. DOI: https://doi.org/10.17645/pag.10468.
Radaelli, C. M. (1999). The Public Policy of the European Union: Whither Politics of Expertise? *Journal of European Public Policy*, 6(5): 757–774.
Sánchez Salgado, R. (2014). Rebalancing EU Interest Representation? Associative Democracy and EU Funding of Civil Society Organizations. *Journal of Common Market Studies*, 52(2): 337–353.
Saurugger, S. (2010). The Social Construction of the Participatory Turn: The Emergence of a Norm in the European Union. *European Journal of Political Research*, 49(4): 471–495.
Schmidt, V. A. (2013). Democracy and Legitimacy in the European Union Revisited: Input, Output and 'Throughput'. *Political Studies*, 61(1): 2–22.
Stratulat, C. and Butcher, P. (2018). The European Citizens' Consultations: Evaluation Report. European Policy Centre. https://www.epc.eu/en/Publications/The-European-Citizens-Consult~267d84. Accessed 2 February 2023.

PART III

EU POLICIES AND THE PROMISE OF DEMOCRACY IN PRACTICE

12
Migration as a Challenge of Constitutional Democracy

Viljam Engström and Katri Gadd

12.1 Introduction

Migration governance has grown into a key area of EU action. The Strategic Guidelines for legislative and operational planning within the Area of Freedom, Security and Justice (AFSJ) for the 2014–20 period recognized the management of 'migration in all its aspects' as one of the priorities of the EU (European Council 2014). Migration is also an area where Member States and the EU share an interest in acting collectively, as migration challenges cannot be resolved by the actions of single states (Rose 2019). At the same time, migration has become one of the most controversial areas of policymaking in the EU. The area of migration policy is broad as it is closely intertwined with several other policy fields such as development and trade, as well as security and conflict resolution (Faustini-Torres 2020). Migration policy has both an internal aspect regarding intra-EU migration, and an external aspect that is interrelated with other foreign policies. The two aspects are also intertwined, as the absence of EU internal border controls is ensured in conjunction with other measures, such as external border controls and coordinated asylum management. EU actions concerning migration consist, first, of frameworks and rules for managing legal migration flows. This includes the migration and movement of asylum-seekers, highly skilled workers, students, researchers, seasonal workers, and family members of migrants through family reunification. In addition, EU migration policies concern the processing of asylum requests, the relocation of asylum-seekers, and readmission agreements for returning illegal migrants.

This chapter discusses challenges in EU migration policymaking in both the internal and external dimension. The emphasis is on asylum policy, which has been the most contested aspect of migration ever since the so-called 'refugee crisis' in 2015. Disagreement on the objectives and functions of migration policies characterizes political debate within EU Member States as well as between them. Although migration management in the EU has been perceived as dysfunctional, the disagreements in effect for a long time prevented the development of the Common European Asylum System (CEAS) (Zalan 2020).

Viljam Engström and Katri Gadd, *Migration as a Challenge of Constitutional Democracy* In: *The Promise of EU Democracy*. Edited by: Jan Wouters, Julie Smith, Kolja Raube, and Ben Crum, Oxford University Press.
 DOI: 10.1093/9780191996191.003.0015

After outlining the current legal context, the chapter discusses the challenges facing EU migration policies through demonstrating the complexity of the disagreement and how it manifests itself in particular contexts. The deeply divisive nature of the migration discourse and the multiple levels on which the disagreement plays out, aggravated by populist rhetoric, the chapter claims, has not only affected the possibility for developing the migration regime, but also affects EU democratic constitutionalism at large. This is the result of the dilemma that the EU faces, where there appears to be no policy choice available that would not further deepen current political fault lines. Taking no action is not an option either, as that raises accusations of incapacity, in itself undermining the EU's credibility in the eyes of Member States. The chapter highlights how this situation has been aggravated by the tendencies to securitize and externalize EU migration policy. At the time of writing, the EU's New Migration and Asylum Pact (hereafter New Pact) had just been adopted (April 2024); the chapter makes some initial notes on how it seeks to navigate this situation.

12.2 The legal context

12.2.1 The regulatory landscape

Article 3(2) of the TEU establishes that the Union shall offer its citizens an area of freedom, security, and justice. Article 67 of the TFEU (2008) further specifies that the Union shall ensure the absence of internal border controls and will frame a common policy on asylum, immigration, and external border control, 'based on solidarity between Member States, which is fair towards third-country nationals', and ensure a high level of security through measures to prevent and combat crime, racism, and xenophobia. Article 80 TFEU requires asylum, border, and migration policies to be 'governed by the principle of solidarity and fair sharing of responsibility, including its financial implications, between Member States'. EU migration law is essentially a regime of secondary law, which means that it is not constitutionalized to an extent comparable, for example, to free movement (in general, see Azoulai and de Vries 2014).

The newly reformed migration and asylum policy framework—the New Pact—consists of:

- Regulation on standards for the qualification of third-country nationals or stateless persons as beneficiaries of international protection (Council Regulation (EU) 2024/1347)
- Regulation establishing a common procedure for international protection (Council Regulation (EU) 2024/1348)

- Regulation establishing a return border procedure (Council Regulation (EU) 2024/1349)
- Regulation on establishing a Union Resettlement and Humanitarian Admission Framework (Council Regulation (EU) 2024/1350)
- Regulation on asylum and migration management (Council Regulation (EU) 2024/1351)
- Regulation introducing the screening of third-country nationals at the external borders (Council Regulation (EU) 2024/1352; Council Regulation (EU) 2024/1356)
- Regulation on the establishment of 'Eurodac' (Council Regulation (EU) 2024/1358)
- Regulation on addressing situations of crisis and force majeure in the field of migration and asylum (Council Regulation (EU) 2024/1359)
- Directive laying down standards for the reception of applicants for international protection (Council Directive (EU) 2024/1346).[1]

The reform aimed to address several shortcomings that had raised criticism among Member States, such as the lack of a mechanism for sharing the burden of the reception of migrants through relocation and the need for an expedited examination of asylum claims. In addition to addressing these concerns, the legislative acts set the criteria according to which a Member State is responsible for examining applications for international protection. The Member States must define responsibilities of relocation of asylum applicants and establish a mechanism to respond to sudden increases in arrivals as well as the instrumentalization of migrants. Additionally, Member States need to outline a pre-entry screening procedure, a common procedure for granting and withdrawal of international protection, and a framework for registration of irregular migrants. The New Pact also sets uniform standards for the recognition of refugee or subsidiary protection status and for reception conditions, and it establishes a voluntary framework on resettlement and humanitarian admission.

Historically, EU institutions have had different priorities in their approaches to migration (Geddes and Lixi 2018). The Commission has been one of the leading actors behind the formulation and implementation of EU external migration policies, with the Directorate-General on Migration and Home Affairs (DG HOME) prioritizing migration control and security. The Council has also tended to adopt a security driven approach. In contrast, the European Parliament has emphasized

[1] The regulations were due to apply in full two years following their entry into force, with some of them applying immediately (Regulation on asylum and migration management: 2024, Article 85). For the reception conditions directive, states have two years to amend their national laws in accordance with it (Directive laying down standards for the reception of applicants for international protection: 2024, Article 35).

root causes for curbing migration and underlined the important role of development and democratization in countries of origin (Carrera, Radescu and Reslow 2016). The New Pact, which received fierce criticism throughout the drafting process owing to its security centred approach, eventually passed the vote in Parliament (although only narrowly), which is perhaps indicative of a more generally changing approach to migration in Europe whereby the need for 'exceptional' means of managing asylum in times of an alleged 'crisis' legitimizes legislation that was previously considered not to be compliant with the rule of law (e.g. Moreno-Lax 2024). The management of migration also engages various agencies, such as the European Union Agency for Asylum (EUAA) (formerly EASO) and the European Border and Coast Guard Agency FRONTEX (for an overview, see Tsourdi 2020). An agencification of migration management and the ever-expanding mandates of these agencies has led to a technicalization and proceduralization of migration management that emphasizes implementation above other aspects (Moutselos 2025).

12.2.2 Migration as a constitutional question

Democracy has been said to owe much of its moral authority to 'a vision of a community coming together, on the terms of equality, to forge a common interest and pursue the common good' (Roth 2000: 500; Morlino et al. 2019). This quote contains two elements. First, democracy is premised on the existence of a community. The very foundation of the EU as a community is set forth in the values it is based upon. According to TEU, Article 2, these include: 'respect for human dignity, freedom, democracy, equality, the rule of law and respect for human rights, including the rights of persons belonging to minorities'. Pursuant to TEU, Article 21(1), the EU's action on the international scene should seek to advance 'democracy, the rule of law, the universality and indivisibility of human rights and fundamental freedoms, respect for human dignity, the principles of equality and solidarity and respect for the principles of the United Nations Charter and international law'.

While the EU's existence as a community does not presuppose that there needs to (or even could) be agreement on all political issues that arise (Weiler 1999; Archibugi 2004; Wolthuis et al. 2025), for EU policies to be justified and acceptable, they should be rooted in the values that have been consensually accepted (Maldini and Takahashi 2017). However, the perception of and prioritization between these values in the context of migration policy varies within and between Member States. Xenophobic sentiments and security concerns are on the rise in many Member States, which at the EU level translates into an emphasis on the protection of EU external borders and avoidance of relocation of migrants. As many of the resulting policy practices raise human rights concerns, they stand in contrast with the commitments at the heart of the EU's normative foundation.[2] The nexus between a dysfunctional asylum system, lack of agreement on the core aims and functions of migration policy, and an externalization of migration governance, all of which are further discussed below, can also be seen to reconfigure the conceptual foundations of the Union, and as such amount to a constitutional crisis (Loxa and Stoyanova 2022).

The second aspect of the quote underlines that democratic legitimacy requires taking into consideration the interests of the entire community. Although initiatives that run counter to migration/refugee law and human rights seem to become more common in domestic policymaking, appeals for stricter immigration policies as such are not necessarily a constitutional or democratic problem, as long as they remain within the confines of the legal obligations of both the Member States and the EU. The concern is rather with the foundational impact of the dilemma in which the EU finds itself, and the consequences of this for formulating acceptable policies. As contentious policy discourse at the level of Member States is reflected in and reproduced on the EU level and vice versa, it becomes ever more difficult to identify policy choices that will not further aggravate the current disagreement or raise a criticism of EU inaction. 'The community', the opinions of which the decision-makers should respect and represent, is nearby non-existent, and the only common ground that can be found is problematic from a humanitarian perspective. The New Pact has been criticized for embodying this situation rather than offering new solutions (Diez, Trauner, and Somer 2021).

12.3 Challenges of EU migration policy

12.3.1 Dysfunctional policy-making and the impact of populist rhetoric

Until the mass refugee flows in 2015, migration and asylum policies attracted somewhat marginal attention in the EU. While these flows generated calls for further deepening and strengthening the integration of migration policies (Maldini and Takahashi 2017), it soon became clear that this was not politically achievable. In fact, any pursuit of further integration has raised fears of a backlash and even disintegration of the EU (d'Appollonia 2019). Quite in contrast to the idea of further integration, claims have also been made that Member States are the proper

[2] This conflict can even be explicitly acknowledged, as in the case of the Finnish legislative proposal to combat instrumentalized migration. See Hallituksen esitys eduskunnalle laiksi väliaikaisista toimenpiteistä välineellistetyn maahantulon torjumiseksi HE 18/2025. Available at: https://www.finlex.fi/fi/hallituksen-esitykset/2025/18 (available only in Finnish), accessed 23 July 2025.

level for policymaking with regard to migration issues, coupled with demands for decentralization (Maldini and Takahashi 2017).

The New Pact establishes more uniform standards for all Member States concerning recognition of refugee or subsidiary protection status and regarding the rights granted to those qualifying for protection. Yet, migration policies are intertwined with several other policy areas, such as development, trade, security, and conflict resolution (Faustini-Torres 2020). Those policies sit at the intersection of migration and foreign policy, while the aims of policymaking in these areas are not necessarily identical or even parallel to the aims of migration policies (Reslow 2019). In addition, the migration agenda is formed by a multitude of actors which contributes to the absence of a single logic or overarching rationale (Hampshire 2016a). As migration to, and movement within, Europe is governed by a complex interplay between institutions and processes operating on local, national, European, and international levels, European migration governance has been called a paradigm of multilevel governance (Hampshire 2016b), and an instance of à la carte integration (d'Appollonia 2019). In respect of the attitude towards migration, there are significant differences among European countries (Davidov and Semyonov 2017). In several countries (including for example France, Greece, Hungary, Italy, Finland, and Poland) right-wing politicians have expressed a hostile attitude towards migration. For instance, France has adopted very restrictive migration policies, which have been described as an 'ideological victory' for the far-right leader Marine Le Pen (Le Monde with AFP 2023). Germany, by contrast, has long been keener to consider migration as an opportunity, and even an inevitability to meet the challenges of a diminishing domestic workforce (Meltzer et al. 2018).

The effects of the dysfunctional state of migration policy became clear in the 2015 'crisis', as several Member States at the EU's external border failed to process asylum-seekers, with the result that both the Dublin as well as the Schengen systems of free movement collapsed, as EU internal borders were reinstated (Loxa and Stoyanova 2022). The events also highlighted that there are (at least) two aspects to this dysfunctionality. On the one hand, one of the most fundamental political controversies in migration policy has concerned the role of border states, which have accused inland Member States of a lack of solidarity in sharing the burden of processing applications, and by extension, questioned the capacity of the EU to impose an obligation to this effect. On the other hand, a notable unwillingness on the part of many EU Member States to receive migrants 'in solidarity' has generated an opposition towards any such policy initiatives, which have been considered oppressive and been deemed to constitute an undue interference in national sovereignty (Karolewski and Benedikter 2018). This created a stalemate that the EU has struggled to overcome. While the New Pact has been presented as a 'fresh start' on migration, critics consider it (the Asylum and Migration Management Regulation in particular) largely as a continuation of the status quo (e.g. Thym 2020).

The dilemmas of asylum policymaking are aggravated by the rise of right-wing nationalism and populist rhetoric in several EU Member States. As a general strategy, populists purposefully create affective and emotional reactions in order to trigger particular opinions (Gadd and Grabowska-Moroz 2021). While recourse to populist rhetoric as such does not presuppose a particular position on the issue of migration (Gruszczyński and Friedery 2022), the dominant right-wing ideological orientation in particular portrays migrants as a source of societal problems. This way of framing migration has also been beneficial for right-wing political parties (in the case of Italy, see Gadd and Grabowska-Moroz 2021; Gruszczyński and Friedery 2022). A case in point is the Hungarian billboard campaign preceding a referendum against allowing the EU 'to mandate the resettlement of non-Hungarian citizens to Hungary without the approval of the National Assembly' (Bárd 2017). Although the referendum failed because the turnout was lower than the statutorily prescribed 50 per cent, it was still successful from the government's viewpoint, as the referendum and the surrounding campaign resulted in a shift of public sentiment against migrants, asylum-seekers and refugees. According to Bárd's (2017) research data, whereas in 2015 two-thirds of respondents expressed tolerance and pro-migrant support, a year later the proportion had decreased to one-third.

In addition to polarizing the migration debate ever further, right-wing populism also highlights how, in areas of shared competence, decision-making at the EU level is dependent on political developments beyond its control. Worryingly for Member States, populism also commonly contains an element of 'twisting' democratic representation (Dieh 2019) and of undermining the role of democratic institutions as checks and balances in decision-making (Kyle and Mounk 2018). In the context of the EU, in particular in countries displaying rule of law backsliding, migration becomes intrinsically connected with a more general hostility towards EU institutions and European integration at large (Schmidt 2019; Grabowska-Moroz and Kochenov 2022). In this way, domestic politics in Member States 'institutionalizes' the challenge to a common asylum policy, and at the same time reinforces the dysfunctionality of EU decision-making through domestic opposition and non-compliance (Loxa and Stoyanova 2022).

12.3.2 Contested goals and the securitization of migration policy

In the right-wing populist rhetoric, migrants become scapegoats for domestic problems that a country faces (Lazaridis and Tsagkroni 2015). Migrants are for example presented as an economic burden, but also as an outright threat. The latter echoes a more general postmodern trend whereby a constant identification of new risks generates calls for increased security in an endless loop (Beck 1992). Political parties which are critical of (or even antagonistic towards) migration, benefit from citizens perceiving migration as threat (Gadd and Grabowska-Moroz 2021). In particular, a discourse on Islam and Muslim migration has been brought to the centre of the European migration debate (Meltzer et al. 2018) and certain parties have harnessed it to generate emotions of insecurity. In presenting migration as a risk and threat, migrants become linked to organized crime and even terrorism. This in turn legitimizes action such as the adoption of coercive policies. The more migration is framed as a risk and a threat, the easier it also becomes to defend a politics of exception, operationalization, and technicalization, which risks foreclosing political debate (Engström and Heikkilä 2014). In addition, the stronger the perceived security risk posed by migration, the easier it also becomes to defend the keeping of policymaking at the domestic level (Erisen and Kentmen-Cin 2017; Erisen, Vasilopou, and Kentment-Cin 2020). After all, domestic security is ultimately considered a matter for the state. The consequent criminalization of irregular migration has also been challenged as a violation of EU law (Case C-821/19 *Commission v Hungary* 2021; Case C-460/23 *Kinshasa* 2023).

In stretching the securitization logic beyond 'migrants as threats', the personal security of the migrant becomes instrumentalized as well. When picturing migrants instead as 'victims to be saved', securitization becomes 'migrant-centred' and is presented as a rights-compliant way of addressing migration. This way the externalization of migration management (discussed further below) is portrayed as a way of avoiding risking the lives of migrants. In the process, human rights end up as a tool for securitization (Moreno-Lax: 2018). Such a linking of humanitarian and security agendas obfuscates the discourse on the goals of migration policies even further as both those with a humanitarian approach and those with a security emphasis can invoke the rights of the migrant (Panizzon and van Riemsdjik 2019).

The absence of a shared conception of the purposes of migration policy is nowhere more visible than in respect of the contentious principle of solidarity, wherein the tension between humanitarianism and securitization has become embodied (Karolewski and Benedikter 2018). The notions of 'solidarity' and 'fair sharing of responsibility' are not defined in terms of their goals or the standards necessary to meet them. Instead, the solidarity principle is to be interpreted in light of general AFSJ policy goals, which can pull in different directions (Vanheule, van Selm, and Boswell 2011: 37). After all, asylum and immigration policies, and external border control, are both focal points of the AFSJ.

The principle of solidarity has predominantly been used to refer to solidarity between EU Member States (Bast 2016; Mitsilegas 2014). This is also the explicit point of departure of the AFSJ (TFEU, Art 67). Furthermore, in respect of solidarity between Member States, it has predominantly applied to measures for securing borders (Murray and Longo 2018). Hence, Karageorgiou and Noll (2022) argue that the very notion of 'solidarity' is a misnomer, and that the way this concept is used (in TFEU, Art 80) is better understood as an alliance clause against an external threat (such as irregular migration). Relocation policies as 'solidarity measures' have met with strong opposition from individual Member States. However, in respect of the refusal by Hungary, Poland, and the Czech Republic to implement relocation, the CJEU (Joined Cases C-715/17, C-718/17 and C-719/17 *Commission v Poland and Others* 2020) established that all asylum measures must respect the principle of solidarity and fair sharing of responsibility. Most recently the CJEU has concluded that failure to abide by the obligation of Member States to ensure the reception of applicants for international protection and examining applications for asylum 'seriously undermines the principle of solidarity and fair sharing of responsibility' which is 'one of the fundamental principles of EU law and is one of the values common to the Member States on which the European Union is founded' (Case C-123/22 *Commission v Hungary* [2024], paras 115–116).

The New Pact offers a flexible solidarity mechanism whereby EU Member States can, in principle, decide on how they want to contribute to asylum management (Milazzo 2023). Member States retain discretion as to the type of solidarity they offer, with no obligation to receive relocated migrants as there are other alternatives open to states (such as paying financial contributions or offering operational support). Instead of being an expression of newly attained solidarity between Member States, this solution has been regarded as confirmation of its continuing absence (De Buycker 2022: 40). Even less is this an expression of solidarity towards the migrant. As Thym (2022) puts it: 'Like it or not, most national capitals define their national interest in terms of minimizing the number of asylum applications', which the Pact allows.

12.3.3 The externalization of EU migration policy

Given the alleged situation of crisis and threat alongside the consequent perception of securitization needs, action is increasingly taken outside democratic processes, which upsets the already complex structure of multi-level migration governance. Migration management is pushed outside of the EU constitutional framework, with consequences both for the rights of migrants and for the uniform application of EU foundational principles and values (Panizzon and van Riemsdjik 2019; Loxa and Stoyanova 2022). At the same time, the externalization of migration management has been one policy which the EU has pursued fairly successfully. One expression of this is the conclusion of readmission agreements with third countries as a central part of migration management (Council Directive 2008/115). These agreements set out the rules for returning individuals residing illegally in the EU to their country of origin or third countries. The agreements have been noted to be differently implemented between Member States, affecting the effectiveness of returns and the standards of protection (European Parliament 2020). The externalization has also led to the creation of a broader toolbox of policy instruments for migration management. These tools display problematic features as the EU as well as its Member States seem to move 'from an externalization of migration control to an externalization of their obligations to afford protection' (Krampe 2020).

The arrangement between the EU and Turkey has become the epitome of the 'informalization' of migration policy (EU–Turkey statement 2016; Loxa and Stoyanova 2022). According to the arrangement, from 20 March 2016 all irregular migrants crossing from Turkey into Greek islands would be returned to Turkey, in exchange for monetary payments from the EU to the Facility for Refugees in Turkey. The arrangement, however, has met with much criticism. First of all, it was adopted outside the purview of parliamentary control (Hanke, Wieuszewski, and Panizzon 2019; Slominski and Trauner 2018). The CJEU has further established in four consecutive cases that the arrangement lies outside the scope of EU law altogether (the first ruling being Case T-192/16 *NF v Council* 2017). Secondly, the deal is problematic also from the perspective of international law (Creutz, Iso-Markku, Raik, and Tiilikainen 2019). Moreover, in its attempt to control and reduce migration, the EU chooses to cooperate with countries with poor human rights records, a criticism that also extends beyond Turkey to similar arrangements with Libya, Afghanistan, Tunisia, Egypt, and Mauritania (Reslow 2019c; Geddes 2018; Monar 2017; Bauböck 2018; Dam 2023). As noted by the Special Rapporteur on the human rights of migrants, many of these arrangements stretch the concept of 'safe third country' to its limits and have 'resulted in violations of the prohibition of collective expulsions and the principle of non-refoulement, and have led to limitations in accessing fair and efficient asylum and other protection-oriented procedures' (United Nations 2022). For these reasons, the arrangements have been subject to strategic litigation domestically (Van der Pas 2024), which again highlights the tension between the domestic level and the EU in migration policy.

A further feature of European migration management is the increasing reliance on bilateral cooperation (Reslow 2019b). In November 2023, Italy concluded a Protocol for the extraterritorial management of migration and asylum management with Albania, for the purpose of establishing detention centres on Albanian territory for the processing of applications and carrying out return operations, raising concerns about its compatibility with EU law (De Leo 2023). Bilateral cooperation also aims to incentivize home and transit countries to cooperate on irregular migration, smuggling and trafficking, and return, through the 'leverage' of non-migration policies (e.g. trade, education, energy, development) (Moreno-Lax 2018; Panizzon and van Riemsdjik 2019). Such arrangements by individual Member States potentially undermine the EU's policies, and risk fragmenting the migration agenda even further (Reslow 2019). Paradoxically, then, dissatisfaction with EU asylum policies creates a political incentive to act on the domestic level, including in respect of the externalization of migration management, which in turn further fragments the EU migration regime.

12.4 Concluding Remarks

The humanism at the heart of the foundational values of the EU meets its nemesis in present-day migration policy. Migration policy has been highly controversial and contested within and among EU Member States for at least a decade. It is contested for different reasons. Mediterranean states question the capacity of the EU to guarantee a fair sharing of responsibilities among Member States, whereas many non-Mediterranean states (especially those that have a hostile political environmental towards migrants), accuse any solidarity mechanisms of lacking respect for their domestic policy priorities. Among the few issues where common ground among EU Member States can be found are the framing of migration as a threat and burden, and the externalization of migration management.

Migration policy constitutes a test-case of the EU as a constitutional democracy for multiple reasons. As EU migration policies promote a minimalistic conception of what it means to be 'fair to third country nationals', the policies raise questions regarding the EU's humanitarian commitment, and in extension, its foreign policy priorities (Gadd and Engström 2024). Use of informal arrangements that in many respects escape the constitutional framework contribute to this development, and the fragmentation of the migration regime through Member State initiatives leads to short-term policy making that deprives EU action 'directed at reaffirming human rights and fundamental freedoms of the required intensity' (European Parliament 2019).

A more profound challenge, however, arises from the fact that every proposed policy action meets criticism from some Member States, which is driven by domestic policy tensions. Every action is either 'too humanitarian' or 'too security oriented' toward the migrant, 'too burdensome' or 'too restrictive' toward some Member State, or 'too far reaching' or 'inadequate' on the part of the EU. A deterioration of political discourse in modern democracies through right wing populist rhetoric on its part undermines the possibility of finding workable compromises. As a result, neither agreement on the goals and functions of migration policy, nor on the meaning of and prioritization between the EU's fundamental values and principles has been attainable. The foundational nature of the situation has been characterized as a 'destructive dissensus' (Hodson and Puetter 2019).

The 2024 New Pact promises to improve the current system. The Pact establishes more uniform rules for EU Member States, which is certainly a welcome development. However, in respect of the questions that have raised most concern, there seems to be little to no improvement. Solidarity between Member States in relation to the relocation of asylum-seekers (and refugees) has been the Achilles heel of EU migration policy. Consequently, the expectations for the solidarity mechanism introduced in the Pact are high. While it remains to be seen how the Pact eventually plays out, at the face of it only minimal changes to the system for sharing responsibility among EU countries are introduced. While the New Pact seemingly addresses the uneven geographies of asylum-seeking in the EU, the 'flexible solidarity' that it introduces comes with the risk of being unable to deliver fair burden-sharing. If that is the case, it would also fail to rebuild trust between Member States (De Bruycker 2022).

The New Pact is also an instrument for balancing the right of EU Member States to control mobility across their borders with an image of the EU as an actor that respects human rights (Pallister-Wilkins 2020). Compared with previous policies, the New Pact promotes and normalizes multiple procedures that can have far-reaching consequences on migrants' agency, dignity, and vulnerability (Häkli, Kudžmaitė, and Kallio 2023), suggesting that the balancing happens at the expense of the fair treatment of migrants (Majcher 2020). As increasing returns and readmission cooperation with third countries are areas in which it is easier to find common ground among Member States, the risk is that these means will be disproportionally opted for in migration management.

There is also an EU external aspect at stake. For the last two decades many third countries have been reluctant to readmit their nationals and now those countries of origin witness migration becoming an inherent and instrumental part of cooperation with the EU (Diez, Trauner, and Somer 2021). As many third countries already perceive the EU as pursuing a double agenda (Gadd and Engström 2024), there is certainly a risk that the New Pact may worsen this image even further, this way extending the constitutional challenge of EU migration policies also to other areas of external cooperation.

References

Archibugi, D. (2004). Cosmopolitan Democracy and its Critics: A Review. *European Journal of International Relations,* 10(3): 437–473.

Azoulai, L. and de Vries, K. (2014). Introduction. In Azoulai, L. and de Vries, K. (eds). *EU Migration Law: Legal Complexities and Political Rationales.* Oxford, Oxford University Press: 1–13.

Bárd, P. (2017). What is Behind the Low Numbers of Hate Crimes in Hungary? *Newsletter of the European Society of Criminology,* 1: 10–11.

Bast, J. (2016). Deepening Supranational Integration: Interstate Solidarity in EU Migration Law. *European Public Law,* 22(2): 289–304.

Bauböck, R. (2018). Refugee Protection and Burden-Sharing in the European Union. *Journal of Common Market Studies,* 56(1): 141–156.

Beck, U. (1992). *Risk Society: Towards a New Modernity.* London, Sage.

Carrera, S., Radescu, R., and Reslow, N. (2016). *EU External Migration Policies: A Preliminary Mapping of the Instruments, the Actors and their Priorities.* Report prepared for the FP7 project 'Transnational migration in transition: Transformative characteristics of temporary mobility of people' EURA-NET, Deliverable 3.1.

Creutz, K., Iso-Markku, T., Raik, K., and Tiilikainen, T. (2019). The Changing Global Order and its Implications for the EU. *FIIA Report 59.* Finnish Institute of International Affairs, Helsinki, Finland.

Dam, P. (2023). EU Commission Should Stop Ignoring Tunisia's Abuse Against Migrants. *Human Rights Watch.* https://www.hrw.org/news/2023/09/28/eu-commission-should-stop-ignoring-tunisias-abuses-against-migrants. Accessed 6 August 2025.

d'Appollonia, A. C. (2019). EU Migration Policy and Border Controls: From Chaotic to Cohesive Differentiation. *Comparative European Politics*, 17: 192–208.

Davidov, E. and Semyonov, M. (2017). Attitudes Towards Immigrants in European Societies. *International Journal of Comparative Sociology*, 58(5): 359–366.

De Bruycker, P. (2022). The New Pact on Migration and Asylum: What it is Not and What it Could Have Been. In Thym, D. (ed.). *Reforming the Common European Asylum System: Opportunities, Pitfalls, and Downsides of the Commission Proposals for a New Pact on Migration and Asylum*. Baden-Baden, Nomos: 33–42.

De Leo, A. (2023). On the Incompatibility of the Italy-Albania Protocol with EU Asylum Law. *SIDIBlog*. http://www.sidiblog.org/2023/11/15/on-the-incompatibility-of-the-italy-albania-protocol-with-eu-asylum-law/. Accessed 8 August 2025.

Dieh, P. (2019). Populist Twist: The Relationship between the Leader and the People in Populism. In Castiglione, D. and Pollak, J. (eds). *Creating Political Presence: The New Politics of Democratic Representation*. Chicago IL, University of Chicago Press: 110–138.

Diez, O., Trauner, F., and Somer, M. (2021). Return Sponsorship in the EU's New Pact on Migration and Asylum: High Stakes, Low Gains. *European Journal of Migration and Law* 23: 219–244.

Engström, V. and Heikkilä, M. (2014). Fundamental Rights in the Institutions and Instruments of the Area of Freedom, Security and Justice. Fostering Human Rights among European Policies. Work Package No. 11, Deliverable No. 1.

Erisen, C. and Kentmen-Cin, C. (2017). Tolerance and Perceived Threat Toward Muslim Immigrants in Germany and the Netherlands. *European Union Politics*, 18(1): 73–97.

Erisen, C., Vasilopou, S., and Kentmen-Cin, C. (2020). Emotional Reactions to Immigration and Support for EU Cooperation on Immigration and Terrorism. *Journal of European Public Policy*, 27(6): 795–813.

European Council (2014). Council Conclusions 26–27 June 2014.

European Parliament (2019). Resolution of 27 March 2019 Post-Arab Spring: Way Forward for the Middle East and North Africa (MENA) Region (2018/2160(INI)), P8 TA(2019)0318.

European Parliament (2020). The Return Directive 2008/115/EC: European Implementation Assessment. European Parliamentary Research Service Study.

EU–Turkey statement (2016). Press release 18 March 2016. https://www.consilium.europa.eu/en/press/press-releases/2016/03/18/eu-turkey-statement/. Accessed 8 August 2025.

Faustini-Torres, L. (2020). Another Nexus? Exploring Narratives on the Linkage Between EU External Migration Policies and the Democratization of the Southern Mediterranean Neighborhood. *Comparative Migration Studies*, 8(9): 1–22.

Gadd, K. and Engström, V. (2024). EU Delegations as Intermediaries of Perceptions of the EU: A View from the MENA region. *Mediterranean Politics*, 30(3): 455–477.

Gadd, K. and Grabowska-Moroz, B. (2021). Relation between Democracy, the Rule of Law, Politicisation and Citizens' Perception of EU Migration Policies. RECONNECT Working Papers.

Geddes, A. (2018). The Politics of European Union Migration Governance. *Journal of Common Market Studies*, 56: 120–130.

Geddes, A. and Lixi, L. (2018). New Actors and New Understandings in European Union External Migration Governance? The Case of EU-Tunisian Migration Relations. In Carrera, S., den Hertog, A., Panizzon, M., and Kostakopoulou, D. (eds). *EU External Migration Policies in an Era of Global Mobilities: Intersecting Policy Universes*. Leiden, Brill Nijhoff: 60–80.

Grabowska-Moroz, B. and Kochenov, D. (2022). The Loss of Face for Everyone Concerned: EU Rule of Law in the Context of the 'Migration Crisis'. In Stoyanova, V. and Smet, S. (eds). *Migrants' Rights, Populism and Legal Resilience in Europe*. Cambridge, Cambridge University Press: 187–208.

Gruszczyński, Ł. and Friedery, R. (2022). The Populist Challenge of Common EU Policies. The Case of (Im)migration. *Polish Yearbook of International Law*, 42: 221–244.

Häkli, J., Kudžmaitė, G., and Kallio, K. P. (2023). Devaluing Personhood: The Framing of Migrants in the EU's New Pact on Migration and Asylum. *Transactions of the Institute of British Geographers*, 49(4): 1–15.

Hampshire, J. (2016a). Speaking with one voice? The European Union's Global Approach to Migration and Mobility and the Limits of International Migration Cooperation. *Journal of Ethnic and Migration Studies*, 42(4): 571–586.
Hampshire, J. (2016b). European Migration Governance Since the Lisbon Treaty. *Journal of Ethnic and Migration Studies*, 42(4): 537–553.
Hanke, P., Wieuszewski, M., and Pnizzon, M. (2019). The 'Spirit of the Schengen Rules', The Humanitarian Visa, and Contested Asylum Governance in Europe – The Swiss Case'. *Journal of Ethnic and Migration Studies* 45(8): 1361–1376.
Hodson, D. and Puetter, U. (2019). The European Union in Disequilibrium. *Journal of European Public Policy*, 26(8): 1153–1171.
Karageorgiou, E. and Noll, G. (2022). What is Wrong with Solidarity in EU Asylum and Migration Law? *Jus Cogens*, 4: 131–154.
Karolewski, I. P. and Benedikter, R. (2018). Europe's Migration Predicament: The European Union's Refugees' Relocation Scheme Versus the Defiant Central Eastern European Visegrad Group. *Journal of Inter-Regional Studies: Regional and Global Perspectives* 1: 40–53.
Krampe, K. (2020). You Can't Build on That: Externalisation as the Cornerstone of the EU Pact on Migration and Asylum. *Heinrich Böll Stiftung*. https://eu.boell.org/en/2020/09/30/you-cantbuild-externalisation-cornerstone-eu-pact-migration-and-asylum. Accessed 4 November 2025.
Kyle, J. and Mounk, Y. (2018). *The Populist Harm to Democracy: An Empirical Assessment*. Tony Blair Institute for Global Change.
Lazaridis, G. and Tsagkroni, V. (2015). Securitisation of Migration and Far Right Populist Othering in Scandinavian Countries. In Lazaridis, G. and Khursheed, W. (eds), *The Securitisation of Migration in the EU*. Basingstoke, Palgrave Macmillan: 207–236.
Le Monde with AFP (2023). What's in France's Controversial Immigration Law? https://www.lemonde.fr/en/france/article/2023/12/20/what-s-in-france-s-controversial-immigration-law_6361995_7.html. Accessed 6 August 2025.
Loxa, A. and Stoyanova, V. (2022). Migration as a Constitutional Crisis for the European Union. In Stoyanova, V. and Smet, S. (eds). *Migrants' Rights, Populism and Legal Resilience in Europe*. Cambridge, Cambridge University Press: 139–164.
Majcher, I. (2020). The EU Return System Under the Pact on Migration and Asylum: A Case of Tipped Interinstitutional Balance? *European Law Journal*, 26: 199–225.
Maldini, P. and Takahashi, M. (2017). Refugee Crisis and the European Union: Do the Failed Migration and Asylum Policies Indicate a Political and Structural Crisis of European Integration? *Communication Management Review*, 2(2): 54–72.
Meltzer, C. et al. (2018). Perceptions of the Impact of Immigration and Attitudes Towards Free Movement Within the EU: A Cross-National Study. *REMINDER Project*.
Milazzo, E. (2023). Asymmetric Interstate Solidarity and Return Sponsorship. *Journal of Common Market Studies*, 61: 1179–1193.
Mitsilegas, V. (2014). Solidarity and Trust in the Common European Asylum System. *Comparative Migration Studies*, 2(2): 181–202.
Monar, J. (2017). Justice and Home Affairs. *Journal of Common Market Studies*, 55: 102–117.
Moreno-Lax, V. (2018). The EU Humanitarian Border and the Securitization of Human Rights: The 'Rescue-Through-Interdiction/Rescue-Without-Protection' Paradigm. *Journal of Common Market Studies*, 56(1): 119–140.
Moreno-Lax, V. (2024). *Crisis as (Asylum) Governance: The Evolving Normalisation of Non-Access to Protection in the EU*. Queen Mary Law Research Paper No. 423.
Morlino, L., Piana, D., Sandulli A., and Corkin, J. (2019). Working Paper on Legitimacy and Authority Regarding the Rule of Law, Democracy, Solidarity and Justice. RECONNECT, Deliverable D4.2.
Moutselos, M. (2025). Expansion Without Mandates: Border Andasylum Agencies in European Union Migration Governance. *Governance*, 38(1): 1–17.
Murray, P. and Longo, M. (2018). Europe's Wicked Legitimacy Crisis: The Case of Refugees. *Journal of European Integration*, 40(4): 411–425.

Pallister-Wilkins, P. (2020). Hotspots and the Geographies of Humanitarianism. *Environment and Planning D: Society and Space*, 38: 991–1008.

Panizzon, M. and van Riemsdjik M. (2019). Introduction to Special Issue: Migration Governance in an Era of Large Movements: a Multi-Level Approach. *Journal of Ethnic and Migration Studies*, 45(8): 1–17.

Reslow, N. (2019a). Horizontal and Vertical Diversity: Unintended Consequences of EU External Migration Policy. *The International Spectator*, 54(1): 31–44.

Reslow, N. (2019b). EU External Migration Policy: Taking Stock and Looking Forward. *Global Affairs*, 5(3): 273–278.

Rose, R. (2019). Referendum Challenges to the EU's Policy Legitimacy – and how the EU Responds. *Journal of European Public Policy*, 26(2): 207–225.

Roth, B. R. (2000). Evaluating Democratic Progress. In Fox, G. H. and Roth, B. R. (eds). *Democratic Governance and International Law*. Cambridge, Cambridge University Press: 493–516.

Schmidt, V. (2019). Politicization in the EU: Between National Politics and EU Political Dynamics. *Journal of European Public Policy*, 26(7): 1018–1036.

Slomisnki, P. and Trauner, F. (2018). How do the Member States Return Unwanted Migrants? The Strategic (Non-)Use of 'Europe' During the Migration Crisis. *Journal of Common Market Studies*, 56(1): 101–118.

Thym, D. (2020). European Realpolitik: Legislative Uncertainties and Operational Pitfalls of the 'New' Pact on Migration and Asylum. EU Immigration and Asylum Law and Policy. https://eumigrationlawblog.eu/. Accessed 6 August 2025.

Thym, D. (2022). Never-Ending Story? Political Dynamics, Legislative Uncertainties, and Practical Drawbacks of the 'New' Pact on Migration and Asylum. In Thym, D. (ed.). *Reforming the Common European Asylum System: Opportunities, Pitfalls, and Downsides of the Commission Proposals for a New Pact on Migration and Asylum*. Baden-Baden, Nomos: 11–32.

Tsourdi, E. (2020). The Emerging Architecture of EU Asylum Policy. In Bignami, F. (ed.). *EU Law in Populist Times: Crises and Prospects*. Cambridge, Cambridge University Press: 191–226.

United Nations (2022). Human Rights Violations at International Borders: Trends, Prevention and Accountability. *Report of the Special Rapporteur on the human rights of migrants, Felipe González Morales*. Human Rights Council, UN Doc. A/HRC/50/31 (26 April 2022).

Van der Pas, K. (2024). Litigating the EU–Turkey Deal. *Verfassungsblog*. https://verfassungsblog.de/litigating-the-eu-turkey-deal/. Accessed 6 August 2025.

Vanheule, D., van Selm, J., and Boswell, C. (2011). European Parliament, *The Implementation of Article 80 TFEU on the principle of solidarity and fair sharing of responsibility, including its financial implications, between Member States in the field of border checks, asylum and immigration*, Report to the European Parliament's Committee on Civil Liberties, Justice and Home Affairs (LIBE).

Weiler, J. (1999). *The Constitution of Europe: 'Do the New Clothes have an Emperor?' and other Essays on European Integration*. Cambridge, Cambridge University Press.

Wolthuis, B., Crum, B., Oleart, A., and Overeem, P. (2025). Democracy and Pluralism After European Integration: Incorporating the Contested Character of the EU. *Critical Review of International Social and Political Philosophy*, 28(6): 1136–1160.

Zalan, E. (2020). Court: Three Countries Broke EU Law on Migrant Relocation. *EUObserver*. https://euobserver.com/migration/arfd652e9f. Accessed 6 August 2025.

Legal documents

Case T-192/16 *NF v Council* [2017] [EU:T:2017:128].

Joined Cases C-715/17, C-718/17 and C-719/17 *Commission v Poland and Others* [2020] [EU:C:2020:257].

Case C-821/19 *Commission v Hungary* [2021] [EU:C:2021:930].

Case C-460/23 *Kinshasa*: *Request for a preliminary ruling* [2023] OJ C338/12.

Case C-123/22 *Commission v Hungary* [2024] [EU:C:2024:493].

Consolidated version of the Treaty on the Functioning of the European Union [2008] OJ 115/47–388.
Treaty on European Union (Maastricht Treaty) [1992] OJ C191/1–112; Consolidated Version of the Treaty on European Union [2012] OJ C326/13–45.
Council Decision 2015/1601 of 22 September 2015 establishing provisional measures in the area of international protection for the benefit of Italy and Greece [2015] OJ L248/80.
Council Directive 2008/115/EC of the European Parliament and of the Council of 16 December 2008 on common standards and procedures in Member States for returning illegally staying third-country nationals [2008] OJ L348/98.
Council Directive (EU) 2024/1346 of the European Parliament and of the Council of 14 May 2024 laying down standards for the reception of applicants for international protection [2024] OJ L2024/1346.
Council Regulation (EU) 2024/1347 of the European Parliament and of the Council of 14 May 2024 on standards for the qualification of third-country nationals or stateless persons as beneficiaries of international protection, for a uniform status for refugees or for persons eligible for subsidiary protection and for the content of the protection granted, amending Council Directive 2003/109/EC and repealing Directive 2011/95/EU of the European Parliament and of the Council [2024] OJ L2024/1347.
Council Regulation (EU) 2024/1348 of the European Parliament and of the Council of 14 May 2024 establishing a common procedure for international protection in the Union and repealing Directive 2013/32/EU [2024] OJ L2024/1348.
Council Regulation (EU) 2024/1349 of the European Parliament and of the Council of 14 May 2024 establishing a return border procedure, and amending Regulation (EU) 2021/1148 [2024] OJ L2024/1349.
Council Regulation (EU) 2024/1350 of the European Parliament and of the Council of 14 May 2024 establishing a Union Resettlement and Humanitarian Admission Framework, and amending Regulation (EU) 2021/1147 [2024] OJ L2024/1350.
Council Regulation (EU) 2024/1351 of the European Parliament and of the Council of 14 May 2024 on asylum and migration management, amending Regulations (EU) 2021/1147 and (EU) 2021/1060 and repealing Regulation (EU) No 604/2013 [2024] OJ L2024/1351.
Council Regulation (EU) 2024/1352 of the European Parliament and of the Council of 14 May 2024 amending Regulations (EU) 2019/816 and (EU) 2019/818 for the purpose of introducing the screening of third-country nationals at the external borders [2024] OJ L2024/1352.
Council Regulation (EU) 2024/1356 of the European Parliament and of the Council of 14 May 2024 introducing the screening of third-country nationals at the external borders and amending Regulations (EC) No 767/2008, (EU) 2017/2226, (EU) 2018/1240 and (EU) 2019/817 [2024] OJ L2024/1356.
Council Regulation (EU) 2024/1358 of the European Parliament and of the Council of 14 May 2024 on the establishment of 'Eurodac' for the comparison of biometric data in order to effectively apply Regulations (EU) 2024/1351 and (EU) 2024/1350 of the European Parliament and of the Council and Council Directive 2001/55/EC and to identify illegally staying third-country nationals and stateless persons and on requests for the comparison with Eurodac data by Member States' law enforcement authorities and Europol for law enforcement purposes, amending Regulations (EU) 2018/1240 and (EU) 2019/818 of the European Parliament and of the Council and repealing Regulation (EU) No 603/2013 of the European Parliament and of the Council [2024] OJ L2024/1358.
Council Regulation (EU) 2024/1359 of the European Parliament and of the Council of 14 May 2024 addressing situations of crisis and force majeure in the field of migration and asylum and amending Regulation (EU) 2021/1147 [2024] OJ L2024/1359.

13
Revisiting TTIP and CETA: Claim-making and Legitimacy in the EU

*Alex Androne-Moylan**

13.1 Introduction

Much has been written about the legitimacy of EU policymaking in general, but especially surrounding trade policy. Over the past fifteen years, unprecedented levels of contestation and politicization have triggered intense debate on the democratic credentials of EU free trade agreements (FTAs) (De Ville and Orbie 2014; De Bièvre 2018; Young 2019; De Bièvre et al. 2020). The challenge, however, is that depending on the vantage point, observers may come to very different conclusions. On the one hand, it has been argued that in this and other policy areas, the EU is at risk of forgetting the importance of legitimacy and democracy. The lack of parliamentary, let alone deliberative, democratic mechanisms ensuring the involvement of EU citizens has been widely criticized, as has the absence of pluralistic and agonistic public debates surrounding alternative policy outcomes (Mouffe 2013; Petersmann 2017; Oleart 2021). On the other hand, it has also been shown that, in comparison with national-level policymaking processes, transparency requirements surrounding EU FTAs are significantly greater, making FTAs more democratic from this point of view (Marx and Van der Loo 2021).

This chapter proposes a distinctive perspective on the role of contestation in policy legitimation; rather than approaching contestation as a legitimation failure, it recognizes contestation as divergence of views on substantive issues, and therefore a crucial part of the legitimation process. Bottom-up contestation and debate on EU issues has become increasingly commonplace (Kriesi 2014; Meunier and Czesana 2019; Rauh 2019), however developing the tools to understand and respond to it effectively in a multilevel setting like the EU remains a challenge. Trade policy is a particularly appropriate context to examine these broader questions about representation and legitimacy in the EU. On the one hand, the Common Commercial Policy (CCP) remains one of the few domains where the EU's prime

* The author would like to express his thanks to Ben Crum and Julie Smith for their valuable feedback on this contribution. All responsibility for its contents remains entirely his own.

Alex Androne-Moylan, *Revisiting TTIP and CETA: Claim-making and Legitimacy in the EU* In: *The Promise of EU Democracy*. Edited by: Jan Wouters, Julie Smith, Kolja Raube, and Ben Crum, Oxford University Press.
 DOI: 10.1093/9780191996191.003.0016

non-majoritarian institution—the Commission—holds an exclusive competence. On the other hand, EU FTAs have the potential to trigger significant levels of contestation, which reflects the fact that transfers of competence in the EU are not always matched by adequate channels of legitimation (Grande and Hutter2016; Zürn 2016). In fact, since the 2009 Lisbon treaty, much has changed as to the procedural legitimacy of EU trade policymaking. The European Parliament is on an equal footing with the Council, particularly when it comes to finally approving FTAs negotiated by the Commission. At the same time, however, it can be argued that the increased role of the EP has eclipsed national parliaments, whose role has become confined, most notably, to deciding on foreign investment matters (which are a shared competence).

Overall, while EU trade policy has become more democratic, it also remains highly supranational in nature, presenting a quintessentially postfunctionalist challenge for the EU (Gheyle 2019). On the one hand, globalization and rising geopolitical challenges, alongside inescapable global value chains, make the functional necessity and benefits of the EU as a unitary trading bloc increasingly apparent. On the other hand, the changing nature of trade policy, from focusing on trade liberalization to involving comprehensive regulatory cooperation, has more deeply connected this policy area to the everyday lives of citizens (Dominguez 2017). The impact of FTAs on issues such as consumer protection or food safety and environmental standards has contributed to raising their salience. This has, in turn, also raised citizens' expectations of, and engagement on, what legitimate trade policy procedures and outcomes look like (Rone 2018): in other words, the EU's promise of democracy in one of its key policymaking processes.

Within this context, this chapter presents an understanding of legitimacy of EU trade policy which is (i) informed by the perceptions of key societal actors on trade and (ii) engages with legitimation as a process in constant flux. Its aim is to understand *how and to what extent societal actors are (mis-)aligned with EU actors in their normative evaluations or demands in relation to TTIP and CETA*. Societal actors are a fairly broad category and include civil society, trade unions, industry, and experts or pundits; they include all societal actors whose views are reported in national media, be they national or EU-level actors. This chapter focuses on mapping whether and how societal actors differ, for instance, in how they conceive of appropriate levels of authority (national versus EU) or whether they understand trade policy as a primarily European or Member State-level matter. As such, this chapter presents an empirically grounded approach to assessing potential legitimacy gaps. To achieve this, it builds on the notion that when legitimacy mechanisms are perceived as weak, bottom-up perceptions of legitimate authority (i.e. sociological legitimacy) become especially important (see discussion in Section 13.2). Finally, it should be noted that this contribution is limited to the discursive dimension of legitimation in the EU. This is related also to the scope of the findings, which is very specific, i.e. media debates within selected EU Member States.

The empirical analysis in this chapter hinges on a set of multinomial logistic regression models which allow an actor-level assessment of divergence and/or convergence primarily among EU-level executive actors (the Commission), civil society actors and industry. This approach is applied to a representative claims analysis dataset on the Transatlantic Trade and Investment Partnership (TTIP) and Comprehensive Economic and Trade Agreement (CETA), in the media of Denmark, France, Germany, Italy, Spain, and Poland. This chapter develops the current literature in two key ways: (i) it highlights how Representative Claims Analysis (RCA) can help make sense of democracy, legitimacy, and representation in the EU; (ii) it also shows the importance of an empirically grounded perspective on the broader *problematique* of the EU's democratic deficit. This contribution points to discourse as a crucial tool in the continuous process of (re)negotiation of the European idea and its legitimacy. By observing how claim-making helps (de-) construct ideas of Europe, legitimacy, and democracy, we may be able to gain insights into the nature of the possible divergences between bottom-up expectations and top-down practices of democratic representation in the EU.

13.2 The sociological legitimacy of trade policy

Sociological legitimacy is defined as 'beliefs within a given constituency or other relevant audience that a political institution's exercise of authority is appropriate' (Tallberg and Zürn 2019: 585). Unlike normative legitimacy, it is not related to the theorization and evaluation of legitimacy criteria, but it is dependent on the beliefs and perceptions of relevant audiences (or *constituencies*). The *normativity* of legitimacy here is limited to perceptions of the appropriateness of the EU's behaviour (*should the EU exercise such authority?*), which is conveyed through acts aimed at legitimizing or delegitimizing the EU, its institutions, policies, etc. (Zürn 2018). This understanding of sociological legitimacy helps to convey that incorporating *beliefs* and *perceptions* into conceptualizing EU democracy and legitimacy might be rather important. Crucially, sociological legitimacy is particularly well suited to conceptualizing (de-)legitimation mechanisms when formal legitimacy mechanisms between citizens and institutions are rather thin (Dellmuth and Tallberg 2015).

However, although sociological legitimacy has its strengths and has gained attention in debates about legitimacy in the EU and other kinds of international organizations, it does seem to display a basic drawback. Following the reasoning of its critics (see in particular: Hurd 2019), bottom-up delegitimation or contestation appears as an indicator of the degree of legitimacy of the organization in question. Contestation is seen as a legitimation failure rather than a key part of the legitimation process. This conception of sociological legitimacy is, therefore, based on the idea that when there is no bottom-up contestation, then the polity has gained the required legitimation. At first glance, the idea of legitimacy as acceptance of the 'appropriateness' of authority is an appealing one and, in some ways, it is also effective. Yet, as Hurd (2019) suggests, the lack of sociological legitimacy might even be seen as a sign of democratic health, i.e., that there is scope for different conceptions of EU integration to be debated. In light of this, the aim of this chapter is not simply to determine the presence or absence of contestation; instead, the goal is to engage with the specific nature of the beliefs and perspectives that contribute to sociological legitimacy. Is the EU seen as the main source of authority in the area of trade? Is trade policy perceived as a truly EU-wide issue, or do national perspectives prevail?

Early instances of trade policy contestation in the EU, such as the Anti-Counterfeiting Trade Agreement (ACTA) in 2012, demonstrated the gradual decline of the sociological legitimacy of EU policymaking, leading to increased civil society mobilization and public pressure (Cabras 2024). The negotiations for TTIP and CETA, however, marked a turning point in the bottom-up acceptance of EU trade policy. These agreements, characterized by their 'deep and comprehensive' nature and the economic significance of the trading partners involved (the USA and Canada), elicited unprecedented public and political contestation, bringing to light a legitimacy gap. By entering domestic policy areas, TTIP and CETA raised concerns about potential regulatory downgrading and limitations on Member States' regulatory autonomy. Issues such as environmental protection, public health, and food safety standards came under scrutiny, fuelling public anxieties and mobilizing civil society organizations and citizens. For instance, Eurobarometer data from 2016 shows how in about half of EU Member States, public opinion was deeply divided on the issue of FTAs, with 50 per cent of respondents or more opposed to either FTAs in general or TTIP in particular (European Commission 2016). The inclusion of investor–state dispute settlement (ISDS) provisions and concerns about regulatory alignment triggered such opposition, further leveraged by civil society groups through widespread mobilization and campaigns (Cabras 2024). The CETA controversy culminated in the Belgian region of Wallonia refusing to ratify the agreement, delaying its implementation and underscoring the growing influence of subnational actors in challenging EU trade policy decisions.

Given these matters had been particularly contentious during the CETA negotiations, the EU Commission adopted a strategy of splitting trade agreements, separating trade aspects from investment provisions (Gheyle and Rone 2023). This approach, combined with a decline in public mobilization, led to a decrease in the salience of later trade agreements, such as those with Japan, Singapore, and Vietnam. National parliaments, facing a diminished role in ratifying trade-only agreements, displayed less interest in engaging with these issues. The EP, while maintaining its important scrutiny roles, also saw reduced engagement in the absence of strong public pressure. Yet, even though the intensity of politicization may fluctuate, public scrutiny and contestation remain integral aspects of trade policy and EU policymaking more broadly, as debates surrounding the EU–MERCOSUR agreement show (see De Bièvre and Poletti 2020). The question that remains is how best to make sense of and respond to such contestation when it emerges.

What makes the case of TTIP and CETA particularly relevant is that within the timeframes and scope adopted in this research, it constitutes an example of *unaddressed* politicization. As has been argued elsewhere (Andrione-Moylan, De Wilde, and Raube 2024), when it comes these instances of EU trade policy, output focused conceptions of legitimacy further entrenched the Commission's tendency to deal with the policymaking process in a depoliticized manner (Schmidt 2013). That is to say that, specifically in the field of trade, the Commission has been found to attempt discursively to reduce the potential salience, polarization, and bottom-up mobilization directed at FTAs (Dür, Hamilton, and De Bièvre 2024). Conversely, engaging with bottom-up contestation counters such depoliticizing logic and would imply recognizing the drawbacks of the one-size-fits-all approach that a supranational policy such as trade implies. Trade policy is not simply about trade liberalization: its consequences can determine who are the winners and losers of both EU integration and globalization. Hence the relevance of recognizing, also from a theoretical standpoint, that decisions on trade are distributional in nature, imply trade-offs, and they are political and, therefore, contestable (Hurd 2019).

The present chapter, while steering away from a typically normative evaluation of the democratic processes surrounding EU policymaking, proposes an approach to sociological legitimacy which is citizen-focused and strives to facilitate the understanding of bottom-up (de-)legitimizing pressures. Considering that empirical observation shows that bottom-up polarization on EU-related issues has grown (Rauh 2019), developing the tools to meaningfully address these kinds of debates seems essential. However, relying on the established understanding of sociological legitimacy entails the risk of limiting bottom-up contestation instead of attempting to understand it or responding to it. The aim here is then to propose a corrective to this established understanding of sociological legitimacy, in the form of the misalignments between the EU and its constituencies. To identify the gaps in the sociological legitimacy enjoyed by the EU and its institutions in trade policy, this chapter examines divergences in how trade policy is framed and conceived between EU actors on the one hand and societal actors on the other. Such an analysis can provide the tools for EU institutional actors to integrate or respond to these such divergences.

The well-known approach to studying politicization introduced by De Wilde et al. (2016) is useful in understanding how the general notion of contestation is captured in this study. The focus is on politicization as a phenomenon that involves contestation but is more precisely characterized by three key components: (i) growing salience; (ii) polarization of opinion; and (iii) the expansion of actors and audiences engaged in EU issues. The increasing, if intermittent, scrutiny of

EU FTAs is effectively encapsulated by this understanding of politicization. Over the past decade, trade policy has often seen an increased relevance within both domestic and EU public debates (salience); this has led to more polarized discussions over the benefits of free trade (polarization); finally, these debates have involved broader and previously unengaged audiences (actor expansion).

Perhaps the most commonly adopted explanatory mechanism of how politicization tends to be triggered is the authority transfer hypothesis, which sees the transfer of competences from the Member States to the EU as a key mechanism (Grande and Hutter 2016; Zürn 2016). Politicization, from this standpoint, is understood as a response to a lack of legitimizing channels which are perceived as appropriate, which implies that politicization is intimately connected to perceived legitimacy gaps. Politicization, therefore, constitutes an important backdrop to the arguments presented in this chapter.

As politicization can be interpreted as a sign of (perceived) legitimacy gaps, the fact that TTIP and CETA remain among the most politicized EU issues to date, constitutes a relevant element in this analysis (Meunier and Czesana 2019; Young 2019; De Bièvre et al. 2020; Oleart 2021). There are, therefore, two key preconditions to the framework adopted in this contribution which relate to the specific nature of the debates surrounding TTIP and CETA. First of all, without salience, mobilization, and polarization, it is unlikely that delegitimizing and legitimizing patterns could be detected in discourse, which implies that the findings in this chapter primarily apply to politicized issues such as TTIP and CETA. Second, the findings and arguments put forward here apply to issues on which EU institutions have explicitly avoided engaging with the politicized debates surrounding them. Within a context of *unaddressed* polarization, salience, and mobilization it seems plausible that civil society actors will display a greater tendency towards misalignment vis-à-vis EU actors. Moreover, it is in a politicized context that distinct views on policy and policymakers emerge; assessing and potentially addressing such legitimacy gaps is dependent on whether and how EU executive actors (the Commission) respond to bottom-up politicization. With this in mind, the first expectation is: *(I) when bottom-up issue politicization goes unaddressed by the EU, there is an overarching misalignment between the claims of societal actors and EU representatives.*

The second expectation is that under those circumstances of unaddressed politicization *(II) among societal actors, civil society actors are more likely to display misalignment on a politicized issue*. Societal actors represent a very diverse category of actors, with the two main sub-categories being civil society actors and business stakeholders. This analytical distinction is relevant as it allows us to assess the positioning and potential impact of societal actors who are faced with major obstacles (financial, know-how) when trying to influence EU policymaking. In other words, how does the (perceived) lack of effective bottom-up legitimation channels affect the behaviour of civil society actors? Business actors, conversely, can dispose of formal and informal channels of influence more easily and have consistently been found to rely on inside lobbying when confronted with a highly politicized issue (Dür, Hamilton, and De Bièvre 2024). This suggests that business actors prefer a strategy that avoids direct confrontation in situations with high salience and contestation. When they do engage in public debate, they tend to advocate for the EU's focus on trade liberalization (Gheyle and Rone 2023). Exploring expectation (II) will provide an indication of whether societal actors rely more than other actors on public debate and politicization to make their views heard. As such, this will provide further insights into whether politicization can be seen as an opportunity for improved EU responsiveness specifically in the eyes of civil society.

13.3 Evaluating legitimacy through claim-making

As discussed, sociological legitimacy depends on the belief within relevant constituencies that a political institution's exercise of authority is appropriate. Claims which more or less explicitly reject the appropriateness of the EU's authority overall, or its concrete policy response, can be considered as displaying misalignment, and therefore a lack of (policy) legitimacy. At the same time, the assessment of such a misalignment is also dependent on the politicized state of the policy issue within Member State media debates; only then is there meaningful bottom-up engagement which has delegitimizing or legitimizing potential. This means that the conditions of salience, polarization, and mobilization, as elements of politicization, need to be met. This also implies that complete alignment between the institution exercising authority (the EU/Commission) and civil society would not allow us to assess sociological legitimacy. Full alignment, and therefore a lack of politicization, is comparable to a permissive consensus scenario, which says very little about true policy acceptance or legitimate authority and is more indicative of a lack of significant engagement on the matter (Hooghe and Marks 2009).

Polarization requires that debates on the issue lead to sufficiently distinct camps which coalesce around either favourable or opposed views: i.e. aligned or misaligned vis-à-vis the EU. The presence of sociological legitimacy in discourse is, therefore, not dependent on complete alignment but rather on whether domestic actors are overall more likely to express claims which align with the EU. As is discussed in Section 13.4, this assessment hinges on the statistical significance of the alignment observed, which determines whether the result 'aligned' is consistently more likely than 'misaligned', or vice versa. It is useful to recall that the assessment of sociological legitimacy as contested and constructed *through discourse* limits the nature and scope of the findings presented in this chapter. These findings reveal, in the first instance, trends *in discourse*, which in turn can provide some insights into the deeper mechanisms potentially at work.

Moreover, it should be noted that the legitimacy 'gaps' surrounding EU trade policy, which are the subject of this chapter do not necessarily entail a flat-out rejection of European integration as a whole; they are simply indicative of differences in conceptions of authority and representation surrounding EU FTAs, which put into question the role played by the EU or its priorities and framing of the policy issue. As outlined in the research question and expectations, the key aim is to identify potential divergences among distinct categories of actors, specifically societal versus EU actors (or, more accurately, claimants). EU claimants include EU-level executive actors, i.e., the Commission and Council, along with the EP and all other bureaucratic or judicial bodies. In fact, in the empirical material to be analysed, by far most 'EU claimants' are Commission officials. As will become apparent in the analysis, societal actors do not necessarily constitute a united bottom-up front when it comes to sociological legitimacy; analysing the views of all societal actors in the aggregate would prevent the more nuanced understanding of bottom-up politicization as a tool to determine the presence of sociological legitimation. Thus, the framework includes industry claimants (business representatives) separately from civil society claimants, which refer specifically to civil society representatives, trade unions but also citizens. It is important to analyse the claims by industry and civil society claimants as separate sources of sociological legitimacy. The behaviour of these two very different constituencies may align in some circumstances but diverge in others.

Saward's notion of representative claims refers to how 'representation is produced by processes of claim-making and consequent acceptance or rejection by audiences or parts of audiences' (Saward 2006: 303). Claim-making in this context is defined as 'a claim to represent or to know what represents the interests of someone or something' (Saward 2006: 306). Representation here is operationalized as the product of 'claim-making and consequent acceptance or rejection by audiences or parts of audiences' (Saward 2006: 303). Claim-making is defined as 'a claim to represent or to know what represents the interests of someone or something' (Saward 2006: 306). Following this approach, the potential misalignment between EU actors and societal actors, can provide valuable insights into the ways in which the EU's authority in the realm of trade policy is contested. De Wilde's (2013) Representative Claims Analysis (RCA), based on Saward's (2010) representative claim and Koopmans and Statham's (2006) political claims analysis, provides the main methodological tool for detecting politicization in the form of salience of the issue, evidence of polarization attempts among claims, and the range of actors involved in claim-making. However, its key strength is its focus on claims made by actors, or 'claimants', who make demands for policy change or evaluations of the issue debated on behalf of a specific constituency and vis-à-vis an addressee who is expected to respond or intervene. In light of the discussion in the previous section, RCA seems particularly well-suited to explore the specific approach to sociological legitimacy which effectively takes into account the views of a variety of stakeholders. In short, RCA is a quantitative methodology for content analysis that enables the categorization of speech acts (claims) assessing policy or expressing demands for policy changes within news sources.

In the context of the present chapter, RCA can capture in which way and to what degree the claims of societal actors diverge from claims made by EU executive actors, highlighting the potential frailty of societal legitimacy. The specific features of politicization which RCA brings to light, precisely because of the focus on representation, can be linked to an idea of sociological legitimacy whereby the debate among diverging views on the appropriateness of the EU's authority, and hence its politicization, is central to bridging the disconnect and re-legitimizing the EU and its policies. In this chapter, RCA allows us to focus on the extent and nature of the gap in the perceptions surrounding the EU's competence on trade policy. The present comparative analysis takes the claims by EU actors as a baseline of sorts and compares them to those of civil society actors (including citizens) and industry representatives. The misalignments captured in the analysis will point to key features indicating misalignment in claims and the concrete aspects of EU (trade) policymaking these claims tend to focus on.

The (mis-)alignment is assessed on the basis of divergences and convergences in the kinds of claim components observed among each category of claimant. The misalignment, as the dependent variable in this study, is captured through five key dimensions which are the hallmark of the RCA approach in analysing media discourse: *object type*, *object scope*, *issue scope*, *structure of cleavages*, *issue position* (Gora and De Wilde 2019). These are the different dimensions that capture the nature of the misalignment between societal actors and the EU; as explained in more depth in the analysis (Section 13.4), the variation across the different categories of actors is assessed in five regression models which allow determining the divergences and convergences among actors, across these indicators.

The *object* of the claim refers to the constituency whose interests are being represented by the claimant. There are two separate coding categories linked to the object: type and scope. *Object type* clarifies who the actor making the claim is representing, bringing to the fore the distinction between representatives and represented, and how narrow or broad the constituency identified is. Often, the object type may coincide with the claimant itself. However, claimants may also invoke object types of other actors whose interests they want to highlight. This analysis distinguishes three object types: polity, industry, and civil society. Polity indicates that the object type (or constituency) is either a state or regional organization; when the main constituency is business or industry stakeholders, it is coded as industry; when the constituency is citizens or civil society organizations, the object type is civil society.

The *object scope* adds a second dimension by focusing on the level of the constituency. On this aspect, the analysis compares own country, third country (both other EU Member States and non-EU countries), and EU. Taken together, the object type and object scope provide relevant insights into distinct conceptions of which constituencies should be represented in EU trade policy and at which level. Whether and how conceptions of representation differ significantly among industry, civil society, and EU claimants can reveal some of the basic disconnects and legitimacy gaps, expressed through claims which contrast with the EU's overarching understanding of its main constituency. Is the EU addressing the right audience? Answering this question will help assess the foundations for the belief in the 'appropriateness' of the EU's authority, i.e., its sociological legitimacy.

Another important window into the relevance of claims on EU FTAs to better understand potential legitimacy gaps is how this issue is framed through the issue scope and structure of cleavages. The *issue scope* answers the question from where the claimant perceives the implications of the issue debated primarily to have emerged. Hence, it captures EU trade as a matter which has mainly an own-country (domestic) scope, or rather an EU scope, or a global scope. This constitutes an important coordinate to detect (mis-)alignment surrounding expectations on the most relevant or 'appropriate' level of governance of this policy area, in relation to the 'geographical' scope of the demands or evaluations made on EU FTAs.

The *structure of cleavages* reveals instead who are perceived to be the main contenders in the public debate on this matter. In this analysis the focus is on claims falling into one of four categories. If the cleavage is between national (EU or non-EU) governments, then it is coded as International. Conversely, if it is framed as pitting EU executive actors against national executive actors, the conflict is coded as EU vs National. Any partisan conflict, among politically affiliated parties (both EU and national level) is coded as Partisan. Finally, a Societal cleavage captures conflict among societal groups, such as elites vs 'the people'. Once again, framing EU trade in one of these distinct ways reveals a further potential for (mis-)alignment as to the perceived stakeholders in the debate and the precise nature of its contentiousness.

Finally, the analysis also takes into consideration the *issue position* expressed in a claim. This refers to the position taken by the claimant, distinguishing three kinds of claims: claims advocating further integration and therefore, in the context of this research, generally in favour of EU FTAs; claims demanding increased demarcation, hence in favour of limiting the EU's involvement in trade policy or more critical of EU FTAs; and claims simply demanding an unchanged status quo. In this case, it will be of particular interest to examine whether there are relevant differences between the two main types of societal actors, and which one aligns more with the claims by EU actors.

13.4 TTIP and CETA debates in six EU Member States

This study covers six EU Member States: Germany, France, Spain, Italy, Poland, and Denmark. The selection of these Member States aims to achieve a balanced geographical distribution, thereby enhancing the representativeness of the sample. The research aligns with Castles and Obinger's 'logic of territoriality', which underlies the family of nations theory—a framework for classifying European countries that effectively predicts convergence and divergence in public policy outcomes (Castles and Obinger 2008). Consistent with this theory, we include two Central/Western European countries (France and Germany), two Southern European countries (Italy and Spain), a Scandinavian/Northern European country (Denmark), and finally an East European/post-Communist country (Poland). Incorporating Member States from these four distinct geographical groups ensures the analysis centres on a sample of countries with a diverse set of structural and path-dependent factors (e.g. economic, political, or geographical) that may influence claimants' perceptions of EU policies.

This chapter relies on freely accessible data collected previously by Gora and De Wilde (2022) (see Table 13.1).[1] To capture both the variation in news sources and include the key newspapers of record, the dataset encompasses articles from one left-leaning and one right-leaning newspaper per country. The newspapers included in the dataset are: *Frankfurter Allgemeine Zeitung* and *Süddeutsche Zeitung* in Germany, *Le Monde* and *Figaro* in France, *La Repubblica* and *Corriere della Sera* in Italy, *El País* and *ABC* in Spain, and *Politiken* and *Jyllandsposten* in Denmark, along with *Gazeta Wyborcza* and *Rzeczpospolita* in Poland.[2] The newspaper articles, which are the source of the dataset of claims used in this chapter, were sampled from the electronic databases Factiva and LexisNexis. Relevant articles were identified using keyword search strings within episodes of contention surrounding the negotiation of TTIP and CETA (October 2015–September 2016) as well as around the launch of the European Commission's 'Non-paper on Trade and Sustainable Development (TSD) chapters in EU Free Trade Agreements (FTAs)' (July 2017–March 2018). Research assistants coded fifty articles per newspaper, randomly selected among the first 100–150 search results: this process resulted in a total of 921 claims made by EU actors, national governmental actors, and a range of societal actors on trade-related issues.[3] Table 13.1 provides a snapshot of the distribution of claims across claimant categories, as well as country cases and data sources.

[1] The data that support the findings of this study are openly available in Sikt—Norwegian Agency for Shared Services in Education and Research. https://doi.org/10.18712/NSD-NSD3047-V3.

[2] For each country, the left-leaning newspaper is mentioned first, followed by the right-leaning newspaper.

[3] For additional details on the codebook and coding rules, please refer to the online handbook by Gora and De Wilde (2019). https://reconnect-europe.eu/wp-content/uploads/2019/09/D2.2-update-July-2019.pdf.

Table 13.1 RCA dataset overview

Claims by Claimant Type											
EU Claimants				**National Governmental Actors**				**Societal Claimants**			
229				424				263			
Claims by Country and Newspaper											
DE (*left/right*)		FR (*left/right*)		IT (*left/right*)		ES (*left/right*)		DK (*left/right*)		PL (*left/right*)	
98	152	76	67	23	63	82	70	61	38	86	105

The analytical approach is focused on unpicking the nature and extent of the divergences in the kind of claims expressed by EU actors, vis-à-vis those by industry and civil society, along the five dimensions discussed in the previous section. Based on this operationalization of the discursive misalignment on trade, the data analysis involves a series of multinomial logit regression models. Multinomial logit analysis allows us to calculate the probability of a correlation when the outcome variable (or dependent variable) is categorically distributed; this means that, unlike binary variables, it has three or more levels. This is true for each of the five indicators of misalignment. The model estimates are calculated against one level of the outcome variable; coefficients are estimated in relation to one of the outcome variable levels. For a unit change in the independent variable (i.e. the claimant), the log-odds estimates the change in the outcome, when all other variables are held constant. The models are reported in Table 13.2, with log-odds replaced by odds ratios, which are more intuitive; the values indicate the chance of the correlation occurring, as compared to the reference category (e.g. an odds-ratio of 1.00 means the chance of occurrence is equal to those in the reference category). This means that the five models tell us how likely it is that, on average, claims by a certain category of actor (e.g. civil society) contain a certain claim component (e.g. EU object scope), when compared to all other actors/claimants. The models are only able to discern this comparative finding when such difference (*more* or *less* likely) is found to be statistically significant, i.e., when only a very small proportion of claims do not follow the correlation pattern. In all models the independent variable is 'claimant type', a three-level categorical variable, including 'civil society', 'EU' and 'industry'; the constant is 'industry claimants'. For instance, in Model 1, 'civil society object' serves as the reference group; the *constant* indicates the odds ratio for 'industry object' and 'policy object', when all other predictors (civil society and EU) are evaluated at zero. This type of analysis allows us to estimate the likelihood of correlations, not in isolation, but in relation to the other levels of both independent and outcome variables.

Multinomial coefficients tend to be difficult to interpret, therefore the analysis and discussion will focus on the plots provided for each of the five models (Figures 13.1–13.5, Section 13.5). On the *x* axis the plots convert odds ratios into predicted probabilities; ranging from 0 to 1, they are the ratio between co-occurrences and total occurrences. Each plot shows the variation of the probability of co-occurrence for each outcome variable in the form of marginal predictions at the mean across the three levels of the independent variable (actor type). In this way, the presence and extent of the divergence between EU actor claims and societal actor claims is measured as differences in the probability of a certain outcome, across the three levels of the claimant variable. Error bars in these are confidence intervals (CI), plotting to what extent the overall predicted values diverge from the marginal predictions at the mean, within a 95 per cent confidence range.[4] On the one hand, if the probability is the same or very similar across industry, civil society, and EU actors, there is no indication of a misalignment from an RCA perspective. On the other hand, if differing probability levels are detected by the logit models, this points to a gap or disconnect, which is indicative of possible weaknesses in sociological legitimacy. When looking at Figures 13.1–13.5, the steeper the incline connecting the estimated probabilities, the more likely is misalignment.

13.5 Mapping out (mis)aligned stakeholders on trade

Overall, the data show that the different categories of actors identified do indeed tend to discuss trade in significantly distinct ways. There are systematic correlations between the actor types and the key elements of their claims which, rather than the result of random co-occurrence, are statistically significant. This is an essential starting point for this analysis as it confirms that the proposed framework is on a sufficiently secure footing; the choices claimants make on precisely *how* they discuss trade are worthy of further examination. However, as detailed in Table 13.2, the level of significance varies across the different variables and models, a limitation which should be taken into account when interpreting this analysis. In addition, the number of claims which are relevant to each model should also be considered: the exact number [N] is reported in Table 13.2, with a higher number of claims implying a greater substantive significance of the model's estimation.[5]

[4] It should be noted that CI bars overlapping by 50 per cent (contrary to most error bars) still display a statistically significant divergence at $^{*}p < 0.1$, a feature which needs to be considered when interpreting these plots (on this see Krzywinski and Altman 2013). Conversely, an overlap greater than 50 per cent shows a lack of statistical significance.

[5] A further technical factor is that the model fit as measured by the McFadden *pseudo*-R^2 also varies across the five models, from 0.198 of Model 2 to 0.060 of Model 4, denoting a decreasing degree of fit, albeit still within an acceptable range. The lower the score, the more cautious the evaluation of the model output needs to be.

Table 13.2 Multinomial logit analysis—TTIP and CETA database

Claimant Type	Model 1		Model 2		Model 3		Model 4		Model 5		
	Object Type		Object Scope		Issue Scope		Issue Position		Structure of Cleavage		
Reference group	*Civil Society Object Type*		*EU Object Scope*		*Global Issue Scope*		*Position Status Quo*		*EU vs National*		
	Industry Object	Polity Object	Own Country Object Scope	Third Country Object Scope	EU Issue Scope	Own Country Issue Scope	Position Demarcation	Position Integration	Int./EU	Partisan	Societal
Civil Society	0.046***	0.031***	0.786	0.346	0.422**	0.751	1.481	0.167***	2.308	2.308	2.692
EU	0.068**	0.543	0.037***	0.175***	0.708	0.033***	0.881	0.767	2.697	0.140***	0.084***
Constant	34.002***	7.001*	2.250**	0.667	2.062**	0.687	0.800	2.667***	0.200**	0.800	0.400*
N	152		158		355		303		243		
Pseudo-R^2	0.163		0.198		0.076		0.060		0.138		

*p<0.1; **p<0.05; ***p<0.01

Model 1 (Figure 13.1) shows the probability of claimants selecting a civil society object, as opposed to an industry or polity object. This model answers the following question: which is the most relevant constituency in relation to EU trade policy, according to each actor category? It should be noted here that it is partly inevitable that each category of claimant will tend to focus on a certain audience or 'constituency': claimants overall tend to be self-referential, by claiming to represent the constituency of which they are a part of. Hence it is not surprising that industry is the most likely to refer to object type industry (0.810); civil society the most likely to refer to civil society object (0.360); and finally, EU claimants are more likely to refer to object type polity (0.535). Yet it remains interesting that civil society claimants are the least likely to take a polity (either national or EU) perspective on EU trade, preferring overall to *represent* industry stakeholders in their claim-making, closely followed by civil society ones. Civil society claimants place themselves the furthest away from the preferred constituency of EU actors, with industry claimants marginally more likely to refer to polity as their object. For EU actors, there seems to be a missed opportunity to bridge an apparent gap; the EU's clear tendency to avoid civil society constituencies in their claims deepens the divide between these two categories of actors, and points to one of the foundations of a fundamental misalignment.

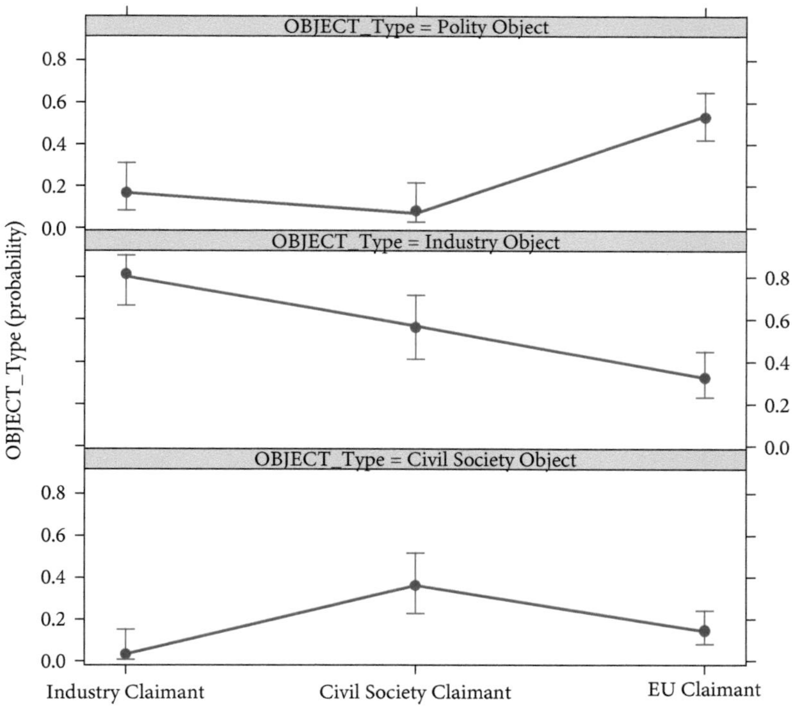

Figure 13.1 Model 1—object type

While it would be unwise to read too much into a certain level of self-referential claims, a gap or disconnect in the preferred conception of constituencies among claimants is clear. While the disconnect is a structural one, it can offer an indication of how the EU could tailor its message to address the concerns of specific constituencies more directly, rather than relying on a theoretical EU-wide constituency. It highlights a first possible sociological legitimacy gap in discourse, which involves both industry and civil society claimants. This constitutes the first validation of Expectation (I): when bottom-up issue politicization goes unaddressed by the EU, societal claimants express claims that are misaligned with those of EU claimants when it comes to the object type. Moreover, as an initial validation of Expectation (II), the extent of the misalignment is not constant across all societal actors, but is particularly apparent in the case of civil society claimants.

Model 2 (Figure 13.2) displays probabilities of correlations between claimant type and object scope, therefore adding another dimension to the constituency component of claims. EU claimants are the most likely to refer to an EU object scope (0.834), confirming how the focus on a polity object implies indeed references to the EU. Both in the case of industry and civil society claimants there is a high chance of references to the claimant's own country as object scope. References in object scope to specific Member States by EU claimants would be captured in

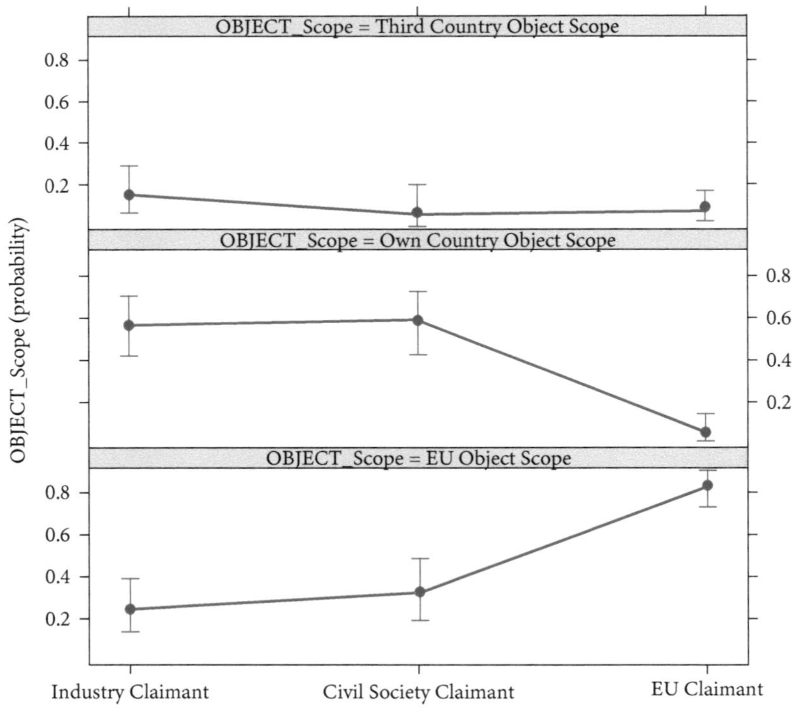

Figure 13.2 Model 2—object scope

the third-country object scope plot, which however highlights an almost zero probability for this category. This adds a further dimension to the misalignment identified by the models: there is a lack of a Member State-specific audience in claims by EU actors, which is a significant focus for both civil society claimants and industry claimants (i.e. own-country object scope).

This is a disconnect which is not easily overcome but is nevertheless noteworthy and in line with research carried out within other policy areas, raising the challenge of how the EU might better adapt its communication on trade issues to different national contexts (De Wilde and Gora 2021; Andrione-Moylan, De Wilde, and Raube 2023). The posited 'misalignment' suggested in Expectation (I) is confirmed, while in this instance there is no appreciable difference when comparing the (mis-)alignment of civil society actors and industry (Expectation II).

Model 3 (Figure 13.3), which switches the analysis to the framing of the issue and the level where its implications play out, shows which polity level different actors associate with the issue of trade. Civil society claimants remain the least likely to portray EU FTAs as a primarily EU-level issue (0.365), and are at the same time more likely to emphasize their global implications (0.419), when compared to industry. Industry claimants do not fully align with civil society claimants, as they privilege an EU framing (0.549) almost as much as EU claimants (0.588), while

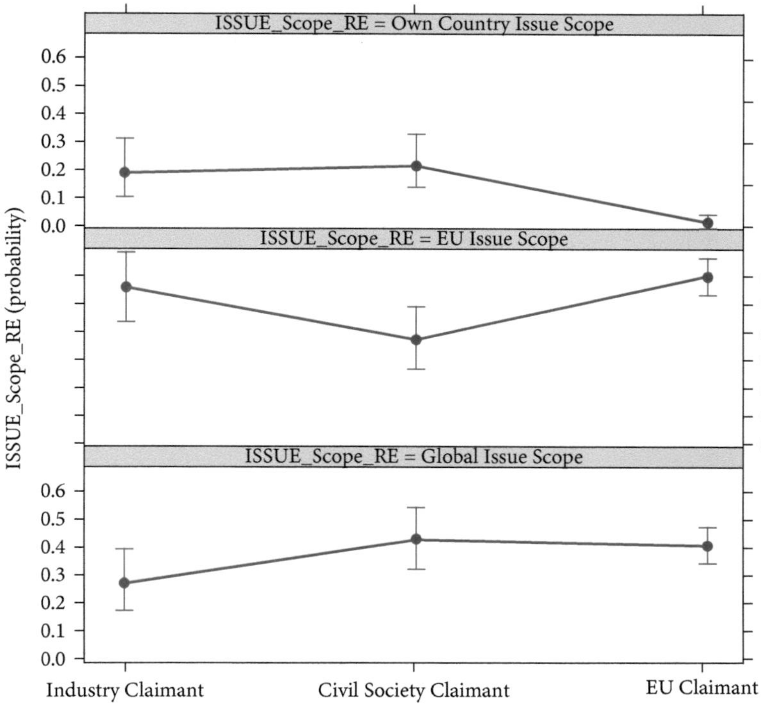

Figure 13.3 Model 3—issue scope

being the least likely to refer to a global framing of FTAs (0.267). Particularly in the case of global issue scope, however, the overlap of the error bars is such that the level of statistical significance is low. Both industry and civil society claimants refer to own-country issue scope to a similar extent, while EU claimants once again steer away from any national framing of the issue, following the pattern outlined in Expectation (I) but showing no evidence in support of Expectation (II). Expectation (II) only finds some confirmation in the EU issue scope plot, where there is a definite misalignment only in the case of civil society.

Model 4 (Figure 13.4) unpacks patterns of support for EU trade policy, through the lens of claims advocating for further integration or, on the opposite end of the spectrum, opposing EU FTAs. First, it is inevitable that there is a rather high probability for claims by EU actors to be in favour of further integration (0.545). At the same time, however, industry claimants display a similar tendency, with a high chance of advocating a pro-EU stance. The major divide is with civil society claimants, who are identified as the claimants with the highest probability of arguing against EU FTAs (0.450) or the status quo (0.380), with only 17 per cent probability that they will advocate in favour of EU FTAs. As is apparent from the graph (Figure 13.4), industry and EU claimants display almost exactly the same

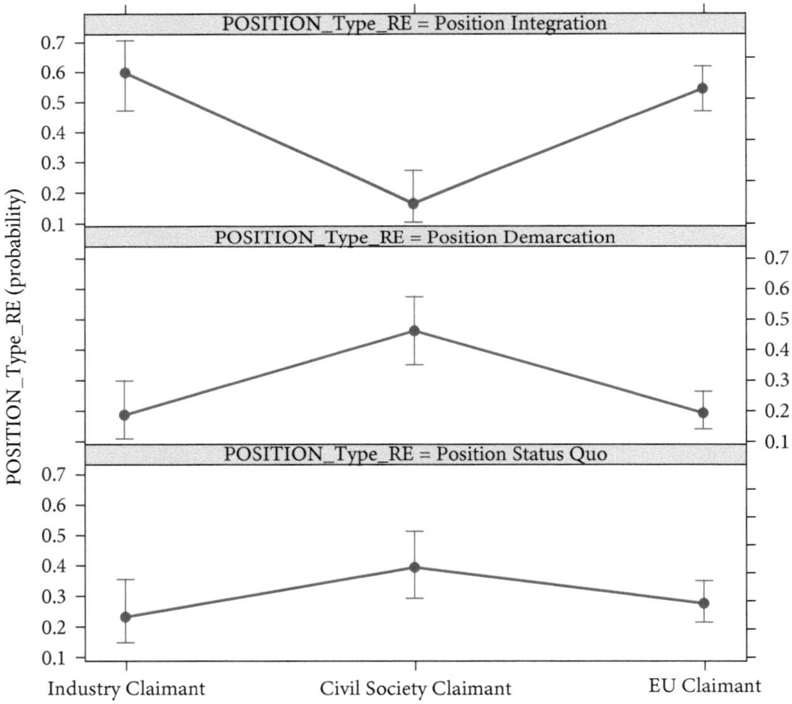

Figure 13.4 Model 4—position type

predicted probabilities, with civil society claimants being singled out as the least supportive of EU FTAs. In line with our expectations, this shows that civil society in the media was consistently critical, even in those Member States, such as Spain, Italy, and Poland, where public opinion was more positive towards EU trade policy (European Commission 2016).

Once again, the model reveals another element of the misalignment between EU actors and other claimants, clarifying the importance of analysing industry claimants and civil society claimants separately, allowing the models to capture a more nuanced picture. Crucially, not all societal claimants display the same disconnect from EU actors, suggesting that levels of sociological legitimacy may in fact vary across different types of actors. In this sense, Expectation (II) definitely finds confirmation in this model, however we do not find support here for Expectation (I), i.e., the notion that all societal actors (including industry) display at least some level of misalignment, within the premised context of unaddressed politicization. Ultimately, it is by paying greater attention to the views of civil society that EU actors may be able to build a pathway towards policy acceptance and, hence, improved sociological legitimacy.

Model 5 (Figure 13.5) is the final multinomial logit model in this analysis, and the only model including four different levels of the outcome variable, the *structure*

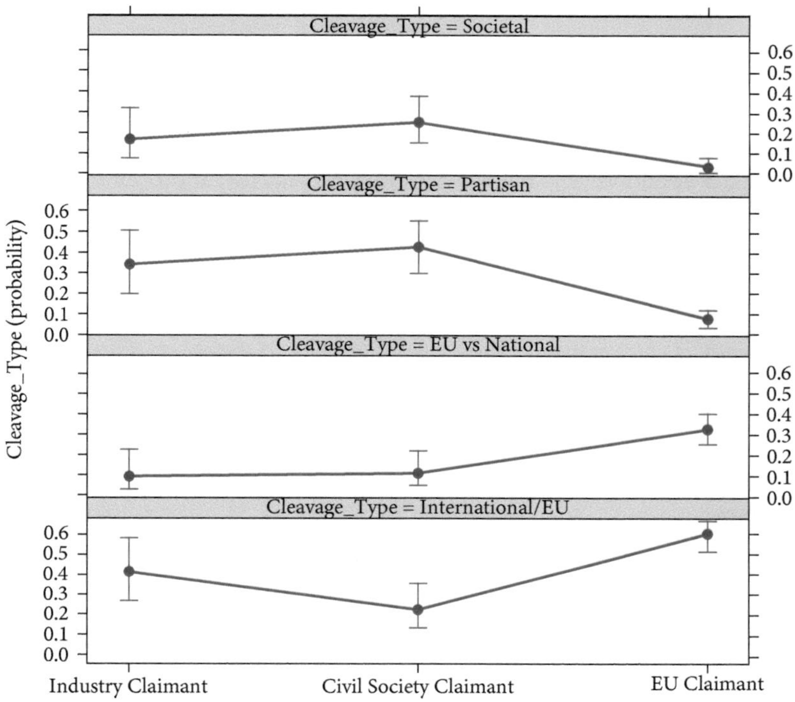

Figure 13.5 Model 5—cleavage type

of cleavages. Both industry and civil society claimants display some level of misalignment with EU claimants. EU claimants tend to see trade policy through the lens of either an international struggle (with an almost 60 per cent probability) or, alternatively, in the context of EU vs EU Member States conflict. Industry claimants, however, even though they display a certain alignment with EU actors at the level of an *international* cleavage, they also display a 33 per cent chance of a *partisan* cleavage and a 16 per cent chance for a societal conflict surrounding EU trade claims, both of which score close to 0 for EU claimants. Claims on trade by civil society actors are the most likely to frame the issue as a *partisan* one (0.421), followed by a 24 per cent chance of societal conflict and finally 22 per cent probability for an *international* cleavage. In this instance too, civil society claimants are overall the least aligned with EU claimants. Instead, they overlap with industry claimants in most regards, with the *international* cleavage being less relevant for civil society claimants. Both industry and civil society tend to understand the conflict surrounding trade policy as primarily a partisan issue, a framing that a non-majoritarian and non-elected body like the EU Commission unsurprisingly shies away from, but one that could significantly boost perceptions of bottom-up sociological legitimacy. This final analysis supports Expectation I, denoting a generalized disconnect among all 'bottom-up' claimants. Expectation II is only marginally reflected in the data, as civil society claimants are more often than not aligned with industry claimants.

The analysis presented in these five multinomial logit models shows how the proposed operationalization of sociological legitimacy from a discursive perspective and its assessment through the methodological tools provided by RCA can help bring into focus dimensions of the EU's legitimacy which arguably deserve greater attention. The models constitute an effective approach to exploring Expectations (I) and (II), both of which found some support in the analysis. Expectation (I), highlighting an overarching misalignment with EU claimants when issue politicization goes unaddressed by the EU, is supported by the analysis, even though the data also suggests that industry claimants remain more likely to align with EU claimants at times (e.g. in Model 4, integration vs demarcation). Regarding Expectation (II), on the 'greater extent' to which civil society claimants were expected to delegitimize EU actors, while there is some evidence to support this claim, it is also clear that civil society claimants are often aligned to industry claimants. Taken together, the findings presented here offer a fine-grained picture of the different pressures and 'beliefs' which shape discursive sociological legitimacy in European public spheres.

13.6 Conclusions

By asking how and to what extent societal actors are misaligned with EU actors in their normative evaluations or demands in relation to TTIP and CETA, this contribution has attempted to highlight how paying greater attention to sociological legitimacy seems to be essential in building (policy) legitimacy. Concretely, this chapter advocates the centrality of beliefs and perceptions in building legitimacy and democracy in the EU. In particular, the absence of contestation is an unsatisfactory measure of legitimacy; the conception of sociological legitimacy put forward in this contribution demands that issues become politicized for true legitimacy to emerge. Under conditions of unaddressed politicization, generalized bottom-up misalignment is more likely to prevail: this can either lead to deepening disconnects, or provide the opportunity for the EU to engage and re-connect more effectively with its citizenry.

Crucially, sociological legitimacy likely hinges on politicized debates that can allow an assessment of the nature and extent of the misalignment. As a result, EU actors should seek to encourage rather than avoid contestation and politicization on EU policies; at the same time, EU actors need to also be prepared to address overwhelming misalignments when they emerge, with a view to building sociological legitimacy instead of over-relying on output legitimacy. If most societal, and particularly civil society actors, are misaligned vis-à-vis the EU, this may be indication of a disconnect that EU actors need to address to avoid its centrifugal potential. This is the scenario that emerges when examining TTIP and CETA debates as instances of unaddressed bottom-up issue politicization. In light of this, future research should reflect on how sociological legitimacy may be the result of debates among differing 'beliefs within a given constituency' on whether 'a political institution's exercise of authority is appropriate', to paraphrase Tallberg and Zürn's (2019: 585) definition.

There are without doubt many reasons why the EU struggles to engage with sociological legitimacy, and therefore politicization. One leading factor is the way in which the EU finds itself in a double bind. Concretely, there is a peculiarity of policy debates in the EU, which is that they can easily shift from debates on specific issues to far reaching discussions on the need for and existence of the European Union. While the exceptional nature of these debates might explain the dodging behaviour of the EU, not engaging with or attempting to contain heightened politicization might further entrench the viewpoints of those who contest the EU. Systematic misalignments as they occur in discourse, particularly when matters are salient and polarizing (i.e. politicized), do have a centrifugal potential if left unaddressed. The toolkit provided by representative claims analysis allowed the operationalization of misalignments in the 'beliefs on the appropriateness of the exercise of authority' as (mis-)alignment among claims. Emphasizing the *relational* nature of sociological legitimacy, claims by societal actors were compared to those of EU claimants, with a focus on media debates on EU trade. Such (mis-)alignment was established within components of representative claims which identify perceptions of the main constituencies involved in the issue, the nature of the issue in terms of appropriate levels of governance, overall rejection, or support for EU integration.

In the research presented in this contribution, the distinct perspective on representation and EU trade policy of civil society claimants emerged quite clearly. These claimants were more likely to refer to societal actors (both citizens and industry) when compared to EU claimants, and although they may at times consider an EU-wide constituency, their preferred constituency tended to be a national one. Civil society claimants often discussed this issue in terms of its global implications. Finally, they were shown to be the most critical of EU FTAs (and EU integration) and tended to see this issue specifically as a partisan one. In order to explore Expectation (I), these views were compared to those of EU claimants, and a misalignment was found in all of these key areas: EU claimants privileged the EU (polity) or industry representatives as their constituency; they discussed trade only from an EU or global perspective; and portrayed conflict around trade policy as EU intergovernmental or EU vs Member States. In most cases the pattern of misalignment was similar to that of industry, however, in areas like EU issue scope, integration, and demarcation, the alignment between industry and the EU was apparent.

The measuring of concrete misalignments in discourse as an assessment of policy legitimacy, is capable of providing a framework that can guide actionable changes in how policymaking processes are communicated and respond to expectations on both policy issues and democratic representation. For example, a distinct factor which deepens current disconnects is the lack of a partisan framing of EU FTAs at an EU level, a feature which would clash with the prominent role of the non-partisan EU Commission; encouraging a more 'agonistic'—indeed, politicized—approach to presenting policy alternatives in a European context is likely to be conducive to providing the necessary premise for further closing the gap between the EU and its citizenry. Crucially, a more agonistic engagement with politicization can only be effective if it is matched with the EU's willingness to address and respond to the views that emerge. Politicization that goes unaddressed is intimately related to a lack of sociological legitimacy. Moreover, the analysis also lent some plausibility to Expectation (II), which showed how this methodological outlook is capable of also distinguishing among different societal claimants; it highlighted how instances of alignment with industry claimants could be an indication of an EU that in areas such as trade tends to cater more to business interests than civil society. These are the kinds of patterns and nuances that could be examined in greater depth in further research, exploring the consistency of a possible link between the nature of the EU's response to bottom-up issue politicization and the prevalence of (mis-)alignment among societal actors.

References

Andrione-Moylan, A., de Wilde, P., and Raube, K. (2023). Varieties of EU Trade Politicisation in EU Public Debates. *Global Policy*, 14(S3): 19–29.

Andrione-Moylan, A., de Wilde, P., and Raube, K. (2024). (De-)politicization Discourse Strategies: The Case of Trade. *Journal of Common Market Studies*, 62(1): 21–37.
Cabras, L. (2024). Explaining the Politicization of EU Trade Agreement Negotiations Over the Past 30 Years. *Italian Political Science Review/Rivista Italiana di Scienza Politica*, 54(2): 138–153.
Castles, F. G. and Obinger, H. (2008). Worlds, Families, Regimes: Country Clusters in European and OECD Area Public Policy. *West European Politics*, 31(1–2): 321–344.
De Bièvre, D. (2018). The Paradox of Weakness in European Trade Policy: Contestation and Resilience in CETA and TTIP Negotiations. *The International Spectator*, 53(3): 70–85.
De Bièvre, D., Garcia-Duran, P., Eliasson, L. J., and Costa, O. (2020). Editorial: Politicization of EU Trade Policy Across Time and Space. *Politics and Governance*, 8(1): 239–242.
De Bièvre, D. and Poletti, A. (2020). Towards Explaining Varying Degrees of Politicization of EU Trade Agreement Negotiations. *Politics and Governance*, 8(1): 243–253.
Dellmuth, L. M. and Tallberg, J. (2015). The Social Legitimacy of International Organisations: Interest Representation, Institutional Performance, and Confidence Extrapolation in the United Nations. *Review of International Studies*, 41(3): 451–475.
De Ville, F. and Orbie, J. (2014). The European Commission's Neoliberal Trade Discourse since the Crisis: Legitimizing Continuity through Subtle Discursive Change. *The British Journal of Politics and International Relations*, 16(1): 149–167.
De Wilde, P. (2013). Representative Claims Analysis: Theory Meets Method. *Journal of European Public Policy*, 20(2): 278–294.
De Wilde, P. and Gora, A. (2021). On the Relation Between Democracy, Legitimacy, Politicization and Citizens' Perceptions in EU Fiscal and Macroeconomic Policy. RECONNECT Working Paper.
De Wilde, P., Leupold, A., and Schmidtke, H. (2016). Introduction: the Differentiated Politicisation of European Governance. *West European Politics*, 39(1): 3–22.
Dominguez, R. (2017). TTIP: Contentious Market Regulation. *Journal of European Integration*, 39(7): 859–874.
Dür, A., Hamilton, S. M., and De Bièvre, D. (2024). Reacting to the Politicization of Trade Policy. *Journal of European Public Policy*, 31(1): 1–19.
European Commission (2016). *Standard Eurobarometer 85 Autumn 2016, Eurobarometer*. https://europa.eu/eurobarometer/surveys/detail/2130. Accessed 4 January 2025.
Gheyle, N. (2019). Conceptualizing the Parliamentarization and Politicization of European Policies. *Politics and Governance*, 7(3): 227–236.
Gheyle, N. and Rone, J. (2023). 'The Politicisation Game': Strategic Interactions in the Contention Over TTIP in Germany, *German Politics*, 32(3): 517–537.
Gora, A. and De Wilde, P. (2019). 'Handbook for Representative Claims Analysis', RECONNECT Deliverable 2.2. https://reconnect-europe.eu/wp-content/uploads/2019/09/D2.2-update-July-2019.pdf.
Gora, A. and De Wilde, P. (2022). RECONNECT Representative Claims Analysis [database]. Sikt—Norwegian Agency for Shared Services in Education and Research. https://doi.org/10.18712/NSD-NSD3047-V3.
Grande, E. and Hutter, S. (2016). Beyond Authority Transfer: Explaining the Politicisation of Europe. *West European Politics*, 39(1): 23–43.
Hooghe, L. and Marks, G. (2009). A Postfunctionalist Theory of European Integration: From Permissive Consensus to Constraining Dissensus. *British Journal of Political Science*, 39(1): 1–23.
Hurd, I. (2019). Legitimacy and Contestation in Global Governance: Revisiting the Folk Theory of International Institutions. *The Review of International Organizations*, 14(4): 717–729.
Koopmans, R. and Statham, P. (2006). Political Claims Analysis: Integrating Protest Event and Political Discourse Approaches. *Mobilization: An International Quarterly*, 4(2): 203–221.
Kriesi, H. (2014). The Populist Challenge. *West European Politics*, 37(2): 361–378.
Krzywinski, M. and Altman, N. (2013). Error Bars. *Nature Methods*, 10(10): 921–922.
Marx, A. and Van der Loo, G. (2021). Transparency in EU Trade Policy: A Comprehensive Assessment of Current Achievements. *Politics and Governance*, 9(1): 261–271.

Meunier, S. and Czesana, R. (2019). From Back Rooms to the Street? A Research Agenda for Explaining Variation in the Public Salience of Trade Policy-making in Europe. *Journal of European Public Policy*, 26(12): 1847–1865.
Mouffe, C. (2013). *Agonistics: Thinking the World Politically*. London/New York, Verso Books.
Oleart, A. (2021). *Framing TTIP in the European Public Spheres: Towards an Empowering Dissensus for EU Integration*. Cham, Springer International Publishing.
Petersmann, E.-U. (2017). Democratic Legitimacy of the CETA and TTIP Agreements?. In Rensmann, T. (ed.). *Mega-Regional Trade Agreements*. Cham, Springer International Publishing: 37–59.
Rauh, C. (2019). EU Politicization and Policy Initiatives of the European Commission: the Case of Consumer Policy. *Journal of European Public Policy*, 26(3): 344–365.
Rone, J. (2018). Contested International Agreements, Contested National Politics: How the Radical Left and the Radical Right Opposed TTIP in Four European Countries. *London Review of International Law*, 6(2): 233–253.
Saward, M. (2006). The Representative Claim. *Contemporary Political Theory*, 5(3): 297–318.
Saward, M. (2010). 'Representation, Legitimacy, and Democracy'. In Saward, M. (ed.). *The Representative Claim*. Oxford, Oxford University Press: 138–168.
Schmidt, V. A. (2013). Democracy and Legitimacy in the European Union Revisited: Input, Output and 'Throughput'. *Political Studies*, 61(1): 2–22.
Tallberg, J. and Zürn, M. (2019). The Legitimacy and Legitimation of International Organizations: Introduction and Framework. *The Review of International Organizations*, 14(4): 581–606.
Young, A. R. (2019). Two Wrongs Make a Right? The Politicization of Trade Policy and European Trade Strategy. *Journal of European Public Policy*, 26(12): 1883–1899.
Zürn, M. (2016). Opening up Europe: Next Steps in Politicisation Research. *West European Politics*, 39(1): 164–182.
Zürn, M. (2018). *A Theory of Global Governance: Authority, Legitimacy, and Contestation*. Oxford, Oxford University Press.

14
The Institutional Architecture Behind the EU Macroeconomic and Fiscal Governance and its Impact on Accountability and Democratic Legitimacy

Carlos Closa, Felipe González De León, and Gisela Hernández

14.1 Introduction

The establishment of an Economic and Monetary Union (EMU) drew significant scholarly interest from the very beginning. The euro was seen as a significant and 'irreversible' political project (Barroso 2011; Draghi 2012), and the initial focus was on understanding the implications of delegating monetary policy to the EU level (Verdun 1998; Elgie 2002; Hodson and Maher 2002). On the other side, the incipient fiscal and macroeconomic governance was viewed as a complementary element of EMU, relying on loose voluntary coordination enforced through peer pressure and consensus-building mechanisms (Hodson 2004). However, early warnings were made about the potential risks of such asymmetrical integration (Eichengreen and Wyplosz 1998; Jacquet and Pisani-Ferry 2001). Since those early days, both processes have undergone several reforms and attempts to achieve further integration. Key milestones include the Stability and Growth Pact (SGP), the Great Financial Crisis (GFC), Covid-19, NextGenerationEU (NGEU) package, and the recent new economic governance framework. These reforms culminated in a complex institutional system which has crucially impacted democratic representativeness (Schmidt 2020; van Rijsgerben and Rogge 2022; Delhomme and Hervey 2023; Christensen and Nedergaard 2024). This chapter aims to delve into this evolution by answering the following research question: what are the accountability and democratic legitimacy implications of the reforms and integration efforts in EMU and macroeconomic and fiscal governance?

Carlos Closa, Felipe González De León, and Gisela Hernández, *The Institutional Architecture Behind the EU Macroeconomic and Fiscal Governance and its Impact on Accountability and Democratic Legitimacy* In: *The Promise of EU Democracy*. Edited by: Jan Wouters, Julie Smith, Kolja Raube, and Ben Crum, Oxford University Press. DOI: 10.1093/9780191996191.003.0017

In order to do so, the first section presents an overall view of the dense institutional architecture that currently governs the macroeconomic and fiscal policy in the EU, offering useful background to those who want to understand it better. Based on this description, we then proceed to identify and discuss the main features of the institutional system and the trends derived from the changes observed: (i) a rebalance of power towards the European level, (ii) the increasing blending of the national and the European level, (iii) a reinforcement of intergovernmentalism, (iv) the existence of weak legislatures, (v) the increasing complexity and fragmentation of the governance framework, and (vi) a growing agencification and technocratization. Finally, we assess the impact of the new institutional system on the channels of input, output, and throughput legitimacy (Scharpf 1999; Schmidt 2020). The conclusion reflects on future trends that may counterbalance the accountability and legitimacy problems of the current governance framework.

14.2 Institutional framework

Macroeconomic and fiscal governance depends on an intricate institutional framework. Figure 14.1 summarizes the institutional architecture derived from the reforms carried out after the GFC (i.e. following the global economic downturn between 2007 and 2009). For the sake of clarity and parsimony, it only includes those institutions that have direct responsibility over one of the two main policy areas, excluding complementary areas such as labour policy, competition, or internal markets (e.g. Eurofound, an agency which focuses on social, employment, and work-related policies). Secondly, the level of detail is limited, excluding the sub-structures of the Council's preparatory bodies and the services/units under the Commission's directorates. Thirdly, we exclude bodies with a transversal competence, i.e. those which may shape policy outcomes, but whose competences transcend economic governance or are designed to act as control mechanisms, such as the Court of Justice of the European Union (CJEU). Finally, given our focus on the fiscal side, we do not examine monetary policy governance, despite the interrelation between these policies. Therefore, the European Central Bank (ECB) is only analysed in respect to its role in the governance of the fiscal policy framework.

As represented in Figure 14.1, there is a stark contrast between the macroeconomic and fiscal side and the financial stability one. At the European level, the former is dominated by the traditional triad: Council of Ministers (hereafter Council), European Commission and European Parliament (EP), plus the European Council (EUCO). Meanwhile, at the national level, national governments and parliaments remain the key decision-makers, although heavily conditioned by what is decided at the European level. Conversely, in the case of financial stability we can see a higher degree of delegation towards technocratic agencies, both at the European and national levels (although the Council, Commission, and

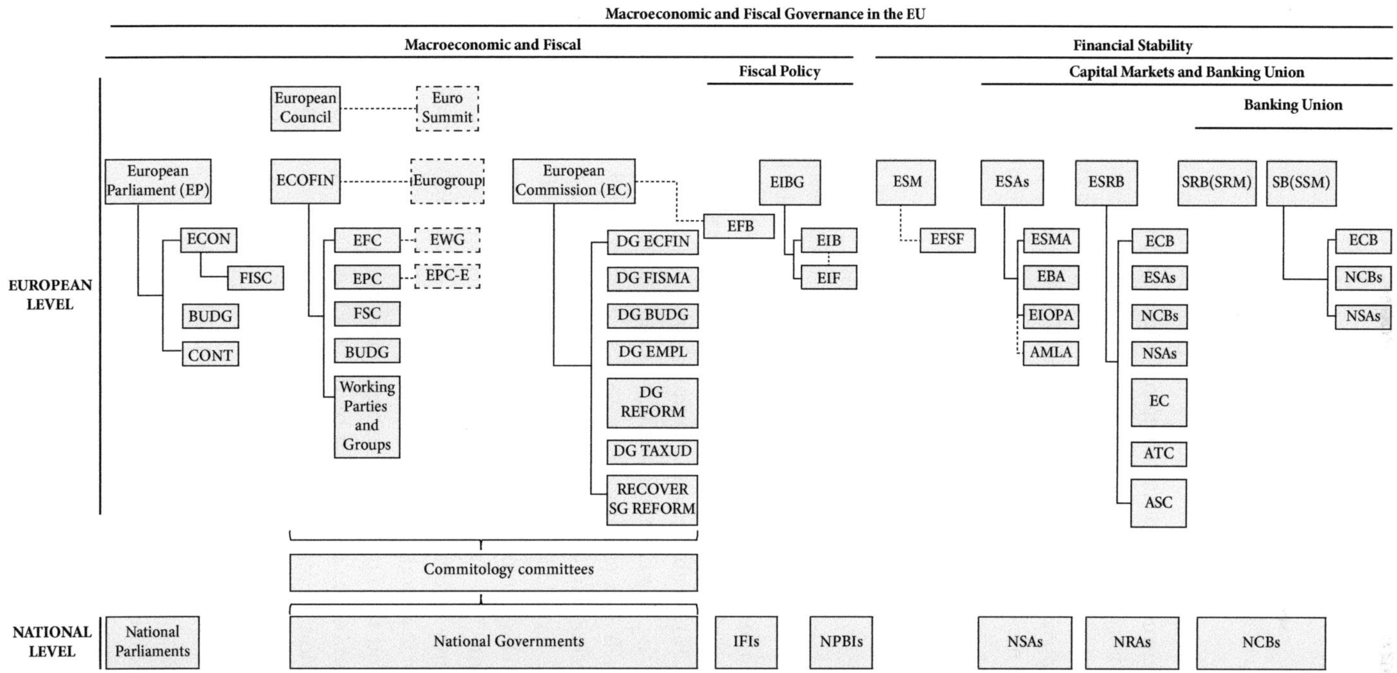

Figure 14.1 The institutional architecture behind macroeconomic and fiscal governance in the EU

Source: Own elaboration

EP set the general direction, oversee the agencies, and maintain their legislative powers).

14.2.1 Macroeconomic and fiscal policy

The institutional architecture of the EU macroeconomic and fiscal policy involves both intergovernmental and supranational bodies, with the former dominating in terms of functions and power. Additionally, some bodies that defy categorization also participate in EMU governance. Several mechanisms (i.e. financial stability policies) complete the picture. To examine these institutional developments, we briefly look at the composition, functions, powers, and evolution of each of these institutions/bodies/policies.

14.2.1.1 Intergovernmental bodies

Both the EUCO and the Council have significant roles in macroeconomic and fiscal governance. In recent years, EUCO has gained prominence in EU governance; its main role is to give a strategic direction and set general guidelines for EU policies, including on the macroeconomic and fiscal fronts. During the financial crisis, the need for rapid decision-making and the political significance of those decisions required European leaders to get involved and reach deals on several areas (Puetter 2012; Fabbrini and Puetter 2016).

In parallel, the Euro Summit has also consolidated as an actor (Fabbrini and Puetter 2016). It was established in 2008 as an alternative composition of the EUCO, gathering the eurozone leaders to deal with the emergency derived from the GFC. Its creation was in itself a clear indication of the lack of an appropriate institutional architecture for the macroeconomic and fiscal governance of the eurozone. The Euro Summit was established as an informal body, which was subsequently institutionalized via the Treaty on Stability, Coordination, and Governance in the Economic and Monetary Union (TSCG).

ECOFIN and the Eurogroup are below the European Council and the Euro Summit. These bodies continue to be the main decision-makers and the main fora of discussion for macroeconomic and fiscal affairs (Puetter 2012; 2016). The Council/ECOFIN acts as legislator, negotiates the allocation of funds, approves the appointment of key positions in other bodies, and is solely responsible for the approval of certain regulations where the EP does not participate such as the European Financial Stabilization Mechanism (EFSM). The Eurogroup performs all these tasks, albeit informally, for eurozone-related affairs.

At a lower level we find the different preparatory bodies of the Council with direct competences. The list includes four key committees (Economic and Financial Committee (EFC), Economic Policy Committee (EPC), Financial Services Committee (FSC) and Budget Committee (BUDG)), and multiple

Working Parties and Working Groups. Additionally, one could add those preparatory bodies from other policy areas that contribute to the work of ECOFIN on an ad-hoc basis and other bodies that may submit reports or appear in front of these committees such as the European Court of Auditors (ECA) or Independent Fiscal Institutions (IFIs; i.e. national bodies that provide independent analysis and monitoring of fiscal policy).

14.2.1.2 Supranational bodies

Although the Commission was initially weaker on the EMU than in other areas, its considerable influence on matters related to macroeconomic policy (i.e. the internal market, trade and competition) gave this institution a certain leverage. During the GFC, the Commission's role was reinforced overall (Bauer and Becker 2014), shaping the policy response and the governance design, becoming part of the so-called Troika, acquiring powers over the control of Member State governments' compliance with the fiscal rules, and expanding its supervision and sanction capacity via the various regulations and the directive included in the Six-Pack and the Two-Pack. More recently, it was also reinforced due to the Covid-19 crisis, acquiring a prominent role in the Recovery and Resilience Facility (RRF) (Closa et al. 2021). The Commission counts numerous departments with competence over macroeconomic, fiscal, and financial affairs, the most significant being the following Directorates-General: Economic and Financial Affairs (ECFIN), Financial Stability, Financial Services and Capital Markets Union (FISMA), Budget (BUDG), Employment, Social Affairs and Inclusion (EMPL), Structural Reform Support (REFORM), Taxation and Customs Union (TAXUD), and the Reform and Investment Task Force (SG REFORM, formerly known as RECOVER).[1] Below each of them sit several units and services.

As for the EP, its limited power on economic and fiscal affairs is commonly identified as a pending issue (Fasone 2014; Juncker et al. 2015; Crum 2018). Historically, the area in which it was most influential was the Multiannual Financial Framework (MFF). During the governance reforms carried out after the GFC, the EP was sidelined and had little impact on most of them (Puetter 2012; Rittberger 2014; Fabbrini 2013; Bressanelli and Chelotti 2016; Schoeller and Héritier 2019). However, the EP did manage to obtain some concessions regarding appointments, institutional matters and accountability procedures in compensation for the little input given in the policy response. More recently, during the Covid-19 crisis, the EP actively sought to exert some influence in the response to the crisis. Nevertheless, the outcome led to only a limited increase in its powers (Closa et al.

[1] The Reform and Investment Task Force or SG REFORM (not to be mistaken with DG REFORM) sits within the Secretariat General, which reports directly to the President of the Commission. This unit has a very influential portfolio connected with the RRF and is headed by an official with the rank of DG. It became operational in February 2025 and succeeded the Recovery and Resilience Task Force (RECOVER).

2021). Currently, there are three EP committees with direct competences over macroeconomic and fiscal affairs (including financial stability): Economic and Monetary Affairs (ECON), Budgets (BUDG), and Budgetary Control (CONT). Additionally, a sub-committee on tax matters (FISC) was set up in 2020.

14.2.1.3 Additional bodies

Some additional bodies play a significant role in fiscal policy. First, it is worth mentioning the European Fiscal Board (EFB), established in 2015 to assist the Commission in the evaluation of the implementation of the fiscal rules and to co-operate with national IFIs. Upon request from the Commission, the EFB can also provide ad hoc advice on fiscal policy matters. Second, the institutional architecture is completed with the European Investment Bank Group (EIBG). It supports the EU's policy priorities and administers a large pool of resources, but without having a high-profile role or acting as a key player in contentious issues, despite its considerable size. The EIBG comprises two institutions: the European Investment Bank (EIB) and the European Investment Fund (EIF). Owned by the Member States and acting as the bank of the EU, the EIB can be described as the parent body. Meanwhile, the EIF is a body focused on venture capital and guarantees.

14.2.2 Financial stability policies

Several emergency mechanisms were created in the midst of the GFC and were further augmented shortly thereafter to prevent future crises. During the first stage the focus was on emergency measures. Later on, attention shifted towards the design of permanent instruments to complete the governance framework.

The Greek Loan Facility and the EFSM were the first instruments created to support countries experiencing financial difficulties under strict conditionality. Its successor, the European Financial Stability Facility (EFSF), was set up as a private facility and separated from the EU legal framework. Strict conditionality was imposed to those requesting support from the EFSF, participating in the bailouts of Ireland, Portugal, and Greece. The EFSF is relatively small in terms of size and still exists to ensure the repayment of the loans made, but it no longer offers financial support. Instead, the European Stability Mechanism (ESM), introduced in 2012, largely subsumed the EFSF as an institution designed to provide support for countries experiencing financial distress. Like its predecessor, the ESM was set up in the margins of the EU legal framework; it was created via an intergovernmental treaty and operates as an intergovernmental organization subject to public international law. Nevertheless, steps to bring it under EU law have been taken, including the amendment of Article 136 of the TFEU and the acknowledgment that the ESM should ultimately be fully incorporated into the EU legal framework (Juncker et al. 2015). In 2021, an agreement to reform the ESM Treaty was reached. The reform linked the ESM with the Banking Union (BU), providing the legal basis for the

ESM to act as the backstop of the Single Resolution Fund (SRF), which was established for the resolution of failing banks within the BU and financed by contributions of the banks.

In parallel, the EU decided to move forward with the Capital Markets Union (CMU) and the BU. The lack of integration in these areas was perceived as one of the failures that facilitated the GFC (Pisani-Ferry et al. 2012; Beck 2012; Howarth and Quaglia 2013). Consequently, the new European System of Financial Supervision (ESFS) was established in 2011. This system relies on two arms: microprudential supervision is carried out by the European Supervisory Authorities (ESAs) at the European level and their national counterparts at the state level, while macroprudential supervision is entrusted to the European Systemic Risk Board (ESRB). Both the CMU and the BU are still under construction with new reforms under discussion.

The three ESAs are: the European Securities and Markets Authority (ESMA), the European Banking Authority (EBA) and the European Insurance and Occupational Pensions Authority (EIOPA). The ESAs are independent agencies which enjoy full autonomy in their respective functions and perform a variety of tasks. However, they are somewhat dependent on national authorities given the way they are structured (representatives of the National Supervisory Authorities (NSAs) are on their Board of Supervisors), the complementarity of their mandates, and their relatively small resources. These authorities are tasked with designing common regulatory and supervisory standards, contributing to the application of legally binding acts, monitoring markets, undertaking analysis and facilitating cooperation. Additionally, ESAs advise the Commission on legislation and have direct supervisory competences over some entities.

In 2021, the Commission proposed the establishment of a new agency, the Anti-Money Laundering Authority (AMLA), which obtained agreement in the Council and a mandate from the EP to enter trilogues in 2023. In February 2024, the Council and the EP reached an agreement for AMLA to start operations in mid-2025. Legally established since 2024, the agency is gradually consolidating: at the time of writing it had opened its office, appointed its authorities, and was on track to complete a setup plan that extends until 1 January 2028 to fulfil its mandate. Once fully operational, AMLA will function independently and will monitor developments and threats on anti-money laundering and countering the financing of terrorism, collect information via direct and indirect supervision, ensure compliance with sanctions, promote regulatory convergence and coordinate with national authorities.

The diagram also includes the ESRB, established in 2010 to exercise the macroprudential oversight of the financial system, preventing and mitigating systemic risks to financial stability. It is only empowered to centralize information, request information to NSAs and issue warnings and recommendations.

Finally, the institutional architecture is completed with the two bodies set up to lead the Banking Union: the Single Resolution Board (SRB) and the Supervisory

Board (SB). The former is entrusted with the governance of the Single Resolution Mechanism (along with the National Resolution Authorities), while the latter (along with the NSAs) is in charge of the Single Supervisory Mechanism (SSM). The SRB is an autonomous body tasked with drawing up and adopting the resolution plans for cross-border groups, significant entities, and those institutions over which the ECB exercises direct supervision. Conversely, the SB is an internal body of the ECB which carries out the preparatory work regarding supervisory tasks and prepares draft decisions.

14.3 Institutional dynamics and trends behind the changes in EMU governance

Having completed our overview of the macroeconomic and fiscal institutional architecture, we now proceed to analyse and discuss the main dynamics and trends derived from the current institutional framework.

14.3.1 A rebalancing of power towards the European level

Macroeconomic and fiscal competences were originally left in the hands of Member States. The decisions were mostly confined to the national level, while the European level was perceived as a technical arena (Majone 1993). However, although the area still largely remains intergovernmental, in recent years, there has been an increasing politicization of the European agenda (De Wilde and Zürn 2012; De Wilde et al. 2016; Börzel and Risse 2018). The Europeanization of fiscal policy is particularly noticeable in the case of EMU and is partly driven by greater economic integration.

Perhaps the most compelling example of this phenomenon is the shift observed in fiscal policy, an area in which Member States have traditionally been more reluctant to accept integration. Although fiscal policy remains a prerogative of national authorities, European institutions now play a major role in the national budgetary cycles. Thus, they are very much involved in the design, assessment, and oversight of national budgets thanks to the constraints imposed by the SGP, the establishment of the European Semester as the coordination framework at EU level, and the new National Medium-Term Fiscal-Structural Plans. Consequently, budgets are no longer negotiated at the national level alone, but also at the European one.

The rebalance of power towards the European level could potentially result in a loss of influence of national actors. However, national institutions have channels to participate at the EU level. Thus, this phenomenon must be analysed in conjunction with other trends such as the rise of intergovernmentalism or the reinforcement of agencies.

14.3.2 The increasing blending of the national and the European levels

In line with the blurred distinction between high and low politics identified by Bickerton et al. (2015), the lines between the European and national arenas have become more blurred. This phenomenon is visible in at least two dimensions: the institutional design, as many European institutions are composed by national representatives or rely on their national counterparts for their activities; and the overlap of their responsibilities. Thus, deeper and cross-cutting integration means that it is not easy to disentangle one policy area from the other. This leads to decisions that must be coordinated or complemented by institutions from different levels and policy spheres.

Several factors contribute to this trend. First, there are not that many policy areas confined to just one of the levels anymore. Although the GFC facilitated this integration, the spill-over and interconnection effects between policy areas was always present. In the case of EMU, delegation of monetary policy without a strong coordination on the fiscal side proved itself unviable and ended up requiring reforms (Alloza et al. 2021). Similarly, the construction of a fully functional internal market may lead to some harmonization in taxation and the development of integrated capital markets.

The participation of national representatives in different institutions also contributes to this blending. This interaction happens at different stages of the policy cycle (e.g. formulation, negotiation, adoption, implementation, or evaluation) and is facilitated by the existence of several channels of communication between the different actors (committees, working groups, bilateral contacts, etc.).

Informal dynamics play a key role too. Even when one institution may not have direct or formal competences in one area, it can take advantage of the powers granted in others. This strategy is frequently used by the EP (Closa et al. 2021). Similarly, informal procedures such as the search for consensus in decisions where it is not required also contribute to this trend; examples can be found in the ECB (Moschella et al. 2020) and in the EFC (Grosche and Puetter 2008). When such practices are in place, national institutions need to negotiate more, making all actors jointly responsible and aligning the decisions across both levels.

14.3.3 A reinforcement of intergovernmentalism

The reinforcement of intergovernmentalism is visible in several dimensions. First and foremost, since the GFC we have seen an expansion in the role of the EUCO, which has gone through a process of institutionalization. This included an increase in the frequency of its meetings and the creation of a permanent President, who competes to a certain extent with the President of the Commission. The role of this institution has evolved remarkably, acquiring a much more active and influential role in macroeconomic and fiscal governance. On the one hand, EUCO has partially invaded the role of the Commission as the agenda-setter on key policy packages. On the other hand, EUCO is also more involved in the legislation process now (Bressanelli and Chelotti 2016), typically providing instructions on key pieces of legislation through extensive and specific conclusions, limiting the scope of action of the Commission or the EP.

In parallel, the Council has also increased its own influence, albeit subordinated to EUCO. This has largely been driven by the need for higher coordination in the economic areas. As a result, ECOFIN and the Eurogroup have consolidated as the main fora for all major economic decisions (Puetter 2012; 2016).

A third element behind the reinforcement of intergovernmentalism is the growing importance of 'informal fora', which shows the relevance of deliberative and consensual intergovernmental traits (Puetter 2012). Besides the Eurogroup, which is now a consolidated and 'institutionalized' formation of the Council, leaders frequently gather in informal meetings of the ECOFIN, the Euro Summit or other configurations to discuss key or contentious issues.

Finally, it is noteworthy that the reinforcement of intergovernmentalism is present not only at the EU level, but also at the national level. Thus, the increasing role of EUCO and the Council gives governments additional leverage over national parliaments. For instance, they benefit from the information and resources of the Council, they can negotiate their preferred policy option without being subject to strong accountability mechanisms, they can narrow the scope of policy options available or justify the need for certain measures as part of a deal at the EU level, and they can exercise pressure through EUCO.

14.3.4 Existence of weak legislatures

The existence of weak legislatures has key implications for the policymaking process and is manifested in the loss of influence of the parliaments and the lack of strong scrutiny capacities, both at the national and the European level.

14.3.4.1 National parliaments

Given that parliaments were sidelined during the design of the new governance framework, it can hardly be argued that the changes incorporated their preferences or input. In terms of policy or legislative influence, parliaments remain largely in charge of most areas, especially in fiscal policy. Nevertheless, they are now subject to more constraints, both in terms of substance and procedures. These constraints may be stronger in times of crisis or for certain countries (e.g. those under a programme).

First, national parliaments face new challenges to their scrutiny capacities of European institutions and national governments, given their logistical, legal and resource constraints. Moreover, they often suffer from a lack of access to information: due to procedural and organizational arrangements, parliaments may only receive information or be able to participate in discussions at a late stage (e.g. during the European Semester). Hence, as Crum (2018) points out, the scrutiny capacities of parliaments have been severally strained, reinforcing governments and intergovernmental bodies. Second, they are exposed to the two-level game in which governments participate. As a result, unless parliaments set the mandate for negotiations beforehand, governments can claim they are constrained by the deals reached in these negotiations. Third, parliaments also face more difficulties in influencing certain policy outcomes (e.g. on fiscal regulation) as their scope of competences is limited by the need to coordinate and comply with the rules set at the EU level.

On a more positive note, parliaments have adapted their procedures to accommodate the new governance framework, e.g. budgetary cycles. Moreover, they have acquired new formal rights, additional scrutiny capacities, and access to some information. Additionally, the new governance framework created opportunities for greater involvement of sectoral committees and, ultimately, gives parliaments the opportunity to participate in areas from which they would otherwise be excluded (Fasone 2015; Jančić 2016).

Overall, the formal balance may be mixed. However, if we look at the actual use of the new instruments and mechanisms, there is a significant cross-country variation. Taking the European Semester as an example, the involvement of national parliaments is very dissimilar, with some countries participating at various stages and actively contributing to the formulation or monitoring of the plans, while others are hardly involved at all (Hallerberg et al. 2018; Hagelstam et al. 2018).

14.3.4.2 The European Parliament

The other element behind the weakening of legislatures is the limited role of the EP. The EP was also sidelined during the eurozone crisis (i.e. the debt crisis that occurred between 2010 and 2015 in several EU countries due to high levels of sovereign debt, which led to financial instability in the eurozone and forced bailouts for countries such as Greece, Ireland, and Portugal) (Puetter 2012; Fabbrini 2013; Bressanelli and Chelotti 2016). The ESM (Rittberger 2014) and the Macroeconomic Imbalance Procedure (Schoeller and Héritier 2019) are some of the examples in which the EP failed to increase its influence and shape the outcome. As a result, the EP did not exert much influence in the design of the existing governance framework.

Not surprisingly, the role of the EP remains fairly limited and indeed faces additional limitations in the case of EMU. For instance, Fasone (2014) accurately describes how the EP has dialogues but not decision-making powers over the new macroeconomic and fiscal framework. Moreover, the EP is involved too late in the Semester, it does not directly receive the national reform programmes, the stability and convergence programmes or the budgetary plans, and it cannot amend the strategic priorities or review the country-specific recommendations once they are adopted by the Council.

14.3.5 Increasing complexity and fragmentation of the governance framework

The enlargement of the institutional architecture, with the creation of several bodies and new layers, has resulted in a much more complex governance system (Fromage and Van den Brink 2018). First, the substructures are more difficult to control by the parliaments and by all those not included in its composition.

Additionally, the fragmentation of competences also adds complexity. Thus, each institution and level involved plays a different role and is responsible for one specific part of the process. Nevertheless, fragmentation should not necessarily be confused with compartmentalization, as there is permanent interaction across the different actors and policy areas.

Finally, this complexity is obviously reflected in the legal framework around macroeconomic and fiscal governance. EMU governance has been built through the Treaties (primary legislation) and through secondary legislation, such as regulations and directives, as well as through intergovernmental treaties and even aspects of private law. Moreover, it has been very dynamic, with many changes being implemented in a short period of time.

14.3.6 A growing agencification and technocratization

In the last decade we have witnessed a clear trend towards agencification in the EU bodies (Busuioc et al. 2012; Closa 2014; Everson et al. 2014; Egeberg and Trondal 2017), with the establishment and reinforcement of independent agencies in several policy areas. In parallel, the number of technical bodies operating below the political level have also grown. Together, these two elements reinforce the power of experts and high-ranking officials, who control information, and can significantly alter policy outcomes and render the policymaking process less accountable.

14.3.6.1 Agencification

The term agencification refers to the process of a growing delegation of tasks and responsibilities to independent non-majoritarian bodies. This process may involve the creation of new agencies or the reinforcement and expansion of the mandate of those already established. There is a wide consensus on the growing influence of these bodies (Busuioc et al. 2012; Closa 2014; Everson et al. 2014; Egeberg and Trondal 2017). Since its inception, agencies have played a key role in EU governance, especially in the field of EMU. Consequently, the ECB has always been the archetype of the European technocratic agency and the one that has acquired the largest influence (Elgie 2002; Heldt and Mueller 2021).

After the GFC there was an 'agency fever' which led to the establishment and the reinforcement of independent agencies (Busuioc et al. 2012; Egeberg and Trondal 2017; Tesche 2020; Pollak and Slomisnki 2021). To give an indication, in the period that goes from 2000 to 2015 the number of EU agencies tripled, from eleven to thirty-four (Egeberg and Trondal 2017). Such a trend is particularly relevant for the macroeconomic and fiscal spheres. Additionally, financial supervisory agencies have substantially increased their budgets over the years and, despite the budgetary decrease caused by the GFC, they received on average more resources than the rest (Migliorati 2020). The agencification trend is not limited to the European level, but is very much present at the national level too, with at least twenty-one Member States creating a new fiscal agency during the last decade (Closa et al. 2020a).

Several reasons explain the creation of independent agencies. First, agencies can enhance credibility of long-term policy commitments (Majone 2001). Second, delegation may be particularly advantageous when efficiency gains can be obtained (Alesina and Tabellini 2007). Thus, delegation is easier when there are no (major) distributional conflicts involved and when the area is perceived as highly technical or requires deep expertise (Blinder 1998; Alesina and Tabellini 2007). Third, contingencies and crises tend to provide windows of opportunities for delegation (Curtin 2007), e.g. the euro crisis (Pollak and Slomiski 2021). Fourth, the willingness to delegate to agencies is also connected with the desire of the Member States to avoid giving too much power to the Commission, mistrust towards the institutions or a preference for stronger integration without supranationalism (Kelemen 2002; Puetter 2012; Bickerton et al. 2015). Fifth, path dependency and institutional dynamics also help to explain the rise of agencies as many of them are built on previous networks or committees (Thatcher and Coen 2008; Levi-Faur 2011). Finally, agencies may have the ability to empower themselves by stealth (Majone 2005; Schmidt 2016), interpreting their mandates in an expansionary way or seeking to increase their resources and influence.

14.3.6.2 An expansion of bureaucratic bodies and networks

The technocratic element is further strengthened by the augmented role of some of the substructures of the Council. Thus, the growing number and influence of committees, working groups and task forces reinforces the power of non-majoritarian bodies.

The empowerment of these bodies can be explained by two elements already discussed. First, the rise of intergovernmentalism, which requires sub-structures to support the tasks assigned to the primary institutions to coordinate the decisions. Secondly, much like in the case of technocratic agencies, most policy areas require a highly specialized knowledge. In that context, delegating parts of the policymaking to national officials presents efficiency and credibility gains.

Ultimately, the advantages and disadvantages of these bodies are similar to those posed by agencies. Thus, the principal–agent logic derived from the delegation to technocrats remains largely the same. The particularity here is that agents come from national institutions and are supposed to represent the interests of the Member States.

14.4 The impact of the new macroeconomic and fiscal governance architecture on legitimacy

Institutional transformations in macroeconomic and fiscal governance and the tendencies derived from these developments have opened a serious debate in terms of legitimacy. In this section, we examine these concerns considering output, input and throughput legitimacy (Schmidt 2020).

14.4.1 Input legitimacy

Input legitimacy refers to 'the exercise of collective self-government so as to ensure government responsiveness to people's preferences' (Schmidt 2020). Debates on the input legitimacy of macroeconomic and fiscal governance thus very much refer to representation concerns. In this regard, the prominence of the Council, derived from the fact that macroeconomic and fiscal policies remain in the hands of national governments, poses a key challenge, since only national executives are seen to have enough legitimacy to introduce certain measures. This constrains the decision-making capacity of national parliaments, leading to a certain disempowerment of these institutions, which are in fact the arenas in which citizens' political preferences are articulated through democratic representation. This phenomenon is accentuated by the limited role of the EP in the new governance framework. Several EU reports (Van Rompuy et al. 2012; European Commission 2015; Juncker et al. 2015) identify the need for reforms of these weak legislatures in order to improve democratic legitimacy. However, EUCO and the Council did not return to their previous activity after the GFC and the eurozone crisis were over.

Additionally, individual governments are also subject to more restrictions now, especially in the case of eurozone governments and particularly those under assistance or surveillance programmes. Thus, following the establishment of the Six-Pack and the Two-Pack and the creation of several supervisory bodies, national authorities are bound by stricter coordination within the framework of the European semester and hence their ability to represent and implement the preferences expressed by citizens is more restricted.

Agencification also imposes a key constraint on democratic governance by limiting the scope of action of democratically elected authorities, and consequently, by limiting the influence of the public in decision-making processes. Agencies exercise their functions at the expense of limiting the scope of action of both parliaments and governments. This issue is particularly controversial when it comes to highly politicized matters, in which ideological differences are deep and influential.

Finally, responses to the GFC were highly creditor-country driven. The institutional trends resulting from this response hardly reflect the preferences of indebted countries, leading to an asymmetric representation of Member States' preferences in the resulting fiscal policy.

Citizens therefore face several constraints in channelling their political preferences into policy results; the reinforcement of the European level in macroeconomic and fiscal governance made them subjects of a legal order in which they are not always included in the scope of decision-making. Consequently, political disaffection, which is one of the drivers of the democratic deficit of the EU, is reinforced by the fact that the increasing role of both intergovernmental and technocratic bodies may limit the transmission of policy preferences.

14.4.2 Output legitimacy

Output legitimacy accounts for policy effectiveness and performance (Schmidt 2020). In terms of output legitimacy, the balance is mixed regarding the EU's financial policy transformations. Macroeconomic and fiscal governance as well as EMU have traditionally been based on output legitimacy and on a transfer of legitimacy derived from support for the European project as a whole.

Some transformations positively impact the EU's financial performance. This is the case of the agencification process; handing over certain parts of the policymaking process to technocrats can lead to more efficiency and trustworthiness. More specifically, for example, the 'no action letters', a specific tool to address shortcomings causing well-defined issues in financial markets introduced in 2020, gives the ESAs more involvement in the policymaking process and enhances them (Van Rijsgerben and Rogge 2022). Independent bodies indeed often highlight their output legitimacy in order to justify their decisions and compensate for their lack of democratic accountability (Christensen and Nedergaard 2024).

Similarly, the response to the Covid-19 crisis benefited from the growing financial coordination at EU level and the intergovernmental dynamic. The risks posed by the crisis to the EU's interconnected economies led to a robust and quick response through the RRF, very much negotiated at EUCO level (Schelkle 2021).

The EU's output legitimacy was enhanced as a result of a response focused on Union-wide economic recovery (Delhomme and Hervey 2022).

Conversely, the strict austerity measures resulting from the supranational response to the GFC challenged the EU's output legitimacy, particularly in the debtor countries, which suffered severe consequences for their welfare systems and high unemployment rates (Katsikas 2021). Hence, the outcomes of the decisions taken to mitigate the GFC asymmetrically impacted the different Member States, deepening the North–South cleavage.

The EU's output legitimacy in fiscal matters is often at odds with input legitimacy. An important example is the existing mismatch between political parties' manifestos and the principles that guide the EU's financial policy, particularly visible in the anti-austerity political positions, which are difficult to satisfy in the financial framework that emerged after the GFC (Closa et al. 2020b). Indeed, establishment parties (particularly left-wing ones) suffer from high electoral costs when it comes to enforcing imposed austerity (Alonso and Ruiz-Rufino 2020). Thus, as put by Schmidt (2020), 'good performance alone does not guarantee legitimacy if citizens do not feel that the regime is sufficiently responsive to their expected desires'.

14.4.3 Throughput legitimacy

The throughput dimension of legitimacy refers to the quality of the policymaking procedure as determined by both technical (efficiency) and normative (accountability, transparency, inclusiveness and openness) standards. Certain tendencies of the current macroeconomic and fiscal governance framework help to increase throughput legitimacy. This is particularly the case of the agencification process; agencies provide better information to the public and to the politicians, reduce information asymmetries between the government and other actors, force the government to use realistic economic forecasts, mitigate common pool problems, raise the reputational cost for the government, and identify and warn against unsustainable trends. Agencification enhances the efficiency and transparency of the decision-making process. In fact, since 2020, ESAs' throughput legitimacy has been reinforced thanks to increasingly transparent and participatory processes. These include, among others, the requirement to publish all stakeholders' questions and ESAs' answers on the Authorities' websites (Van Rijsgerben and Rogge 2022).

However, some features of the macroeconomic and fiscal institutional setting seriously hinder throughput legitimacy. One is the weakening of parliaments vis-à-vis national governments; not only do parliaments often encounter problems in accessing information, but the Council is in fact also considered as the least transparent institution in the EU's institutional framework. Scrutiny and accountability processes are thus weakened as a result of an intergovernmental style of decision-making in fiscal matters. Similarly, the growing complexity of the governance system arising from the agencification process renders very difficult the task of identifying those responsible for a policy decision and even more difficult the task of holding them accountable.

The EU's institutional action as a result of the GFC also posed a challenge in terms of throughput legitimacy. Some of the provisional measures and quick responses to the pressing constraints imposed by the crisis were developed outside the legal framework provided by the Treaties, thus endangering the legal certainty principle. This is notably the case of the Fiscal Compact, concluded through an international treaty. Similarly, the Troika mandate gave the International Monetary Fund (IMF), an institution outside the EU setting, a key say in the rescue programmes. This approach contrasts markedly with the response to the Covid-19 crisis, undertaken within the EU's legal constraints (Delhomme and Hervey 2022).

14.5 Conclusion: the future of macroeconomic and fiscal governance

In April 2024, the new economic governance framework of the EU entered into force. This came after the Commission presented a set of legislative proposals to implement the most comprehensive reform of the EU´s economic governance rules since the GFC. This new framework modifies the SGP via the derogation of Regulation (EC) 1466/97 and the amendment of Regulation (EC) 1467/97, and the Six-Pack, by amending Directive 2011/85/EU on requirements for budgetary frameworks. The main elements of the reform revolve around: (i) a stronger national ownership through National Medium-Term Fiscal-Structural Plans, (ii) simpler and more transparent rules for fiscal adjustment paths formulated as multi-year spending objectives, (iii) more gradual adjustment paths if accompanied by credible reforms and investments, (iv) enhanced enforcement and common safeguards, and (v) new EU-wide standards for independence, technical capacity, tasks and powers for national IFIs. Thus, despite the significant changes in certain areas, this new economic governance framework seems to maintain the spirit and key trends discussed in this chapter.

In parallel, other developments appear to continue the tendencies derived from the scheme emerged after the GFC. For example, the institutionalization of AMLA as a separate entity in February 2024 rather than reinforcing EBA's mandate in this area points towards a preference for further consolidation of the fragmentation process by delegating competences into the hands of technocratic experts, thereby exacerbating the input legitimacy concerns linked to this trend in exchange for an increased output legitimacy.

However, other recent trends can contribute to reinforcing both the input and output legitimacy of the EU fiscal scheme. First, regarding the former, the role of the EP has been reinforced in the aftermath of the Covid-19 crisis. The EP secured a seat at the RRF negotiating table, not guaranteed at the beginning, by successfully linking several instruments. It is true that the EP failed to maximize its governance powers over the instrument in exchange for policy concessions; however, it remains to be seen whether it succeeds in extending its limited scrutiny power over national plans in the following years (Closa et al. 2021). Second, the 2020 Conditionality Regulation strengthens the output legitimacy of fiscal policy by linking the disbursement of EU funds to compliance with the rule of law. Activated for the first time against the Hungarian government in 2022, measures to prevent disbursing funding to Hungary were still in place at the time of writing (although it is worth noting that the Commission decided to unlock part of the withheld Cohesion funds under rule of law criteria at the end of 2023). The true impact of this conditionality on promoting significant and lasting reforms thus remains to be seen. Nonetheless, the Regulation is a key step toward reinforcing the democratic protection of the Union's financial interests. In this sense, fiscal agencies could and should play a fundamental role in monitoring the proper use of EU funds by national governments.

Several reforms are still pending in order to improve the democratic accountability of fiscal governance. Particularly relevant would be the formalization of the Eurogroup as an EU institution and the codification of its tasks. Some steps have already been taken in this regard, such as its incorporation in the Treaties (TFEU, Art 137), the approval of Protocol 14, the election of a permanent president since 2005 and its inclusion in the TSCG. However, the current informality of the meetings and the lack of transparency still hinder the throughput legitimacy of the Eurogroup. Similarly, further involvement of national parliaments in macroeconomic governance, and concretely in the European semester, would enhance both the input and throughput legitimacy of the policymaking process (see also Crum 2018).

Finally, some pending questions emerge as regards future developments. The creation of a common budget for eurozone countries, as proposed by French President Macron in 2017, would work as a stabilization mechanism, enhancing resilience vis-à-vis economic shocks as well as facilitating the provision of common goods. Likewise, the RRF marked a critical juncture for fiscal integration (Schelkle 2021), but it remains uncertain whether it will become a permanent instrument. The reticence shown by certain governments (in particular the so-called 'Frugals', i.e. Austria, Denmark, the Netherlands, and Sweden) may prevent further fiscal integration in these regards; however, the Union might be forced to advance them if new critical situations emerged. The current macroeconomic and fiscal governance is very much the result of the EU's response to crises. Advancing reforms in order to improve this scheme and its legitimacy appears imperative to achieve a Union that is more resilient and robust vis-à-vis future shocks.

References

Alesina, A. and Tabellini, G. (2007). Bureaucrats or Politicians? Part I: a Single Policy Task. *American Economic Review*, 97(1): 169–179.

Alloza, M., Andrés, J., Burriel, P., Kataryniuk, I., Pérez, J. J., and Croissier, J. L. V. (2021). *The Reform of the European Union's Fiscal Governance Framework in a New Macroeconomic Environment.* Banco de España Ocassional Papers, No. 2121.

Alonso, S. and Ruiz-Rufino, R. (2020). The Costs of Responsibility for the Political Establishment of the Eurozone (1999–2015). *Party Politics*, 26(3): 317–333.

Barroso, J. M. (2011). *Speech by President Barroso at the EP debate on the conclusions of the December European Council.* European Parliament plenary session, Strasbourg, 13 December 2011. https://ec.europa.eu/commission/presscorner/detail/en/SPEECH_11_880. Accessed 31 July 2025.

Bauer, M. W. and Becker, S. (2014). The Unexpected Winner of the Crisis: The European Commission's Strengthened Role in Economic Governance. *Journal of European Integration*, 36(3): 213–229.

Beck, T. (ed.) (2012). *Banking Union for Europe: Risks and Challenges.* London, Centre for Economic Policy Research.

Bickerton, C. J., Hodson, D., and Puetter, U. (2015). The New Intergovernmentalism: European Integration in the Post-Maastricht Era. *Journal of Common Market Studies*, 53(4): 703–722.

Blinder, A. S. (1998). *Central Banking in Theory and Practice.* Cambridge MA/London, MIT Press.

Börzel, T. A. and Risse, T. (2018). From the Euro to the Schengen Crises: European Integration Theories, Politicization, and Identity Politics. *Journal of European Public Policy*, 25(1): 83–108.

Bressanelli, E. and Chelotti, N. (2016). The Shadow of the European Council. Understanding Legislation on Economic Governance. *Journal of European Integration*, 38(5): 511–525.

Busuioc, M., Groenleer, M., and Trondal, J. (eds). (2012). *The Agency Phenomenon in the European Union.* Manchester, Manchester University Press.

Christensen, S. E. and Nedergaard, P. (2024). All Along the Watch Tower: The European Central Bank and Legitimation Strategies in Times of Crisis. *Journal of Common Market Studies*, 62: 451–467.

Closa, C. (2014). Los cambios institucionales en la gobernanza macroeconómica y fiscal de la UE: hacia una mutación constitucional europea. *Revista de estudios políticos*, 165: 65–94.

Closa, C., Fernández-Albertos, J., and González De León, F. (2020b). Democratic Legitimacy in EU Fiscal and Macroeconomic Policy. An Overview from Parties' Manifestos. RECONNECT Deliverable 10.1.

Closa, C., González De León, F., and Losada, F. (2020a). Democracy vs Technocracy: National Parliaments and Fiscal Agencies in EMU Governance. RECONNECT Deliverable 10.2.

Closa, C., González De León, F., and Hernández González, G. (2021). Pragmatism and the Limits to the European Parliament's Strategies for Self-empowerment. *Politics and Governance*, 9(3): 163–174.

Crum, B. (2018). Parliamentary Accountability in Multilevel Governance: What Role for Parliaments in Post-Crisis EU Economic Governance? *Journal of European Public Policy*, 25(2): 268–286.

Curtin, D. (2007). Holding (quasi-) Autonomous EU Administrative Actors to Public Account. *European Law Journal*, 13(4): 523–541.

De Wilde, P. and Zürn, M. (2012). Can the Politicization of European Integration be Reversed?. *Journal of Common Market Studies*, 50: 137–153.

De Wilde, P., Leupold, A., and Schmidtke, H. (2016). Introduction: The differentiated Politicisation of European Governance. *West European Politics*, 39(1): 3–22.

Delhomme, V. and Hervey, T. (2022). The European Union's Response to the Covid-19 Ccrisis and (the Legitimacy of) the Union's Legal Order. *Yearbook of European Law*, 41: 48–82.

Draghi, M. (2012). *Speech by Mario Draghi, President of the European Central Bank, at the Global Investment Conference.* London, 26 July 2012. https://www.ecb.europa.eu/press/key/date/2012/html/sp120726.en.html. Accessed 31 July, 2025.

Egeberg, M. and Trondal, J. (2017). Researching European Union agencies: What have We Learnt (and Where Do We Go From Here)? *Journal of Common Market Studies*, 55(4): 675–690.

Eichengreen, B. and Wyplosz, C. (1998). The Stability Pact: More than a Minor Nuisance? *Economic Policy*, 13(26): 65–113.

Elgie, R. (2002). The Politics of the European Central Bank: Principal–Agent Theory and the Democratic Deficit. *Journal of European Public Policy*, 9(2): 186–200.

European Commission (2015). Communication from the Commission to the European Parliament, the Council and the European Central Bank On steps towards Completing Economic and Monetary Union. COM/2015/0600 final, 21 October 2015.

Everson, M., Monda, C., and Vos, E. (eds) (2014). *European Agencies in between Institutions and Member States*. Alphen aan den Rijn, Kluwer Law International.

Fabbrini, S. (2013). Intergovernmentalism and its Limits: Assessing the European Union's Answer to the Euro Crisis. *Comparative Political Studies*, 46(9): 1003–1029.

Fabbrini, S. and Puetter, U. (2016). Integration Without Supranationalisation: Studying The Lead Roles of the European Council and the Council in post-Lisbon EU Politics. *Journal of European Integration*, 38(5): 481–495.

Fasone, C. (2014). European Economic Governance and Parliamentary Representation. What Place for the European Parliament? *European Law Journal*, 20(2): 164–185.

Fasone, C. (2015). *Taking Budgetary Powers Away From National Parliaments? On Parliamentary Prerogatives in the Eurozone Crisis? On Parliamentary Prerogatives in the Eurozone Crisis*. EUI Department of Law Research Paper, No. 2015/37.

Fromage, D. and van den Brink, T. (2018). Democratic Legitimation of EU Economic Governance: Challenges and Opportunities for European Legislatures. *Journal of European Integration*, 40(3): 235–248.

Grosche, G. and Puetter, U. (2008). Preparing the Economic and Financial Committee and the Economic Policy Committee for Enlargement. *European Integration*, 30(4): 527–543.

Hagelstam, K., Lehofer, W., and Ciucci, M. (2018). *The Role of National Parliaments in the European Semester for Economic Policy Coordination*. In-depth Analysis, Economic Governance Support Unit (EGOV), PE 614.494 – 5 April 2018.

Hallerberg, M., Marzinotto, B., and Wolff, G. B. (2018). Explaining the Evolving Role of National Parliaments under the European Semester. *Journal of European Public Policy*, 25(2): 250–267.

Heldt, E. C. and Mueller, T. (2021). The (Self-)Empowerment of the European Central Bank during the Sovereign Debt Crisis. *Journal of European Integration*, 43(1): 83–98.

Hodson, D. (2004). Macroeconomic Co-ordination in the Euro Area: The Scope and Limits of the Open Method. *Journal of European Public Policy*, 11(2): 231–248.

Hodson, D. and Maher, I. (2002). Economic and Monetary Union: Balancing Credibility and Legitimacy in an Asymmetric Policy-Mix. *Journal of European Public Policy*, 9(3): 391–407.

Howarth, D. and Quaglia, L. (2013). Banking Union as Holy Grail: Rebuilding the Single Market in Financial Services, Stabilizing Europe's Banks and Completing Economic and Monetary Union. *Journal of Common Market Studies*, 51: 103–123.

Jacquet, P. and Pisani-Ferry, J. (2001). *Economic Policy Co-ordination in the Euro-zone: What Has Been Achieved? What Should Be Done?* London, Centre for European Reform.

Jančić, D. (2016). National Parliaments and EU Fiscal Integration. *European Law Journal*, 22(2): 225–249.

Juncker, J. C., Tusk, D., Dijsselbloem, J., Draghi, M., and Schulz, M. et al. (2015). *Completing Europe's Economic and Monetary Union*. Brussels, European Commission.

Katsikas, D. (2021). European Union's Democratic Legitimacy after the MoUs: The Political Legacy of an Economic Crisis. In De Souza Guilherme, B., Ghymers, C., Griffith-Jones, S., and Ribeiro Hoffmann, A. (eds). *Financial Crisis Management and Democracy*. Cham, Springer: 111–124.

Kelemen, R. D. (2002). The Politics of 'Eurocratic' Structure and the New European Agencies. *West European Politics*, 25(4): 93–118.

Levi-Faur, D. (2011). Regulatory Networks and Regulatory Agencification: Towards a Single European Regulatory Space. *Journal of European Public Policy*, 18(6): 810–829.

Macron, E. (2017). President Macron Gives Speech on New Initiative for Europe. Elysée News, 26 Septembre 2017. https://www.elysee.fr/en/emmanuel-macron/2017/09/26/president-macron-gives-speech-on-new-initiative-for-europe. Accessed 31 July 2025.

Majone, G. (1993). *The European Community: An Independent Fourth Branch of Government?* EUI Working Paper, SPS.

Majone, G. (2001). Two Logics of Delegation: Agency and Fiduciary Relations in EU Governance. *European Union Politics*, 2(1): 103–122.

Majone, G. (2005). *Dilemmas of European Integration*. Oxford, Oxford University Press.

Migliorati, M. (2020). The Post-agencification Stage between Reforms and Crises. A Comparative Assessment of EU agencies' Budgetary Development. *Journal of Common Market Studies*, 58(6): 1393–1412.

Moschella, M., Pinto, L., and Diodati, L. M. (2020). Let's Speak More? How The ECB Responds To Public Contestation. *Journal of European Public Policy*, 27(3): 400–418.

Pisani-Ferry, J., Sapir, A., Véron, N., and Wolff, G. B. (2012). *What Kind of European banking union?* Bruegel Policy Contribution, No. 2012/12.

Pollak J. and Slominski P. (2021). EU Agencies in Times of Crisis: An Introduction. In Pollak, J. and Slominski, P. (eds). *The Role of EU Agencies in the Eurozone and Migration Crisis: Impact and Future Challenges*. Cham, Palgrave Macmillan: 3–19.

Puetter, U. (2012). Europe's Deliberative Intergovernmentalism: The Role of the Council and European Council in EU Economic Governance. *Journal of European Public Policy*, 19(2): 161–178.

Puetter, U. (2016). *The Eurogroup: How a Secretive Circle of Finance Ministers Shape European Economic Governance*. Manchester, Manchester University Press.

Rittberger, B. (2014). Integration Without Representation? The European Parliament and the Reform of Economic Governance in the EU. *Journal of Common Market Studies*, 52(6): 1174–1183.

Scharpf, F. (1999). *Governing in Europe: Effective and Democratic?* Oxford, Oxford University Press.

Schelkle, W. (2021). Fiscal Integration in an Experimental Union: How Path-Breaking Was the EU's Response to the COVID-19 Pandemic? *Journal of Common Market Studies*, 59: 44–55.

Schmidt, V. A. (2016). Reinterpreting the Rules 'By Stealth' in Times of Crisis: A Discursive Institutionalist Analysis of the European Central Bank and the European Commission. *West European Politics*, 39(5): 1032–1052.

Schmidt, V. A. (2020). *Europe's Crisis of Legitimacy: Governing by Rules and Ruling by Numbers in the Eurozone*. Oxford, Oxford University Press.

Schoeller, M. G. and Héritier, A. (2019). Driving Informal Institutional Change: The European Parliament and the Reform of the Economic and Monetary Union. *Journal of European Integration*, 41(3): 277–292.

Tesche, T. (2020). Supranational Agency and Indirect Governance After the Euro Crisis: ESM, ECB, EMEF and EFB. *Journal of Contemporary European Studies*, 28(1): 114–127.

Thatcher, M. and Coen, D. (2008). Reshaping European Regulatory Space: An Evolutionary Analysis. *West European Politics*, 31(4): 806–836.

Van Rompuy, H., Barroso, J. M., Juncker, J. C., and Draghi, M. (2012). *Towards a Genuine Economic and Monetary Union*. Brussels, European Council.

Van Rijsbergen, M. and Rogge, E. (2022). Changes to the European Financial Supervisory Agencies' Soft Law Powers: Legitimacy Problems Solved or New Puzzles Created? *European Journal of Legal Studies*, 14(1): 219–254.

Verdun, A. (1998). The Institutional Design of EMU: a Democratic Deficit? *Journal of Public Policy*, 18(2): 107–132.

Legal documents

Consolidated Version of the Treaty on European Union [2012] OJ C326/13–45.

15
Democratic Legitimacy and Covid-19 Responses

*Julie Smith and Naman Karl-Thomas Habtom**

15.1 Introduction

The Covid-19 pandemic was a global crisis with European and national level consequences, precipitating a wide range of policy responses that transformed the European Union (EU) in various ways as the European Commission under President Ursula von der Leyen and Member States, led by France and Germany, sought solutions to transnational problems. Health policy is ostensibly a national, not an EU-level competence (see for example Brooks et al. 2023). The initial reactions to the pandemic were thus also national, as so often in previous crises (Quaglia and Verdun 2023: 600, 605; Wolff and Ladi 2020: 1025), reflecting a lack of solidarity among the twenty-seven Member States. So significant was the apparent rift within the EU that both Russia and China saw an opportunity to exploit the perceived divisions. Each offered support to Italy, the first EU country to be affected, which seemed to be ostracized by fellow EU Member States, with Austria swiftly closing its border with Italy (Krotz and Schramm 2022: 531) and other countries, notably Germany, reluctant to export personal protective equipment to other EU states. Russia and China offered supplies of medicines and personal protective equipment, which meant relatively little in practice but was highly symbolic; Russia sent medical supplies in planes emblazoned 'From Russia with love' (Foy and Peel 2020). China's actions also served as a reminder that Italy was a rare example of an EU Member State being part of the Belt and Road Initiative.

It swiftly became clear that what had started as a health crisis went far beyond health policy, having implications for the Schengen area and for national economies and, by extension, for European budgetary matters, as extensive lockdowns saw national borders reinstated and severely damaged national economies. The Covid-19 pandemic was thus an issue that impacted the whole EU, although the Member States were affected asymmetrically and responded in quite different ways, with varying consequences for democracy and public support. Emergency

* The authors would like to thank Charlie Fox for his invaluable research assistance during the Horizon Europe Reconnect project, when this chapter was originally conceived.

Julie Smith and Naman Karl-Thomas Habtom, *Democratic Legitimacy and Covid-19 Responses* In: *The Promise of EU Democracy*. Edited by: Jan Wouters, Julie Smith, Kolja Raube, and Ben Crum, Oxford University Press. © Julie Smith and Naman Karl-Thomas Habtom 2026. DOI: 10.1093/9780191996191.003.0018 powers were invoked by most governments, with some profound implications for democratic accountability within those states. Moreover, certain policy decisions were rapidly undertaken by the EU, despite the lack of any obvious legal basis for it to do so (Grogan 2022: 23), and by the end of the pandemic the Union had increased its role in public health (Brooks et al. 2023), without any reference to its citizens or any formal shift in legal competence. Overall, reactions to the pandemic thus raise questions about their democratic legitimacy at both national and European levels.

The aim of this chapter is to consider European reactions to the Covid-19 crisis and their democratic consequences, looking at both the national and EU levels. At the national level, the use of emergency powers and dangers of executive creep raised questions about democratic accountability, as the lockdowns that were imposed in most states, and their consequences for rights of assembly and the holding of elections or referendums, reduced citizens' ability to hold governments to account effectively. Given space constraints, the chapter will look primarily at the situation in five countries, including the two largest Member States, France and Germany, whose bilateral cooperation allowed ambitious EU-level initiatives to take place, even if formally all Member States needed to agree to the proposals before they could come into effect (Krotz and Schramm 2022). We also look at Italy, given its initial isolation and the significant impact Covid had on that country, as well as Hungary, a state that had already witnessed democratic backsliding prior to the pandemic and whose prime minister was swift to take on enhanced executive powers when Covid hit. Lastly, we look at the case of Sweden, which was a marked outlier among EU states, adopting more liberal, laissez-faire policies, looking to 'herd immunity' rather than lockdowns to tackle the health crisis. At the EU level, the responses included policy or 'mission' creep by the Commission (for example over vaccine procurement), which seems to have become institutionalized without any formal approval by national parliaments or the peoples of Europe. In this it is redolent of the 'permissive consensus' of the early years of integration when it was assumed that the citizens endorsed what their representatives were doing yet were never formally asked for their opinions on European matters (Lindberg and Scheingold 1970). Longer-term consequences can also be seen in the budgetary package for 2021–27, NextGenerationEU, adopted in 2020, which linked support for Covid recovery measures to rule-of-law backsliding, providing a creative way in which the crisis was used to enhance rather than reduce democratic resilience.

The chapter will first briefly outline the nature of the pandemic before turning to European responses. We look initially at states' decisions to impose emergency powers, and the frameworks within which such decisions were taken, before looking at one particular use of emergency powers in practice, namely lockdowns. Next, we turn to choices about whether or not to hold elections during the pandemic, noting that the choice to postpone elections can sometimes have more equitable outcomes than holding them regardless of an ongoing crisis. We then consider the EU-level responses and the drive of Commission President von der Leyen as a policy entrepreneur seeking European solutions to the crisis, before turning to public opinion regarding national and EU-level responses in the five selected countries.

15.2 Covid-19: a brief introduction

The Covid-19 pandemic originated in China in late 2019 and reached Europe in early 2020, with the first case being reported in France in January 2020.[1] The Director-General of the World Health Organization (WHO) declared a public health emergency of international concern (PHEIC) on 30 January 2020, barely a month after the first cases had been acknowledged in Wuhan, China (see WHO 2020; Colfer 2020). Just three years later, 676,609,955 cases had been recorded globally and 6,881,955 people had died with this particular coronavirus (COVID-19 Dashboard, no date).[2] Infection and mortality rates were especially high across densely populated parts of the world including Europe and North America. By January 2023, 2,169,191 Covid-related deaths had been registered across the continent of Europe, including a significant number in Russia (Statista 2023). Nor were the recorded statistics notably better within the EU, as Table 15.1 shows.

Table 15.1 Covid-19 infection and mortality rates in selected European countries, 2020–23

Country	Number of infections	Number of deaths	Size of population	Deaths per 1000 inhabitants
France	39,866,718	166,176	68,401,997	2.43
Germany	38,249,060	168,935	83,445,000	2.02
Hungary	2,196,804	48,762	9,584,627	5.09
Italy	25,603,510	188,322	58,989,749	3.19
Sweden	2,699,339	23,777	10,551,707	2.25

Sources: Incidence and mortality statistics from the COVID-19 Dashboard; Population figures from Eurostat

[1] The terms Covid-19 and coronavirus are frequently used interchangeably in common parlance, although there are many different types of coronavirus. More precisely, Covid-19 is caused by the SARS-CoV-2 coronavirus.

[2] The Dashboard website gives data up to 3 January 2023, towards the end of the pandemic. It is those figures that are cited here. Most other databases, including Statista (2023) cited elsewhere in this chapter, also only provide comprehensive data up to 2023, reflecting the fact that the WHO declared the pandemic to have ended in May 2023. At the time of writing (early 2025) Covid-19 was still prevalent; the crisis had ended but the virus persisted in ever-changing variants.

The catalyst for the global crisis that followed the spread of the Covid-19 coronavirus was a matter of public health, but the consequences went far beyond healthcare, entailing considerable constraints on civil liberties and fiscal discipline in many countries as political leaders sought to limit the number of infections and, crucially, deaths resulting from the virus. For most governments, whether democratic or authoritarian, from China to Canada, from Arctic nations to Australasia, the preferred option initially was to limit people's movements outside the home. The concept of 'lockdown' became commonplace within the European Union as elsewhere, but the restrictions came with severe economic consequences, arising from budget-busting bailouts for businesses and other exceptional fiscal policies, and they frequently lacked the sort of legislative scrutiny expected in democratic systems. Moreover, the constraints on free movement jeopardized the very practice of democracy, one of the most fundamental principles of the modern Western states and a key value of the European Union (see Radjenovic et al. 2020: 2). The lockdowns introduced in the vast majority of European countries inevitably limited citizens' right of assembly and, hence, created problems for democratic practices that have rarely been discussed in the scholarship on Covid, despite their undoubted significance for the rise of populism and tensions between citizens and governing elites.

There is a substantial literature on the Covid-19 crisis, covering many disciplines, including political science (e.g. *Round Table* 2021), law (*Common Market Law Review* 2020), public policy (*European Policy Analysis* 2020) and medicine (National Library of Medicine 2023). Much of this scholarship emerged during or immediately after the pandemic, enabling authors to provide timely commentary on the causes and consequences of Covid-19, especially from medical and public health perspectives, but not permitting more in-depth reflection on the wider ramifications of governments' policy choices or their democratic implications. A few authors have begun to look at questions of legitimacy in European responses to 'emergency politics'. For example, Schmidt (2022) considers the legitimacy of two executive actors, namely the Council of the EU and the European Central Bank, particularly focusing on rhetorical power. She pays little attention to the EU's main executive body, the European Commission. We seek (partially) to fill this gap by providing a description of certain key policy responses at the national and EU levels before analysing popular reactions to political responses to the pandemic, including the interplay between EU and national responses and their joint and separate consequences for democratic legitimacy.

15.3 Declaring an emergency: taking power from the people?

The health emergency triggered by Covid-19 provided the conditions for states of emergency to be declared in many countries. States of emergency are, by their very nature, responses to an ongoing—and frequently not fully understood—challenge. Faced with incomplete information, governments wielding emergency powers may bypass legislative bodies, weakening constitutional norms that typically prevail in democratic states.

States of emergency can have important ramifications for democracy and democratic legitimacy, not least as there is a danger they will lead to increased executive dominance, which may become entrenched. As Grogan and Donald (2021: 7) argue, 'emergency powers are inherently problematic where they have been made permanent features, sometimes extending over years, or where they can be invoked with limited or no scrutiny, or where their exercise, extent and duration is dictated by the executive alone'. Consideration thus needs to be paid to the actions taken by governments and what scope there was for parliamentary scrutiny. Were the powers of national parliaments reduced either formally or informally, for example? Did opposition parties challenge governments' proposals for changes that contributed to executive dominance, or did they mutely acquiesce to them? Since responses to emergencies are typically time-critical, established practices of parliamentary oversight may be curtailed in favour of approving governmental decisions with minimal scrutiny. Thus, as Jonathan White noted a decade ago, 'representative democracy . . . risks being marginalized amidst the actions and rhetoric of emergency' (White 2015: 300). This was certainly the case in many European countries' responses to the pandemic of the early 2020s.

Despite facing a common threat in the form of Covid-19, governing elites made very different policy choices, reflecting constitutional and cultural differences as well as varying party political preferences regarding individual liberty versus societal resilience. Not only did EU Member States have differing constitutional provisions regarding triggering states of emergency and the rules that should prevail during times of emergency, but they also took quite different approaches regarding the extent and duration of the states of emergency that were declared and the policies adopted during the emergency. Some states declared a specific health state of emergency, others used more general emergency provisions, not specifically targeted at health emergencies; other states introduced measures that did not require a suspension of regular governance structures or indeed any other extraordinary measures. The declaration of general or health-related states of emergency during the pandemic reflected both existing legal frameworks and political dynamics within each country, as well as the predisposition of governing parties to adopt extraordinary measures.

In France, the initial measures taken by the Health Minister in 2020 were grounded in the pre-existing Public Health Code (*Code de la Santé Publique*) (Platon 2020: 296). On 23 March 2020, the country established a 'state of health emergency' via the Emergency Response to the Covid-19 Epidemic Act (2020-290) (ibid.: 293). States of health emergency in France can differ from 'normal' states of emergency by permitting general rather than individual measures to be implemented (ibid.: 300). Thus, compared to the 2015–17 state of emergency following terrorist attacks in Paris, there were greater restrictions during the pandemic and less scope for parliamentary oversight. During the 2015–17 crisis, the National Assembly engaged in 'real-time monitoring of the implementation of the state of emergency' through its Law Committee, whereas during the pandemic there was only an 'information mission' (ibid.: 303). In addition, the Council of State, which is responsible for judicial scrutiny, suggested that the government adopt rules for a month at a time, rather than the twelve-day limit that exists under normal states of emergency (ibid.: 304).

In Hungary, where no specific framework for health-related states of emergency was in place prior to the Covid pandemic, the government relied on broader state of emergency provisions. The Fundamental Law (i.e. Hungary's constitution) allows for six types of 'special legal order', one of which is tailored to the 'danger of crisis' such as natural disasters and formed the basis for the emergency declared during the pandemic (Drinóczi and Bień-Kacała 2020: 175). Such 'special legal orders' have a 'sunset' provision, meaning they should end automatically after fifteen days unless they are reapproved by the Hungarian parliament. However, the Fundamental Law is silent on how such reapproval should be granted, for example whether parliament is required to reapprove the powers every fortnight or can approve a longer extension of emergency provisions. In fact, the second authorization was made without any time limits (ibid.). As Győry and Weinberg argue, 'The Authorization Act thus gave Parliamentary assent to decrees that did not yet exist, undermining the principle of legal certainty' (Győry and Weinberg 2020: 339).

Hungary, which was already known for its democratic backsliding and illiberal democratic turn before Covid, witnessed considerable growth in executive dominance during the pandemic. According to Győry and Weinberg (2020: 329):

> the Hungarian case stands out because the government was granted via legislation by Parliament (The Authorization Act) almost unlimited, though revocable, authorisation to rule by decree without temporal, jurisdictional or other legal restrictions, aside from those limits enshrined in the constitution protecting the most fundamental rights.

Although the Hungarian government formally ended the emergency period relatively early (after the end of the first wave), it sought to make certain aspects of the emergency arrangements permanent by incorporating 'many of the emergency decrees into ordinary statutory law' (ibid.: 330). The government lost some parliamentary support, owing to its inflexible stance. For example, it sought to use a fast-track procedure that requires the support of four-fifths of the members of Hungary's unicameral parliament to remove the fifteen-day sunset period that would normally apply in emergency circumstances. Some opposition MPs would in fact have supported a period longer than fifteen days, but wanted 'oversight' (Drinóczi and Bień-Kacała 2020: 183). Thus, even authoritarian governments could not presume to override their parliaments in all circumstances.

By contrast, the German government had no power to call a national state of emergency in the face of the pandemic (Hegele and Schnabel 2021: 1065). Meanwhile, Sweden's government chose not to move into emergency mode, responding quite differently from the vast majority of states, including opting not to go into lockdown to prevent the spread of the virus.

15.4 Lockdowns: emergency powers in action

The adoption and implementation of lockdowns broadly reflected the divergent approaches and interpretations of emergency powers in individual states, as well as attitudes towards individual liberties. Lockdowns were in part determined by constitutional constraints, although the differences between Member States reflected individual circumstances arising from a mixture of legal differences, domestic political dynamics, and governmental predisposition to top-down measures.

Sweden stands out for its relatively laissez-faire response to the pandemic, notably its decision not to go into lockdown (Ludvigsson 2023). As a result, the country operated largely as normal, albeit with greater deference to the government and public health authorities. This marked it out not just from the EU as a whole but even from its Nordic neighbours with similar forms of government and cultures. While some restrictions were introduced, such as around nursing homes, they tended to be exceptions rather than the rule. Voluntary actions like social distancing, increased working from home, and a drop in use of public transport came to be defining features of the Swedish approach, which did not see blanket school closures or the compulsory closure of hospitality venues, unlike in other European states. The absence of lockdowns was not the only Swedish deviation from the European norm. A general reluctance by the national health authorities to advocate the use of face masks (and at times even to discourage it) was symptomatic of a broader divergence from the European approach (Vogel 2020). Meanwhile, the Swedish government's deference towards the Public Health Agency alongside parliament's deference towards the government resulted in a relatively low profile for the government during this period compared to other national governments in the EU.

Constitutional arrangements also impacted the formulation and implementation of lockdown restrictions *within* states. For example, Germany had decentralized, though generally coordinated, decision-making processes between the federal government in Berlin and the *Land* governments (Hegele and Schnabel 2021). The pursuit of an informal approach relying on coordination rather than compulsion in the case of a federal state like Germany reflected two realities: restrictions on the national/federal government's powers and the nature of power distribution between the federal government and the governments of the *Länder*, with the latter at times exercising powers usually reserved for national governments. In 2001, Germany had passed the Infection Protection Act (*Infektionsschutzgesetz*, IfSG), which provided that the federal government may set out recommendations but that the *Länder* would actually make and implement the ensuing decisions (Hegele and Schnabel 2021: 1064). While some decisions such as the closure of the national borders remained within the remit of the federal government, Germany pursued 'coordination aimed mainly at harmonising the measures enacted by the Länder' (ibid.: 1068). While there were initially attempts to have some uniformity regarding the implementation of lockdowns, towards the end of the first wave, decisions regarding the relaxation of lockdown arrangements increasingly tended to be made unilaterally by the governments of the *Länder* (ibid.: 1067). Opposition parties at the federal level—the Greens, the Free Democrats and die Linke—were less hostile to the Federal government's proposals than were opposition politicians in countries like France. This was perhaps in part because several of the parties in opposition at the federal level were members of governments at the *Land* level and thus participated in lockdown decisions in a way that was not the case in unitary states. Additionally, the lockdowns were less restrictive in Germany than in France, where initially written permission was required for people to leave their homes.

Lockdowns were especially controversial because, by definition, they imposed restrictions on people's liberty (Platon 2020: 300), particularly their rights to move freely in their own countries (and more widely in the EU) and of freedom of association, which, as Radjenovic et al. (2020) remind us, is essential for democracy to function. Freedom of movement, a right enshrined within the EU, was effectively paused and Schengen borders were re-imposed by one state after another. While Member States have the right to reinstate national border restrictions in exceptional circumstances such as a health emergency, the wholesale nature of such decisions in 2020 and delays in removing them set an unwelcome precedent in terms of European (dis)integration.

15.5 Democratic moments, undemocratic delays

A further challenge to democracy during the pandemic related to the holding of elections, specifically whether or not to proceed with elections and referendums that had already been scheduled for spring/summer 2020. In some cases, constitutional provisions took the decision out of politicians' hands (see Radjenovic et al. 2020) but elsewhere policymakers were faced with a choice whether to continue with the elections as planned, postpone them, or hold them by other means, namely by post or digital (electronic) voting.

One might assume that deferring democratic moments should be avoided at all costs in order to avoid undermining the democratic process and strengthening the powers of executives, further exacerbating the dangers of executive dominance. However, as Rajdenovic et al. discuss, the decision is not so straightforward. In particular, as they point out, 'Democracy is unthinkable without a credible electoral process, which includes not only voting but also *equal possibilities to campaign for all the candidates*, *freely exercising the right of assembly* and *participating collectively in the political process* and ensuring pluralism of ideas' (Radjenovic et al. 2020:2; emphasis added). An emergency situation characterized by lockdowns inevitably limits these conditions for a 'credible electoral process'. Thus, delaying an election may, in certain exceptional circumstances, be the most appropriate decision, even from the perspective of democracy. As the Venice Commission noted, 'Postponement is a restriction to the periodicity of elections and has to be foreseen in the law, be necessary in the concrete circumstances and be proportionate' (Venice Commission 2020: para 93). There are times when postponement might be appropriate. Indeed, the Commission points out that the European Convention on Human Rights and the UN's International Covenant on Civil and Political Rights allow for derogations in cases of public emergency, which 'may relate to war or other ongoing armed conflicts, high level terrorist attacks, natural disasters or epidemic' (Venice Commission 2020: para 95). A priori, the pandemic provided a context in which deferring elections might indeed be the correct decision.

If voting were allowed to go ahead in such conditions, democratic inequalities might compound health and economic inequalities, as the healthiest people, who will often also be the more affluent in the prime of life, rather than the vulnerable and elderly, would be better able to engage in democratic processes, primarily by casting their ballot in person, while those worse affected by the pandemic might not be able to participate. The asymmetric turnout that would thus be likely to occur would then further privilege those least impacted by the pandemic. Yet, if elections were deferred, how could citizens have their say on Covid policies or, indeed, any other government policy that they might normally seek to reject or challenge at the ballot box? After all, periodic free and fair elections are a hallmark of democracy.

States took differing stances on whether to hold elections during the first wave of the pandemic, with a growing propensity to postpone from late March 2020 onwards when the scale of the pandemic became more apparent. Thus, some countries went ahead with planned elections, albeit under specific, adapted conditions, while others opted to postpone them on grounds of public safety and health as the severity of the public health crisis became clearer. Differences occurred not just between countries but also within them, as shown by the German *Länder*. Bavaria held municipal elections in March 2020 despite high infection rates (Radjenovic et al. 2020: 5). The first round, which took place on 15 March, went ahead in person, albeit with some modifications. Strict hygiene rules were introduced, voters were told to bring their own pens, and proxy voting was allowed. However, voting in the round on 29 March was conducted entirely by postal vote. This required an amendment to the municipal electoral law, which the Bavarian state parliament duly adopted. This decision may even have had a positive impact on the elections, as turnout in the second round was 4.1 per cent higher than in the 2014 municipal elections (Radjenovic et al. 2020: 5). By contrast, both Hessen and Saxony postponed their spring 2020 municipal elections, while North Rhine Westphalia kept to its scheduled 13 September 2020 date (ibid.), by which time the first wave of the virus had receded.

France, meanwhile, initially seemed keen to press ahead with elections despite Covid, committing to holding local elections on 15 March 2020 as planned. Certain precautionary measures were taken (e.g. permiting people to bring their own pens, and the provision of hand-sanitizing facilities). Nevertheless, voter turnout was considerably down on normal levels, falling from 63.5 per cent in 2014 to 44.66 per cent in 2020 (ibid.: 7). President Macron was reluctant to postpone the second round of the elections, but the Minister of Interior made the decision to do so on 17 March 2020 (ibid.). Italy was scheduled to hold a confirmatory constitutional referendum on the question of reducing the numbers of MPs and Senators on 29 March 2020. However, the government proposed that the presidential decree setting the date for the referendum be revoked and the vote was accordingly deferred to September 2020. Terms for elected regional officials were extended in order to allow for a postponement of regional elections (ibid.).

Given that the first wave of the pandemic, certainly the period before an effective vaccine was introduced, was of relatively short duration, the limitations on elections and referendums were quite limited across most of the EU. However, the issues raised are important and would need to be considered carefully in any crisis moment, particularly one of prolonged duration. One exception during the Covid pandemic that demonstrates the significance of such choices was the decision over whether or not to hold the election for the President of Poland, which was due to be held on 10 May 2020. Following a highly controversial attempt by Law and Justice to persist with the election which their candidate, the incumbent President Andrzej Duda, was the favourite to win, despite the health risks and in the absence of any legal basis to hold elections wholly by post, the decision was eventually taken to postpone the elections (Shotter 2020). This case showed clearly the issues at stake in determining whether to hold elections during a health emergency; an incumbent has, or may have, the advantage of (favourable) media coverage and opposition parties lack the ability to campaign on equal terms, suggesting that from an equity perspective it may be preferable to postpone an election. In the event, Duda narrowly won the rescheduled elections, suggesting that the deferral did not ultimately have a major impact on this particular electoral moment, even though it appeared highly significant at the time.

15.6 European level responses

At the EU level, Commission President Ursula von der Leyen was anxious to respond to the crisis, but was initially impeded by the EU's lack of competence in public health, which remains a national competence. Thus, as Robinet-Borgomano (2020) noted, 'The European Commission was conspicuously absent from initial efforts to manage the crisis'. Within just a few months, however, von der Leyen had seized the Covid opportunity to push for further integration in health policy, pressed for EU-level vaccine procurement, and overseen a new budgetary package. The 2021–27 Multiannual Financial Framework (MFF) included a growth package—NextGenerationEU—based on loans and grants that could inter alia assist those states facing the worst economic consequences of the pandemic. Inevitably, these policy innovations were not all down to the Commission President, or even to the Commission. Rather, they were the result of negotiation and cooperation among the Member States, led by France and Germany, in addition to the activities of the Commission and indeed the European Council President, Charles Michel, and in the case of the budgetary provisions they had to be approved by both the Council of the EU and the democratically elected European Parliament. There was no formal mandate for the EU's collective responses, yet the determination of national leaders as well as the Commission to avert an existential crisis ensured that ground-breaking policies were introduced at speed.[3]

While the medical consequences of the pandemic such as the need for hospital beds and ventilators had to be tackled by individual Member States, the economic consequences had implications for the whole EU. By mid-March 2020, the European Council comprising leaders of all twenty-seven Member States was seeking a common European response (Krotz and Schramm 2022: 532). Yet, a desire to act does not necessarily translate into effective policy outcomes, as the interests of the twenty-seven may well diverge. Thus, as with many budgetary questions, discussion of how best to tackle some of the financial consequences of Covid united a group of the richer states, typically known as the 'Frugals', unwilling to contribute financially to assist their EU partners (ibid.). However, on this occasion, German leader Angela Merkel, who had been resistant to fiscal transfers during the eurozone crisis a decade earlier, was persuaded by French President Emmanuel Macron of the need for an innovative 'recovery fund' in what Schmidt (2022: 987) argues was 'the culmination of France's persuasive power *through* ideas via discourse with Germany'. For the first time, Germany was willing to accept transfer payments, seemingly as a way to ensure intra-EU solidarity (see Miró 2022), and the EU agreed to issue bonds. This result of bilateral negotiations led

[3] The European Court of Auditors (ECA) highlighted clearly the interplay of the Council, Commission and Member States in decisions on vaccine procurement. See ECA 2022.

to an EU-level agreement, with von der Leyen managing to link the proposals to the ongoing MFF negotiations (Drachenberg and Vrijhoeven 2021). As Krotz and Schramm note, she 'called for turning the MFF into "the mothership of our recovery"' (Krotz and Schramm 2022: 533–534). On 21 July 2020, the European Council agreed the 2021–27 MFF, which included the innovative €750 billion NextGenerationEU recovery fund, composed of €390 billion in grants and €360 billion in loans (European Parliament, no date). A key innovation was that the new funding included 'rule of law conditionality', meaning that those states that failed to meet EU standards on the rule of law, notably Hungary and at that time Poland, would see funding withheld. Having for many years failed to tackle democratic and rule-of-law backsliding, particularly prevalent among the Central and East European states that joined the Union in 2004 and 2007, policy entrepreneurship in response to the pandemic had finally allowed the EU to act.

A second crucial area of innovation relates to the vaccine procurement programme pursued by von der Leyen at the behest of the Member States (see European Court of Auditors 2022). At the outset of the pandemic there was no vaccine for the SARS-CoV2 coronavirus; by October 2021, three-quarters of EU adults had been vaccinated; by mid-2022 that number had risen to almost nine in ten (European Council, no date). Indeed, the European Commission managed to secure sufficient doses 'to vaccinate all adult EU citizens and to make donations to third countries' (ECA 2022: 38). The aggregate statistics for vaccination were impressive, although the EU's response was slower than either the UK or US, and neglected certain questions about security of supply (ECA 2020). The Commission, alongside representatives from seven EUMS (including the three largest states as well as the Netherlands, Poland, Spain, and Sweden), negotiated on behalf of the EU. Their focus was on ensuring equity of supply, which would not have been guaranteed had states each negotiated individually—smaller states would almost certainly have struggled to secure the necessary vaccines in the urgent rush to the pharmaceutical market.

The process of vaccine delivery was left to the Member States. Take-up rates differed quite significantly between countries as did public attitudes towards vaccination, as discussed in the next section. Rapid vaccine development by various pharmaceutical companies was met by fierce competition to procure vaccines, with the EU and the recently departed United Kingdom competing both to develop and procure vaccines. Eventually, the EU procured vaccines from eight different companies (ibid.). For the European Council, the fact that the EU had worked together from March 2020 'showed solidarity, supporting each other in the distribution of vaccines and providing medical equipment to those most in need' (European Council, no date). In 2025 the European Commission's Health Emergency Preparedness and Response Authority signed a further joint procurement contract with Moderna (European Commission 2025), highlighting the Commission's continued role in procurement even after the pandemic was over, and reflecting an institutionalization of processes occurring without any obvious democratic input.

The vaccine procurement and distribution processes undertaken at the height of the crisis lacked transparency as well as democratic accountability. Decisions on collective procurement and distribution were particularly beneficial to smaller countries that would not have gained traction in the competitive international market for vaccines. However, perceived problems with the procurement process led to legal action, the other remedy in a democratic system if legislative solutions are not available. By 2024, von der Leyen and the Commission were facing two legal cases regarding vaccine procurement, both of which they would lose in the General Court. The first case, brought by Green Members of the European Parliament, related to a lack of transparency in the Covid vaccines contracts, with the EU General Court ruling that 'The European Commission unlawfully concealed details of its Covid-19 vaccine procurement contracts' (Bounds et al. 2024). The second case, in which the General Court ruled against the Commission on 14 July 2025, was brought by *The New York Times* (*Stevi and New York Times v Commission* 2025). This case arose from von der Leyen's office's refusal to release private text messages the Commission President had exchanged with the head of Pfizer in 2021 while procurement negotiations were ongoing, leading to questions about her credibility in 'defend[ing] standards of transparency, efficiency and probity' (Politico 2024). Both cases suggest a failure by the Commission to meet its transparency standards. Although this could arguably have been linked to business requirements for confidentiality, the General Court appeared unpersuaded by this suggestion (Bounds et al. 2024). In any event, such concerns do not appear to have impacted citizens' attitudes or to have played any significant role in the 2024 European Parliament elections.

15.7 Public opinion

Despite legal concerns over the vaccine procurement process, most EU citizens were supportive of vaccination per se, believing that the advantages outweighed the disadvantages (European Commission 2022: 3). Those who had not been vaccinated included some who would refuse all vaccinations on principle and others who expressed concern at the speed at which the vaccines had been developed (ibid.: 14). Across the EU, by February 2022 67 per cent expressed the view that getting vaccinated was a civic duty, with 83 per cent of Italians holding this view, but just 41 per cent of Hungarians (European Commission 2022: 19). Overall, 56 per cent believed that vaccination should be compulsory, with Italians, Germans, and Swedes particularly strongly in favour, although a majority of Hungarians and many of the Central and East European neighbours opposed mandatory vaccines (ibid.: 20). Overall, respondents tended to be more positive about the EU's response than that of their respective national governments. Swedes and Italians were the most satisfied with their national government's vaccine strategy; they were also among the most pro-vaccine. French and German citizens were also above the EU average in support for the vaccine, whereas Hungarians were among the more vaccine-sceptic (ibid.: 28). Seventy-one per cent of respondents acknowledged the EU's role in ensuring Covid-19 vaccines, with Hungarian and French citizens second and third most sceptical, after Czechia, regarding the EU's involvement in enabling access to the vaccine (ibid.: 30). It is notable that the Swedes, who accepted a very relaxed pandemic response in terms of the absence of lockdowns and emergency powers, were very positive about the need for vaccination. Meanwhile, Hungarian voters were more likely to follow the vaccine-sceptic approach articulated by populists elsewhere, including the US.

European citizens were broadly very supportive of the NextGenerationEU recovery programme as well as the vaccine delivery from which all EU Member States benefited, although the statistics differed markedly between Member States. As of December 2022, half of EU citizens (51 per cent) were 'aware of a Recovery Plan for their country to support economic recovery from the COVID-19 pandemic', with 78 per cent of Portuguese and 74 per cent of Italians being aware, but just 28 per cent in Estonia and Sweden (European Commission 2023: 2). Significantly, there was strong support for intra-EU solidarity, with three-quarters of respondents (74 per cent) 'agree[ing] it is a good approach for the EU that Member States provide financial support to each other to emerge stronger from the COVID-19 pandemic' (ibid.: 4–5). These figures again mask considerable variations between states: 86 per cent of Portuguese and 85 per cent of Maltese respondents felt that the approach was good for the EU, compared with just 66 per cent in the least enthusiastic state, Sweden (ibid.). These responses are perhaps explained by the fact that the Maltese and Portuguese were also most likely to perceive the approach to be beneficial for their country, while Swedes, among the EU 'Frugals', were least likely to see benefits. Hungarians were quite positive about the scheme, believing they would benefit, whereas French voters were more hostile (ibid.).

Regarding national policies, support for lockdowns tended to be highest at the outset of the pandemic, waning in the months that followed before seeing a further uptick (Hurst 2021). Pre-pandemic partisanship and levels of trust in government tended to be good indicators for public sentiments during the first wave of the pandemic. Comparison between France and Austria undertaken by Kritzinger et al. (2021) provides one example of national differences. They found that although there was initially an increase in the confidence in the government in both countries, Austria saw opposition parties supporting the government's response to the pandemic in a way that was not seen in France, where traditional political antagonisms prevailed (Kritzinger et al. 2021: 1206).

The significance of pre-pandemic attitudes towards government also holds true when comparing very similar countries. For example, comparing trust in government and health authorities in Sweden and Denmark, differences in attitudes were more reflective of existing levels of political polarization than a reaction to the pandemic (Nielsen and Lindvall 2021: 1181). Overall confidence/trust in the government was lower in Sweden than in Denmark in the early stages of the pandemic (not just lower in terms of ability to handle the spread of Covid) while decline in trust was similar in both countries, suggesting that the lower trust was not fundamentally the result of performance evaluation during the pandemic (Nielsen and Lindvall 2021: 1190–1191, 1194).

Attitudes towards experts and institutions constituted a major talking point during the pandemic, yet it seems their views did not necessarily persuade citizens. A survey conducted in Germany and the United Kingdom (by now outside the EU) in May 2020 found that 'the endorsements of the mentioned public experts [health ministries, public health agencies, universities and the WHO] did not influence support for COVID-19 measures' (Heinzel and Liese 2021: 1259). Perhaps surprisingly, the survey found that older German citizens 'credit the ministry, institute and university with significantly less expertise than the youngest age group (18–24)' (ibid.: 1274).

Attitudes within countries were not simply for or against Covid measures, as some citizens who were broadly supportive of governmental action could be critical of the specifics. Again, Germany is illustrative: in the summer of 2020 the German government enjoyed the support of 60–90 per cent of the population for its pandemic-related measures (Schieferdecker 2021: 309). Yet, despite the high level of support for the measures generally, there was some dissatisfaction. As Schieferdecker (2021: 312) points out, '[S]upporters commonly wished for a more uniform legislative response', believing that the government's messaging should have been more 'straightforward' and 'consistent', as well as less 'nebulous' (ibid.: 312). Opponents of containment measures did not deny the virus's existence but tended to have different threat perceptions (i.e. they were less likely to perceive Covid as serious) while being more concerned about the economy and issues of freedom than supporters of such measures (ibid.: 312–313). Interestingly, both opponents and supporters of containment measures were unhappy with the 'omnipresence' and 'alarming tone' of the media coverage, although supporters were generally content with the information received while opponents viewed the coverage as one-sided (ibid.: 313).

Trust in governmental institutions was a strong predictor of compliance with government measures during the pandemic. In the case of Germany, 'Overall agreement to follow a measure (no matter if voluntary or enforced) is higher when the government is perceived as trustworthy', while 'control aversion' was higher among those who trusted the government less (Schmelz 2020: 3). Moreover, Charron et al. (2022: 800) found that states with 'lower social or institutional trust, as well as greater social and political polarization may have ended up costing lives in the first wave of COVID-19 in Europe'. The relationship between institutional trust and compliance applies to a range of measures, such as mask-wearing and social distancing, albeit to varying degrees. This high correlation can also be found in the case of vaccination even in countries with very different responses to the pandemic. A study comparing attitudes in Sweden and Italy found that 'Perception of trust in authority was strongly associated with adherence to vaccination campaigns in both countries' (Raffetti et al. 2022: 806).

15.8 Concluding remarks

By the time the Covid pandemic broke out in 2020, after a decade of crisis, the EU and its Member States had become accustomed to dealing with seemingly existential challenges, typically starting with separate national responses before shifting to EU-wide policy responses (Quaglia and Verdun 2023). There had clearly been some policy-learning between crises and the responses to COVID were relatively swift and effective, although they raised some questions about how the decisions were taken and with what consequences for democratic legitimacy. There was little scope for public debate as national governments and the European Commission took swift executive action to try to mitigate the multiple public policy challenges they faced separately and collectively. Thus, as Boin and Rhinard note, 'major policy choices were made without a significant public debate about potential effects on the future character of the Union' (Boin and Rhinard 2023: 655), thus limiting democratic input into policy solutions. To an extent this was inevitable in an emergency situation, as leaders sought to minimize the incidence of the virus and, more importantly, the number of deaths it would cause. However, one of the policy tools adopted almost universally, namely some form of lockdown, had direct ramifications for democracy within Member States. Citizens' normal democratic rights were constrained in several instances as states or regions cancelled or postponed elections during the crisis. Most Member States also saw national executives take on emergency powers, frequently limiting the role of parliaments and limiting democratic practices in addition to reducing citizens' freedoms (see Grogan and Donald 2021).

Overall, the temporary arrangements such as lockdowns and Covid passes were generally accepted at the time, with high levels of compliance and relatively few protests, leaving few long-term democratic challenges. In most cases, the emergency powers adopted by national governments were also temporary; the long-term consequences feared by the Venice Commission and others in 2020 and 2021 did not in the event lead to permanent executive creep, Hungary being a notable exception (Batory 2024). Moreover, the European Commission's policy entrepreneurship was broadly accepted by national political leaders and was endorsed up to a point in the EP elections of 2024, when von der Leyen's European People's Party again secured the largest number of seats. Yet, the rise of populists and the far right in Europe includes many vaccine-sceptics and Covid-deniers, reflecting a growing division within many Member States between the political mainstream, which broadly favoured the decisions taken during the pandemic, and those who sought to reject such constraints.

Arguably, the fact that the pandemic had consequences that affected the whole EU and required supranational and/or transnational responses justified the Commission taking a leading role alongside the European Council. Indeed, the whole principle of European integration historically was for states to cooperate to ensure mutually beneficial outcomes that could be achieved by 'pooling sovereignty', with popular consent due to the output legitimacy that successful policies provided. Similarly, in the early 2020s in the face of a pandemic there was again popular support for European integration, notably for moves towards a European health policy, even without a formal mandate, certainly not one on which voters had been consulted ex ante.

Overall, we see a shift towards enhanced EU competences, but is this temporary or destined to be more enduring? And under what authority—or legal base? For the EU formally to acquire competences in public health policy, treaty change might be required. Increasing EU competences is a testing business, as seen over the first quarter of the twenty-first century. The failure of the Constitutional Treaty in 2005 followed by difficulties in ratifying the alternative Lisbon Treaty two years later ensured that once Lisbon was finally ratified in November 2009 national leaders were reluctant to envisage any further treaty reform (see Chapter 2 of this volume). Yet by 2024, European leaders and transnational parties had again begun to float the idea of treaty reform (ALDE 2024; EPP 2024; PES 2024), which could pave the way for a new legal base for health policy.[4] Having successfully campaigned to be re-elected Commission President on the manifesto of the European People's Party,[5] von der Leyen now had a popular mandate to act. Yet the nature of decision-making at EU level and the need to secure the agreement of all Member States to revise the treaties meant that there were many hurdles still to jump—including persuading the leader of the EU's most awkward (and vaccine-sceptic) Member State, Hungary, of the benefits of reform. The Covid pandemic provided a catalyst for reform, but not the guarantee that it could be brought about by the will of the peoples of twenty-seven Member States.

[4] Whereas the ALDE manifesto made a clear commitment to treaty reform, the EPP made a more modest commitment 'to have a European convention in the coming years to discuss and decide on possible improvements to the Treaties' (EPP 2024) and the PES advocated 'us[ing] the next parliamentary term to strengthen the EU's capacity to act in an enlarged Union, with targeted Treaty changes' (PES 2024).

[5] The EPP 2024 manifesto argued that 'We stand for . . . Europe that invests in health research, guarantees high health and care standards and fights disease' and expressed support for 'creat[ing] a true European Health Union' (EPP 2024, Introductory paragraphs and section 3.5).

References

ALDE (2024). Your Europe, Your Freedom: Delivering Change for You. Political manifesto.

Batory, A. (2024). More Power, Less Support: The Fidesz Government and the Coronavirus Pandemic in Hungary. *Government and Opposition*, 59: 1017–1033.

Boin, A. and Rhinard, M. (2023). Crisis Management Performance and the European Union: the Case of COVID-19. *Journal of European Public Policy* 30(4): 655–675.

Bounds, A., Foy, H., and Mosolova, D. (2024). Brussels Concealed Covid Vaccine Contract Details, Court Finds. *Financial Times*. https://www.ft.com/content/36cc0a5c-6102–4ab5–839d-5dc3fea6ba3c. Accessed 26 January 2025.

Brooks, E., de Ruijter, A., Greer, S. L., and Rozenblum, S. (2023). EU Health Policy in the Aftermath of COVID-19: Neofunctionalism and Crisis-Driven Integration. *Journal of European Public Policy*, 30(4): 721–739.

Charron, N., Lapuente, V., and Rodríguez-Pose, A. (2022). Uncooperative Society, Uncooperative Politics or Both? Trust, Polarization, Populism and COVID-19 Deaths Across European Regions. *European Journal of Political Research*, 62(3): 781–805.

Colfer, B. (2020). Public Politics Responses to COVID-19 in Europe. *European Policy Analysis*, 6(2): 126–137.

COVID-19 Dashboard (no date). COVID-19 Dashboard by the Center for Systems Science and Engineering (CSSE) at Johns Hopkins University (JHU). https://gisanddata.maps.arcgis.com/apps/dashboards/bda7594740fd40299423467b48e9ecf6. Accessed 7 January 2025.

Drachenberg, R. with Vrijhoeven, M. (2021). *The Role of the European Council in Negotiating the 2021–27 MFF – Continuity and Change in the Politics of the EU's Latest Seven-Year Financial Settlement*, PE 662.611, European Parliamentary Research Service, April 2021.

Drinóczi, T. and Bień-Kacała, A. (2020). COVID-19 in Hungary and Poland: Extraordinary Situation and Illiberal Constitutionalism. *The Theory and Practice of Legislation*, 8(1–2): 171–192.

Editorial comments (2020). Editorial Comments: Disease and Recovery in (COVID-Afflicted) Europe. *Common Market Law Review*, 57(3): 619–630.

European Commission for Democracy through Law (Venice Commission) (2020), Respect for Democracy, Human Rights and the Rule of Law during States of Emergency-Reflections, May 2020.

European Commission (2022). Attitudes on Vaccination Against COVID-19 – February 2022, Flash Eurobarometer 505 Report.

European Commission (2023). EU Recovery Plan 'NextGenerationEU', Flash Eurobarometer 515 Summary.

European Commission (2025). Commission Signs Joint Procurement Contract for COVID-19 Vaccines to Ensure Preparedness and Continued Protection of Citizens. News Announcement, 24 January. https://health.ec.europa.eu/latest-updates/commission-signs-joint-procurement-contract. Accessed 26 January 2025.

European Council (no date). Stronger Together – The Incredible Journey of COVID-19 Vaccines. https://www.consilium.europa.eu/de/stronger-together-the-incredible-journey-of-covid-19-vaccines. Accessed 26 January 2025.

European Court of Auditors (2022). Special Report – EU COVID-19 Vaccine Procurement – Sufficient Doses Secured after Initial Challenges, but Performance of the Process Not Sufficiently Assessed. https://op.europa.eu/webpub/eca/special-reports/covid19-vaccines-19–2022/en/#:~:text=EU%20COVID%2D19%20vaccine%20procurement%20Sufficient%20doses%20secured%20after%20initial,up%20to%204.6%20billion%20doses. Accessed 23 April 2025.

European Parliament (no date) Multiannual Financial Framework. *Fact Sheets on the European Union*. https://www.europarl.europa.eu/factsheets/en/sheet/29/multiannual-financial-framework. Accessed 2 February 2025.

European People's Party (2024). Our Europe, a Safe and Good Home for the People. Political manifesto.

European Union (no date). Facts and Figures on the European Union. https://european-union.europa.eu/principles-countries-history/facts-and-figures-european-union_en. Accessed 7 January 2025.

Foy, H. and Peel, M. (2020). Russia Sends Italy Coronavirus Aid to Underline Historic Ties. *Financial Times.* https://www.ft.com/content/b1c5681e-6cf9-11ea-89df-41bea055720b. Accessed 7 January 2025.

Grogan, J. (forthcoming). Global Health Emergencies and the Rule of Law: the Case of COVID-19. In Wouters, J. et al. (eds). *Upholding the Rule of Law in the EU.* Oxford, Oxford University Press.

Grogan, J. (2022). COVID-19, Rule of Law and Democracy – Analysis of Legal Responses to a Global Health Crisis. Reconnect Work Package 11 – Deliverable 5. www.reconnect-europe.eu. Accessed 9 August 2025.

Grogan, J. and Donald, A. (2021). Policy Paper on the Implications of COVID-19. Insights into State Governance and the Rule of Law, Human Rights and Good Governance during the COVID-19 Pandemic Reconnect Work Package 11 – Deliverable 2. www.reconnect-europe.eu. Accessed 9 August 2025.

Győry, C. and Weinberg, N. (2020). Emergency Powers in a Hybrid Regime: The Case of Hungary. *The Theory and Practice of Legislation*, 8(3): 329–353.

Hegele, Y. and Schnabel, J. (2021). Federalism and the Management of the COVID-19 Crisis: Centralisation, Decentralisation and (Non-)Coordination. *West European Politics*, 44(5–6): 1052–1076.

Heinzel, M. and Liese, A. (2021). Expert Authority and Support for COVID-19 Measures in Germany and the UK: A Survey Experiment. *West European Politics*, 44(5–6): 1258–1282.

Hurst, Luke (2021). Majority of Europeans Think Lockdown Benefits Outweigh Economic Damage. Euronews. https://www.euronews.com/2021/06/03/majority-of-europeans-think-lockdown-benefits-outweigh-economic-damage. Accessed 29 April 2025.

Kritzinger, S. et al. (2021). 'Rally Round The Flag': The COVID-19 Crisis and Trust in the National Government. *West European Politics*, 44(5–6): 1205–1231.

Krotz, U. and Schramm, L. (2022). Embedded Bilateralism, Integration Theory, and European Crisis Politics: France, Germany, and the Birth of the EU Corona Recovery Fund. *Journal of Common Market Studies*, 60(3): 526–544.

Lindberg, L. N. and Scheingold, S. A. (1970). *Europe's Would-be Polity: Patterns of Change in the European Community.* Englewood Cliffs NJ, Prentice-Hall.

Ludvigsson, J. F. (2023). How Sweden Approached the COVID-19 Pandemic: Summary and Commentary on the National Commission Inquiry. *Acta Paediatr*, 112: 19–33.

Miró, J. (2022). Debating Fiscal Solidarity in the EU: Interests, Values and Identities in the Legitimation of the Next Generation EU Plan. *Journal of European Integration*, 44(3): 307–325.

National Library of Medicine (2023). The Most Influential COVID-19 Articles: A Systematic Review. https://pmc.ncbi.nlm.nih.gov/articles/PMC9918314/. Accessed 9 January 2025.

Nielsen, J. H. and Lindvall, J. (2021). Trust in Government in Sweden and Denmark During the COVID-19 Epidemic. *West European Politics*, 44(5–6): 1180–1204.

PES Socialists and Democrats (2024). The Europe we Want – Social, Democratic, Sustainable. Political manifesto.

Platon, S. (2020). Reinventing the Wheel. . . and Rolling Over Fundamental Freedoms? The Covid-19 Epidemic in France and the 'State of Health Emergency'. *The Theory and Practice of Legislation*, 8(3): 293–309.

Politico (2024). Von der Leyen's Private Texting Habits Face Court Scrutiny. https://www.politico.eu/article/ursula-von-der-leyen-pfizer-ceo-text-messages-vaccines-court-case/. Accessed 26 January 2025.

Quaglia, L. and Verdun, A. (2023). The COVID-19 Pandemic and the European Union: Politics, Policies and Institutions. *Journal of European Public Policy*, 30(4): 599–611.

Radjenovic, A. and Mańko, R., with Eckert, G. (2020). Coronavirus and Elections in Selected Member States. Briefing PE 651.969 June 2020 (EPRS: European Parliamentary Research Service).

Raffetti, E., Mondino, E., and Di Baldassarre, G. (2022). COVID-19 Vaccine Hesitancy in Sweden and Italy: The Role of Trust in Authorities. *Scandinavian Journal of Public Health*, 50(6): 803–809.
Robinet-Borgomano, A. (2020). Leaders Revealed by Covid-19: Ursula von der Leyen, or the Reaffirmation of a European Ambition. Institut Montaigne. https://www.institutmontaigne.org/en/expressions/leaders-revealed-covid-19-ursula-von-der-leyen-or-reaffirmation-european-ambition. Accessed 26 January 2025.
Round Table (2021). Special Issue on COVID-19 and Commonwealth Countries. *Round Table – The Commonwealth Journal of International Affairs*, 110(1).
Schieferdecker, D. (2021). Beliefs, Attitudes, and Communicative Practices of Opponents and Supporters of COVID-19 Containment Policies: A Qualitative Case Study from Germany. *Javnost - The Public*, 28(3): 306–322.
Schmelz, K. (2020). Enforcement May Crowd Out Voluntary Support for Covid-19 Policies, Especially Where Trust in Government is Weak and in a Liberal Society. *Proceedings of the National Academy of Sciences*, 118(1).
Schmidt, V. A. (2022). European Emergency Politics and the Question of Legitimacy. *Journal of European Public Policy*, 29(6): 979–993.
Shotter, J. (2020). Poland Postpones Presidential Vote after Bid to Defy Pandemic Fails. *Financial Times*. https://www.ft.com/content/d167724e-2dd9–4ae4–8d86–8afc26e0fca4. Accessed 2 February 2025.
Statista (2023). Incidence of Coronavirus (COVID-19) Deaths in Europe as of January 13, 2023. https://www.statista.com/statistics/1111779/coronavirus-death-rate-europe-by-country/. Accessed 7 January 2025.
Venice Commission (2020). Report – Respect for Democracy, Human Rights and the Rule of Law during States of Emergency: Reflections by Nicos Alivizatos (Member, Greece), Veronika Bílková (Member, Czech Republic), Iain Cameron (Member, Sweden), Oliver Kask (Member, Estonia), Kaarlo Tuori (Member, Finland). https://www.venice.coe.int/webforms/documents/default.aspx?pdffile=CDL-AD(2020)014-e. Accessed 7 January 2025.
Vogel, G. (2020). Sweden's Gamble. *Science*. https://www.science.org/content/article/it-s-been-so-so-surreal-critics-sweden-s-lax-pandemic-policies-face-fierce-backlash. Accessed 22 April 2025.
White, J. (2015). Emergency Europe. *Political Studies*, 63(2): 300–318.
WHO (2020). COVID-19 Public Health Emergency of International Concern – Global Research and Innovation Forum: Towards a Research Roadmap. https://www.who.int/publications/m/item/covid-19-public-health-emergency-of-international-concern-(pheic)-global-research-and-innovation-forum. Accessed 7 January 2025.
Wolff, S. and Ladi, S. (2020). European Union Responses to the Covid-19 Pandemic: Adaptability in Times of Permanent Emergency. *Journal of European Integration*, 42(8): 1025–1040.

Legal documents

Case T-36/23 *Stevi and New York Times v Commission* [2025] [EU:T:2025:483].

Index

For the benefit of digital users, indexed terms that span two pages (e.g., 52–53) may, on occasion, appear on only one of those pages.

Tables and figures are indicated by an italic *t* and *f* following the page number.